A BIT OF A BLUE

The Life and Work of Frances Fuller Victor

by Jim Martin

To Don and Barbara,

With best wishes from the author,

Jim Martin

July 19, 1996

DEEP WELL PUBLISHING COMPANY
Salem, Oregon
1992

Copyright © 1992 by Jim Martin
All rights reserved.
No part of this book may be reproduced, transmitted, copied or retrieved by any means whatsoever without the prior written permission of the publisher, except for brief quotations which may be used in critical articles and reviews.

Cover photo: Frances Fuller Victor in San Francisco, 1878; I.W. Taber, photographer. Courtesy of Oregon State Library.

Library of Congress Catalog Card Number 91-90607
ISBN 0-9632066-0-5

PRINTED IN THE UNITED STATES OF AMERICA

First printing. . . . .March 1992

DEEP WELL PUBLISHING COMPANY
1371 Peace Street SE #12
Salem, Oregon 97302-2572

I don't see the motive for wearing a mask —
I will answer you true — I'm a bit of a "blue"

Frances Fuller Victor, in a poem, 1875

CONCORDIA UNIVERSITY LIBRARY
PORTLAND, OR 97211

To my whole family, especially Julie, George, Nicholas, Christina, Elizabeth, Raymond, Joel and Michael — and to all present and future generations of Americans — I offer Frances Fuller Victor as an example of the difference one individual can make, and also as a reminder of how good women and men could be — if only they would make the effort and accept the sacrifices it sometimes requires.

Contents

Acknowledgments

A writer's work is necessarily solitary, a matter of filling up blank pages with words. But writers are never alone, for they draw inspiration from the world around them in its many forms.

I came upon my subject in a library, and I had help and assistance from a number of others along the way. In particular, I wish to express my thanks and deep appreciation to the following institutions for their generous sharing of material — without which this book could not have been written:

Credit is due the Oregon Historical Society for permission to quote from Mrs. Victor's letters to Matthew Paul Deady, Frederic George Young and William Gladstone Steel; *Women's War with Whisky*, a pamphlet she wrote supporting an 1874 temperance movement in Portland; a scrapbook of hers (No. 120 in the OHS collections); various selections from the *Pacific Christian Advocate*, the *Evening Telegram* and the *Oregon Historical Quarterly*, all in Portland; *"Literary Industries" in a New Light* by Henry L. Oak; Jesse Applegate to Elwood Evans, a letter dated 13 October 1867.

From the Special Collections of the Knight Library at the University of Oregon in Eugene came correspondence between Mrs. Victor and Oliver Cromwell Applegate, and approval to use the same. The library also has a microfilm copy of *Anizetta, the Guajira; or, the Creole of Cuba*, a fiction novel she published in Boston in 1848.

Quotations from the Portland *Morning Oregonian* appear with the permission of the Oregonian Publishing Company.

Thanks also are due the Oregon State Library in Salem, which holds copies of most of Mrs. Victor's books and yielded a good bit of supporting documentation, including, primarily, a feminist weekly newspaper in Portland, *The New Northwest*. In addition, OSL has a microfilm copy of Mrs. Victor's correspondence with Elwood Evans (the originals are in the Western Americana Collection of Yale University's Beinecke Rare Book and Manuscript Library, New Haven, Connecticut); microfilm from the U.S. Veterans' Administration containing her pension records; and microfilm that includes part of an 18 August 1894 letter she wrote to a sister-in-law in Salem. Through it all, the library was a pleasant place to work and the reference room staff has remained friendly and helpful.

I wish to acknowledge the Oregon State Archives in Salem for providing the following: Oregon Supreme Court Records, Supreme Court Case File Number 01524, Frances Fuller Victor et al. vs. Walter S. Davis.

Permission to quote from several early issues of the Salem *Daily Oregon Statesman* was extended by Statesman-Journal Newspapers.

I am grateful, too, to the California Section of the California State Library in Sacramento for their assistance, and permission to quote from early San Francisco newspapers. Mrs. Victor wrote regularly for the weekly *Golden Era*, the *Evening Bulletin*, the *Morning Call*, and *Overland Monthly* magazine. These sources, plus items in the *Daily Alta California*, also provided useful background information.

Of the material provided by the Bancroft Library at the University of California, Berkeley, letters written by Mrs. Victor to Benjamin P. Avery, then editor of the *Overland Monthly*, proved especially helpful.

The Salt Lake City Public Library provided articles from the Salt Lake City *Daily Tribune* for 16 February 1893 and 14 April 1893, both of which were interesting; and the latter I quote briefly in my work, regarding Mrs. Victor's labors for the Bancroft history series.

To the Burton Historical Collection of the Detroit Public Library I am indebted for information about Mrs. Victor's early days in journalism as a writer and assistant editor of the *Monthly Hesperian and Odd-Fellows' Literary Magazine* in Detroit, from which I extracted material in connection with my work.

I also acknowledge the Michigan State Library, in Lansing, for providing records from the Michigan Historical Commission on the Barritt family. These proved helpful in my research.

The State Library of Ohio, in Columbus, deserves thanks for letting me quote from William T. Coggeshall's *The Poets and Poetry of the West*, which contains a biographical sketch of my subject as well as examples of her early literary work.

I also wish to express my appreciation to the Library of Congress in Washington, D.C., for providing "A Stage Ride in Oregon and California," an article by Mrs. Victor that appeared in *The American Publisher* (Hartford, Connecticut) in August and September 1871.

My thanks, too, to the General Research Division, The New York Public Library, Astor, Lenox and Tilden Foundations, for supplying, and granting permission to quote from, several articles in *The* (New York) *Home Journal*. The library also has a copy of *Poems of Sentiment and Imagination*, a collection published in 1851 by Frances and her sister Metta.

In addition, I am pleased to acknowledge the Interlibrary Loan and Reference Desk of the Salem Public Library, whose staff, over the past decade, obtained much information that aided my research and made my book more complete.

Advanced Typographics, Inc., of Salem, Oregon, did production, design and layout work on the book; and I am glad for their assistance.

I also received able and efficient help from Carol J. Smith, of Silverton, Oregon, who typed the manuscript and to whom goes my sincere thanks and appreciation for a job well done.

Finally, I'd like to express deep gratitude to my sister Terry and my mother for their kindness and generosity in helping me move this project forward.

Preface

Like much other historical work, this book had its origin in something shorter and more limited. I at first thought of writing a magazine piece to give Frances Fuller Victor credit and recognition for several volumes of Pacific Northwest history that she had ghost-written in the 1870s and 1880s for San Francisco publisher Hubert Howe Bancroft as part of his "Works," a massive 39-volume study of the Pacific coast, from Alaska to Central America, and the western United States. The last book in the series included brief biographies of his writers, but no credit for what they had done, and his estimation of each. This piqued my interest. That Mrs. Victor was the only woman writer in Bancroft's library I thought interesting enough, but my research soon showed that she was a gifted woman of broad experience and accomplishment whom people today might like to know. Though I wrote and eventually published my article, it was no longer enough. A book would be necessary.

I decided that the best course would be simply to find and read as much of her work as possible. However, other scattered sources of information were interesting and proved helpful. These include articles by William Alfred Morris in the December 1902 and December 1903 *Oregon Historical Quarterly*; Hazel Emery Mills in the October 1954 *Pacific Northwest Quarterly* and the December 1961 *Oregon Historical Quarterly*; Albert Johannsen's two-volume *The House of Beadle and Adams and Its Dime and Nickel Novels, the Story of a Vanished Literature* (University of Oklahoma, Norman, 1950); and John Walton Caughey's *Hubert Howe Bancroft, Historian of the West* (University of California Press, Berkeley and Los Angeles, 1946) — as well as short passages in various encyclopedias and atlases.

Introduction

When Frances Fuller was born, this country's two greatest founders, ex-Presidents John Adams and Thomas Jefferson, were still alive; and John Quincy Adams, the son of one, occupied that high office. It was also a time of growth and change. The Erie Canal had opened only the year before, in 1825, connecting the Great Lakes with the Hudson River and the Atlantic Ocean. Her birthplace, Rome, New York, was an important town along the canal, which facilitated the westward movement of people and commerce.

Lumped into one of three categories — "domestic machine, fool, saint," as she later described them — a woman wasn't supposed to need much education. If not fully conscious of this injustice as a girl, then Frances certainly must have realized it several years later when she visited New York City after her work became widely known. Newspapers printed a declaration by 100 women who met 19-20 July 1848 in Seneca Falls, New York, urging that women be given the right to vote and opportunities for a "thorough education." It was to be only the first of many such meetings all over the United States in the decades that followed.

Although Frances was fitted naturally for such a career, literary work, with its low pay, was one of the few employment opportunities for women in those days — when stories were handwritten and then set in type.

Many of her contemporaries were among those who succumbed to ailments like influenza, pneumonia, scarlet fever, tuberculosis and smallpox, that modern medicine can now control or eliminate. Surgical techniques were primitive and unsanitary. The hazards of ordinary life, as well as the stresses and strains of daily existence, also took their toll. Families were usually large to compensate for the loss of individual members.

Efforts to politically resolve the slavery question were further complicated by the purchase or acquisition of new territory from France in 1803, Spain in 1819, Great Britain in 1846, and Mexico in 1848 and 1854. Most northerners were willing to tolerate slavery in the South, but not elsewhere. Southerners thought slavery could only be preserved by extending it into new territory. Both sides always echoed the insistent question:

Is it to be slave or free? That, plus the growing economic inequality between North and South, and sectional antagonisms, caused the nation's slide into civil war in 1861.

At its end four years later 620,000 mostly young men were dead. Much of the South lay in ruins under a military occupation that lasted until 1877; this "Reconstruction Period" became one of the darkest in American history.

With the war over, the federal government looked toward Mexico and issued an ultimatum to the French emperor, Napoleon III, to end his intervention there. A large, battle-tested U.S. Army was now ready to enforce the Monroe Doctrine. The French withdrew in 1867, after six years' fighting against stubborn Mexican resistance.

While the Civil War caused death and destruction and inflationary finance, it also triggered an economic boom for most of the country, based on industrial expansion. Immigrants from Europe and the Far East swelled the work force. Steel replaced iron as a raw material and more efficient energy sources — electricity and the internal-combustion engine — were developed. Railroad mileage in the U.S. increased almost sevenfold by 1900, to 200,000 miles. Automatic machinery required a higher degree of specialization. Education became more important. Inventors and scientists contributed in many practical ways to the development of a modern and broad-based economic system.

Monopolies, corporations and trusts tried to control various parts of the economy, but ordinary farmers and working people fought back. They organized, picketed, staged strikes and work stoppages, and importuned politicians and the courts to recognize their grievances and enforce their demands. Of course, capitalists, their managers and agents, used some of these tactics, too. In addition, they could rely on strikebreakers and private security men — occasionally even state militias and federal troops — to maintain or extend their influence. These labor-management confrontations were often violent, and many people on both sides were injured or killed — to win rights Americans today take for granted.

Besides all these events, natural and man-caused disasters, the Indian wars and more, Frances lived through the assassinations of three presidents — Lincoln, Garfield and McKinley. (Two others — William Harrison and Zachary Taylor — also died in office.) She saw America go to war against Spain and not long afterwards send a large military force to the Philippines to suppress the Filipino independence movement. The death of Britain's Queen Victoria in 1901 must have contributed to the feeling that an era was passing.

Literature enabled Mrs. Victor to survive. But her finances were always marginal and, particularly in later years, she received help from friends and acquaintances. Two unhappy marriages — the first ending in divorce, the second in separation — added to life's pain and uncertainty. She shook off all these disappointments, however, and kept trying. She loved to be free, and paid its price. But she was a path-breaker who helped make possible the gains of American women, and society in general, since then.

Frances was curious, a trait in any good journalist; she poked around a lot. She hated being frightened, and sometimes went places no woman had been before. Fortunately, she always took a notepad and pencil to record her impressions. She combined deep sensitivity, an eye for detail and a graceful style that put life into her writings. She gained a national reputation as an able and entertaining writer. Between 1865-1902, she wrote eleven books and many magazine and newspaper articles about the life and history of the Pacific Northwest; her efforts preserved much valuable information that would otherwise have been lost.

"She was an able writer of essay, and possessed an insight into the evolution of civilization and government rare, not only for an author of her sex, but for any author," a friend recalled. "Combining the qualities of poet, essayist and historian, she occupied a position without a peer in the annals of Western literature."

Frances valued the truth above all else, and was never shy about putting forward her view of it. A restless yearning for something better was her defining characteristic. She always thought of the future, tried to do painstaking and conscientious historical research, and offered practical advice. Her insights, enriched by contact with a wide variety of people, remain direct, clear and relevant.

Mrs. Victor spent as much time among men as with women, and she tried to understand and explain them both. Her mind was alive with the possibilities for men and women, but she realized that only conscious, persistent and general effort could make these a reality. Progress, therefore, would necessarily be slow. With education and the passage of time, however, she hoped the two sexes could begin to realize their potential.

Looking backward can help us move forward. The world gave Mrs. Victor a hard time but she bore it no animus and went on leading an active, interesting and productive life. May her example reach across the years and continue to serve as a guide. It is in that hope that this book was written.

1

Childhood Literary Fame

Frances Fuller was born 23 May 1826 in Rome, New York, the eldest of five daughters. According to an early genealogical sketch, her father, Adonigh, belonged to an old colonial family, some of whom were among the founders of Plymouth, Massachusetts. Her mother, Lucy Williams, "a passionate lover of the beautiful in nature and art," was a descendant of titled and distinguished ancestors, who could trace their lineage through thirty-nine generations to Egbert, the first king of England.[1]

The Fullers took their children to Erie, Pennsylvania, when Frances was four years old. The family in 1839 moved to Wooster, Ohio, and Frances continued her education at a girls' school there.

Her career as a writer, as she herself recalled, "began very early in life, as no doubt did that of other authors, whose aspirations are cruelly nipped in the bud."[2]

Frances started to write poetry when she was nine, and within three years she was collecting her original verses in albums. But not until the age of fourteen did she consider publishing her work.

She was especially pleased with one of her creations, a poem of five eight-line stanzas entitled "The Soldier Boy," and decided to submit it to the editor of a local paper for consideration.

"My five stanzas looked so grand and martial that I could not but wish to see them — no, to have others see them — in print," Frances wrote twenty-four years later. "I did not know what obliging people editors were in those days of inexperience, and I did not like to ask anybody about them for fear of betraying my little secret."[3]

She enclosed with her poem a modest note — asking the editor not how much he would pay for the verses, but how much he would charge for publishing them.

Frances, elated when the editor replied that he was glad to have the poem to publish, was determined to exploit this opening for her literary aspirations. She figured she wrote a poem each day that summer.

"I could not keep my secret either; so I got it kept for me by a school-mate who could not keep it without the help of the whole school; and

at last the whole town had to help the schoolgirls in the keeping," Frances
recalled. ". . . I could not stop writing the poetry, but that editor could
have stopped printing it."[4]

She also wrote a short story — "Seventy Times Seven" — for the
Philadelphia *Saturday Courier*, then a highly popular journal of light
literature.

Within a year, poetry had become routine, so she wrote a play. It was
published by a rival editor, jealous of the appearance of her original verses
in his competitor's paper.

"There wasn't a word of fair criticism in his notice . . . nothing but
unmitigated praise," Frances lamented. "Therefore I understood it to be
all right, and wrote several more no better."[5]

Most of her early work appeared in the Cleveland *Herald* and Sandusky
Register.

"I never thought of being paid until the Herald surprised me by sending $15 for a short poem, 'The Old Man's Favorite,' which was copied by
an English journal," Frances recalled. "When I received this money I was
dismayed, for my poems had always been something so sacred to me that
I felt a sort of guiltiness in selling them. Moreover, I had another feeling
that I was no longer my own mistress, and would have to write what the
publishers wished. For a few months I ceased to publish altogether."[6]

By the time she was sixteen, Frances had published a number of things
there, and she began to consider herself "a real live author" now that she
was getting paid for her submissions.[7]

But then someone leveled scathing criticism at her work, which she
considered "so aggravatedly unjust as to affect me contrariwise to the
critic's intention."[8] Frances was determined not to be put down, so she
wrote more than ever.

She tried her hand at novel-writing, and found in its many facets a
challenge for her youthful exuberance.

"All winter I wasted precious time in getting together the proper portions of love-making and heart-breaking, and descriptions and 'connip-
tions,'" Frances related. "Then I cast about for a publisher."[9]

Getting a book into print, she discovered, however, was not nearly so
easy as publishing poetry in the local papers. "Book publishers *did* ask
something for printing," she noted ruefully, whereas in her earlier work
there were "no expenses incurred except for stationery."[10]

At last a friend offered to help get Frances' book published, and to obtain
for her some monetary benefit from it.

"In the course of six months it began to appear in a sensation paper,"
she recalled, "and at the end of another six months the publisher sent
me *five dollars*."[11]

As a young lady, Frances "in fact was, in a way, quite a belle," and she
was often courted by her male peers.[12]

Her novel that ran serially was now generously reprinted by the owners
of the sensation paper as a paperback book. One of her suitors, a young
man whom she considered to have good sense, bought a copy and told
her that he had read it.

"What do you think of it?" Frances inquired anxiously.

"The preface is splendid," her beau replied, "the book nothing!"

Crestfallen, she asked: "You mean that I have a talent for writing prefaces?"

"Just so," he answered, lightly squeezing her hand in sympathy, "don't write novels any more."[13]

This criticism "somewhat crushed" Frances, though she knew it was just.[14] She took his advice and stuck to poetry, but her ambition was growing. She sent a few verses to a lady editor in New York City who had a high reputation for learning and other attributes.

In a note, Frances modestly admitted that she was young and unknown. This was a mistake, for a short time later her verses were sent back with the cryptic sentence: "Returned for the reasons stated in your note."[15]

Undeterred, she submitted the poem to "a famous and leading literary paper in the same city," which published it with very flattering notices in May 1848.[16]

This was The Home Journal, a leading exponent of belle-lettre literature that published such celebrated authors as Honore de Balzac, James Fenimore Cooper, Charles Dickens, Alexandre Dumas, Henry Wadsworth Longfellow, Herman Melville, Edgar Allan Poe, George Sand and John Greenleaf Whittier.

In 1848-1849, Frances and her seventeen-year-old sister Metta, also a writer of marked ability, often visited New York City and met people prominent in the literary and publishing world.

Among the writers with whom Frances made pleasant acquaintance were Rufus W. Griswold, Bayard Taylor, Grace Greenwood, Anne C. Lynch, J. T. Headley and Francis Osgood.

"During my visits to New York I was invited to literary receptions at the home of Miss Lynch, where came statesmen, authors, actors, artists, musicians and all people of note," Frances recalled.[17]

Metta soon followed her sister into print. On June 10, the editors published verses she wrote under her nom de plume of "Singing Sybil," and in a prefatory note asked readers: "Have we discovered a poetess in the writer of the following poem — or not? . . . Send us an opinion — some fair-fingered critic in seclusion, who has nothing else to do!"[18]

They quoted from a letter Metta had written on May 18th to accompany her poetry:

GENTLEMEN: — Would you care to take under the strong arm of your protection, a little, timid warbler, who has hardly yet essayed to trill her young song amid the green leaves and bright flowers of her own secluded home? . . .

. . .

So she trusts fearlessly to you to uphold the timid pinion just fluttering out into the world. And whether she sings to that world, or only to her own spirit, the well shall sparkle, and the flowers spring, and the music gush forever from the soul of

SINGING SYBIL.[19]

With a great talent for inventiveness, and a rapid writer, Metta was more prolific and successful than her sister. But observers thought Frances possessed a wider range of intellectual powers, of the less popular because more solid order. According to George P. Morris and N. Parker Willis, editors of *The Home Journal* and well-known writers themselves, Metta attracted "a larger share of attention" for her poetry "than any *first* publications of a new author, masculine or feminine — and they are not few — that we have been the medium of presenting to the world."[20]

One young gentleman, who had just returned to New York City after an extended ramble through the more remote areas of the country, and taking note of the acclaim Frances and Metta had received, wrote *The Home Journal* to describe a visit he and a friend had almost a year earlier, one Sunday in November 1847, with the Fuller sisters at their home in Monroeville, in northern Ohio.

It dazzled "Manuel" to find two young women of such beauty, intelligence, gentleness and poise in that part of the interior. Both had "fine forms" and were a "little above the medium height."

The sisters were almost ready for church, "and as joyous as birds in spring," he wrote.

> At church Frances was thoughtful and attentive. The bearing of an argument, or the application of an important truth to a great principle she seemed to see and appreciate at a glance, and her remarks upon the discourse would have done credit to a student in theology. In a long conversation upon various truthful and important subjects, I was interested, and indeed surprised, at the pure, vigorous and original thoughts that seemed to be as familiar to their minds as household subjects, and which they would clothe with a strong and elegant diction. It was indeed a pleasure to meet with females who loved the solid, the truthful and beautiful things of life, and who could appreciate them, and utter the glowing words of description, and who had hearts noble and generous to feel. O, how gladly could I turn away from the insipid and arrogant conversation of "ladies of rank," and from most fashionable circles, to be instructed by the happier thoughts and more fitly spoken words of these gifted sisters.[21]

Metta related that friends had given her various names, but she wanted none. "Singing Sybil" would be well, if she deserved it; but she preferred to be known as "Metta" by her friends, and not at all by the world. She wanted to nestle in solitude and write verses that would "find no dying cadence" in her heart.[22]

"Manuel" averred that "the minds of common females could not gather up so many bright gems of thought in half a century" as had Frances in her twenty-one years.[23]

With perhaps one exception, no poet that he had ever seen was more spiritual than Frances.

"There is a deep thought running through much of her poetry that typifies the currents of her feeling," he commented. "No one can trace [Frances' and Metta's] poems without being assured of the uncommon genius they possess. Their stories also show their inventive skill, and are given with all the charms of luxuriant description. Their styles are much alike and I speak of them both as of congenial spirits.

"... Not soon, from my mind, will be lost the memory of the morning when the sun shone brightly upon the pleasant village of M_____, and, with a warm shake of the hand, we said 'good-bye' to 'Singing Sybil' and to her noble and spiritual sister Frances."[24]

In Frances and Metta, the editors of *The Home Journal* wrote that they "discern more unquestionable marks of true genius, and a greater portion of the unmistakable inspiration of true poetic art than in any of the lady minstrels — delightful and splendid as some of them have been — that we have heretofore ushered to the applause of the public."[25]

Accordingly, on 14 October 1848, they were pleased and honored to announce the formal connection of the Fuller sisters with *The Home Journal* as contributors.

Frances and Metta were very happy together, "making out," as Charlotte Brontë said, the plan of a story or poem by their own bright fireside in winter, or under the delicious moonlight of a summer evening in Ohio.[26]

Frances also published, in Boston in 1848, a vividly written romantic novel entitled *Anizetta, the Guajira; or, the Creole of Cuba* — which helped to make her literary reputation in the East.

For more than a year, the Fuller sisters' contributions appeared in *The Home Journal*. Frances wrote poetry. Metta did so, too; but she also wrote a number of serials, two of which, "The Tempter" and "Mother and Daughter," were widely acclaimed.

Rufus Wilmot Griswold, a prominent and well-known litterateur, who, Frances recalled, "had a penchant for standing as godfather to young writers," sponsored the Fuller sisters, and in 1849 gave them a place in his *Female Poets of America*.[27]

Edgar Allan Poe, in a somewhat noted review, classed Frances Fuller among the "first dozen" of the ninety-five poetesses listed, as well as one of the "most imaginative."[28]

A 264-page volume of the Fuller sisters' verse, *Poems of Sentiment and Imagination*, was published in New York City in 1851 on the recommendation of Griswold. Frances later termed it a mistaken kindness which induced friends to advise publication of these youthful poems.

One reviewer for a literary paper in the city remarked that Frances found her strength in the "portrayal of *real* suffering, the recital of *actual* strife and endurance, yet, withal, in poetic language and exalted imagery. . . . She recognizes . . . a reality in the poet's mission — a substantive subject-matter for heart and soul to evolve." He continued:

FRANCES FULLER has a great deal of dashing, blood-heat energy about her, and will enough to force it, if she but guide it aright, into a winning race with fame. She need never be tame, and has too much good sense to be wild. Like most young poets, especially American, she wants schooling, not of the heart, (that her poetry proves,) but of the head. She will yet learn to be more practical even than she is — more earnest — more self-sacrificing of pet ways — in a word, more concentrating of her powers on such subjects as she can handle lovingly. She has ten times the real poetic stamina of half a hundred much-lauded lady-writers of our literary republic, but she must not fall into one of the common diseases which easy delivery induces — that of blank verse dropsy or rhyming plethora; we do not apprehend anything of the sort, yet a word of caution is never amiss.[29]

2

A New Beginning

In the spring of 1850, as she was about to sail for a tour of Europe with some friends, the death of her father compelled Frances to return to Ohio to help support the rest of the family. By July 1850, she and Metta were working in Detroit as assistant editors of the *Monthly Hesperian and Odd-Fellows' Literary Magazine*, which started publication three months before.[1]

The family was settled in St. Clair, Michigan, by 1851, and Frances remained on the magazine's staff until late the following year. Then for a time she gave up journalistic work.

Metta had already left to chart her own literary course, ultimately in New York City. She was considered one of the most charming and popular writers of her time, and gained wide recognition primarily as an author of fiction though she also produced numerous critical essays, letters on popular or special themes, and poetry.*

On 16 June 1853 Frances married Jackson Barritt of Pontiac.[2] His parents were Hiram and Lucinda Barritt, who came to Oakland County, Michigan, in 1833 from Wheeler, New York, where Jackson had been born in 1827.

Hiram Barritt, a farmer and surveyor, built the first frame house, and school building, in Oakland County. He later helped to write the state constitution and served in the legislature.

The couple decided to try their luck on the frontier — in search of what a chronicler described as "that 'New Atlantis' which speculators would fain have us believe lies west of the Missouri."[3]

In 1855 they staked out a claim near Omaha, Nebraska, and for several years they struggled with the land.[4]

"In the excitement and hardships of a pioneer life," an early biographer observed, Frances "had little incentive to write."[5]

She could well see, however, that it was historic ground. Nearby, leading to Salt Lake City, passed a trail beaten by Mormons in 1846-1847 after their forcible eviction from Nauvoo, Illinois, an attractive city of 15,000

*For biography, see p. 239.

they had developed for seven years as the "Zion" from which Christ would reign after his second coming.

Mormon refugees passing over the trail were soon followed by throngs of California-bound wayfarers drawn by news of the great gold discovery. "When the gold-fever had abated somewhat . . . we went out upon it for a day's ride," Frances recalled, "and beheld it stretched like a garland of roses among the green swells of prairie, as far as the eye could reach. For the breaking of the strong sod by the heavy wheels of loaded wagons had given encouragement to wild roses and other prairie flowers, and the most luxurious growth of these marked the track of the emigrant trains, and pointed out their course."[6]

The marriage failed. Frances returned to New York City in 1859 to resume her literary activities as a contributor to leading prose and poetry magazines.

Drawing on her experiences of frontier life, Frances wrote several novels for the publishing house of Beadle and Adams. The firm was founded in Buffalo in the 1850s by Erastus Beadle and his younger brother Irwin; and Robert Adams, a partner. In late 1858, the establishment was moved to New York City, where it pioneered in the literary genre known as the "Dime Novel" — small sextodecimo booklets of about 100 pages, with clear type and with orange wrappers upon which was painted a stirring woodcut in black, that sold for ten cents and were issued in continuous series.

The stories gave fairly accurate portrayals of the struggles, hardships and daily lives of the American pioneers. They were intensely nationalistic and patriotic. Although the adventures were to a great extent fictitious, many of them were based on fact. But even when pure fiction, the adventures had to be plausible to satisfy the many readers who were familiar with western conditions. The "Dime Novel" was popular for roughly a quarter of a century, from 1860 until its decline in the early 1880s.[7]

Frances produced three dime novels and one of the *Pocket Novels* series; two other novels written by her were published by the Beadle subsidiary in London as part of the *American Library* series. She wrote for another of the Beadle publications, *The Home*, a magazine edited by her sister Metta, who became one of Beadle's most faithful and prolific authors — even while sending numerous poems, sketches and stories to other outlets. Frances also compiled a *Youth's History of America* for an eastern publishing house, but the outbreak of the Civil War prevented its appearance.[8]

It was in New York City that she met Alice and Phoebe Cary, lately of Cincinnati, Ohio, who as poets had also come to fame in the metropolis.

The papers touted the Carys and the Fullers as Ohio's "pair of sister poets."[9]

"I had corresponded with Alice, previously, and after they came to reside in New York [in 1850], our families became intimately acquainted," Frances recalled.[10]

Metta and another sister were frequent guests of the Carys who, in addition to their literary work, were known for bringing together an ever-widening and disparate circle of writers.

In their modest and unpretentious home on Twentieth Street, every Sunday evening for more than fifteen years, gathered the great and lesser-known habitues of New York City's literary and cultural worlds — all men and women of aspiring tastes and refined sensibilities.

"The distinctive characteristic of these Sunday evenings," an observer noted at the time, "[was] that they opened welcoming doors to all sympathetic souls, without the slightest reference to the state of their finances or mere worldly condition."[11]

Horace Greeley was said never to have missed a Sunday evening at the Carys while in the city. The famed editor would "drink his two cups of sweetened milk and water, say his say, and then suddenly vanish, to go and speak at a temperance meeting, to listen to Dr. Chapin [the well-known Universalist preacher], or to write his Monday morning leader for the 'Tribune.'"[12]

Other luminaries attending included the poet John Greenleaf Whittier; editors Samuel Bowles of the Springfield, Massachusetts, *Republican*, Robert Bonner of the New York *Ledger* and Mary L. Booth of *Harper's Bazaar*; woman's rights advocate Elizabeth Cady Stanton; Phineas T. Barnum, showman and observer of human nature; and Thomas W. Knox, correspondent of the New York *Sun*, whose vignettes of Russia and Siberia were widely reprinted.

The Court of Common Pleas for Fairfield County, Ohio, in March 1862 granted a petition for divorce in which Frances alleged that her husband "has been willfully absent . . . for more than three years immediately prior to the filing of the . . . petition, and that for the same length of time he has grossly neglected his duty towards her."[13]

The court restored her maiden name and other legal rights. Jackson Barritt was required to pay her $500 in alimony, plus costs.

(Jackson Barritt enlisted in the Union Army during the Civil War. He died at Stone Mountain, Georgia, on 27 October 1864, while serving as a member of Company "G," Ninth Michigan Cavalry.)[14]

Frances married Henry Clay Victor, a naval engineer, on 14 May 1862, in Philadelphia.[15]

He was assigned to the U.S.S. *Canandaigua*, one of the Union warships blockading the port of Charleston, South Carolina, as first assistant engineer.[16]

On 29 January 1863 a British steamer trying to run the gauntlet was captured. The *Princess Royal* carried cargo worth an estimated $1 million — including a large amount of arms and ammunition, plus the necessary machinery to build ironclad rams.[17]

Mr. Victor was one of the officers chosen to bring the prize ship to Philadelphia.[18]

3

Crossing the Isthmus

Henry was granted a short leave. Then new orders arrived and, one snowy Saturday morning, 14 March 1863, he and his wife left New York City aboard the steamer *America* on a voyage, via the Isthmus of Panama, to join the U.S.S. *Narragansett,* which was to sail against Confederate privateers in the Pacific.

"There were the crowd, the noise, the jostling; there were the partings, where people fell into one another's arms and wept, and the partings where [farewell] was gayly spoken, to conceal a little trembling of the lip; and the *bon voyage* with a shake of the hand," Frances recalled. "Then the bell was rung to warn loiterers ashore, and the leviathan began to tremble and chafe at her moorings."[1]

A fellow-passenger observed that the chaos which marked the vessel's sailing left steerage passengers in cabins and cabin passengers in steerage, but this condition was soon remedied.

"There is a sure and speedy sifting of the conflicting elements of society," commented Charles H. Webb, a well-known New York writer and bohemian, who was on his way to San Francisco.

> Tickets are called for and stations are allotted; divisions of caste and of mould are instituted; and bars are placed between the different grades of humanity, which even democracy's self cannot overleap. We of the first cabin are the nobles of the deck, representing, so to speak, the blue blood of the ship. We can go forward among the "people" who play unambitious games of Seven-up, with greasy packs of cards, for insignificant antes, but they cannot come aft to us — though they were our peers on the piers and jostled us rudely there by way of proving it.*[2]

The steamer at last swung into the channel, amidst the last shouts of adieu and a confused flutter of handkerchiefs.

---

*Seven up is a card game for two or three players, and originated in England in the seventeenth century. Other names by which it is known are: All Fours, High-Low-Jack, and Old Sledge. For more detailed information see *The Way To Play: The Illustrated Encyclopedia of the Games of the World* by the Diagram Group (Paddington Press Ltd., The Two Continents Publishing Group).

The first couple of days out, Mrs. Victor recalled, were cold and dismal. The ship was jammed with people, about two or three hundred more than there were berths for, even after a small boatload of people who lacked tickets, or the money to pay for them, had been put off in the harbor and towed back to the pier by a tug.

"Paying for accommodations on board a steamer bound to California, in those days, did not seem sufficient to secure them," she wrote.[3]

Passengers slept on tables and floors, and supped as best they could on the meagre provisions. Many people were seasick at first. They gazed patiently and intently over the ship's side — or nibbled on turnips, which were said to be a "sovereign cure" for the physical discomfort and distress they experienced.

"The wife of an Army Captain, of aristocratic antecedents, once found herself roomless on one of these steamers, and obliged to lie upon the floor with a mixed herd of men and women, and with no opportunities for toilet privileges other than could be begged in some ladies'-room already overfilled," Mrs. Victor related. "Before I had seen the same thing, I had laughed at her energetic 'I have never quite recovered my self-respect since!' Doubtless, the incidents of the war, which made her husband Major-General, have obliterated those lesser horrors from her mind; but I often remembered the expression when on board the . . . *America*."[4]

The steamer crept down the coast of the Carolinas and Florida, a wary lookout being kept for Confederate privateers. The Union navy's blockading squadrons were nowhere to be seen, though the *America* passed very near their stations, and some passengers were worried lest a Rebel marauder slip north up to Massachusetts or Maine.

Two or three days' voyaging brought the ship into warmer climes, Frances recalled, and the discomfort was lessened somewhat as passengers could stay on deck all day.

> . . . Then people thawed, and made acquaintances; sympathized with the consumptive young lady, and the dying soldier, whose mother was bringing him all the way to California only to bury him; gossiped about each other, and grumbled at the officers of the ship; cursing Vanderbilt in the interims. Then we ran from side to side to see a porpoise; exclaimed at flying-fishes; went into ecstasies over a fleet of "Portugese men-of-war" (*nautilii*); and declared a very ordinary sunset display "gorgeous." So sped the days, ending with card-playing in the evening, or a quiet walk by starlight on deck at night.[5]

The gentlemen lounged about the decks in relaxed postures, puffing large pipes in a calm, thoughtful manner, and discussing various issues of the day.

"All of them are immensely patriotic, and avow a determination never to submit to the South, but to take the field themselves if necessary," Webb observed. "As might naturally be expected, this patriotism develops itself each day with crescent ardor as we increase our distance from the seat of war and the Conscription bill."

> A celebrated traveler — a Frenchman, of course — stated as the result of his experience that he had found the world inhabited by only two sorts of people — men and women. So on shipboard, the men may be mostly divided into two great classes: those that have wives and those that have not. The latter are in a sad minority. It is fortunate for these latter wretches that California-bound ships are provided with other spare objects of utility than spare spars and ropes. . . . In like manner, besides carrying out any number of spare old maids, the California ship generally carries out a varied assortment of spare wives. We have several on board. They go out to rejoin husbands, not lost but gone before. Perhaps we should not blame them for receiving innocent little attentions from *fellow*-passengers, nor the latter for paying them; for it is not good for man to be alone on the sea. . . . The sea air is highly conducive to flirtations — perhaps because it is so bracing.[6]

The *America* was "clean, well-behaved, and kept under excellent control," according to Webb. "No bustle or confusion is visible on board; but everything seems to go on with the precision and regularity of clockwork."[7]

Webb reported that there was a lack of water, even though many passengers did not use it for cleansing purposes, but wine abounded.

"Claret . . . is an excellent substitute for water," he wrote. "It is quite as good to wash in, and very much better for drinking purposes."[8]

The steamer skirted the coast of Cuba and one night passed tantalizingly close to Havana.

"Seen through our opera glasses the city seemed a garden blossoming with roses of fire," Webb wrote. "I have always been anxious to visit Havana, and it was aggravating to go so near it and not stop. Many, perhaps all of the passengers would have liked to go ashore for a few hours, and it was rather unkind on the captain's part not to gratify them."[9]

At last, the *America* arrived at the Isthmus of Panama. Frances and her husband disembarked to continue their journey by rail. Charles H. Webb stayed aboard — to go to Greytown, Nicaragua, and an overland passage from there to the Pacific.

> . . . What joyful confusion! To be on shore again; and on shore in the tropics! To eat an execrable breakfast of bad eggs and detestable coffee at [a] hotel; and go wandering around Aspinwall [Colón] buying oranges of native women, and shells of basket-carrying native boys in an abbreviated costume. Two hours of this; then summoned to the train.
>
> How jolly everybody was on the train! No more grumbling, no sea-sickness, not the least grudge at Vanderbilt; mirth and good feeling reigning riotously. Some people eating foreign fruit enough to keep the ship's doctor busy for the next week. Some talking animatedly of every thing they saw; some eager to buy all the trinkets, fruits, and animals offered at all the stations. Occasionally somebody closely observant, and enjoying all he saw silently. One, in the seat just in advance of us, making sketches of the orange-venders — beautiful, native women, with round shapes; golden-tinted, creamy complexions; faultless white teeth; and silky black hair, coquettishly adorned with scarlet flowers.[10]

Her husband, too, was an artist, and Frances asked what he thought of the passing scenes; but Henry "only looked fierce, and stroked away at his sketch-book on the window-sill of the Panama R.R. Company's carriage."[11]

What a delightful ride! I do not remember the fellow of it in all my many experiences of travel. The strange and excessive luxuriance of the vegetable growths beside our way; the brief glimpses of planters' houses nestled in beds of bloom; the curious crowds of natives in holiday dress at every station; the clear, fine atmosphere; the beautiful violet haze hanging over the Andean ridge connecting the two continents; but chiefly the unspecked happiness of being on shore with good health and good weather.[12]

Even after New York City had quite faded from view, Frances retained "a cockneyish spirit of enthusiasm at the magnificence of that Eastern village," and not until the highest grade of the Panama Railroad was reached — "where you fancy you can see the identical hills which link the great mountain ranges of the two Americas; and where the very form, coloring, and golden warmth . . . of the Andes lie before you" — did she discard her regional pride and like other "New Yorkers, Chicagoans, Bostonians, and Cosmopolitans" changed "into Californians, about five miles from Panama."

How do you account for it? Is it because we never before saw majestic forests, nor trailing vines, nor gaudy flowers, nor sunshine on the hills? Or is it because the native women in their flounced skirts and white chemises, with scarlet flowers in their hair, and baskets of yellow oranges on their heads; their white teeth and saucy laughter, and delightfully easy manners, turn our heads?[13]

Three hours to Panama — mossy, venerable, quaint, but fever-haunted Panama. Just such square towers pennoned with green vines, as in our country we only find in pictures. We wish to risk our lives to explore a little; but inexorable companies forbid. Therefore, we are placed on board a lighter, crowded to suffocation, and kept broiling in the sun, with the privilege of admiring the lovely Panama Bay, for two mortal hours, while the ship gets ready to receive us.[14]

The travelers' good humor wilted in the hot, steamy confinement. Mrs. Victor was "nearly delirious with headache" — and alone.[15] Henry learned the *Narragansett* had gone up the coast, probably to Acapulco, and he went to the flagship, anchored in the harbor, for orders to proceed.

"Thus," Frances confessed, "while I had to contend single-handed with the unpleasantnesses of the transfer to the [Pacific Mail] Co.'s steamer *Golden Age*, I was glad that I was not to leave my husband at this port."[16]

The passengers finally boarded at twilight that Sunday, March 22, prior to the ship's departure at 9 p.m. There was the usual scramble for accommodations, which apparently contradicted assurances Frances had received from veteran travelers that matters would improve "on the other side," where "everybody was to have access to his or her baggage," she wrote. "Clean linen for gentlemen, and handsome toilettes for the ladies were to be permitted. There was to be twice as much wine drunk; and we could have all the ice we wished for, at two bits per pound. We were to have a clean ship too, and good discipline."[17]

Henry did not board until the last moment, and all the other passengers were ahead of him in the matter of rooms.

"It might have been disappointment, or it might have been headache; but I enjoyed a 'good cry,' after the fashion of weary women, before I received information of 'the best they could do for me,' and went supperless to bed," Frances recalled.[18]

Next morning, things actually seemed much better. The ship was roomy and clean, and the breakfast tasted good. Acquaintances became friends, and some friendships blossomed into loves.

"It was now possible to tell who was handsome, or agreeable, or desirable. People settled down to ship-life comfortably; were good-humored and happy. Only the poor mother of the soldier, who was evidently dying," Mrs. Victor related.

The second night out we watched late for the Southern Cross, with its glory of great gem-like stars. After that, every night we kept on deck until rather a late hour, enjoying the balmy airs, and hushed into repose of soul by the murmur of human life and ocean murmurs mingled. "Steeped in delicious languors," is the phrase for an evening at sea in the tropics.

The days sped on. To rise early, take a cup of coffee on deck, and an orange, became a habit. The late breakfast, lunch, and early dinner, with intervals for light reading and lighter talk, filled up the day. It is astonishing how much idle people can eat with impunity. In fact, their immunity from harm would seem to suggest that people who eat a good deal ought not to labor much — for how can Nature support the double tax? Our little isolated world, representing all classes and professions of people, was having a holiday, while the good ship plowed steadily onward toward the Golden Gate, thousands of miles distant from her starting-point.[19]

Capt. Hudson kept us all straight, including himself. He put a man in irons for not ordering a second cabin passenger (lady,) off the quarter deck. He threatened a young gentleman who wore the Navy buttons with a like ignominious fate if he did not cease paying his attentions to a certain handsome lady passenger, to whom the Captain and Doctor were afterward very confidential. People "found their places," just as the old Californians had assured us they would, on "this side!"

. . . There were quite a number of handsomely dressed women on board our ship, on this side; and diamonds were plenty as stars in the sky. I presumed the owners were army contractors' wives; though their husbands must have been left behind, to finish their contracts. These ladies had most of them just passed the winter in Washington. And of course must have seen a great deal of society; principally from the army, I suspect. That being the case, less experienced ladies seemed a little shy of them — owing to people having found their places.[20]

4

Twelve Days in Acapulco

When the Victors arrived in Acapulco, at 10 p.m. "one delicious evening" after six days at sea, the *Narragansett* was gone, and they decided to wait until it returned.[1]

Their baggage was sent ashore and "an old Californian," familiar with the entire coast, offered to chaperone the couple to a good hotel. A young officer also assigned to the *Narragansett* intervened, however, and said he would take them to the house of acquaintances whom he felt certain could provide agreeable entertainment.

"It was a strange walk we had that night through the streets of decayed old Acapulco. The moon, nearly full, poured down a flood of light, illuminating the Plaza and showing the *adobe* church to advantage. Late as it was, the people were astir, most of them being down at the steamer with fruit, flowers, and shells, to dispose of to the passengers. The unusual commotion had set the thousand-and-one curs of the town to barking, so that their continual noise was monotonous, like the barking of young seals heard at night in quiet bays," Mrs. Victor later wrote.

"With a sort of feeling as if in Mexico, one might look for a bandit in every angle of a wall, I looked well at everybody I met, and peered sharply into all the black shadows the moonlight threw across our way. Two or three rough-looking fellows followed and watched us — out of curiosity, no doubt, to see where we were going. The house was a little retired, and was larger and neater-looking than most of the houses we had passed, so that I prayed silently we might meet a favorable reception. But my desire was not granted — was not even denied me, which would have been some satisfaction."[2]

There was no answer to their knocking and talking. The house was dark, doors and windows remaining shuttered and barred, and cloaked with silence. The group then recrossed the plaza and down a narrow street to the hotel suggested by the Californian.

We entered, at length, a long, large room, of a long, large *adobe* building. In one corner of it was a bar, lighted by a tallow dip. Inside the bar stood a short, rather stout person, of about fifty years — possibly, not so old — in dark-blue, cotton trowsers and coarse, white shirt, with hair cut short. "Madame Moreno — old John's wife," whispered our guide in my ear. I tried not to stare very much, but fear I failed.

Old John, himself, was a large, finely built man; Spanish, most likely — certainly of a Spanish name; but French when the army of Maximilian occupied Mexico. The Madame was undoubtedly French. They were from New Orleans, and reached Acapulco overland by way of Arizona. It was in this journey that Madame adopted male attire, which, proving convenient, she retained for constant use.[3]

Old John showed the Victors to their apartment — in another building looking out on the garden — which by the dim light of a tallow candle, or "dip," resembled Mammoth Cave converted to hospital use, with a row of cot-beds down it.

"The floor, like all the floors, was of earth, a strip of matting being laid beside each bed," Frances observed. "The beds consisted of a thin mattress, two sheets, and a pillow, each. A small pine table with a tin wash-basin, and a stone water-jug, stood against the end wall. Above it, and up in the peak of the roof, was a large square opening to admit the air, and give a glimpse of the sky. No ceiling, no white walls — nothing but one immense shadow, relieved a little by the white cots."[4]

She admitted that she "shivered secretly" over having to stay in such a place, described by their host as the best accommodations in Acapulco.

"You can not stay here; you must go back to the ship," Henry told his wife.

"*You* will have to stay here until the *Narragansett* returns," she replied. "And I can live here if you can, I presume."[5]

The couple went back to the saloon to say good-bye to some of the other passengers, who had come ashore to look around. The soldier's mother, learning the Victors had left the ship, sent her farewell and good wishes, for Henry had been kind to her boy.

The Victors were very tired, it being past midnight, and went to bed. The young officer had said enough about centipedes and other noxious creatures to excite Frances to vivid imaginings, for which her dark, mysterious quarters seemed a most fitting abode. To allay any fears, she began to survey the place.

"Taking my 'dip' in hand, I first examined the two beds selected, nearest the entrance, then the matting; and while continuing my investigations on the wall near where my baggage was placed, came upon the most immense spider I ever beheld, which, finally escaping pursuit, gave me great uneasiness until forgotten in the sleep of exhaustion," she related. "My researches, though often repeated, never extended far into the depths of shadow beyond my couch; in fact, in the twelve days I occupied that room I never explored the farther end of it."[6]

First impressions are misleading, however, and in the morning she awoke delightedly.

> . . . Whether it was the cooing of the pigeons in their cote beyond and adjoining my apartment, or whether it was the sudden piercing of my eye-

lids with the morning beams which shot in at the opening in the gable, I could not have told. But I was conscious that I had never seen such a morning — no long twilight, no clearing away of mists, but a sudden burst of clear, bright day. To a certainty, it must have been the same on shipboard; but by reason of lacking the accessories of that cocoa-palm showing through the gable window, and the roses in the garden in front of my door, it had not the same charm.[7]

The morning seemed a "new creation" to her.[8] She was lying on her cot, contemplating the sensation, when the voice of Madame Moreno could be heard in the corridor announcing coffee. Ship's coffee was "vile stuff" to Frances, and the thought of good French coffee, as she judged Madame could make, brought her quickly to her feet.[9]

The brew was "nectar" that morning — as were the large, flat, light, very slightly sweetened cakes that came with it. Frances and her husband sat indolently in night-robes and slippers at a table in the corridor, facing the garden in the hacienda's interior court, breaking fast and comparing impressions of the morning and the night before.

She quickly learned to make use of the early morning, because from 10 a.m. to 4 p.m. the heat was scorching. Lounging, reading and writing occupied those hours.

"Everywhere we found the people disposed to be polite, inviting us to partake of fruit, or offering a glass of cocoa-nut milk," Frances recalled. "To see one of the native boys — little fellows, not more than six or seven years old — climb the perfectly straight trunk of one of these palms to bring down a nut in his teeth, was a sight . . . [and] they do it so expertly: up like a squirrel, sixty or seventy feet; detaching a nut that would crack in the falling; taking the stem in their teeth, and scrambling down again."[10]

Americans, French, Spaniards, Natives — it mattered not to Frances and Henry.

"We fellowshipped everybody and caricatured a good many — in the sketch book," she wrote. "We utterly contemned busy life and daily newspapers."[11]

The Victors occasionally relaxed in hammocks in the shade — "too animated for slumber, too indolent for action" — and swapped stories of past experiences.[12]

Mrs. Victor averred that there was nothing more soothing in nature than palm trees.

. . . A grove of them is like a cathedral for stillness and grandeur, without the cold and gloom of the stone building. . . . The round, straight shafts shoot up far, far above us, crowned at the top by an umbrella-shaped tuft of long, slightly rustling plumes. Not a bird haunts them: they do not seem social. Born of the sun and the sea, they have the impressive character their parentage would warrant.

I learned to love the solitary one which stood in a portion of the court walled off from the garden, and whose top I always saw at night as I lay in my cot, with one great star shining between the branches as they moved slowly in the land-breeze. It became to me the type of royalty — of all stately and serene qualities. One day, I saw open a narrow door in the wall separating us from this court, and ran quickly to get a view of the whole tree. What a shock it gave me to find the court a little patch of abominable dust and rubbish, tenanted by a couple of shabby little mules, who were making themselves still more repulsive by rolling in the dirt. "Ah, my palm," I thought, "how often a great soul has stood alone like you in the midst of uncongenial and repulsive surroundings — its feet in the filth, its brow to the stars!" Then I sighed at the profanation, and ran away from the sight of it.[13]

Going out in the morning, Frances found that many Acapulco men were lounging on the earthen pavement where they had passed the night.

"These lazzaroni may be found during the day asleep under trees; by night, they gamble in the Plaza; and, taking a nap on the sidewalk, half rise on one elbow when the market-women come around in the morning with coffee, fruit, and *tortillas*," she commented. "Picking one's way among them . . . was a delicate piece of engineering."[14]

Mrs. Victor saw Mexican women occasionally in the evenings when she and her husband were invited to enter their households, at church, or in religious processions "of which there seemed to be one for each alternate day."[15]

The ladies seemed to prefer dressing in black, and "the appearance of a crowd of them in a procession was rather sombre," Frances added. "The poorer class wore common calicoes, of large and showy patterns, and all marched and knelt together in the dusty streets. In the church we saw the same thing: many women, very few men. In Mexico, as elsewhere, the same custom exists — men do the sinning, women the praying: it is consistent, I suppose."[16]

With time, Frances slowly discarded her fear of poisonous creatures. She rather liked the way the gray lizards on the walls came down when she and her husband were eating, "and peered at us so saucily, and perked their little heads so curiously, as if doubtful about being invited to take a crumb."[17]

A previous visitor, a lady, used to allow the lizards to eat with her. But Mrs. Victor said her intimacy did not go that far. She recalled that her husband liked to frighten them, and in the scramble see one fall to the ground and break its tail clean off.

"They tormented him, too," Frances added, "for every night I would hear him slapping his face with an exclamation, imagining or dreaming that a lizard had fallen from the rafters upon it."[18]

Her own well-being also suffered a narrow escape. One day, as she sat writing at a table in the corridor, Mrs. Victor heard something suddenly fall from the tiles above onto the matting beside her.

Sensing danger, Frances at once stood and saw a scorpion, which hurriedly scuttled off.

"I darted after it," she recalled, "and set my slipper down viciously upon a spot on a piece of matting, just under which I knew . . . it must be. And there it was, crushed to death by my foot."[19]

Frances carried it triumphantly on a stick to old John. "An *alacran*?" she asked.

"Yes," he told her, "you were lucky to kill it."

"It just escaped my shoulder in falling from the tiles. What would it have done to me had it hit me?"

"Stung you," John replied. "There is a bean grows in Mexico which cures the sting. Every family who has one values it very highly."[20]

The doctor on the *Narragansett* later told Frances there were about fifty cases annually. The insects hid in the coal and wood used to fire the ship's boilers, and the men handling it were often bitten. The wound caused delirium and great pain; ammonia and alcohol were used to treat it.

She wondered if Shakespeare had seen someone affected by an alacran's sting when he wrote: "What ho! the fellow is dancing mad! he hath been bitten by a tarantula."

Mrs. Victor remarked that she was afterwards careful not to sit under the tiling's edge.

Chocolate was available to eat in the middle of the day if one wanted it, but Frances oftener squeezed one or two limes from the garden into a glass and added sugar and water. This, with a cake saved from breakfast, made her a better lunch. Dinner was at four.

"I could not enjoy warm food at the hours when our meals were served," she later wrote. "The dinners were excellent, but my appetite was wanting. Had I ordered the arrangement of meals, I should have eaten the principal one at sunrise."[21]

In 1858 the Indian patriot Benito Juarez, a lawyer and former governor of Oaxaca, was elected President of the Republic. His efforts at liberal reform — including the disestablishment of the Catholic Church, which owned much property and exercised considerable political influence — drew opposition from the aristocracy.

Two years later, Juarez was forced to suspend payment on foreign debts. Emperor Napoleon III of France, who wanted to obtain power in Mexico, used the issue as a pretext to send an army in 1861. Juarez retreated into northern Mexico, where he led opposition to the invasion.

The United States was embroiled in the Civil War, and the emperor brushed aside Lincoln administration protests that the French were violating the Monroe Doctrine.

Four warships, part of the French fleet supporting Napoleon's army, entered the harbor on 10 January 1863 and conducted a sustained bombardment of the town and its defenses. The people had been forewarned of the squadron's approach, however, and they sought refuge in the neighboring hills.

Within two hours most of the Mexican artillery batteries were silenced, and the French began a more concentrated and systematic assault on their targets. One observer estimated that Acapulco was hit by about 500 shells during the three-day barrage.

"It appears to me astonishing that the whole town was not destroyed," this man wrote, "which undoubtedly must have been the intention of the French, as scarcely a house remains that has not been riddled by their balls." He averred that "a general conflagration" was prevented only by Acapulco's adobe walls and stone floors.[22]

"The Mexican soldiers, uniformless, often hatless, unintelligent in countenance, and sluggish in manner, were not able to inspire foreigners with
respect," Frances wrote after her visit about three months later. "They
were braver than they seemed, and fought well under the Juarez command.
. . . Only one of their batteries, situated on the brow of a mountain behind
the town, proved effectual, and did some damage to the French fleet."[23]

Although Frances was not allowed inside the fortress guarding the city,
she sometimes sat on its low, outside wall, watching iguanas slipping
among the rocks, and counting the marks of French cannon balls on the
fort's seaward side.

"They were the merest dents — not a breach made anywhere," she
noted.[24]

The French vessels had withdrawn, although not before landing parties spiked several of the Mexican guns and dumped others into the bay.
The garrison was surprised by the French gunners' sixty-pound shells and
lost some fifteen men killed in the engagement, but the soldiers felt very
proud of their successful defense of the town.

"All were desirous that the enemy should land, to give them a taste of
their determination to resist invasion," a correspondent reported.[25]

The French were expected to return at any time, and because of the
uncertainty Mrs. Victor was not able to make a tour of the interior.

An American trader owned a schooner in which he transported goods
to a port about seventy miles south of Acapulco. The cargo would then
be loaded onto mules for an overland journey to the ancient city of Oaxaca.

The trader's wife suffered from tuberculosis, and he wanted her to try
this journey over the mountains for health reasons, but would not take
her unless another woman accompanied them.

"The scheme suited me very well," Frances recalled. "I was willing to
run the risk of banditti for the gratification of my curiosity — Oaxaca
being one of those cities out of the line of travel, where an American
woman had never been seen, and where we had the promise of being
greatly lionized by the inhabitants. Such an opportunity (of being lionized)
might never occur again; therefore it was with a pang of regret that I
accepted my husband's ultimate negative, based upon the ground, that,
should the French blockade the port in my absence, it would be impossible for me to return there while the blockade lasted. As I must return there,
for various reasons, the plan was reluctantly abandoned."[26]

Before long, the *Narragansett* returned to Acapulco, and her officers
came ashore daily to call.

Mrs. Victor boarded the captain's "gig," and was rowed over the shining waters of the bay to the rhythmical plash of three pairs of oars.

From this perspective, she could easily discern the bay's landlocked
character — "with beautiful green headlands, and low, sandy beaches,
backed by cocoa-nut groves — it is one of the handsomest harbors in
the world."[27]

Sometimes, in the evenings, Mrs. Victor and her husband would go down
to the bay to experience one of Acapulco's great pleasures.

They were not unmindful of sharks, however, and while bathing they stayed in among the rocks, "where these creatures dare not venture, for fear of scratching their delicate hides," she recalled. "O, the luxury of *warm* sea-water . . . northern bathing is a dangerous and shuddering task; but in tropical seas, where the water is the same temperature with your blood, to move about in it, and feel its soft plashings, is the greatest luxury in the world."[28]

Frances also liked to take evening walks towards the mountains behind the city. Her path crossed a narrow, beautifully designed stone bridge. This bridge, she wrote, bore

a date which carried one back to the prosperous days of Acapulco, in the middle of the sixteenth century, when richly laden galleons sailed into her beautiful bay from East Indian ports, and when she built her splendid fort to keep off rakish buccaneers like Sir Francis Drake. Proud, violent, aggressive Spain! At the bidding of her officers, the native Mexicans transported from the mountains those stones, one by one, which went to build the walls of the fort — about the only memento left of her pride and greatness, in miserable, dilapidated Acapulco.[29]

5

"Florence Fane" in San Francisco

And so, leaving her husband "to live, perhaps die," in the harsh Mexican climate, Frances boarded the steamer *Sonora*, which docked at San Francisco in the early evening of Saturday, 18 April 1863, and she set about re-focusing her journalistic insights.[1]

"I found myself rather out of sorts, as the printers say, for a variety of pastimes . . . And as very few people in this city had letters of introduction to me, and I did not much effect the favored few, I was used to yawn, and occasionally to grumble a little, *sotto voce*, though grumbling is not a ladylike habit by any means," she explained.

"In the midst of these unsettled humors I bethought me of an old habit of mine . . . of dotting down notes about people and things."[2]

She contributed articles "quite regularly both on inside and outside matters" to the *Evening Bulletin*, "and received liberal pay."[3]

But it was under the nom de plume of Florence Fane that she gained a literary reputation on the Pacific coast — by writing for *The Golden Era*, then the literary journal of California, a series of society articles which won much favorable comment for their humorous observations.

In her very first column, on 9 August 1863, Frances announced that she had become a confirmed Westerner.

Mrs. Victor discovered, however, that the first step towards achieving that estimable goal was simply getting the wrinkles out of her clothes. San Franciscans, even if in town just long enough to be clad in creaseless attire, could tell that "the steamer is in" from the rumpled wearing apparel pulled from trunk or suitcase by disembarking passengers.[4]

She took "a sort of terrified delight" in strolling along the main city streets and getting a feel of the night life she saw.[5] Frances liked to window shop wherever the beautiful was displayed — fabrics, forms, colors.

"Everything gay and enchanting from the brilliantly illuminated theatre whose name in gas jets is over the door, to the tempting confectioner's window, and the gorgeous chemical jars of the druggist," she observed.

"Beautiful men and women flit past, looking their handsomest in the sudden blaze of the gas lights. Toil and elbowing business men have retired from the scene. Only gaiety and careless satisfaction remain."[6]

In uncurtained parlor windows Frances saw "pleasant family groups, set like pictures in the blank walls of the town."[7] She had never guessed how many such scenes were hidden by daylight behind those walls, and thanked God that they continued to exist despite the world's toil and turbulence.

But Mrs. Victor also recorded the sinister and terrifying aspects of night life:

> . . . Guilt, skulking out of the broad glare of the street lamps into dark alley ways. Shame, with shameless effrontery flaunting itself in our face. Crime dogging the innocent and bringing the unoffending to sorrow. Want gazing piteously at us from the curbstone, hoping ever so despairingly for a morsel of our charity.[8]

What, she asked, would next morning's paper tell of these things?

— A morning stroller on the wharf might see a body, possibly that of a woman, "with long, wet, clinging hair glistening in the sun," as it floats on the water's surface. "That woman's wretched story is known unto the night — to us it will be never," Frances commented.[9]

— The proprietress of a boarding-house, not seeing one of her tenants for some time, forces open the door to find the man dead on the floor, a suicide.

— A mechanic opens his shop early, only to find someone was there before him and had taken a heavy or sharp-edged tool. During the day he is arrested on the evidence of his own deadly instrument having been used in a murder.

— A policeman, walking along a seldom-traveled street, picks up an emaciated, lifeless body and conveys it to the morgue. The coroner's verdict: death by starvation.

A reporter might tell of all these things. "But the thousand secret sins, and the thousand hidden griefs of a night, who shall tell?" she inquired.

"Cannot spirits see through walls and roofs. Fancy the angels looking down between the stars of a night, upon all the doings, open and secret, of a great city! I am no angel . . . but I have often fancied myself taking such a view, and have congratulated myself that I was only human with a limited human vision. It is well for us that He who's slow to be angry is quick to be pitiful."[10]

To mark Union victories at Gettysburg, Port Hudson and Vicksburg, President Lincoln proclaimed August 6 as a day of national thanksgiving, praise and prayer.

As thousands of San Franciscans jammed city streets that Thursday morning in patriotic demonstrations and rallies, Frances climbed several flights of stairs to the roof of her boarding-house. There she sat in solitude, gazing at the panorama of San Francisco's hills and valleys.

"A great city, yet with the air of having sprung up in a night? As many hills as Rome; yet these are only sand-hills, graded but yesterday. Everything is dust-colored. Even the shrubbery in the tiny gardens attached to the dust-colored houses. The people themselves, flowing like a turbid river along the yellow canons of streets, are touched with th[e] prevailing hue.

The waters of the bay, the air through which we see the hills beyond, the country itself, is of the universal yellow tint," she wrote.[11]

This drab hue, Mrs. Victor thought, was not pleasing to the eye; but she loved San Francisco for other reasons.

"What a golden warmth in the air! What animation in the busy life of the streets! What rude beauty in the tawny landscape! What promise of future elegance — future magnificence — in the happy combination of climate, enterprise, wealth and taste, which is apparent here!" she wrote.

"I fell into a reverie, and noticed dreamily how the dark-gowned celestials glided cat-like along the roofs far beneath me, attending to the drying of Occidental linen.

"I noticed too, a great number of wind-mills; and I wondered if in those queer things were ground out the gales that buffet us daily in our walks about town."[12]

She asked *The Golden Era* editor to speak to city and county officials — "whoever have the charge of such a matter — and get them to grind out a lighter article."[13]

Thousands of American flags waving in the breeze aroused in Frances a singularly ecstatic emotion:

"An army with banners!"

As Mrs. Victor contemplated that sentence, she envisioned mighty columns of men moving to the sound of martial music, and the fluttering of many banners.

> March, march, with a strong, firm, thunderous tread: — young men and middle-aged, even a few grey-haired veterans.
>
> March, march, leaving home, friends, wives, babes, — all common interests and common affections behind them. On they go, over toilsome roads, in clouds of dust, through deadly marshes, in sun and rain, in cold and heat, in sickness and in health, to meet the enemy on his chosen ground. On to battle — to glorious victory, or still glorious defeat. On to wounds, to agony, the maddening thirst of fever, the ghastly death on the field, the indiscriminate burial in trenches.
>
> How the waving of those flags blurred my vision more and more, till all San Francisco was an indistinguishable mass of red, white and blue.
>
> I was thinking of how we felt and acted when the Seventh Regiment left New York. But that was only the beginning. Bull Run!! — What a spasm seized our hearts when the dreadful report came home of that first of many terrible and disastrous battles! How anxious we were for every breath of tidings. How eagerly we grasped the paper from the newsboy's hands, while others just as eager crowded around to hear. But no! we could not! The choking sensation in our throats when we read of the mad terror, agony and exhaustion of our brave men, fighting unsustained against such fearful odds, stifled us. Oh, how we cried for days over those horrible scenes!
>
> And thus the tragedy proceeded; the agony on the battle field; the other agony at Home.
>
> The banner that waved over those scenes has acquired a terrible beauty and significance in the last two years![14]

Frances patiently awaited an opportunity to see the view from Telegraph Hill, and "accomplished it before the wind had risen one [summer] morning, early riser though it is. You see I had written to Mrs. Winslow to ask if her inestimable Soothing Syrup would not be good for wind in San Francisco, and the old lady had sent me a bottle with directions for use: — hence a quiet morning," Mrs. Victor related.

"The view . . . was enchanting. Such a lovely azure overhead — such a soft, white, floating mist along the hill-tops! The bay reflected the beauty that smiled down upon it, and over city, country, blue waters and tawny hills, our ships silently swinging at anchor and dwellings of men on shore, brooded a silver-winged spirit — the beautiful presence of Peace. Even fiery Alcatraz basked harmless in the genial sun, and her dogs of war forgot to show their fangs."[15]

Frances attended an opera one Friday evening, at the Metropolitan Theatre on Montgomery Street, and enjoyed the performance and its musical accompaniment.

"Operatic representation is of all kinds the most difficult to excel in," she contended. "It is one thing to be a good singer, and another thing to be a good actor; and one does not necessarily imply the other. Besides the effort required in singing must interfere with that required for action; therefore the two are very rarely harmonious."[16]

Mrs. Victor admitted having "heretical opinions" on a wide variety of topics of interest to cultured men and women.[17] She preferred thinking her own thoughts rather than adhere to a professional critic's.

"It is a dangerous habit," she wrote. "It frequently brings us in collision with established authorities in a very disagreeable manner, besides endangering our caste with those who believe in the critics by inheritance."[18]

Early on, Frances demonstrated a creative energy and intelligence which, coupled with her experiences of city and frontier life, helped her surmount the barriers to women taking an active part in affairs of the age.

By the time of her arrival in San Francisco in 1863, Mrs. Victor was a mature, experienced woman of thirty-six. Her views on the status of women had evolved gradually, but were strongly held, and in *The Golden Era* she found a congenial outlet for them.

Her writings for that literary journal on the subject were the first she would produce at intervals during a period of almost forty years in letters and in various periodicals.*

"I am not an advocate of woman's rights. In my humble opinion, the more rights she has, the worse off she is. No; all the right I want . . . is the right to make some man responsible for all my little happinesses — and for all my little debts; — the latter, particularly," she wrote.

> There may be something extremely improper in it . . . but I have several
> times wished to be a man. I told my good old [A]unt Mitty . . . of that
> predil[e]ction of mine for the masculine estate, and the old lady looked so

---

* "But the trouble with these social problems is that emancipation comes before the knowledge which makes it of its full worth," she would write in 1895. "The freedom has to be achieved first, and the understanding of its value is learned by experience afterwards." *Oregon Historical Society Scrapbook No. 120, pp. 85-86.*

reproachfully at me over the tops of her spectacles that I immediately hastened to change the subject. If I had said I wished to have been a spirit of the outer darkness, I could not have shocked her more. Evidently she thought I must have been lost to all propriety, to wish to be anything so low in the scale of humanity as a man.

The discussion I hoped to provoke with Aunt Mitty having fallen through in that weakminded manner, after brooding over my concealed fancies for some time, I finally ventured to give them utterance before an M.D. cousin of mine. Without a shadow of occasion, as far as I could see, he burst into a loud, long, irrepressible fit of laughter, and without stopping to make any comments, rushed out of the house into the garden, where I saw him walking up and down talking to himself, and laughing heartily still. Now why my aunt should see anything so improper, or my cousin anything so ridiculous, in my wish, I never yet have found out. But the fact that they should treat it in this manner, very naturally set me to thinking the subject over to see if I could not justify myself in my peculiar views.[19]

Even after the apple-eating affair in the Garden of Eden, Frances asserted, Adam never had any reason to complain, because he was given the power to rule. And Eve, if she had any perception at all, often must have shed tears for her plight even as Adam labored in the cornfield as God commanded him. Even so, she couldn't have seen how being a woman would work out.

"It is not that women cannot enjoy either riches, or rank, or honors, except as they derive them from men, that I complain," Frances wrote. "It is not that we are compelled to endure the society of children, gifted with uncommon talents at making themselves disagreeable, during the term of our natural lives. . . .

"It is not that we are expected to smile with a head-ache or a heart-break. Nor that our fists are not big enough to knock down on the spot the fellow that deserves knocking down. Nor that we are not privileged to ask the man we love to marry us, though that perhaps is the greatest of our disadvantages in a psychological point of view . . . Not that we are obliged to have an attendant when we might prefer our own company, or cannot get one when we would like to have one. Not that we cannot go to balls whose managers have not been introduced to us. Not that we are snubbed when we are not pretty, and made fools of when we are — perhaps."[20]

In this connection, she found the cumbersomeness of women's apparel particularly irritating.

Imagine that I walk through Montgomery street in a pretty silk dress short enough to clear the tops of my gaiters, — as a comfortable dress would! I advise any lady who is fond of a sensation to try it. But all the time ladies are promenading in clothes so long that they are compelled to hold them up in order to walk at all. Besides the labor of carrying all this heavy drapery in the hands, it is sure to drag in some parts and be held too high in others. Or perhaps it is allowed to drag without restraint? Bah! how can any woman consent to become a mop-handle![21]

She told the story of the little boy who did not want to be ''born again'' because God would make him a girl next time.

Frances admired the lad's honesty, though she thought many of them would be of better service to the world as second or third rate girls than as fifth or sixth rate men.

A precocious girl of ten once told an audience, of which Mrs. Victor was one, that she wanted to be a boy.

"A boy can divert himself with *sensible fun!* — while I can only do certain things that I don't like," this girl explained. "If I want to have a good rough-and-tumble time, mamma always interrupts me with, 'that is not proper for girls, my dear.' I always wish to be a boy when mamma says that."[22]

Mrs. Victor reported that some young ladies of the 1860s smoked cigarettes, or rode in steeple chases.

Frances professed to have done neither. But her husband, a crack shot, with whom she often went on excursions, persuaded her to learn how to use a rifle and hit a target.

"It was no use telling him that I didn't like the noise, and that the gun hurt my shoulder," she recalled. "His only answer was, 'you'll soon get used to that;' and so I did."[23]

After a summer in California, Mrs. Victor found, to her dismay, that it was not a sentimental country.

"How are a young couple to fall in love without the usual adjuncts of dewy roses, bewitching moonlight, whispering trees, gorgeous sunsets and the like?" she asked. "Whereas, here, all is dry, dusty, windy and horribly practical."[24]

A friend one evening asked if Mrs. Victor had "a talent for happiness." She replied she liked being happy, if that was what he meant.

"Your sex possess the opposite capacity chiefly," this man told Frances. "They love to be miserable!"[25]

She was at a loss to answer him. How could she explain that it was men who on so many occasions caused women to be sad.

> Doesn't a boy forever delight in making a girl cry? Whether it is his sister, or cousin, or school-fellow, he always has some little feminine victim to vent his mischievous propensities on, with a view to seeing her "dissolved in tears;" when he adds insult to injury by denominating her a "cry-baby."
>
> When she is older, don't some other boy exert all his fascinations to make her "fall in love" with him; and if she is simple enough to drop into the snare, don't he tell all the fellows at school that Lily or Rosa is dead in love with him, and call her a little goose?
>
> Later still, isn't the same game carried on by some invincible male flirt, whose profession in society is to "wring the hearts" of susceptible young ladies?
>
> When at last she comes to be married, under the fond delusion that marriage secures to her somebody to love, and somebody who will love her, don't her husband tell her he has no time for nonsense now? What he wants of her is to get up good dinners, and keep the baby quiet while he is in the house! And dont he give her a lecture on domestic excellencies, instead of giving her a kiss and a new bonnet, on their wedding anniversary? If these repeated disappointments are not enough to give one a talent for being miserable, I'd like to be told what would do it.[26]

Aside from the abuse and harassment many women experienced in private and public life, they also had to contend with unfair journalistic portrayals of feminine character.

"They ridicule our dress, and tell shocking stories about us; causing vulgar men to sneer, and good men to frown at the allusions," Mrs. Victor complained. "Yet they insist, with curious inconsistency, upon our keeping bright all the virtues; for, they argue, it is necessary that somebody should do it; and for themselves, they have neither time nor taste for practising these things."[27]

Frances feared San Francisco would die of tuberculosis because it neglected to develop parks to offset the city's dusty dreariness. She boarded a public conveyance to South Park in eager anticipation of relaxing on green sod underneath a shade tree or by a splashing fountain.

"I am afraid the conductor laughed in his sleeve when he noticed my lunch-basket and drawing-book, and heard my request to be set off at South Park gate," she wrote.

"I laughed too, when I got over my vexation. Poor little flower-plot, I was so afraid of doing it an injury by setting my foot on it, that I only walked round it two or three times, peeping at it over the fence, as if it had been a box of wax-work."[28]

In *The Golden Era* she urged the city fathers to provide young ladies "some better place to canter their horses than through a crowded thoroughfare, with the dust covering them like a cloud from our admiring vision."[29]

Mrs. Victor asked if babies riding in their carriages must endure similar conditions, or if mothers did not deserve a quiet place of recreation to watch their children play, or if the elderly and the sick did not need a respite from home life and the hubub of the city.

"The absence of simple and harmless recreation makes young men, and young women too, resort to injurious means of 'killing time,'" Frances wrote, ". . . no character is perfect that has not a touch of romance in it."[30]

She saw nothing in the city to develop "the romantic in the minds of the rising generation; and that as a consequence in a genial climate like this the sensual nature will get long strides ahead of the esthetical."[31]

A metropolis like San Francisco, she argued, "needs a huge pair of lungs, where the mental, moral, and physical atmosphere may be vitalized to any extent demanded by a growing population."[32]

Frances threatened not to vote for San Francisco officials at some future election unless they pledged to use some of the city's money for woods and fields for the public's "delectation, preservation and sanctification."[33]

She recommended that the new park not be planted with chaparral, scrubby pines or cedars — adding that if there was a transmigration of souls in the afterlife, she would like to return to earth as a tree.

"A stately, graceful elm; or a noble maple, showing by its uniform growth and upright form the symbol of a well-developed mind; or a murmuring aspen with its immortal sorrow, so gentle and so sweet," Mrs. Victor wrote.

"I do not love to buffet storms, therefore I would not be the mighty oak; neither the lofty tulip tree, lifting its golden chalices up to the face of heaven; nor yet the mournful willow, to remind men of their graves."[34]

But Frances would rather have been any of those three than "a prim, dark, never-changing evergreen" — which she detested except among its native rocks and hills.[35]

Mrs. Victor remarked that the trees she loved "put out little faintly colored buds in the spring-time, and keep growing in beauty till summer's perfection is upon them; and after doing their sweet duty, when the autumn comes scatter their faded foliage to the winds and rest from their labors until another spring. They are full of grace and expression. They rejoice and they lament; they clap together their millions of little palms when the frolic winds caress them, or throw up their arms in wild dismay when the fierce gales sweep over them. They are sentimental too, if one might judge from the sounds one hears of summer nights beneath the moon — such whispering and sighing," Frances continued.

"Then there is the lofty palm, that loves the sun and sea, and that I loved when I was in Mexico. And the heaven-reaching *Palo Santo* which holds its white clusters up to the blue sky and golden stars — that grows in Mexico; and the *Itos* whose shade is so cool as to chill the blood."[36]

On 9 September 1863 Californians celebrated the thirteenth anniversary of their state's admission to the Union.

"Notwithstanding the bad conduct of her elder sisters on the other side of the continent, she was not dis-spirited, but sustained her reputation of promising to be the flower of the family," Mrs. Victor commented.[37]

The weather was perfect. No clouds, no fog; just blue sky, a warm sun and gentle breezes.

Festivities in San Francisco concluded with a ball. Many people were there, but Frances did not attend. Being a recent arrival in the city, she was not personally acquainted with the managers who put on the gala.

Mrs. Victor also failed to engage a hairdresser the week before the ball, and would not have had her hair dressed until after it was over. All the coiffeurs in San Francisco, she noted, were busy until the last possible moment getting the ladies ready.

> Think of that, Mr. ERA. Think of having to take off your head and leave it on your dressing-table, for two nights previous to the ball, because you cannot go to bed in curls, puffs, and frizzed fronts! It requires some courage to be a pioneer, I should think.
>
> If I had been personally acquainted with the managers, and had gone to their ball, I should not have objected to dancing, for I like it. It requires a [great] deal of self-restraint to hold my feet still when other light fantastic toes are twinkling round. Still I think if I could have made up my mind to go to the ball before the managers had been properly introduced to me, I should have endeavored to have been dignified about it, and not have danced more than nine times out of ten.[38]

Though San Francisco society soon accepted Mrs. Victor, she had special regard for its younger members who were articulate, creative, intelligent, witty, and occasionally disdainful of the conventions.

Frances professed to know but few individuals who understood the "sacredness" of true friendship. The behavior which passed for it in conventional society she regarded as a shallow imitation.

Mrs. Victor also took note of the hardy breed of pioneers who matched the strength of their "young and buoyant" lives "against the perils of a long journey, and of a new, wild, inhospitable country" as they arrived in California to search for gold and adventure.[39] Many lost. Their graves in the mining regions, she observed, were primitive and neglected, marked only by wooden crosses painted with the name, native state and approximate age of the deceased.

"It was little by which to identify a lost friend — but it was all those who buried him knew," Frances thought, pausing by the grave of one miner, a man of about thirty. "The history ended there. He was a stranger among strangers. No familiar face bent over his couch of languishing. He was then too ill to be questioned by kind but unfamiliar attendants. Evidently no one had been informed where were his home and family, else those inscriptions would not have been so very brief and unsatisfactory."[40]

This young man was willing to tempt fate, she added, but the risks had been too great for him.

> . . . He had drawn a blank from the wheel of fortune, and never more been heard from. In vain they have waited for him a[t] home all these years: they will find him at last "over the river."
>
> Those pioneer graves reminded me of what it is to be homesick. Every one of those silent sleepers had known what i[t] was, before delirium, or apathy, or death had abated their wild yearning. The sickness, the nausea, the pitiless pain had been little in comparison with that other sickness of the heart for which the most learned leeches have no remedy.[41]

A few years more, she asserted, and those wooden markers will have rotted away, concealing forever the resting places of the pioneers.

"The tear of some passing stranger is the only tribute their sorrowful story exacts, but rarely, now," Frances lamented. "Very soon they will cease to be remembered at all. Peace to their ashes."*[42]

Her husband was in one of his "spells," ostensibly because he had to stay in an apartment. After dealing with salty seamen in wartime, the last thing Henry wanted was to be cooped up on land with people — some of them Frances' friends — whose views he detested. He was determined to have his own lodgings.

---

*Mrs. Victor fared much better. On the strength of her reputation as "Florence Fane," she was "welcomed . . . to the mountains with a present of stock from every mine-owner in the district." Although the shares afterwards were allowed to lapse (see Chapter 18), Frances treasured the memory of her experience. In 1896 she wrote:

> Ah, those were the happy days of writers before the Associated Press dispatches were substituted for their more human sympathies and conceits. The newspaper readers of to-day do not know what they have missed by coming upon the stage when "correspondents" are abolished and telegraphic brevities are made to take their place.
> . . .
> . . .[M]uch stress is . . . laid upon the ill-judged saying of . . . one of the founders of the Golden Era, that it "was killed by letting women write for it; they killed it with their namby-pamby schoolgirl trash." Now, there were 218 writers . . . who contributed to that paper, seventy-eight of whom were women, giving a preponder[a]nce of forty to the men's list. . . .

"He is as cross as two sticks and will not listen either to pleasantry or reason," his wife remarked.

"Nothing I can say about the disagreeableness of eating at a restaurant, or the inconvenience of having to wear one's walking dress all the time, or the loneliness of lodgings, has power to move him. He is going to be independent. He will not eat *his* salt with men whose hands are at the nation's throat. His house shall be his castle, where no disloyal sentiment shall be uttered; no disloyal guest sheltered."[43]

Frances submitted very reluctantly to her husband's wishes, on grounds it is woman's fate to subordinate her views to a man's and "because if I let him alone he will do just what I wish he would."[44] Off the couple went in search of a more permanent abode.

It was not a pleasant walk. The wind seemed to blow from all directions at once. Sand filtered into mouth, nose and eyes, and at length Henry declared that he felt like an hour-glass with a strong inclination to stand on his head and let the sand run out again.

"I thought the ladies whose crinolines *would* invert themselves over their heads, *looked* a great deal more like hour-glasses," Mrs. Victor admitted. ". . . I resolved thereupon to put a few pounds of lead in the bottom of my dress before I ventured out again in the city of St. Francis."[45]

At last, through one half-opened eye, Henry discerned the words "Furnished Rooms" on the front of a good-looking house in a respectable part of town. With alacrity his wife mounted the steps and took shelter in the windward corner of the doorway while the ceremony of ringing and being admitted was enacted.

As they climbed the staircase, they dodged several children in dirty pinafores "whose sole business in life seemed to be that of making pictures in oil of buttered bread on the stair-carpet and wall, or on the gowns of thoughtless mortals who go about seeking furnished rooms," Frances observed.[46]

The accommodations, she thought, would be much nicer if they had been larger, newly furnished and decorated, and overlooking a flower garden instead of an odiferous back yard. When Henry asked her opinion, Frances later wrote, "I told him I was delighted that such lodgings were to let; and if I was consulted in the matter I should certainly let them alone."[47]

. . .[T]he women . . . , if they did not make, certainly did not unmake the reputation of the Golden Era. In fact, a large degree of the support received by that "remarkable paper," as Horace Greeley called it, was due to the bright things said by the women who wrote for it. The decline of the Era's period in literature was due to new conditions. The men who had fostered it by their abilities had found wider and more remunerative fields, and the women likewise. The weaker majority could not sustain the reputation of the paper. Besides the overland railroad had opened the East to us with its monthly magazines, its great weeklies and dailies, and as I have already pointed out the form and fashion of journalism was changed. So unique had been the character of the Era that at this day it requires a "key" to enable the reader to understand its localisms. Such a paper, when its peculiar period is past, becomes a sealed book, and such the Era became, not on account of its women writers, some of whom no doubt were vapid enough, but because the world moves. *Frances Fuller Victor, "Early California Literature," San Francisco Sunday Call, 19 April 1896, p. 28 c. 2-3.*

After conferring briefly with the lady of the house, Mrs. Victor looked around for her husband. She saw Henry at the bottom of the staircase, beckoning her to come down. As Frances descended, the proprietress gave earnest assurances there were no finer rooms in San Francisco and that she could have them for less than the price first mentioned. The Victors, in the course of their search for suitable living quarters, "made a dozen or two flights up narrow, dusty stairs, which ended, like the first one, in ignominious retreat."[48]

Her husband liked to draw pictures of everything — from San Francisco belles to long-tailed Chinamen, warehouses to public monuments. Frances sometimes liked to go with him on these excursions as a pleasant way to spend a morning.

"The only objection I find to it is, that it gets one in the habit of studying faces rather too earnestly, and is apt to give one an air of impertinence," she explained. "Especially in church this habit pursues one. The sermon may be tedious and our attention wander. To keep from getting fidgetty we take to sketching people in our minds, and directly we have found out the handsomest face in the congregation and are taking notes of that instead of the sermon. This mode of passing time during church service is more delightful than orthodox. More particularly if the music has been good, and has put you in a happy frame of mind."[49]

Frances also spent an afternoon at the U.S. Mint unraveling the mysteries of money-making.

> Nothing interested me so much (if I except the good-looking gentlemen in some of the offices) as the process of assaying as explained to me by the gentlemanly assayer. It would not do to have us humans put into such nice balances! — we should kick the beam directly. A hair's weight turns the balance. It would almost weigh a man's conscience. What a good thing it would be could we establish an assay office for the proving of loyal sentiments. Wouldn't some folks find themselves filliped in the face of the indignant stars by the flying up of their end of the beam! I should like to be there to see. There would be a good many spread eagles on brass buttons going up along with the rest, if the rule of "birds of a feather flock together" means anything in some cases.[50]

6

The Russians

In the fall of 1863, Czar Alexander II of Russia sent his navy to the east and west coasts of the United States — ostensibly on a goodwill mission. The Lincoln administration suspected, however, that the ships had left their bases to avoid being bottled up, destroyed or captured if hostilities developed with the other major European powers over Russian military involvement in occupied Poland.

His father, Nicholas I, had ruled Poland with an iron hand, after suppressing a rebellion in 1830. Alexander pursued a more liberal course, but the Poles remained dissatisfied. A new wave of nationalism swept the country. Open opposition to the government manifested itself on 25 February 1861, and grew to such an extent that all Europe became concerned that a general war would follow.

Thinking the movement would die out if its leaders were seized, the police on the night of 15 January 1863 arrested many young dissidents in Warsaw, with the idea of conscripting them into the Russian Army. This draconian tactic not only failed but sparked a revolt against Russian rule. Young men fled into the forests. One week later, a revolutionary committee called for an insurrection, and as its first decision granted the peasants ownership of the lands they tilled.

For more than a year the Poles fought a guerrilla war against the Russian Army, then the largest in Europe and most feared, whose vastly superior numbers proved decisive. Wholesale executions, confiscations and deportations followed, as authorities tried unsuccessfully to bring Poland even more firmly under Russian control.[1]

But official reports concerning the warships' visit, from Edoard de Stoeckl, the Russian minister in Washington, were deliberately ambiguous. By refusing to state clearly his nation's motives, Stoeckl performed a valuable favor for Lincoln's government that cost the Russians nothing and gave the Union the benefit of every doubt that would arise in European diplomatic circles.[2]

On 11 September 1863, a Russian steam frigate sailed unheralded into New York harbor, and anchored in the Hudson River within sight of seven visiting British and French warships. During the next two weeks, two more Russian frigates and two steam corvettes arrived, including the flagship of Russia's Atlantic fleet.[3]

On the Pacific coast, the lead vessel of a Russian fleet bound for San Francisco Bay ran aground on a sandbar near Point Reyes on September 26. The weather that morning was very foggy, and the officers of the steam corvette *Novick* had misjudged her position. The vessel struck the beach about 5 a.m. Her engines were immediately reversed in an attempt to back off, but heavy incoming surf tossed the ship broadside onto the sand in about five or ten feet of water. Only one crew member died; 176 officers and men were rescued and brought to San Francisco. Most of the equipment, personal belongings, and other movables, also were saved, but the hull was battered to pieces.

During the next six weeks, four more Russian corvettes and a frigate steamed into the bay. Rear-Admiral A.A. Popov, "a very able officer" who commanded Russia's Pacific fleet, previously visited San Francisco in 1859 and 1862 and already had many friends there.[4]

When he heard rumors that the Confederate cruisers *Alabama* and *Sumter* planned to attack California, the Russian admiral ordered his ships "to put on steam and clear for action . . . to repel any attempt against the security" of the city.[5]

This unauthorized order alarmed the Russian minister, who warned Popov not to become involved in America's war. But Stoeckl acknowledged that the admiral had "the right, in the name of humanity, and not for political reasons, to prevent" a direct Confederate attack on San Francisco.[6]

Although Popov saw no combat with the Confederacy, he did win public esteem for heroic service.

About 1:30 a.m. on Friday, October 23, San Franciscans woke from the reveries of sleep to the clanging of bells and the sharp rattle of fire engines over the pavement. A blaze had broken out in the business district, in the block bordered by California, Sacramento, Davis and Drumm streets.

Admiral Popov ordered 300 of his men ashore to help in fire-fighting efforts and they "rendered as efficient service as men accustomed all their lives to the control of water might be expected to," a reporter noted.[7]

Nobody died in the blaze, but several firemen and a number of Russian sailors were injured. Scores of families were made homeless and several businesses were destroyed. The area consisted primarily of wooden buildings, mostly two-story, used for storage and manufacturing purposes, with many of the upper rooms serving as residences.

A grateful city raised funds to aid the Russian sailors injured while fighting the blaze or trying to save property. Handsomely embossed resolutions of appreciation, ordered by the Board of Supervisors, were presented to the officers and crews.

On Tuesday, 17 November 1863, the Russian officers were the guests of honor at Union Hall, on Howard Street near the corner of Third, at a lavish soirée arranged by the people of San Francisco.

"Every preparation has been made to make it the entertainment of the season," a journalist said of the occasion, "and it assumes an importance from the political complexion given it, as an expression of the good feeling existing between Russia and the United States, which it would not possess were it merely a social and fashionable demonstration. The affair has been gotten up wholly by subscription, and the tickets to it are complimentary. It is expected that all the Governmental officials and army and navy officers will be present."[8]

The ballroom itself was elegantly and tastefully decorated with arches of evergreen, banners, emblems and inscriptions. A portrait of George Washington smiled at likenesses of the Czar and Czarina, which occupied places of honor on either wall further down the room.

"The double-headed eagle perched above the stars and stripes on divers emblematic shields, and the Russian arms quartered themselves with our national device, while the Russian banner and bear lovingly intertwined with the Federal flag," a local newspaper reported. "Russian navy officers, Admiral Popoff preëminent, and the officers of our own army and navy, shook hands together in a desperate attempt to pronounce each other's names or perish in the attempt."[9]

One guest was mortified to see "that the Russian officers had twice the gold lace and buttons on their clothes that our own had," but he felt this was "a defect on costume merely, that can be remedied by special act of Congress."[10]

The business, military and political sectors were well represented; and the many ladies who attended looked so "superb" as to cause gloom on their husbands' faces when they passed or anyone complimented them.

"Intellectually speaking, it was a tremendous success. The ladies looked Gay and I say it with a big 'G,'" wrote one observer. ". . . The whole thing was a *feat*, well 'worthy of our steel.'"[11]

The guest also related that the flotilla's commander, Admiral Popov, "confidently told me he was still on good terms with the Czar, and thought the decorations of the hall brilliant in the extreme."[12]

The admiral's dress uniform "was highly embellished with legions of medals, generously bestowed on him — for great meritorious conduct in the late Crimean conflict — by his true friend the Czar."[13]

Mrs. Victor was present at the affair with her husband. She looked radiant; and, because her finery was considered more in harmony with Russian taste than that of other ladies present, she opened the ball by dancing with Admiral Popov.

"The music was excellent and loud enough for any battle-field," one observer remarked. Dancing began about 9:30 and continued for several hours.[14]

It was indeed an elegant occasion; euphoria and good spirits reigned. Frances must have been ecstatic that evening, gliding around the dance floor with her stately, bemedalled partner while the city's best society watched. Her raiment was stunning, and she was not the least bit reticent in describing it:

> . . . [My] skirt, which was of rose-colored satin, had a view of the city of St. Petersburg worked in silver on the front breadth, a diamond being

introduced here and there to represent the glitter of its distant spires in the morning sun. At one side was a hunting scene in a forest of silver. At the other side a winter festival, also in silver; and on the back breadths the Russian fleet in a shimmering sea of silver. A fringe of silver around the bottom of the skirt (which was not a trailing one,) was headed by a delicate band of ermine. The body was made up in the peasant style, pink satin laced over a very full undershirt of white tulle, coming up to the throat, and having long full sleeves fastened at the wrist with bracelets of gold and pearl. A necklace to match, finished it at the throat. The body was without sleeves, and was elegantly embroidered with pearls and diamonds put on in the shape of bunches of fern leaves. The cord which laced it, and shoulder-straps, were of silver, the latter worked with diamonds. My hair was worn in the style of Catharine II.'s portraits, and dressed with pink and white feathers fastened with a butterfly of gold and pearl, with diamond eyes. Slippers embroidered with silver and brilliants. I carried a fan of white silk embroidered to match my dress, and having a pearl handle, in which was set a fine portrait of Alexander II. Handkerchief of point lace, with a small cambric centre bearing my initials in silver thread and fine pearls.[15]

A fringe of seed pearls lining her gloves at the wrist got caught on a button of the admiral's uniform. A good many pearls were scattered, and Mrs. Victor presumed some of them were found when the hall was swept the next day.

Secure in the knowledge that she looked beautiful, Frances also had no fears about her dancing. "If my feet were set to going by a strain of good dancing music," she wrote, "they would keep right on without further trouble as long as it would be expedient to dance with one partner."[16]

She persuaded Henry, who usually liked to slouch around in old clothes, to dress up for once — and he did.

"Rose-colored lining to his coat skirt, gold braiding on his vest, emblems on his sleeves, faultless gloves and boots, and a perfume of some delicate bo[u]quet floating about him," she noted with approval. "If he colored his moustache, or whitened his forehead with powder, I didn't see him do it; but he looked splendidly."[17]

The confections upon the banquet table were elegant and unique, with a distinctly Russian ambience.

Especially noteworthy, Frances wrote, "was an immense cake, representing something like a mountain. Trees covered with frost(ing) imitated a deep forest. Through this forest lay a narrow and dangerous road, down which a sleigh was flying at the heels of two wild horses, tandem; and a whole pack of wolves made of red sugar was pursuing, evidently with the intention of making a dinner off the two yellow candy figures in the sleigh."[18]

Mrs. Victor lost her appetite contemplating that exciting scene. She made a show of eating, however, and relied on having a mouthful of food to account to her left-hand neighbor, a Russian naval officer, for her poor pronunciation of the German in which they were trying to have a conversation.

. . . I could not help reflecting upon my culpability in making the polite Lieut. beg my pardon a dozen times for not comprehending me, when it was utterly impossible for me to comprehend myself. But I managed to divert his attention by losing my fan, and getting half-a-dozen gentlemen to look for it, the Lieut. among the rest. Just before supper was over I found it in the folds of my dress.[19]

"The grand supper was well rendered, and reflected great credit on the getters up thereof," remarked another writer, of obviously well-refined culinary tastes. "The Russian cranberry sauce was particularly fine. . . . The Russian pickles were too sour to be perfect. The sponge-cake was good, however, and no doubt consisted of the best material. The Castle of Ice was also well done, though a little too cold. 'Young pidgeons, containing champagne sauce, fried on a hot stove' fully realized all expectations. It exactly suited the public taste."[20]

The menu was so long that a supplement had to be issued, "and the lusciousness of the reading fully compensated hungry ones for the impossibility of getting anything to eat in the general melee of the supper room."[21]

Wine was more abundant than water, and one wag noted that many of the guests wished they could reverse the miracle of Galilee. The supply of champagne would have run out, however, but for the timely arrival of the ship *Fabius* from France. A special permit allowed the landing of fifty baskets of Napoleon's Cabinet, direct from the vineyard and presses of Bouché Fils & Co. in sunny Champagne, expressly for the occasion.

Mrs. Victor had a very pleasant time, as did many others. The festivities, she wrote, "were protracted to a late hour" — until almost 5 a.m. — and departing guests were so sleepy that many grabbed the wrong hats and overcoats as they left, "to the loss of some and the gain of others."[22] These mishaps, she felt, made the occasion more interesting and would contribute to its being long remembered by local citizens.

7

City and Country Episodes, 1863-1864

In early December 1863, the Victors decided to go to the head of San Francisco Bay on a hunting trip. Frances told *The Golden Era* editors:

> . . . I carry the ammunition, and count the game. I have [Henry's] promise not to make game of me; but, should he do so, mistaking me for the goose he often calls me, you will of course write a neat farewell address for me to the readers of the ERA, and sign yourself, very regretfully,

> FLORENCE FANE.[1]

The couple left very quietly, with only a compact traveling bag or two. Frances and Henry had nothing to look after but themselves, and they found Mother Nature in one of her more benign moods.

"She never once breathed roughly on us, nor wore a clouded face. She led us through pleasant meadows, by lagoons swarming with myriads of water-fowls, into vall[eys] just growing green again, over wild mountain declivities, and among the haunts of the grizzly. She permitted us to explore her deep forests, and search out her hidden springs of moisture. And, oh, what a joy was that to the sand-blinded eyes of a San Franciscan! Real woods! Genuine thickets where ferns and other water-loving plants grow gigantically," Mrs. Victor wrote *The Golden Era* enthusiastically upon her return.

"Then such views! Where have your artists been that they never sketched these scenes? Why was there nobody to tell Bierstadt* where to find the choicest California landscapes? We wondered not a little over the question, and somebody who overheard us volunteered the remark that Ross Browne* had declared that he had seen nothing finer in Europe. Considering that Ross Browne is so careful an observer, we felt proud of the sanction."[2]

*For biographies, see pp. 239-240.

Their tour was not a professional one "by any means," Frances emphasized. "I am horrified at professional tourists. Haven't I traveled with them often? — and don't they always carry guns, and dogs, and fishing-tackle, and boxes, and blankets, and geologists' hammers? — and don't they smoke in your face, and laugh immoderately, and often refer to a flask of something — cologne, I presume — which they carry in an inside pocket? Defend me from the company of your regular tourist! Especially if he has ever seen the inside of a German University, or any University whatever."[3]

The Victors paused for awhile in a small village, where the more civilized amenities were lacking save several subscriptions to *The Golden Era*. When Frances learned this, she feared that the simplicity of the place would be found departing, and resolved that once she established residence she would somehow stop the circulation of Sunday papers.

Frances declined to publicly identify the place that proved so attractive to her and Henry, for fear someone would jump their claim. She did reveal that it was by the ocean and backed by mountains.*

"It is free from winds and fogs," she wrote, "and abounds in all types of beauty from grand to lovely scenes, with a charming variety of either, and just enough wildness to make cultivation a delightful work of art."[4]

Mrs. Victor returned to the city for the holidays because she wanted to see San Franciscans on a Christmas binge. She gazed into "the many elegant bazaars that lay in wait for plethoric purses," but had heeded her husband's advice to leave hers, which was none too full, at home. "I found the experiment a safe one," she admitted.[5]

Frances spent a couple of days "in the commendable exercise of walking, and looking and admiring."[6]

She couldn't help hoping that some of the gifts she saw in Montgomery Street store windows would be in her room on Christmas morning. The things she wanted, however, were not mentioned in the commandment against covetousness.

> For Beauty, you see, . . . like light and air, is free to the enjoyment of all God's creatures. Nothing but the loss of sight can make a man so poor that he may not revel in beautiful visions, and in visions of the beautiful, quite as rapturously as the rich man. The old Scotchman's philosophy, who was as rich as his master when he had looked at his gold, was the true one. The rich man's riches consist in his hoards of other treasure purchased with gold. He looks at it, and his enjoyment soon palls through familiarity. The poor man who sees it seldom, has livelier emotions of pleasure than does the owner. So true and strong is this principle, that the poorest people used to living in cities where every form of elegance may be constantly seen, have their tastes for the artificially beautiful so cultivated by contact, that they can never be persuaded to live in the country, not having learned to estimate properly the more majestic beauty which may be found in even the wildest haunts of Nature.[7]

---

*It could well have been Half Moon Bay.

Frances did not retract anything she had said about "the execrable climate of San Francisco," but felt much better knowing that within 100 miles there was a haven she could retreat to, shaking the dust of the city off the soles of her shoes at its threshold.[8]

While in San Francisco, Frances visited several Chinese families who were celebrating their New Year. What most impressed her was the absence of other women.

"Only one Chinese Madame made her appearance," Mrs. Victor recalled, "and she only that she might parade her little black-eyed boy with his tinseled cap, who was learning no doubt, to receive New Year's calls like his papa."[9]

She shook hands with the youngster, and talked outside with his father after bowing to the mother through the open doorway.

Frances asserted that she could never be satisfied with a society in which men were the only active and representative portion.

"*I* wouldn't stand quietly by and see my lord making tea for other ladies, while I looked on through a half-closed door!" Frances exclaimed. "And happy will be the day for the China woman when she says, 'I will not!'"[10]

Mrs. Victor spent most of the spring and summer of 1864 enjoying a rural life. She was "only a little weary of uninterrupted innocent simplicity" by the time of her return to "earthquake-threatened and stock-ruined" San Francisco.[11] But instead of "restless pining after a taste of the wicked though fascinating falsehoods of Metropolitan society," she got caught up in preparations for the Christian Commission Fair.[12]

"The money that goes to the Christian Commission, goes for the most part in small sums," Frances explained. ". . . It goes for a cause sacred to the hearts of all the people of this land — its benefits reach even to our foes, in the truly Christian spirit, ministering to all alike who are in peril and in sadness; and its demands can no more be refused, than could the suffering or the dying soldier be turned away, could he crawl for help to your doorstone."[13]

She went early on opening day to get a good look at all the fine things before the hall filled with people. The effort was worthwhile, she thought.

"We came very near casting ourselves away in that charming grotto at the left of the door as you enter," Mrs. Victor told her readers. "We wished we were a mermaid, and had such an apartment in the bottom of the sea. We fancied ourself sitting on one of those sea-green rocks, smoothing our cheeks upon one of those polished shells, while some gentle merman wound our long, green tresses with a wreath of sea-mosses ready pressed and dried, like those to be purchased at this alcove."[14]

Table after table, laden with beautiful and useful items, vied for the patronage of fair-goers. The prices, Frances noted with pleasure and relief, were not exorbitant, and she hoped the money would purchase "more substantial comforts" for wounded and sick soldiers.

"Pleasant faces smiled at us from behind the tables, willing hands served us both at the booths and the refreshment tables — flowers scented the air — gay promenaders moved in masses about the hall — cheerfulness, goodwill, and pleasant visions of beauty greeted us at every turn," she related.[15]

Talking about prices of things at the fair led Mrs. Victor to reflect on impulse buying, which trait men found so annoying in women.

"We poor feminines are quite used to that, and having to endure it every day of the week, Sundays excepted, at the hands of the other sex, it is but natural we should enjoy retaliation when the opportunity affords," she declared.[16]

Frances averred that she always entered a store in San Francisco, save one or two, "with a trepidation experienced under no other circumstances. There is something about the bearing of every clerk in it which says as plainly as print, 'If you want anything short of a *moire antique* be quick about it. Cannot stop to show you anything less: hurry up, can't you?'"[17]

Mrs. Victor wrote that since she had a firm belief in her own good taste, and a desire to gratify it, she wanted

> five minutes at least in which to select a new dress. But the clerk does not want you to have it; and if he has not got the article you desire, he insists on your taking one you do not desire. He tells you to your face that you are a goose — that you don't know what is fashionable, or becoming, or proper. He assures you that a scant pattern is ample, or a monstrous number of yards little enough — no lady thinks of having less — in short, he treats you as if he had worn petticoats all his life and quite understood the thing, while you — well, you might have worn the breeches, or you might have dressed *a la* "poor Cassimer," [a handsome young man in trouble as a spy, a stage character in drama] for all you know about clothes. And then if you should venture to disagree with him; to think that the article he recommends is not what you were looking for; to doubt if he has what you desired to purchase — none, I assure you, having once experienced the effect of such a bold proceeding, can ever venture upon it again without more than the ordinary amount of courage. Especially she would never again be so foolish as to wilfully encounter like treatment in the same place. Why I have been so effectually wilted, quenched and annihilated before now, that I went home to hide my confusion in the dimness of my own curtained room, where no prying eyes could possibly discover what a shabby, know-nothing, despicable individual I was, and spent the remainder of the day in reflecting upon the superior wisdom of men-clerks in the department intended to furnish female clothing, and in resolving that when I take a lady's maid to Happy Valley it will be one selected from among the gentlemanly clerks of this virtuous and happy city.[18]

The fourteenth anniversary of California statehood was near, and Frances looked forward to attending the Society of California Pioneers' annual ball, an event she had missed the preceding year being new to the city and unfamiliar with its society. Imagine her dismay when their program of scheduled events did not include a ball.

"It *was* a great oversight in the Pioneers, because now they have been introduced to me, and I might have gone to their ball without compromising my dignity, as I could not have done last year," Frances lamented. "It seems odd that men of their varied experience should not have understood the case better."[19]

Other socialites did not take the absence of a ball so philosophically. One friend, Mrs. Victor reported, "was quite daft for a whole afternoon" after hearing the news.[20]

Frances was more peeved, however, that a poem she had written was not chosen for the ceremonies marking statehood. The honor went instead to Bret Harte, a better-known Western litterateur.

Frances disliked the tendency of pioneer gatherings to heap encomiums upon their male forebears and exclude the women, whose sacrifices were often as great or greater.

"I have often wondered, when I have heard of the Pilgrim Fathers, where had been the Pilgrim Mothers. Was the zeal which inspired them to leave homes and kindred, for a shelter in the wilderness, less holy in them than in the Fathers?" she asked pointedly. "Perhaps their zeal was not for their religion, but only for their lords. Ah? Let their wifely devotion be remembered, then. Could not waves drown, or winds beat upon, nor ice freeze, those delicate women? Could not savages kill, and sickness destroy those brave and faithful women? Pilgrim Fathers, forsooth! These mutual admiration societies all on one side of the house do not recommend themselves to my admiration."[21]

As the Civil War dragged on, with many bloody and sometimes inconclusive battles, the North's superiority in manpower and materiel gradually made itself felt.

Still, as the 1864 presidential campaign got underway, there was such war-weariness as to make the question of Abraham Lincoln's re-election an interesting one.

Frequent displays of patriotism were the rule. In October, Frances saw one being arranged in a shop-window nearly opposite her apartment. For two days, she watched the proprietor arrange and rearrange an assortment of eagles, pedestals and flags until he had what he thought was an appropriate motif.

Frances herself was preparing to put lights in her window to show solidarity with a parade that night in support of the Union.

"We have had enough of soft speaking and equivocation," she asserted. "I hate equivocation; and I despise fashionable, silken-handed amiability, — that is, too delicate to be anything decided. A downright knave is more easily met, and more pardonable, than the vacillating 'good man' who never knows when to do right until the occasion is past. Sins of omission are fully as reprehensible as sins of commission, though people are not apt to think so. If you see a man drowning, and make no effort to save him, or his house on fire and offer no assistance, can you walk away with no feeling of criminality in your conscience? Small would be the conscience that would not suffer guilt."[22]

Mrs. Victor felt that in time of national crisis, anyone who remained passive, showing neither support nor opposition to the government, gave covert assistance to the enemy.

"I would prefer an open enemy, an avowed traitor, to the apparent friend who should fail me in a time of need: even to the non-committal and conditional friend whose numerous mental reservations nullified what faint feeling he might have for me," she wrote.[23]

A San Francisco paper contended that the war, with all its fiery carnage and extreme opinions on either side of the issues, had brought about an unprecedented display of party spirit.

The principles espoused by the Republican and Democratic parties, the editor wrote, "have been ventilated in extremest virulence upon the thoroughfare, and in parlor and counting-house, and through the press and upon the hustings. Everywhere the eyes of our fellow-citizens were dilated with nervous excitement, and their voices were animated and tremulous in discussive heat. It was the fiercest and most unrelenting civil contest since the travails that accompanied our governmental birth. Never before in newspaper literature did the press steep its arrows in such poison of vituperation."[24]

Amid the tragic news of war and the harsh rhetoric of politics, Frances found relief when a small quail landed on her windowsill in search of food.

"He don't realize, poor little wanderer, that we should be much more likely to put him into our own mouths than to put anything into his mouth," she reflected sadly. "He does not understand the ways of the world, being fresh from the southern fields, where grass-seed used to be plenty, and he led a quiet, happy life."[25]

Perhaps, she thought, the young bird was one of her own Happy Valley family, who thought it was time for her to come home and care for him and Henry.

"I agree that it nearly is, little quail, but not quite yet," Frances whispered reassuringly, "not quite yet," as she fed him some crumbs.[26]

On Tuesday, 8 November 1864, approximately 21,000 San Francisco men cast their ballots in ten hours at twelve polling stations. Most of them undoubtedly heeded, at least in part, the advice Frances gave two days before:

> Rise early, say your prayers, putting in a good petition for the Union; eat a plain substantial breakfast; avoid all excitement; call on your wavering next-door neighbor with the proper ticket, and ask him kindly to come out like a man; — come out like a man yourself when the polls are opened, and deposit in the ballot-box your unconditional vote for LINCOLN AND JOHNSON.[27]

In marked contrast to the campaign, election day passed without "a solitary attempt at infraction of law." Citizens voted "silently and solemnly," the editor noted approvingly, "and that accomplished, they as peacefully retired to await in eager expectancy the portentous result."[28]

Frances donned hat and shawl to go out and look around herself. From a horse-car, she saw long lines of voters stretching away a block or two from the polling places. It was a heartening sight, for she knew most were loyal Union men.

"When I see a fine exhibition of genuine loyalty — good faith in the masses, it rouses my enthusiasm, till I feel like huzza-ing," Mrs. Victor wrote.[29]

The days and weeks passed swiftly, until one beautiful November morning Mrs. Victor decided to arrest the process by spending the day in utter idleness and contemplation.

There were times, she thought, when it seemed impious to do the usual things — "where merely to live, enjoy, and thank God seems enough to do, and by far the most natural and suitable thing to do."[30]

Frances considered herself "a simple fraction only of the great autumnal picture lying warm and ripening in the soft November sunshine."[31] She was relaxed, and everyday considerations — "flat, stale and unprofitable" — had been banished from her mind. "But all that is spiritual rises untold degrees by comparison," she wrote.

> Truly there are days when "idleness *is* sweet and sacred" — go your ways, you of the sordid souls who never knew its sacred sweetness! — I "have a day to be idle:" I shall be "idle for a day." But not to all alike, even of those who could find spiritual rest and gladness in such golden seasons as this, comes the enjoyment of its peace. Those there are, who like Rachel mourning for her children and refusing to be comforted, are blind through tears, and insensible through pain, to the delicious 'sense of being alive' on days like this. To them joy is a mockery, and peace unknown. They have not found the meaning out, that lies in wrong and pain and strife; they know not why they walk through grief, to reach the crowning joys of life. They see the world so bright and fair, the heart with beauty often aches — but ere they quiet this sweet pain, some cross so presses, the heart breaks. To-day, this lovely, golden day, when heaven and earth are steeped in calm; when every lightest air that blows, sheds its delicious freight of balm: if they but ope their lips they sob; if but an eyelid lift they weep — they deprecate all good, all ill, and only wish for endless sleep. . . .
>
> . . . The very way to cure melancholy people of their sadness is to humor them to the top of their bent. Encourage them in every possible way to feel themselves abused, and directly they begin to assume a doubtful expression, which after going through several shades of relief, finally becomes one of positive pleasure. If it makes people happy to be thought miserable, why make them happy in their own way; sooner or later they will tire of it and come out on the happy side of their characters voluntarily. But do not tell me that there are some who are perforce miserable — too unhappy to be comforted even by the most genuine sympathy. For all such on this lovely day I say, God help them. For myself I am too happy and too idle to be pricked very deeply with other[s'] griefs.[32]

Mrs. Victor had read, in a San Francisco newspaper, about the pleasures of visiting Oakland and the tribulations faced by residents there. She resolved never to be persuaded to make an excursion to "those trans-Francisco shores" lest while "wandering about the rural Oakland streets, in simple enjoyment of sand and sunshine and dusty-rusty shade," she be mistaken as a tourist desiring only a free lunch.[33] In fact, she "much preferred having my own crackers and cheese in my pocket."[34]

But Frances' "earthly resolves" crumbled when she and Miss Rosemary, a friend, were invited to enjoy the hospitality of a lady who had a residence on the other side of the bay — "a sort of sight draft for a welcome and a lunch whenever I choose to present it."[35]

One day, at 9 a.m., the two women rode over on the "neat and comfortable" ferry-boat *Louise*. They were, Frances wrote, "as blithe and gay as youth and clear consciences could make them."[36]

Her only regret was in not bringing a basket of goodies for them to enjoy leisurely "in the glorious air of a clear autumn morning," as the vessel glided over the pellucid waters of the bay.[37] She was consoled by the thought that Mrs. Barberry would be so glad to see them that she would be willing to sacrifice "a couple of hours out of the best of the day."[38]

Alas, that estimable lady was not so inclined. Mrs. Barberry appeared not to remember having invited the two young women to come over and visit some day that week. She said she had a cold, which Frances thought may have accounted for her uneasiness.

"The cold I think seemed to have got into her manners more than into her head; she might have said it was upon her lungs, but I thought she acted like a person suffering from a cold on the heart," Mrs. Victor wrote.[39]

Mrs. Barberry replied "Ah" and "Yes" when her guests said they intended to do a lot of walking and perhaps make several sketches.

"I think she considered it a good thing," Frances recalled, "and rather wished we should go about it; which we directly did, bidding her an affectionate — and final — good-by."[40]

Strolling around Oakland, she noticed that the whole town had an absent, "not at home" sort of look, and wondered if it had become so through the same forgetfulness that affected Mrs. Barberry.

"Miss Rosemary thought not — she says Arcadians are always invisible; and now that I think of it, I believe they are so; certainly the greater number of people we met were not Arcadians," Mrs. Victor wrote.

> Now it might have put some young ladies out to have had to change their plans as we did that day; but not Miss Rosemary and I. We sauntered about the sandy streets in a "gay and festive" manner; found a lunch at a place where we had not been previously invited; made surly watch-dogs bark by peeping over fences, and practiced our ideas of happy independence as we liked . . . Walking up to San Antonio we beheld all that is beautiful in the different views of Oakland. We also saw much that at this season of the year is ugly enough. If Ross Browne had sent Arizona up to Oakland he couldn't have sent a more arid-looking piece of mother earth than his own place presents at present.[41]

When Frances got home, her husband asked if she had cold chicken or cold ham for lunch.

"I told him I had cold shoulder," she related. "Poor innocent! he does not see the point of that joke, and really believes I lunched off boiled mutton and currant jelly."[42]

The situation in Mexico had been the topic of much discussion in San Francisco and elsewhere for several years.

At a distance, it was possible for Americans to be light-hearted; and one of Mrs. Victor's acquaintances attributed the lack of rain in California to the extraordinary fall of "Maximilian's reign" on Mexico. He insisted that because of the drought "events no longer had a current, but had taken to their bed and dried up."[43]

Though the supply of paper money was growing, this man told Frances, greenbacks were not yet widely used on the Pacific coast.*

---

*For more about the financing of business transactions in California at that time, see p. 247.

"He thought it would be a long time before they could get over the bars of gold and silver which obstructed their course," she wrote. "The only event of the week that according to his knowledge was current, was the pudding on Thanksgiving day — that was a currant pudding."

> Are you such a natural that you cannot be sensible? Do be serious, and tell me what I wish to know.
> No, I'll not be Sirius. Sirius is the dog-star, and it is always on the ascendant in San Francisco — always current — if you want a current event. Nothing but dogs, live dogs, and dead dogs, in San Francisco. No, thank you, I'll not be Sirius.
> Be amusing, then.
> I always am a musing: — especially of late I think I have mused too much on some subjects. In my musings I have tried to discover a new method of squaring the circle: — how to get a square meal within the circle of a dime; but I cannot make it out; I don't think I have a mathematical brain.[44]

When Frances agreed with this opinion, the gentleman scowled and grabbed his hat to leave. But at the door he relented, and came back to tell her that the week's current event was a wheelbarrow ride down Montgomery Street, at which thousands of spectators assisted, besides a giant, a clown, a Lilliputian pony, and a brass band.

> . . . Now the story had been told to me before, therefore it was no news, yet was said to be quite a nuisance to the Police; to passengers in street cars who did not pass, but remained stationary, though never before had they been known to be inside of a stationers; to stationary people who had an ink-ling of what was going on, yet "couldn't see it," and kept in-quiring where all those persons were bound, and what so many editions of cheers were all about. As for the windows, the balconies, the roofs and chimneys of San Francisco, these were swarming with the boot-y and gall-antry of our city, who in a very carnival-iverous manner, made themselves merry at the sight of one butcher wheeling another butcher over the cobble stones to the tune of the "Pauper's Funeral" — "Rattle his bones over the stones" *etc. Vive la bagatelle!*[45]

Mrs. Victor stayed awake all of one late fall night in eager anticipation of seeing a meteor shower that was predicted by Benjamin Silliman (1816-1885), a noted professor of chemistry and mineralogy at Yale University, known also for his study of meteorites. But the vigil kept by many citizens was of no avail, and Frances wrote irritatedly:

> Blessed are they that expect nothing, for they shall not be disappointed. With this happy motto I console myself when I have been so foolishly confiding as to expect something, and get — nothing. . . . If Prof. Silliman had prophesied meteors, why didn't he have meteors? Why did he induce people by irresponsible statements to ruin their good looks catching colds in their heads, besides losing a night's sleep?
> Why do not scientific men keep the run of things to some purpose? If we had known that the top of Mt. Baker was going to sink into itself, and the mountain going to emit fire and smoke, we should have gone on an excursion to see the interesting phenomenon. What a hard drinker the old mountain must be, to swallow so much of "the crater" at one gulp! I don't care

much for meteors nor earthquakes, nor for burning mountains, but I dote on comets — comets with long shining tails — starry birds of paradise. If any of the Professors see one coming this way at present, shall be glad to be notified; but shall not sit up any more for meteors. The fireworks the Union Clubs sent up the heavens were the most beautiful kind of falling stars when they were coming down: besides we knew what they meant, which is more than can be said of meteors. If there has been a Presidential election among the planets, and they have elected a Union candidate, why don't the Professors say so? In that case I might sit up another night, out of a sentiment of sympathy with staunch planetary principles. But if there has been a rebellion in space, and the falling stars are disunion fireworks, I couldn't be brought to take the least notice of them; — no, not if they should rain all around me — they might consider themselves quenched with contempt.[46]

Despite the many signs of the city's apparent prosperity, hundreds of San Franciscans struggled to survive, in miserable conditions.

Mrs. Victor looked into the "vulgar reality" faced by a poor widow living with three children in a decrepit old tenement building.

The one-room apartment, Frances reported, contained all the woman's worldly possessions, "which are few and insignificant enough."[47]

She cleaned other people's dirty clothes. And when she was lucky enough to have customers, the washer-woman had to carry water from a nearby street corner up to her third-floor residence to wash and rinse the garments, and then carry it down to the street again.

Mrs. Victor suggested that young men, recently released from army service and who felt they could not afford to marry, ought to consider the advantages they had in being able to support a family:

. . . If men absorb all the paying occupations, and leave women only the most menial and ill-paid of work by which to live, what is their evident duty? Why, to make up the deficit out of their own pockets. Again, a man has all his time in which to earn his living — he, be he rich or poor, being waited upon to food, clean, ready-made clothing, and all that; while the woman who earns her living must take time and strength to prepare her food, make, mend, and wash her clothes, and keep her house decent; and often all this for several children besides. What would the fine, soldierly young man do in a situation of this sort? Would his courage sustain him, do you think?

But suppose the poor washer, or the soldierly young man, cannot obtain the even employment which, through the severest labor, would furnish a subsistence? Suppose the children must be taken care of by this one guardian, because the Asylums were not made for "half-orphans?" What is the temptation of the poor striving wretches who cannot find bread for their mouths? Do you think it never comes into the care-crazed brain to make them altogether orphans, in order that they may be fed and clothed by reluctant charity? Never doubt but it often does; haunting the weary mind in the dreams of night as in the despairing thoughts of daylight. Yet newspaper reporters jeer at the hopeless would-be suicide who attempts to end her life, which hinders her children's welfare.

I don't want to make you blue, dear ERA, but I fear we go on too much as if everybody was as happy and as fortunate as ourselves.[48]

Frances talked with her friend Miss Rosemary, who agreed that something should be done to help such overworked and underfed women.

Miss Rosemary believed she would establish a center, similar to those in Paris, where, for a small fee, working mothers' children were cared for during the day.

Mrs. Victor, on the other hand, favored construction of "a washer-woman's row — tenements made suited to their calling and for their convenience — while the mother is away earning their support — where they could live decently and afford to pay a fair rent."[49]

She subscribed to the sentiment then prevalent on the Pacific coast against Chinese labor, and felt the poor and starving should be given work in preference to the "thriftless competition" posed by Orientals, whom she considered merely slaves earning money for their masters to send to China.

She conceded that some readers might consider these matters too serious for a "Florence Fane" column, for it was not often she presented a thoughtful face.

"There are many who will want for food this winter unless they have help from the prosperous ones," she explained. "The different societies, with whose managers I have talked, have their hands full of poor, but not their treasuries full of money, but quite the contrary. Will not somebody who chances to notice this appeal, constitute and resolve themselves into a committee to help the societies, or to look out cases of suffering for themselves?"[50]

On 20 November 1864, "Florence Fane" told *Golden Era* readers that she would be leaving San Francisco "for an indefinite period of time."[51] It was a decision Frances made reluctantly, for one and one-half years of poking around and looking into things had made her "familiar with [the] city, and tolerably conversant with the characteristics of the country."[52] She met many San Franciscans, admired many and condemned a few of their habits. "Just at the moment of parting they seem all admirable," she confided.

> Dear ERA, mine is the same California story — I came, I saw, I went away again. To make the analogy complete, I shall have to return here once more, hungering and thirsting for the brightness of California skies; languishing for the tonic of San Franciscan airs.
> . . .
> I think with affection even of the frowsy winds, the blinding sands, and the racking sidewalks. I am willing to risk being run over by a half dozen express-wagons, two horsemen, and one truck, at every street-crossing. I don't mind paying three prices for everything as long as I have any money to pay with. I am proud of the good order and loyalty of your city, of the generous hearts, and charitable hands of its people. But this is praise to which you were long ago accustomed, and which I shall not dwell upon, through a fear of being tiresome. I only cast lingering glances behind me at the many hills, crowned some with palatial residences, and some with picturesque looking shanties, of which a windmill is the chiefest part. I saunter again in imagination along Montgomery street, elbowed by Chinamen, and crowded off the crossings by sublimely unconscious street brokers. The beautiful show-windows, the inviting fruit stores, the various elegant snares for purse-strings tempt me yet a little longer. I am busy once more comparing this city with others, and drawing distinctions by which to give it a personality of its own:

for cities are like individuals in their points of difference and correspondence; some being wise and prudent, some wise and wicked, some wicked and reckless, and others either dull and commonplace, or wild and witty. Shall I name the class to which *belle* San Francisco belongs? — or is her character too mixed?

It often happens that the wild and witty ones get more love than the wise and prudent — which proves nothing in favor of the former, but only goes to show the total depravity of human affections. If you care for counsel, try the prudent wisdom first, and if that does not win love, there is time enough for the witty wildness afterward.

Yes, I shall go away from you, Queen o the Pacific, and you will continue to grow in beauty and wisdom to be the astonishment of all observers. As that eminently poetical writer, Walt Whitman, would say:

Your streets will be lengthened and graded —
Montgomery, Market, and Second and Third streets,
Kearny will also be widened; your hills
Will sink before the pick and the shovel;
Telegraph and Russian — barring a place for the
        reservoir —
Will be spaded away into levels, over which
Horse-cars can run with their passengers
Going and coming to business or pleasure.
Chinadom will be removed from Pacific
And Jackson, and also from Sacramento,
Away from under the sensitive noses
Of men and women and children
Of the superior races of white men.
You will have a Pacific railroad;
And a floating bridge of steamers
To the Sandwich Islands and China;
With a pre-empted title to Mexico.

Well, so be it. I have only let Happy Valley to good paying tenants: and years from now, when I am world-weary, sad and old, I shall return to claim possession, and die in peace. Meantime, dear ERA, you can shoot game, and gather grapes off my premises when it suits you to do so; and while so doing give an occasional thought to your wandering friend and correspondent,

FLORENCE FANE.[53]

8

On to Oregon

In early December 1864, Mrs. Victor went with several friends to the coast for a last outing, and experienced what she considered "one of the saddest and dreariest things in nature" — a heavy rain over the sea.

"Poor old Ocean! how melancholy, abashed, and crestfallen he seems!" she reflected. "The saucy deluge pours down upon him, subdues his sparkle, sobers his hues, tames his wild freedom — in fact makes him seem quite another thing than the ocean he was yesterday. If the comparison were not peculiarly odious, I should say he looked as dejected as a damp chicken. But I will not make such a comparison — I have too much respect for the dignity of his Oceanship; besides it would not be a sea-sonable simile."[1]

Frances' heart felt a sadness at seeing so many forces under restraint, even though "the spectacle of great power in action is often exceedingly terrible to witness."[2] The ocean was like a strong man chained in the marketplace, who, though she might prefer to keep him in check, was so impressive that she couldn't go away and easily forget him.

"*His* heart would be beating in *our* breasts, and *our* nerves would be tingling with the wild fever of *his*," she thought. "And so I kept saying to myself 'poor old Ocean!' as the floods bound his mighty billows in sudden bondage, though Heaven knows his waves are one of the things in this world I do fear!"[3]

A lady companion told Mrs. Victor it was "very imprudent, and improper, and improvident, and every other imp," for her to expose herself to such a dreadful rain.[4] But Frances had read of Noah and the ark, and wanted to get an idea of what that Biblical mariner experienced.

"I think now that I have it," she wrote that evening in the cozy comfort of her seaside retreat. "He could not see a dozen yards from his vessel, whether there was anything ahead or not. Doubtless the world looked drowned to him, as to all intents and purposes it was; and he must have had a sad time during those forty days, if it rained all the time as hard as it did here to-day."[5]

The stormy weather did have at least one beneficial effect: it made everybody amiable indoors. Irritability was all right — but only if one could run away, or be run away from, at any moment. On the other hand, Mrs. Victor noticed, "good humor only is allowable when you are cribbed up with people by necessity. Even I condescended to make myself agreeable, and with remarkable success."[6]

If Alexander Pope had written "the proper study of *woman*-kind is man," Frances would have endorsed the sentiment and felt she made some progress in the time spent at the coast.

"You may meet people very often in town, and not know anything about them; but place half-a-dozen of these same townsmen under one roof in the country, and lo, a revelation!" she explained. "I am not altogether sure but I have undergone a transformation — in the eyes of my sea-side acquaintances."[7]

Mid-December found Mrs. Victor back in San Francisco, making final arrangements before her departure.

On Monday evening, the 19th, she sat alone in her room at the Occidental Hotel, at the corner of Montgomery and Bush streets, deep in thought as she gazed at the fire burning in the stove.

"The heaviness of departure was upon my heart," Frances related. "My trunks were covered and strapped, standing against the walls."[8]

More than a year earlier, on 9 November 1863, her husband, Henry, resigned his naval commission on account of ill health and disability. He was carried on the rolls as an invalid, until honorably discharged in the spring of 1864 as being unfit for duty. He had developed a romantic admiration for Oregon, based on his reading of Vancouver's *Voyages* and other early books about the region.[9]

When Mr. Victor was partially recovered, he went north. In the fall of 1864 he took a job with the Oregon Iron Works, in Portland.

Henry was "a sort of shooting star on his own account" who "cannot be long content in any part of the globe, and as I am only a lesser light, following in his wake like phosphorus after a vessel at sea, I fall in naturally when he takes up the line of march. Tents being struck in the nighttime, the morning shines on only the ashes of our camp-fires," Frances wrote.[10]

In those days, she recalled, steamers went alternately to Portland or Victoria, B.C., for their first landing.

Frances boarded the *Brother Jonathan* on 20 December 1864. The town and bay of St. Francis never looked better than on that sunny Tuesday morning. Mrs. Victor gazed intently at the scene in an effort to fix "its details in my mind's hall of pictured memories," lest she never return.[11] Then she turned her back on it, consoling herself with the thought that "blessings brighten as they take their flight."[12]

On the ship, "all the odd samples of the genus *homo* seem to have been jumbled together in a fashion the most disorderly."[13]

Newsboys came aboard to peddle their papers to departing passengers. Frances studied and listened to these "San Francisco imps" with a good deal of fascination. She continued:

> . . . Like all imps, they have their dash of fun in their composition, however much mixed it may be with the diabolical. You may hear any subject dis-

cussed, moral, social or political, in their peculiar dialect. Listen to a cri-
tique upon theatrical affairs: "I say, Bill, I saw a soldier cry at Maguire's, last
night." "*You* did! Humph! *I* like tragedy — none of your *East Lynnes*; want
to see plenty of blood on the stage — seventeen murders in one play, suits
me! Here's the morning papers — who wants to p'ruse the *Alta?* — latest
news from the Atlantic States! — I say, Bob, wasn't that a tip-top murder in
New York?"[14]

Mrs. Victor watched as baggage was lowered away into the hold, and
"handled in that reckless manner known to steamboat and railroad
porters."[15] Several other women looked on from their stateroom doors
and worried aloud at the peril to which their trunks and boxes were
exposed. Frances remained silent, though she "winced when my favorite
'Saratoga' dropped its whole weight with a violent strain on one handle."[16]
What irritated her more was the way male onlookers "exchanged looks
and smiles of amusement or contempt at the irrepressible alarm exhibited
by the women — as if it were absurd or ridiculous to be careful! — a sentiment I think in which nearly all men share."[17]

That evening at dinner, Mrs. Victor was honored with a seat to the captain's left, at the head of the table. But next morning the *Brother Jonathan* began encountering rough seas, and Frances was confined to her
cabin with a severe case of seasickness.

"For thirty-six hours I lay in my berth, shifting from head to foot of
it like a shuttle, or rather like a half-filled sandbag on a tolerably smooth
see-saw," she wrote. "I found myself wondering at the tenacity of the spinal
column which so long resisted that jerking strain."[18]

She found some entertainment in the goings on of a card party, "which
was in pretty constant session during the whole voyage," just in front of
her door.[19]

After the vessel entered the Strait of Juan de Fuca, there was smooth
sailing and a fine coast view. Frances regained her feet, and decided to
explore the ship more thoroughly. She discovered that the upper saloon
had a good fire, which was fortunate, for the weather had turned "tolerably clear," cold and windy. But showers soon intruded; and by the time
the *Brother Jonathan* reached port near Victoria, at 1 p.m. on the 23rd,
it was raining, which at least modified the chill somewhat.

(Victoria was only three miles away by a fine graded road, but its beautiful harbor was inaccessible to large steamers on account of rocks.)

> . . . Esquimalt harbor is a gem. Small, land-locked, bounded by forests and
> hills, and set in a basin of most picturesque rocks covered with beautiful lichen
> of every shade of yellow, brown and green, it makes a lovely picture. . . .
> I heard much of beautiful walks and drives about Victoria, which I could
> well believe; also of small romantic bays and inlets along the coast, which
> I could well believe also. There is no doubt but Vancouver must sometime
> become a popular resort — whether or not it has any other brilliant future
> appears questionable.[20]

She wished some of the California artists would come up to do portraits of the wild northern scenery.

The "beautiful little harbor," she recalled, was "made doubly picturesque by the presence of the Indian canoe with its gaily blanketed paddlers, darting from point to point with the swiftness and silence of winged creatures."[21] The *Brother Jonathan* slipped from its moorings about fifteen hours after it arrived, and by 9 a.m. it was back upon the turbulent ocean. This time Frances was ready. She breakfasted early, locked her cabin door, and with crocheting in hand retreated to the upper saloon to ride out the storm.

> . . . I said to the sea: "Now, I am ready; toss away if you like, and boil and seethe, and misbehave yourself generally; I am not going to be sick on account of you, but am going to sit all day in this chair as near the centre of motion as I can get it, and amuse myself with your caprices and my crocheting." Well, I kept my promise, though it cost me my dinner, and some weariness besides. One by one the weaker sex disappeared, until only I and one other remained to afford the sterner half of humanity the entertainment of wondering how long we would hold out. Before noon my one companion was limp and speechless, though she resolutely kept her seat. As for me, I knotted away with great industry, occasionally studying the appearance of the sea, the shape, height and direction of the waves, and listening to the remarks of the dozen or so gentlemen who were determined, like myself, not to give up to sea-sickness nor alarm. I even made a feeble attempt at some doggerel which, as near as I can now remember, made some distinction between seeing a ship and shipping a sea. There was a good deal of uneasiness coined by a portion of the passengers as to whether we should bring up at last in an earthly or a heavenly haven, and I fancied that some wondered at the apparent want of effect which these remarks had upon me and my crocheting. I was not mistaken either, for by and by came a gentleman who had often looked my way, and finding an excuse for introducing a conversation, finally found an opportunity to remark upon my "stoicism." Of course I declared I was not stoical, only calm — if I had to die I wanted to have my thoughts clear — I hated being frightened. This view of the case seemed to strike my companion favorably, and he thereafter helped to keep a clear head by some agreeable conversation relative to a variety of topics.[22]

The vile weather lasted all the way to the mouth of the Columbia, which the steamer entered on Christmas Day "through a seething sea of breakers."[23] The officers and crew on duty were lashed fast, to prevent their being carried away. But what most impressed Mrs. Victor was the pouring of oil upon the waves, with marvelously calming effect. Here, she thought, was "oil upon troubled waters" to some purpose.[24]

Not until the ship crossed the bar into peaceful waters that afternoon was Frances able to meet passengers who had boarded at the northern stop. At Christmas dinner at the captain's table, she was amazed to learn that the *Brother Jonathan* still had 110 miles to go, up the Columbia and Willamette rivers, before it reached Portland.

"I never had heard of the Wallamet [as it was also called], and had always believed Portland was on the Columbia," she admitted. "It was put down so when I studied geography . . . and all Eastern people thought as I did."[25]

The vessel arrived in Portland at 5 a.m. on December 26; Mr. Victor was on hand to greet his wife in the "strictly Oregonian" downpour of rain.[26]

"The winter rains will keep me prisoner for some time to come, probably," Frances lamented.[27] But what good weather there was since her arrival revealed enchanting views of Mt. Hood and Mt. St. Helens.

"Summer must convert Portland into a very charming residence for any of nature's familiars, who, like myself, can find sweetest company in clouds and trees, streams and mountains, and all the delicate shades of light and shadow from dawn to dusk of a summer's day," she wrote. "The business of Portland is thriving, and the pioneer State of the Pacific promises to achieve a future for herself by rapid strides henceforth."[28]

For the first year or two, the couple lived in a house in Portland. The first person she formally met happened to be Addison C. Gibbs, owner of the Oregon Iron Works, then serving as governor of the state.

Frances laughingly confessed that she knew little about the country. Gibbs said that wasn't surprising since so little had been written about Oregon, and he suggested that she publish a book to correct false impressions among people in the East.

"Oh," she said, "if that is what is wanted, it is just in my line, and I should enjoy studying the country with the purpose of writing it up."[29]

The governor suggested that the legislature would probably make an appropriation to defray the expenses of publishing such a book.

"When I came to Oregon . . . nothing was known by my generation in the East, or even in California, about the Pacific Northwest," Mrs. Victor recalled. ". . . The people and their history were in obscurity. The very aloofness and uniqueness of the country interested me, and I began at once to study its characteristics."[30]

Gibbs suggested that she visit Matthew Paul Deady, the U.S. District Court judge in Portland, an early pioneer whose library, the governor said, would be useful in historical research; the judge was also of a literary turn, and served as a correspondent for the San Francisco *Evening Bulletin.* Gibbs permitted Mrs. Victor to use his name.

Frances went, expecting a favorable reception, but to her surprise Deady huffily remarked that Oregon "had suffered enough at the hands of itinerant scribblers."[31]

This comment was prompted by the judge's memories of a woman calling herself a writer, who shortly before Frances' arrival had been in Oregon collecting subscriptions for a publication of some sort.

"She had proven a fraud, whether intentionally or not," Mrs. Victor recalled, "and people were, on her account, suspicious of me."[32]

Deady also was irritated by an account of the Columbia River that Fitz Hugh Ludlow had written for the December 1864 *Atlantic Monthly.*

It was, the judge tartly observed in a letter to the *Evening Bulletin* the following month, "readable *per se,* but is fully three parts pure fancy. But I suppose it will take in Boston as well as anything. . . . When the readers of the *Atlantic Monthly* have regaled their fancy with Fitz Bigblow's romance of the Columbia river, they will do well to turn to [Washington] Irving's *Astoria* and read the homely truth."[33]

Although somewhat embarrassed by her reception, Frances told Judge Deady that she "could not see how knowledge of a country was to be obtained without itinerancy."[34] She added that she always traveled intending to acquire knowledge about what she saw, that she was a paid correspondent of the *Evening Bulletin* and had already sent several letters about Oregon which she believed the people would approve if they read them, and that her only purpose in visiting him was to increase her knowledge of the subject at hand.

No sooner had Mrs. Victor mentioned the *Bulletin* than the judge's demeanor softened. "The interview ended by a cordial permission to use his library as if it were my own, and from that day until his death Judge Deady was the staunchest and most helpful of my Oregon friends," Frances later wrote. "Blessed be his memory!"[35]

She often traveled around Oregon, and became acquainted with many of the state's founders and leading men. Several gave her access to their books and papers, and assisted in procuring material from other sources.

By collecting documents and taking down personal recollections, a biographer explained, Mrs. Victor "performed a service of inestimable value to the state," since the "facts concerning the beginnings" of Oregon "were well known" to these men and "which, had it not been for Mrs. Victor's efforts, would have been lost to posterity."[36]

This distinction earned her a place as one of six women whose names (along with those of 152 men) have been inscribed on the walls of the legislative chambers in the state capitol building in Salem as being prominent in early Oregon's affairs.

About the status of women then, Mrs. Victor wrote that her experience "has forced upon my observation this truth — that while men, even men of no great intellectual or moral value to society, can create a constituency which will bring them profits of reputation, position, and hard cash by means of which women cannot or will not avail themselves, the woman of no matter how much industry, ability, or moral worth is not recognized because of her refusal to adopt certain of their methods, as well as on account of her inferiority from a political point of view."[37]

9

Start of a Northwest Odyssey

In May 1865 was the first of Mrs. Victor's trips to see Oregon for herself. Portland, she quipped in a letter to the San Francisco *Evening Bulletin*, "was the Monumental City of the Pacific coast . . . and . . . the monuments were very tall and very black."[1]

These "carbonized relics of a past age," she went on, strongly reminded her "of what Oregon was, and . . . is. Marble shafts might be handsomer, but those of charred fir are perhaps most appropriate, since Oregon was founded by the fur trade, and still continues to flourish by traders in fir."[2]

Mrs. Victor embarked by steamboat for a "voyage of observation up the famous Wallamet Valley."[3] (She preferred the original Indian spelling, as opposed to the present "Willamette.")

She observed that a canal was being considered to bypass the Willamette falls, near Oregon City, but said the money would be better invested in railroads since navigation of the river "half the distance to Eugene" was hampered by low water much of the year.[4]

The river could never open the valley as effectively as railroads, she added, because freight and passenger capacity by rail was unlimited and tracks could be laid in any direction desired.

She noted that the federal Donation Land Law of 1850 put control of most of the valley's land in the hands of the first settlers. She believed these families could not properly cultivate the land, and stated that if they could be persuaded to donate part of their property for railroads, all would benefit. Land values would be enhanced, and markets for produce created.

As it was, Frances wrote, the Donation Land Law "is sufficient to account for the fact, that with so fine an agricultural country of their own, the Oregonians still purchase hay, vegetables, etc., of California."[5]

Mrs. Victor thought that Salem was well designed. The streets were "regularly laid out, wide and clean. A large public square and other small parks reserved . . . for the enjoyment of the public, add much to the beauty and future healthfulness of the town."[6]

Salem's "thoroughly comfortable and tidy look" was in marked contrast to Portland, but official buildings were still lacking. "The legislative hall and the State offices are now only rented in a commodious fire-proof building on the principal street," she wrote.[7]

There was a good prairie road for most of the seventy miles from Salem to the Santiam gold and copper mines. Mrs. Victor examined several ore samples, which she described thusly:

> . . . Fancy a circular cavity of the diameter of six inches, more or less — a "hollow" like that in the heart of an overgrown potatoe — and imagine the hollow lightly filled with a fine-spun web of threads of gold, brittle and crisp-looking as crystals of frost, quite filling with its delicate fibres the space within, yet nowhere so compactly as to destroy its beautiful, thread-like appearance.[8]

Frances noted that the common schools everywhere in Oregon lacked organization, but that some localities were trying to deal with the problem.

"Many communities divided on the Slavery question in 1862," she wrote, "and still remain divided, sending their children to separate and generally very poor schools."[9]

She thought that Corvallis ranked second to Salem as the most attractive townsite on the river, and had several advantages for settlement: "It is situated in the midst of the best agricultural region of the State. It is at the head of navigation for a considerable portion of the year; and it has what few points in the valley can have, easy communication with the sea coast."[10]

Yaquina Bay, she added, "is becoming a point of some interest" as a commercial outlet for much of the Willamette Valley.[11]

Mrs. Victor transferred at Corvallis to a stagecoach to continue her journey south, as far as Jacksonville.

The way over the Calapooya Mountains was "not necessarily a bad road," she commented, "[but] on this part of the route, one must have considerable elasticity not to [be] seriously bruised up after a 20-mile ride. A fine prospect, however, could always entice me into the endurance of any temporary discomfort, and I felt very well repaid for the bruises I got, by the fine views and the novelty of the [forms of vegetation] which I discovered."[12]

Jesse Applegate, a prominent early pioneer who came to Oregon in 1843 and was known as the "Sage of Yoncalla," wrote Mrs. Victor to say that if she wanted information she "must come to me for it," but had not expected her to take up the offer, and was surprised to learn that she was coming.[13] The ride from Corvallis to Yoncalla took a night and part of the next day. Frances recalled:

> I shall never forget my reception . . . He stood at the gate when the stage drove up. His philosophical head close shaven, with its large ears standing almost at right angles to his face, his large mouth stretched wide in a cordial yet half quizzical smile, together with his gaunt figure and farmer's garb made altogether a most unexpected picture — for I had heard a great deal about this Oregon statesman, and looked for something different . . . Of all the minds I have ever come in contact with I think his the most independent; for though stored with learning he did not draw his ideas from other men's

stock, but thought for himself. As he liked to talk, in his deliberate, reflective way, I only had to listen. The only subject on which I discovered we were opposed was that of woman's rights. Mr. Applegate had the old-fashioned opinion that all a woman needed of education was enough to make her a good wife according to the same ancient standard. But I succeeded in upsetting some of these notions, and when I came away he said to me, "I should be proud if I could call you my daughter." [14]

For ten days they visited, and after she left — two years later, in fact — Applegate was still thinking about their encounter.

In a 13 October 1867 letter to his friend Elwood Evans, Applegate, while stating that he "generally succeeded in escaping from male authors and think I could still fight them off," also confessed that he was "no match for the 'ladies of the pen'" and that Mrs. Victor "pumped me so dry of historical matter that the stores both of memory and imagination were utterly exhausted . . . there was nothing I could conceal or withhold from the keen scrutiny of this lady, and yet she is as little grateful for the information thus wrung from me as you seem to be for my strictures on your 17th chapter [part of a draft Evans was writing on the history of Oregon] . . . . If you really seek truth go to her. Perhaps she will give you the benefit of her investigations — what she derived from me is now hers. I cannot object if she now gives you my auto-biography." [15]

In July, Frances resumed her Oregon odyssey — this time along the Columbia River. She decided to start at the beginning, so she "went down the river in order to come up it again." [16]

She spent a week in Astoria, at the mouth of the great "River of the West" where Americans first appeared.

"With a copy of Irving's *Astoria* in my pocket, and some extracts of Lewis and Clark's *Journal* fresh in my mind," Mrs. Victor was ready to consider the town as being something more than merely the site of a U.S. Customs house.[17]

Frances had already seen Astoria, briefly, on Christmas Day, 1864, from the wildly gyrating deck of a steamer laboring through storm-tossed waters, and wondered how a town could exist in such circumstances. But Astoria then and Astoria on a summer's day are two different things, she acknowledged.

"With the inquisitiveness usual to me," she explained, "I set out shortly after my arrival . . . to peer into the past, the present and the future of the place." [18]

She visited the old Fort, and "sat down in the sun to gaze upon that majestic yet tranquil scene" which Capt. Robert Gray first saw on 11 May 1792.[19]

As Frances relaxed, she imagined how it looked in 1811, when the *Tonquin* crossed the bar and unloaded, by "this very bluff," the stores of the Pacific Fur Company, set up under the auspices of John Jacob Astor, America's greatest fur magnate, to compete with the North West Company, a British firm based in Montreal.[20]

The American firm within two years sold out to the North West Company, but before transfer was made of its stock and outpost at Astoria, the British navy seized them during the War of 1812.

The Treaty of Ghent, that in 1815 ended the war, returned Astoria to the United States, but Astor never resumed operations in Oregon. (The Hudson's Bay Company absorbed the North West Company in 1821.) When the *Tonquin* arrived in the Columbia, Mrs. Victor wrote, "doubtless these waters were black with Indian canoes . . . their occupants curious to know the meaning of this unsolicited visit from the white men."[21]

By 1849, "gold-hunters by the hundreds" were camped at the same spot, "wearing out weeks in waiting for a passage to the mines [in California]; and in this little cove at our feet were 800 Indian warriors, in their slender canoes, watching curiously the motions of these erratic white visitors."[22]

At the time of her visit sixteen years later, Frances wrote that there was not a canoe to be seen. "The white race to the red are like the sun to snow: as silently as the snow the red men disappear, dissipated by civilization."[*][23]

From a steamer up the Columbia, Frances saw Mt. St. Helens, which, she wrote, had erupted in 1839, spewing ash one or two inches deep all over the countryside.

She enjoyed being aboard such a powerful vessel on the Columbia in July, for "in the stormy season there are high winds, rough seas, and tempests of rain or of sand to encounter, by no means easy to battle with. It is at our peril that we invade the grand sanctuaries of Nature in her winter moods."[24]

Steamboats began running on the upper Columbia in 1852, but the Yakima Indian War four years later gave the first real impetus to waterborne passenger and cargo traffic.

In 1861, a portage railway was completed on the south side of the Cascades, a series of rapids which fell 37.3 feet in 5¾ miles. The Oregon Steam Navigation Company purchased it the following year. Iron rails were laid, and from a San Francisco foundry came a locomotive to begin service. The first train ran on 20 April 1863. That same day, a portage railway from The Dalles to Celilo was also opened.

Six miles by rail — past an "exciting spectacle of rushing, boiling, foaming, dashing, impetuous water," as Frances described it in 1865 — brought passengers to the Upper Cascades and another steamer to resume their journey.[25]

(The Cascade rapids no longer exist; they are submerged beneath the waters impounded by Bonneville Dam.)

So grand and tall were the mountains above the rapids that, Mrs. Victor wrote, they "cannot be described . . . only . . . felt."[26] She then reflected on the history borne by the Columbia as it flowed to the Pacific:

> . . . Down this strong, rapid, high-walled river, fifty years ago floated the annual "brigade" of the Hudson's Bay Company, bringing the year's accumulation of peltries and the annual express from the Red river settlements and Canada. Ten years [before that] Lewis and Clark had descended this great river in the service of the Government; and a few years later a part of the

---

*But these things didn't just happen, as Mrs. Victor well knew. She looked into the matter and revealed her grim findings in an October 1871 essay, portions of which appear on pages 248-249.

Astor Expedition suffered all but death passing these rugged mountains in the winter. Only twenty years ago the yearly immigration to Oregon, arriving at the Dalles destitute and sick, late in the season, were dependent on the Hudson's Bay Company's boats to bring them down to the settlements. It was a terrible passage, and many, both of boatmen and immigrants, lost their lives in the fearful rapids. These were the incidents of pioneer life . . . while we, tourists at leisure, dream and gaze from the deck of a first class steamer, with all our wants anticipated.[27]

The steamboat stopped at The Dalles. Mrs. Victor went ashore and found "rocks, nothing but rocks, on every side but the heavenward one; and if it be a warm day, the very heavens will seem to be a concave of red hot basalt."[28]

Frances visited with Thomas Condon, pastor of the Congregational Church, who even then was known for his collection and study of geological, mineralological and paleontological specimens.

"From the contents of his cabinet, it is evident that the northwest coast is rich in the remains of extinct species of animals, together with numerous indications of the ocean life which once existed where now are elevated mountain peaks," she later wrote.[29]

Next morning, a train took the travelers to Celilo, past more rapids, and at the Oregon Steam Navigation Company's immense warehouse they boarded a third steamer.

Most of the scenery between Celilo and Umatilla consisted of Indians and Cayuse ponies. The steamboat entered the Snake River, and at a place called Pine Tree Rapids was stopped by shallow water in a channel. The cargo was unloaded, and next morning the captain tried to return to Wallula and exchange his ship for a smaller vessel to make the passage.

"We . . . were going down stream gallantly; but all at once . . . bump, thump, jump, crash, tear — we knew what had happened, and so did everybody, when we headed up stream again with all haste, and beached our craft, pretty well water-logged, in less than four minutes."[30]

After eight hours, enough water was removed to allow the steamer to continue. Damage, fortunately, was confined to one side of a bulkhead; but pumps had to be kept operating all the way to Wallula as one side of the lower deck was under water.

"It was to the fact of the *Chief* being bulkheaded that we were indebted for our ability to get back to Wallula," Frances wrote. "True, in the present condition of the Snake river, there was no danger to our lives from sinking; but in the rapids of the Columbia, this would not be true; and the Company show their wisdom by building their boats in a manner to provide against such accidents."[31]

On July 30, the *Brother Jonathan* sank in the Pacific Ocean, northwest of Crescent City, California, with the loss of about 200 lives. Had that vessel contained bulkheads, Mrs. Victor noted, "the late terrible disaster" might not have been so catastrophic. "When will ship-builders and ship-owners learn humanity?"[32]

Her own adventure was not yet over. After the *Nez Perce Chief* returned to Wallula, some of the passengers rowed across the Walla Walla River in a small boat to look around. Mrs. Victor tried climbing a bluff to get a view of the countryside, but, fearing exhaustion, turned back after getting about halfway up.

"The sun was setting gloriously," she recalled, "the young moon sailing silvery white in the southwest, the river shining luminously below us." In the fading light, she suddenly confronted "a good sized rattlesnake . . . erecting itself for a spring." Carefully, she backed away; the snake "thought better of it, and quickly uncoiling, crawled off." Frances later regretted not having had the courage to capture her interloper by using "some of the rocks at hand, but many accidents had probably weakened my nerves."[33]

10

Mt. Hood Erupts

At about 5 a.m. on Saturday, 23 September 1865, several soldiers on guard duty at Fort Vancouver saw Mt. Hood erupt in flame and smoke. Fragments of rock shot up a considerable distance and fell immediately after; there was "a rumbling noise not unlike distant thunder."[1] Hundreds of people in Portland witnessed the event, which was the first volcanic activity seen on the mountain in some time.

Mrs. Victor's attention was drawn about 8 o'clock to "a singular looking cloud that was hanging off from the top of the mountain."[2] Five minutes' observation convinced her it was smoke from deep within Mt. Hood itself.

"It was black and dense, and puffed out at intervals of about one or two minutes. Being much interested, I continued to watch the phenomenon for two hours, during which time there was first black smoke, then alternate puffs of smoke and steam, and finally steam alone," Frances reported in the San Francisco *Evening Bulletin.* "The morning had been very bright, as also the preceding day; but the weather soon changed to cloudy and rainy, thus excluding any further observations. The rain continued for nearly a week, during which the eruption may have continued without allowing any one to observe it."[3]

Two weeks after the first eruption, Mrs. Victor saw that Mt. Hood was giving off great volumes of steam. That Saturday was bright and cloudless, and she resolved to spend all of it waiting to see "what the grand old Titan was doing, that he needed to be puffing away at that rate."[4]

For eight hours she watched as the volcano fumed almost without interruption. "Frequently the whole mountain was enveloped in vapor, which was carried away almost immediately by the wind; when for an instant the mountain stood out clear and sharp as usual in the brightest weather," she wrote.[5] The steam formed clouds, which floated away one by one and settled along the horizon. By about 4 that afternoon it was quite overcast, and five hours later several large raindrops fell. Sunday, October 8, was rainy; and Frances felt certain that it resulted from Mt. Hood's activity the day before.

"I have several times during the summer noticed that Mt. Hood was in action; yet the action was so slight as to create little or no curiosity, being confined to an occasional half-hour of smoking in small volumes," she wrote. "Mt. St. Helens also has shown the same slight indications of internal heat, and was throwing off steam only ten days ago, in small puffs, that looked like the smoke of a cannon."[6]

There was much speculation whether all this volcanic activity in the Pacific Northwest accounted for a massive earthquake that struck the San Francisco area on October 8th. The 12:45 p.m. temblor — an undulatory motion from northeast to southwest — caught everyone by surprise.

"The uproar caused by falling walls, glass coming down in showers on the sidewalks, the frenzied stampede of thousands of people, horses, running away, bells ringing, & c., was indescribable," one witness wrote. "Women fainted and men screamed, church congregations piled over each other in the excitement to escape, and many people jumped from second story windows, in some cases receiving severe injuries."[7]

Several buildings were destroyed, or had to be razed because the damage to them was so serious. The city hall was cracked throughout. Walls of some structures were thrown out of line so that doors could not be opened or closed, and others were moved from their foundations. The city's gas works and some piers on the waterfront were damaged. Some destruction also was reported in San Jose and Santa Cruz, but the quake was not felt in Visalia or Los Angeles.

"Might it not be that the convulsions felt first at Honolulu, and following the first eruption of Mt. Hood, were caused by the displacement of some of the elements of the earth through the escape of so much steam and more solid matter, thereby causing a vacuum toward which other matter rushed with violence?" Frances suggested in her letter to the *Evening Bulletin*. "And in the same way might not the second eruption . . . have been a primary cause of the earthquake in San Francisco, which happened on the following day? At all events, it is sufficiently suggestive of a collusion between the volcanic elements of Oregon and the earthquake forces of California to warrant telegraphic communication on the subject; and I would recommend that when the operator at Portland telegraphs an eruption of one of our volcanoes, San Franciscans should make fast all their loose property and sit with open doors, ready for an exit."[8]

11

"The River of the West"

Mrs. Victor had decided to write a hand-book describing the land and resources of the Pacific Northwest, especially Oregon, and in her search for information she contacted Elwood Evans in Olympia.

"I am convinced we have very nearly the same understanding of the interest, the moral, and the romance of that history which attaches to the Northwest Coast," she wrote him in November 1865. "Your synopsis of subjects sounds almost as if I had been giving an outline of my own sections of history. It is true however, as you say, that 'the theory underlying our respective works' may be widely different; and from the fact of this difference, future historians looking back to us may be able to make philosophical deductions in support of the truth. As 'distance lends enchantment,' so also it often lends clearness of view. We in our humble way may be serving posterity by presenting the several sides of an argument to the dispassionate criticism of another generation."[1]

Mrs. Victor also revealed her native skepticism, a quality essential in the writing of history, when she asked Evans:

"Would it be impertinent in me to inquire if you are convinced by the evidence before us, of the complicity of the Hudson's Bay Company, and the Catholic Fathers, in the massacre at Wai[i]latpu? I ask the question because I was so assured by one of the old missionaries . . . I do not believe it, and am of course more or less curious to know what facts unknown to me have served to so convince you."[2]

Frances also told Evans that it "would give me great pleasure, and profit also I do not doubt," to talk in person with him about historical matters, "but an Oregon winter is so full of horrors for me that I could not . . . visit Olympia except after it is over, and the disagreeableness of travel is somewhat abated.

"[T]here are so few people who are sufficiently literary, or public spirited, or progressive, to apply to for aid or appreciation, that the few must bear the burden of all such demands, whether they will or no," she added.[3]

The *Morning Oregonian* in Portland had already published a two-column essay by Mrs. Victor on Oregon's lack of railroads and other means of transportation.[4]

Summarizing the article in his regular letter to the San Francisco *Evening Bulletin*, Judge Deady noted that Frances "raps us over the knuckles, in a kindly way, about our special peculiarity — *slowness*" — which he insisted

> has its good as well as evil results. Our kind of "slowness" implies sureness, pay your debts, crawl before you walk, live within your means, individual independence, moderate taxation, etc., etc. . . . Doubtless Oregon is approaching that period in her growth, when she can safely and legitimately . . . improve her means of transportation by building railroads and the like; and it is equally certain that it is to her advantage, now and in the future, that she has been blessed with sufficient "slowness," not to attempt it before she was ready and able.
>
> Mrs. Victor is a good writer, neither flashy nor foggy; has a clear and correct eye for the natural resources, scenery and material of a country. She has examined the State and its surroundings to a greater extent than any one else that I know of, or who has attempted a book or pamphlet about it.[5]

A delegation led by Schuyler Colfax, of Indiana, speaker of the U.S. House of Representatives, visited Portland in July. The party included Albert D. Richardson, a famous war correspondent for the New York *Tribune*, who spent time in the notorious Confederate prison at Andersonville, Georgia, and was assassinated four years after he visited the Pacific coast.*

Mrs. Victor told Richardson she was having trouble selling her manuscript, and he offered to take it and find a publisher when he returned to the East.

On 11 December 1865 Frances boarded a steamer for San Francisco to spend the winter. Three months later, she corresponded with Judge Deady about the difficulties she was encountering in getting her hand-book published.

Frances told him in March 1866 that Richardson had sent her *Harper's* note on the subject. This note, she said, "stated that the high price of material and labor, and the difficulty of finding sale for a work of that kind, would deter them from undertaking it, unless they could receive assurance that the State of Oregon (meaning the Legislature) would make a purchase of two thousand copies."[6]

Mrs. Victor feared the state would not appropriate the $2,000 necessary for such a purpose, adding that there was "not the least prospect" she would profit from her work. "I shall be quite content if it pays the publishers," she wrote.[7]

In 1865, Judge Deady introduced Mrs. Victor to one of early Oregon's most interesting and picturesque characters. He was Joseph L. (Joe) Meek, born in 1810 in Washington County, Virginia, and raised on a plantation, who preferred outdoor sports with the youthful bondsmen of his father to learning "the alphabet on a paddle" at school.[8]

---

*For biography, see pp. 240-241.

Meek left home at the age of eighteen, and early in 1829 at St. Louis he enlisted with the veteran frontiersman William Sublette, who was in town to purchase supplies and recruit for the fur-hunting service.

Meek was one of them, but he was not accepted into their comradeship for several years, during which time he learned — as many recruits did not, to their eternal regret — to live by his skill and resourcefulness in the western wilderness where Indians and wild animals roamed aplenty.

By the time early settlers in Oregon were making the first tentative moves to establish a provisional government, Meek had taken up homesteading in the Willamette Valley, and was active in these meetings.

"Meek sent me a batch of notes in pencil every little while for a year or more," Frances later wrote, and the two talked often.

> On one occasion he came to [Portland] to have a photograph taken by Mr. Joseph Buchtel, from which an engraving was to be made, but did not come near me. By chance I met him as he came down the stairs from Buchtel's, and he was looking dissipated enough — limp and white from drinking. When he recognized me the gentleman in him asserted itself, and he said with a deeply apologetic air: "Punish me any way you please, Mrs. Victor, I know I am unworthy to speak to you; and I promise on my sacred honor not to be seen by you in this condition again." Nor did I ever see him really intoxicated afterwards — perhaps because when he came to town he usually reported to me, and I took measures to prevent him from meeting too many of his acquaintances on the street.[9]

Her husband, Henry, had received a large sum of money from the U.S. government for helping to capture the *Princess Royal* while on duty with the Union fleet blockading the Charleston, South Carolina, harbor.[10]

In November 1865, undoubtedly as a speculative venture, the Victors purchased the St. Helens townsite. Henry also invested in Santiam gold mines and engaged in coal, iron and salt mining. He apparently was a visionary speculator with little business acumen, however, and all these ventures failed.[11]

His greatest mistake was buying thirty shares of stock in the Oregon and California Wagon Road Company. This investment earned only large assessments which he eventually could not pay and so became involved in a lawsuit.

In June 1867, Judge Deady ruled on a case involving the separate property of married women. The decision stated that though the law did not entitle a woman to claim property acquired directly from her husband, there apparently was nothing to prevent the husband from giving it to the wife as a gift.

Frances had been puzzling about how to save some of the St. Helens property for herself. After reading press accounts of the decision, Mrs. Victor wrote the judge three days later, on June 28, to ask if Henry could deed her a certain house and lot in the town and whether she could then register it as her own. If this alternative was unacceptable, she asked if Deady instead could advise her of a proper course to secure some separate property. Frances acknowledged it might be inappropriate to consult the judge on the matter, and expressed her willingness to be sent elsewhere for legal advice.

Though the couple sold much of their St. Helens property, by 1868 they were in financial difficulties and evidently agreed to go their separate ways. Despite these troubles, Mrs. Victor had toured the state every summer since her arrival, gathering material for a book on Oregon history that she wanted to do. Frances at first resisted the idea of writing up Meek's adventures as a mountain man and pioneer, but gradually she became more intrigued by the story of his life and decided to make him the central figure in the narrative, which included an account of early Oregon events as she understood them.

In July 1868, Mrs. Victor asked Judge Deady for any stories, papers or facts that he had about Meek, so she could give a correct view of his official acts.

"My time is limited," she told Deady, "and whatever you can do for me will be gratefully remembered — for really it is as much a matter of bread-and-butter with me now, as of literary reputation. I must publish my book this winter, and I must get off to New York as early as possible."[12]

A week later, on August 5, Frances sent a reminder that she would be coming to Portland for an interview, and advised the judge "that although anecdote constitutes the principal capital in writing Meek's life I wish to impart what dignity can properly be imputed to him in a more serious light, and so try to remember what is good and useful about him, as well as amusing."[13]

A year later, on her way home from the East, Mrs. Victor stopped over in San Francisco to see Bret Harte, whom she had known when both were writers for *The Golden Era*. Harte was editor of the *Overland Monthly*, and Frances offered him her first historical article, "Manifest Destiny in the West." Harte was delighted and published it in the August 1869 issue of the magazine.

Mrs. Victor then returned to Oregon, and went to Salem for a few months. She stayed at the home of Oregon's governor, George L. Woods, whose wife was apparently her friend.

It was a fortunate choice of residence, for as soon as Oregonians began to read her book — *The River of the West* — Frances found herself under attack.

Harvey W. Scott, editor of the Portland *Morning Oregonian*, praised the book. It supplied "a tolerably full and well connected narrative of early events in Oregon. It is certainly the best that has yet appeared," he commented.[14]

The editor said the book made Meek quite a hero, and that the story was told very attractively and would be popular.

"Doubtless there will be some who think that certain parts of the narrative are not fair, for Mrs. Victor has positive opinions and does not hesitate to state them," he added, however, "and in her study . . . of early times in Oregon, she has found matter for censure as well as for praise."[15]

Then, after quoting some of her observations about the missionaries, Scott wrote:

We give the above as a specimen of the writer's independent style of criticism, and leave her to those who may be disposed to take a different view
of these things, as doubtless such there are.[16]

The missionary contingent in Oregon was deeply offended by *The River
of the West* and they never forgave the author. Mrs. Victor did make a number of provocative statements about missionaries, and inserted on page
274 a clever cartoon captioned "The Missionary Wedge."

Frances was astonished by all the fuss being made over her work, and
on 25 March 1870 she wrote Judge Deady:

> . . . Quite to my surprise I find myself much talked about, having forgot-
> ten that writers of co-temporaneous history were liable to notoriety — some-
> times unenviable. Up here in Salem there is a good deal of feeling among
> the class connected either in former times or now with the Methodist Mis-
> sion and Church; however as they avoid me and only quarrel with my friends,
> there seems to be no present opportunity of "reasoning together" to the end
> that a compromise of opinions may be made.[17]

In answer, the judge criticized one of her statements about the missionaries, to which she replied, "I am such a scorner of hum-bug that really
I cannot find it in my nature to be very sorry that I said it!"[18]

12

Beyond the Cascades

In May 1870, Mrs. Victor moved to Portland. She soon embarked on a tour that took her east through Oregon and Washington to Lewiston, Idaho Territory.

According to Indian legend, she wrote, enroute up the Columbia once more in a steamboat, the Cascade rapids were formed when "Mount Hood had a quarrel with Mount Adams, and these two giants threw fire stones at each other, and tore up and shook the earth for a great distance, causing . . . the fall of a natural arch of stone which spanned the river . . . thereby choking up its channel and forming the present rapids."*[1]

Congress was then considering a bill, she noted, to devise ways and provide funding to make the rapids safe for passage. (Not until 1896 was a system of locks completed to help ships bypass the turbulent waters.)

The steamer to take passengers to The Dalles was two hours late arriving at the Upper Cascades, because of strong headwinds the vessel encountered while coming downstream.

"Nor did she escape without feeling the force of such waves as can be met with on the Columbia at certain times of the year," Mrs. Victor wrote. "One of her bulkheads had been crushed in, — the wave that did it rushing up the starboard gangway just in time to carry on its crest one of the cabin boys who was in the act of descending, and laying him sprawling like a jelly-fish as it spread over and ran off the deck."[2]

Frances was delighted with the changes that had taken place in The Dalles in the five years since her last visit.

"It was hastily and poorly built of boards, with the usual single fire-proof building belonging to Wells, Fargo & Co.," she recalled. "The streets were thronged with rough looking men; every bit of ground was bare and dusty; there was no shade anywhere . . . Now there is a general appearance of order and cozy comfort; trees are already grown large enough

---

*Geologists today believe that about the year 1170 an earthquake caused cliffs on either side to collapse, and a wall of rock estimated to be 180 feet high thundered across the river. The slide may have blocked the Columbia for several years, during which time a lake backed up to where The Dalles is now.

to shade the sidewalks; flowers and ornamental shrubbery are seen in every street."[3]

Mrs. Victor also related the origin of "Wasco" — "wacq-o" to the natives — a term, she wrote, that came about long ago when Indians gathered three miles from Winquat to fish for salmon.

> . . . One . . . was so unlucky as to lose his squaw, the mother of his children, one of whom was yet only a babe. This babe would not be comforted, and the other children being young, were clamorous for their mother. In this trying position, with these wailing little ones on his awkward masculine hands, the father was compelled to give up fishing and betake himself to amusing his babies. Many expedients having failed, he at length found that they were diverted by seeing him pick cavities in the rocks in the form of basins, which they could fill with water or pebbles, and accordingly, as many a patient mother does every day, adapted himself to the taste and capacities of his children, and made any number of basins they required. Wasco being the name of a kind of horn basin which is in use among the Des Chutes, his associates gave the name to this devoted father in ridicule of his domestic qualities; and afterward, when he had resolved to found a village at Winquat, and drew many of his people after him, they continued to call them all Wascos, or basins.[4]

At 5 a.m. on May 24th, Mrs. Victor boarded a train for a 15-mile trip to Celilo to connect with another steamboat for the run along the upper Columbia. As the only lady passenger, and a stranger to the other occupants, she could devote full attention to the scenery.

The scene that most impressed her was the "narrow, dark-looking current" of the Columbia River as it passed between the walls of dark volcanic rock; and she was moved to poetry:

"How it swirls, how it twirls, how it eddies and boils; how it races and chases, how it leaps, how it toils; how one mile it rushes and another it flows, as soft as a love song sung 'under the rose;' how in one place it seeths, in another is still, and as smooth as the flume of some sleepy old mill; — A rock entroughed torrent, like none else, I pledge; and in truth is a river set up on its edge."[5]

Before leaving Portland, Mrs. Victor had heard that several steamers would attempt to run through The Dalles and over the Cascade rapids. She wanted to take the ride, but a view of those waters had changed her mind.

"I concluded to wait until I was so weary of life as to be able to endure it no longer, when I had no doubt a distinguished exit could be made, in the manner above hinted at," she remarked.[6]

Aside from the river, there was little else of interest on the journey to Celilo. She did note, however, that there were several Indian lodges "with salmon drying inside, whose rich orange color shows through the open doorways like flame."[7]

Several Indians were fishing with a net. Their long black hair draped their shoulders and blew into their eyes "in a most inconvenient manner," she wrote, and disapprovingly added: "But everything about an Indian's dress is inconvenient except the ease with which it is put on! Some of the younger [ones] had ignored dressing altogether, as a fatigue not to be undertaken until with increasing years an increase of strength shall be arrived at.''[8]

At Celilo, passengers quickly boarded a "fine commodious steamer" lying alongside the Oregon Steam Navigation Company's huge 900-foot warehouse.[9]

Still the only lady passenger, Mrs. Victor had a cabin to herself, and she passed the day in reading and taking notes on the scenery.

"Larks are pouring their liquid melody upon the air; and a few prairie hens are seen shyly stooping their long necks among the bunch grass," she wrote. "At long intervals a cabin, or a flat-boat, or a herd of Indian ponies, give indications of human habitation; and thus the current of both time and tide flow by us.''[10]

The vessel stopped about 6 p.m. at Umatilla, a small town serving as a port of entry to the mining region of northeastern Oregon, and then steamed twenty-five miles to Wallula in a "rosy sunset and purple twilight."[11]

The steamboat arrived in the darkness at Wallula, where Frances discovered, to her dismay, a hazard that tired and weary travelers in the early West often stumbled into.

> . . . A hotel it does not boast; but a sort of boardinghouse, with beds for way-bound travellers like myself . . . The art of not knowing how to "keep a hotel" has been brought to considerable perfection all over the northwest coast; but it does not surprise one so very much when occurring in places like Wallula. Little hillocks of sand were piled up in the corners of the wash stand, and a sand beach was found in the bottom of the basin. The pillows betrayed a clear grit when I dashed my weary head against them, and retaliated by throwing dust in my eyes. The breakfast also was well seasoned with sand — a by no means useless condiment when the indigestible nature of hotel breakfasts generally is taken into account. . . .
>
> On taking my seat in the coach after breakfast, for Walla Walla, I found that the female element was in the minority again. Eight specimens of the noble sex, and one insignificant woman! Of course I subsided into my corner over the right hind wheel, and submitted to have the sand thrown in my face by handsful without venturing to utter a word of remonstrance. The simple audacity of being a woman up here in this masculine territory was so powerfully impressed upon my mind, that I felt compelled to sit in speechless immobility during the whole drive of thirty-five miles.
>
> Fortunately one may *think* without committing any impropriety . . . The comments of my fellow passengers were not without interest . . . although I confess to a slight feeling of mistrust when one of them declared that the soil of Powder River valley was so rich that if a man chanced to leave his crowbar sticking in the ground at night, in the morning he would be sure to find it had sprouted eight-penny nails![12]

The sandy drive between Wallula and the Touchet River crossing was "necessarily disagreeable," Mrs. Victor wrote.[13] The alkaline soil extending a few miles beyond the Touchet "must be exceedingly tedious to get over in midsummer. So light is it that the earth, powdered by the wheels of wagons and tramp of animals, is blown away by the wind, leaving the wagon track in some places several feet below the level of the ground, rendering it impossible to turn out should two teams meet in one of these dusty canyons."[14]

Walla Walla's "cheerfulness and thrift" surprised Frances, and she also found its residents "generally hospitable and social."[15] During a week spent in the town, she saw "ample evidences of prosperity of a sure and steady kind."[16]

More money seemed to be in circulation in Walla Walla, she noted, than in the Willamette Valley; and commerce among merchants, miners and farmers had proven beneficial for all.

Mrs. Victor termed fruit growing "a specialty of Walla Walla farming."[17] She also "had the pleasure of walking through a field when the rye stood seven feet high, with occasional bunches a foot higher."[18]

Frances rode out to Waiilatpu, the site of the Whitman Mission, where Dr. Marcus Whitman, his wife Narcissa, and eleven others were killed by Indians on 29 November 1847, and the buildings burned.

"Having been built of adobe . . . the walls dissolved into mounds of clay undistinguishable from the earth around; unless, in thrusting a stick into one of the heaps you came to bits of burnt glass, iron, charcoal, or broken earthenware. Another mound of dry alkali earth, enclosed with a rough board fence, mark the spot where Dr. and Mrs. Whitman and their fellow victims lie buried in one common grave."[19]

Waiilatpu, she added, is the Indian word for "rye grass people" — so-called for the coarse grass that grew on the mission grounds.

Two or three fruit trees, she observed, escaped the general destruction, and scarlet poppies were scattered over the creek bottom near the houses.

"Sad it is that that flower whose evanescent bloom is the symbol of unending joys should be the only tangible witness left of the womanly tastes and labors of the victims of savage vengeance and superstition," she wrote.[20]

The Whitman Seminary, commemorating the work and suffering of the late missionary, had been chartered in the winter of 1859-1860, and was built in 1867 by subscriptions from Walla Walla residents.

Teachers of sufficient ability were difficult to obtain for the salary being offered, and the school was closed. Frances noted, however, that there were two high schools in Walla Walla, one each for Catholics and Protestants.

Mrs. Victor also suggested that western Oregon was uninformed about the eastern part of the state.

"It is our fashion to grumble because Californians do not understand or appreciate us," she added. "With equal propriety the people east of the mountains may complain of our ignorance concerning them, their institutions and resources."[21]

Leaving Walla Walla in a two-horse hack, she found herself the only passenger. The wagon drove across a rolling prairie, through the valley of Dry Creek. Frances thought it was one of the most beautiful farming sections she had ever seen. Farmhouses, ancillary structures and fences were common in the region despite the fact that residents had to go at least fifteen miles for timber in the Blue Mountains.

She observed many signs of plenty in the "excellent pasture lands undulating miles away on either side [of the road]. Fat, sleek-hided cattle feed in herds on a hundred hillsides."[22]

Mrs. Victor found amusing the "noisy, silly ways and awkward style of flying or running" of the curlew, a bird she never before had seen.[23] She asked the driver of the coach — a Maine Yankee — what the use was of the curlew's four or five inches of bill. The man replied that he didn't know, "unless it was to eat out of a bottle."[24]

At 10 a.m., the coach stopped in Waitsburg, a town of 100-200 people on the banks of the Touchet River. A flouring mill had been built there in 1864, and soon traders, stores and a hotel were established around it.

Waitsburg had no church, Mrs. Victor recorded, but its schoolhouse — which was used for religious services on Sundays — was the largest and best she had seen outside of Portland. There also was a Good Templar's lodge of eighty members and "only one very sickly saloon" in the town.

"Contrary to Walla Walla, which is Democratic, Waitsburg is strongly Republican," she wrote.[25]

Upon leaving Waitsburg for Lewiston, Frances discovered that the road through the Touchet Valley was lined with a "constant succession of thrifty looking farms, with a neat, commodious white-painted school house every few miles," she wrote.

"From the greatest elevation there are splendid views — wonderful for extent, and rather awful, inasmuch as one is able to realize that we are traveling like the fly on the rind of an orange, and can look down its slopes to dizzy descents of curvature."[26]

Descending the hill of the Tucannon was "frightful."[27] So steep was the grade, she wrote, that the coach seemed ready "to tumble over the backs of the horses."[28] Walking down, she thought, would have been far preferable and safer.

Frances was quite relieved when the bottom of the hill was reached. After crossing the Tucannon River, the coach stopped for the night at the farmhouse of a settler who provided bed and board for travelers.

"Plenty to eat and a good bed seemed almost more than could be expected in so isolated a situation," Mrs. Victor wrote.[29]

Getting from the Tucannon to Lewiston was the "most tiresome, warm and dusty" part of the overland journey from Wallula.[30] The weather had been growing hotter for two or three days, she commented. "We had a heavy coach, and an easy driver, who let the horses take their own way, and so we moped along in the sunshine at a very wearisome rate."[31]

After a stop for lunch at noon, Frances immediately was "inspired" to climb a high hill. "But the walking up hill was nothing to the heat and fatigue of walking *down* [it] into the valley of the Alpowah — the hottest place probably to be found above ground."[32]

She described the Alpowah as a "shallow, but unfailing stream, very crooked, and bordered with much flowering shrubbery. Its narrow bottom is occupied by the Indians as farming land."[33]

Mrs. Victor was parched when the coach arrived at the Snake River crossing, and the ferryman gave her a glass of ice water. By the time she got to Lewiston, she was also a very dirty looking traveler. She was dissatisfied by the hotel life there, but after a few hours friends unexpectedly came to the rescue and took her home with them, "to the comforts of private life and social intercourse."[34]

Lewiston was then a rather dull town, but she felt that commercially its location, on a sandspit at the confluence of the Clearwater and Snake rivers, was "a good one whenever the development of the country, by settlement, and by means of roads, navigation, etc., shall demand a commercial centre."[35]

The only impressive sight Mrs. Victor saw in Lewiston was a pack train depot, where miners' goods were received, kept and released to their owners upon payment of certain fees.

She noticed with disapproval the city's Catholic seminary "to which . . . Protestants are compelled to send their children or allow them to remain out of school."[36]

Mrs. Victor wrote that she was tempted to do an essay, "here and now, on the singular apathy with which the Protestant world of *free thought* regards the education of the young in schools where freedom of thought is regarded as sinful. How many Protestant American children — girls more particularly — are now growing up who will believe in the Papal infallibility? And if the women of this generation, or the next, believe it, who is going to save their children from the same faith? What is it about an ounce of preventive being worth a pound of cure?"[37]

Mrs. Victor also saw the agency for the Nez Perce Indians at Lapwai; she thought the Lapwai Valley was exceedingly pretty. Frances' guide for the tour of the reservation was Perrin Whitman, a nephew of the late missionary, who showed her places of special interest — most notably the old mission buildings, then falling into decay.

Mrs. Victor observed that a new, stone-walled mission church was being constructed. It would be little better than a ruin, she said, because a roof was lacking.

"Uncle Samuel must be a very good natured relative to allow so many of his nephews to set up expensive monuments to themselves out of his material; and to pay themselves handsomely at the same time for doing it," she noted wryly.[38]

She complained further that it was a "stupendous piece of nonsense" to provide "handsome buildings" or "enlightened institutions" for the "average aborigine."[39]

The Nez Perces, Mrs. Victor wrote, behaved "certainly . . . much better" than other Indians, "but to regard them as civilized or half civilized, or to expect them to become such, is an error."[40]

Only fifteen of the 3,000-member tribe were enrolled in school at the agency, she added.

> . . . It is true that they cultivate a little ground under superintendency which looks well, but it is only a little. They have an orchard too, at the Agency,

but the fruit is all stolen while it is green, and never does them any good. They parade themselves in their blankets of red or white, lounging about, full of impertinence, and very Indian altogether. Some of them are fine enough looking fellows and many of the young women are pretty. The latter can learn to sew quite nicely, but are too indolent to keep themselves decently clad without constant urging. They prefer lounging like the men, and amuse themselves in the Indian room at Mr. Whitman's by chanting together their low, lazy, not unmusical though decidedly barbarous and unpronouncable sing-song.[41]

Mrs. Victor interviewed Lawyer, a prominent Nez Perce chieftain, whose father had kept Lewis and Clark's horses while the expedition went on to explore to the mouth of the Columbia.

"He is [a] rather short, stout-built, man, with a good face of the Indian type, very dark — almost African in complexion — and dressed in a rusty suit of white men's clothes, with the inevitable high silk hat. His manner on being introduced is a very good copy of the civilized man's; but his English is quite too imperfect for much conversation," she wrote.[42]

Perrin Whitman told Frances that "Lapwai" meant the place of meeting, or boundary, between two peoples, and that Lapwai Creek in fact divided the Nez Perce tribe. The Upper Nez Perces hunted buffalo, while the Lower Nez Perces were fishermen and root-diggers.

Mrs. Victor said that Congress enacted a law donating a square mile of land to Oregon missions established before 1850. This, she noted, benefited Methodist missions west of the Cascades because, between 1848 and 1859, the country east of the mountains was closed to settlement by U.S. military order.

But after 1853 when Washington Territory was established, the territorial government conferred benefits of the federal legislation upon missions within its jurisdiction.

The federal government later took possession of the Lapwai claim for a military post. In opposition to this, the mission's agent, Henry H. Spalding, sold the claim to a private party. A legal brouhaha then arose over rights to the mission grounds.

"The law on the subject seems very much mixed: — I think if I were an advocate I should like such a case," Frances observed. "Whether it is U.S. *versus* U.S., or *versus* Washington Territory, or *versus* private individual seems difficult to determine."[43]

Another attraction, she wrote, was a "small, deep, clear lake," about twenty miles from Lewiston, "where trout abound, and pleasure parties delight to go."[44]

Mrs. Victor admitted ruefully that she had been unable to get to the lake on her visit, but that it would be "in reserve for me when I have exhausted the more common pleasures of travel and sight-seeing."[45]

Frances found the weather rather hot during her three days in Lewiston. Then her hosts saw a little cloud, no bigger than a man's hand, and predicted the onset of a sandstorm which happened on a Sunday afternoon.

. . . First, the wind came in full force, lifting the loose sands of the streets roof-high, and blowing it into every aperture of every house. Doors and win-

dows were hastily closed, and people left to suffocate with heat, in preference to being suffocated with sand. Before night, fortunately, the clouds
accumulated with an appearance of rain. Presently we had, which is a rarity
in Oregon, a rousing thunder shower. Ah! how refreshing it was, after the
heat and sand![46]

When Mrs. Victor returned to Portland from her tour east of the mountains, she found that J. Quinn Thornton had challenged the veracity of
her book in an extremely long review in the Portland (Oreg.) *Pacific Christian Advocate* in May 1870.*

Thornton charged that for "some strange and inexplicable reason"
Frances had "conceived an inveterate prejudice against Methodist preachers
in general, and against Methodist Missionaries in particular," and then laid
out evidence which he said would support the allegation.[47]

Mrs. Victor's reply on June 11 was prompt and uncompromising, and
it included the earliest statement known of her historical methods:

> . . . My course had been from the first, in gathering the material for my
> book, one of impartial hearing of all sides; that I had sought information
> far and wide, of all classes and denominations alike . . . I felt that I had shaken
> together and sifted the beliefs of all Oregon in writing my book. . . .
>
> . . . It is enough for me to say that while I gave Mr. Meek's mountain sto-
> ries as he furnished them to me, as the exponent of a class of men and style
> of living now passing away, and while I do not doubt the truth of them myself,
> leave them to the judgment of the public as the tales of a well known moun-
> tain man, — I claim something more than that for the historical sketches inter-
> woven with the adventures. Having access to old files of papers — all the
> books previously written about the country and its history — private papers
> and public documents, it would be strange if, with a disposition to write
> the truth without fear and without favor, I had not arrived at something
> approximating to it.[48]

---

*For biography, see pp. 241-242.

13

Northern Notes, 1870

On 18 June 1870, at 6 a.m., Frances boarded a steamer in Portland for a six-hour trip to Monticello, Washington Territory (now Longview, Washington), on the first leg of a two-week excursion north to Victoria, British Columbia.

This part of the Cowlitz Valley — and the mountains around it — had fertile land, extensive coal deposits and an almost inexhaustible amount of timber. She predicted that railroads and an increase in population would draw notice to these benefits.

Olympia-bound passengers found one or more stagecoaches waiting at the landing in Monticello. Competition for business, Mrs. Victor observed, had pushed fares ridiculously low. But she warned newspaper readers not to have false expectations of being carried from Monticello to Olympia for four dollars, as was her party, because of a rumor that the fare would be doubled for the rest of the season.

The conveyance for Mrs. Victor, and three other passengers from the steamer, was a long, light, open wagon with three wide seats. It also was weighted down with mail and freight, making enough work for the two stout horses doing the pulling.

Frances and another woman passenger were without umbrellas but, with the aid of a gentleman in the back seat, they were able to unfurl a "large cotton affair" over their heads to shade all three from the sun.[1]

"A warm dress with a linen duster over it; a heavy shawl for morning and evening, and a sun hat and sun umbrella are requisites for comfort," she advised.[2]

The road over the Cowlitz Mountains was so bad that Mrs. Victor wondered how it would be in winter. Yet, she admitted that not for a "pretty sum" would she have missed the ride.[3]

The forest was memorable for its "solemn and stupendous grandeur. Fir and cedar are the principal trees. They stand thickly upon the ground, are as straight as Ionian columns, so high that it is an effort to look to the top of them, and so large that their diameter corresponds admirably to their height," she added.[4]

Mrs. Victor's companions were friendly. The fine weather, bracing mountain air, and the beautiful scenery, made them all merrier still.

"We felt like mischievous children, and longed for an adventure,"
Frances wrote. "No bears, cougars or road-agents appearing to satisfy our
craving, we were forced to be content with the prospect of breaking down
which began . . . when about seven miles from our sleeping station. Walking over bad coupons of road, mending the wagon, and locking the wheels
with rope, amused and belated us together; so that it was nearly eight
o'clock when we crossed the Aliquot creek and climbing a sharp ascent
found ourselves at Pumphrey's [Landing], where we were to sup and
sleep."[5]

The food was good and the beds were comfortable. But the travelers
did not enjoy them as long as they might have wished, for they got up
at 2:30 the next morning to resume their journey. The effort, Frances
wrote,

> proved a trial to the merry mountaineers of the previous afternoon, who had
> not been particular to save their strength, and could not have saved it if they
> had been particular. A cup of coffee . . . fortified us as well as might be for
> an ante-breakfast ride of fourteen miles. But I did not like the coffee — it
> made me sick; and right here, for the benefit of those who do not know how
> to make good coffee, let me give a [recipe] for preparing that delicious bever-
> age in the proper manner. First, roast the grains yourself, and grind it properly
> — neither too coarsely nor too finely; make it into a paste with a little white
> of egg and water; then put it into the pot and pour on hot water until the
> pot contains as much as is wanted. Then let it stand where it will *steep* —
> not boil. It may *steep* from ten to twenty minutes, according to quantity, keep-
> ing just below the boiling point. When it begins to boil up, set it off immedi-
> ately, and stirring it with a long spoon to dislodge any grounds from the sides
> of the pot, let it stand and settle from three to five minutes. If ever I could
> hope to have a cup of such coffee in traveling, I think I could endure any
> amount of fatigue, with that in anticipation — especially if I knew there would
> be sweet, rich cream to go with it.[6]

After crossing the Chehalis River, they passed through Claquato, a
"pretty little village . . . which boasts, if we may believe a sign-board,
of an academy of that euphonious name."[7]

So attractive was the place that it seemed only poetry could describe
it. And poets, Frances observed wryly, "are not very reliable as real estate
agents."[8]

She also remarked, as the wagon passed through Grand Mound prairie,
that it hurt her "patriotic Oregonian pride" to acknowledge Mount Rainier as "the chief of the snow-peaks, and the one altogether lovely."[9]

Mrs. Victor considered Tumwater a suburb of Olympia. It was finely situated as a lumbering village at the head of Puget Sound, where the Des
Chutes enters, and a sawmill was located at the falls. Nearby were Tumwater's other industries, a flouring mill and a tannery.

"The falls of the Des Chutes are very pretty; but their beauty will ultimately be hidden by all manner of mills, which will be made to avail themselves of this fine water power," she wrote.[10]

Olympia, being cut out of the forest, had to contend with the primitive aspects of its environment — stumps, fallen timber and burnt trees.

"Still it is a cheerful looking place," Frances observed, "with pleasant houses, good sidewalks, and the longest and most delightful bridges! In time it must become a second Venice. The habits of its people are eminently social, and the tone of its society good. Its business is not of the noisy and bustling kind of the lumbering towns. There are large and commodious wharves, but as yet but little commerce."[11]

Commerce in western Washington, she thought, would depend on minerals and timber rather than agriculture.

Of most interest to Mrs. Victor in Olympia was the historical collection of Elwood Evans, the prominent lawyer and territorial statesman.

"Mr. Evans has taken pains to collect every volume by every author relating to the Pacific coast," she wrote. ". . . All the matter printed in newspapers referring to the early history of Oregon and Washington has been carefully preserved and as carefully arranged for reference. I do not know of any one in Oregon who has anything like so extensive a collection of such matter; and I would suggest . . . that the Portland Library Association is the proper party to commence and prosecute the work of collecting similar material for Oregon. By advertising, no doubt a great many valuable books and papers might be obtained for preservation which are now lying in dusty corners of old pioneer houses, and which will be destroyed as waste paper by the rising generation, if not secured in the lifetime of the present one."[12]

The town, at the time of her arrival, was agog over the beginning of survey work for the proposed North Pacific Railroad (which arrived on Puget Sound seventeen years later).

At 7 a.m. on 23 July 1870, in Tumwater, surveyors tamped down the first stake, "in the center of Adams street, between Third and Fourth streets, at tide water," according to the Tacoma *Daily Tribune*.[13]

Mrs. Victor observed that the railroad was much talked about by Olympians:

"Grave men discuss it gravely; lighter minded individuals talk of cutting up that first stake for toothpicks, to be sold as *souvenirs*; ladies mention the matter flippantly, as if still doubting their prospective good fortune; children rush to the scene of the survey, and young misses talk railroad while playing at grace hoops or croquet."*[14]

Frances was taken for a ride on Chambers' prairie — a plain of only a few miles' diameter — "past two lovely little lakes" and a "belt of noble woods."[15] Puget Sound's porous, gravelly soil, she wrote, created roads "smooth as a floor, and dry without being dusty."[16]

The prairie was divided into farms whose most productive portions bordered on the timberland where the rain gave the soil a "yearly accession of a certain quantity of leaf mold," which Frances observed was characteristic of all prairies between the Cowlitz Mountains and Puget Sound.[17]

---

*A game in which two or more players throw to each other and catch a small hoop by means of one or two sticks held in the hands of each person.

Chambers' prairie, she wrote, was named for its first settler, a "colored individual" from Missouri, who married a white woman.[18] The oldest orchard near Olympia was Chambers' orchard, and residents of the town remembered when they paid 25-50 cents for three or five common seedling apples, although by 1870 fruit was "plenty and good" in the area.[19] The wet weather that prevailed in Olympia during Mrs. Victor's stay prevented a clam bake, "on which my heart was very much set," from taking place.[20]

"Clam-bakes, boating parties, riding parties, and all that," were popular recreational activities among the townspeople, and in dressing for church they showed good taste.[21]

"A more stylish looking congregation . . . I have never seen north of San Francisco," she wrote. "Not that 'style' in a church makes us more devout, but that it rather takes one by surprise up in this wooden country to come upon a large assemblage of people with a look of culture and refinement about them, and arrayed, besides, in the latest fashions."[22]

She boarded the *Olympia*, a "large, commodious, and handsomely fitted up" steamer that also had "a most obliging corps of officers."[23]

One hundred-thirteen miles was the distance to her next destination, Victoria, B.C., but Frances estimated that detours to various ports along Puget Sound added at least seventeen miles to the journey.

"The only objection to be made to the present arrangement is the price of fare, ten dollars being passage money for [the] voyage . . . And it used to cost twenty dollars to make this little voyage — then fifteen, now ten, which, when it is once more halved, will be about right," she wrote.[24]

Because of the early hour of departure, Mrs. Victor could not see Steilacoom, from which Mt. Rainier was to be viewed to best advantage.

"Every one here speaks enthusiastically of the fine views, and beautiful drives about Steilacoom; but the difficulty in the way of seeing all these places is that there is but one steamer a week to Victoria, and without taking chance conveyances from port to port, one would be obliged to spend a week at those points chosen for special visits; and that is quite too much time to give to sight seeing in small new towns," she commented.[25]

Seattle, the largest place on Puget Sound, had "an amount of wharfage which would do credit" to an even larger city, Frances observed.

> . . . Here were several ships loading and unloading, and a great buzz and whirr of mills in operation. Small steamers were plying back and forth between this point and [Port] Blakely and Freeport, opposite, — the one a high, round promontory — and the other a long, low neck of land projecting into the Sound so as to form a bay with the first.
> . . . Seattle, though busy looking, did not impress me so pleasantly as Olympia, nor is it so pretty a town as Port Madison . . . It has a new interest being developed, a coal mine, which lies some miles to the east of the Sound. It is reached by land and water carriage, and is a resort much visited by tourists. The alternation of carriage, steamer and railway makes the excursion one of interest and enjoyment. Lake Washington (or Dwamish) is about thirty miles in length by four or five in width, and is now furnished with a small steamer which connects with the travel at either side of the lake; furnishing not only easy conveyance, but an opportunity for sight-seeing which is very desirable.[26]

On July 26, Mrs. Victor was on a steamer enroute down the Sound to Victoria. The air, she wrote, was "very bright and bracing. A slight breeze just rippled the blue waters . . . the summer sky was just mottled with flecks of foam-white clouds; seals sported below, birds flitted from shore to shore overhead; a 'golden silence,' only broken by the paddle wheels of our steamer, wrapped all together in a dreamy unreality very charming to the tourist. Occasionally a white sail, gleaming in mid distance, added a beauty to the view."[27]

The vessel went fourteen miles out of its way to reach Port Gamble, a milling town she termed "most important in respect to the amount of lumber produced."[28]

Travelers also got "a peep" at Hood's Canal, "that remarkable arm of the Sound . . . which is fifty miles or more in extent, yet whose entrance seems scarcely [wide enough] for the passage of a ship," Frances wrote.[29]

Further down was Port Ludlow, another milling community "and a right pleasant looking spot."[30] Most of its timber came from the western shore of the Sound and Kitsap County.

Milling companies in the vicinity owned five steamers and twenty sailing craft of various sizes. Many of these vessels, however, remained in port because of a depression in money matters, which also slowed operation of the sawmills.

Port Townsend, at the Sound's entrance, was the site of a U.S. Customs house. Here, as elsewhere, small groups of people awaited arrival of the steamer, if only to bid its passengers hail and farewell.

"In these isolated situations the arrival of the weekly steamer with mail, news, and perchance an acquaintance from some other point, is an event, and one which all seemed to enjoy equally," Mrs. Victor observed.[31]

Enroute to Victoria, Frances passed over waters that were the subject of a longstanding dispute between the United States and Great Britain.

On 15 June 1846 the two countries signed in Washington, D.C., a treaty fixing the boundary at the 49th parallel and drawing the line south from "the middle of the channel which separates the continent from Vancouver's island; and thence . . . through . . . Fuca's straits to the Pacific ocean."[32]

This vague phraseology brought about conflicting claims to, and near warfare over, San Juan Island in 1859. Cooler heads prevailed, however, and joint Anglo-American occupation of the island began, pending a negotiated settlement of the dispute.

The British felt the boundary should run through Rosario Strait, east of San Juan, while the U.S. believed it was Haro Channel on the west.

"But as the Island of San Juan will go to whichever party prevails in the contest, there is an apple of discord of considerable size to be fought over; and the matter rests in abeyance while the island is held by joint occupancy as Oregon used to be," Mrs. Victor wrote as she traveled through the region in 1870. "From the appearance of the channels as represented by the best maps we have it would seem that the British claim is unfounded; yet in this, as in all other matters of boundary between two

great nations, the question will be decided according to which one has
the heaviest account against the other."[33]

(On 8 May 1871, in Washington, D.C., an Anglo-American Joint High
Commission signed a treaty to submit the San Juan dispute to Emperor
William I of Germany for arbitration. Article 35 of the treaty stipulated
that Emperor William's award "shall be considered as absolutely final and
conclusive, and full effect shall be given to such award without any objection, evasion or delay whatsoever."[34] On 21 October 1872 the emperor
ruled in favor of the U.S. claim that "the boundary line between the territories of Her Britannic Majesty and the United States should be drawn
through the Haro channel."[35] British troops withdrew on 25 November 1872 but not until mid-summer 1874 were U.S. soldiers taken off
the island.)

After waking from a pleasant hour's nap as the steamer was crossing
the head of Fuca's Straits, Frances saw an enticing mélange of scenery.

> . . . Looking back to the east . . . one sees the snow peaks of Rainier and
> Baker towering over a blue line of mountains, with an archipelago of islands
> intervening. On the southern view the Olympian range . . . seeming to lave
> their feet in the waters of the Straits, surpassingly beautiful in outline, deli-
> cately colored, tipped and rimmed with silvery lines and crests of snow —
> a marvel of ariel effects — a poet's dream — a vision of the air.
>
> Turning . . . one sees on the north the rocky but picturesque shores of Van-
> couver and Quadra's island. Neither high nor low, but handsomely rising out
> of the water; indented with numerous coves, bays and arms of the sea; being
> dotted with trees, rather than heavily wooded, and having some fine resi-
> dences in sight from the steamer. Vancouver's Island presents a charming
> appearance at the moment of approach. First impressions being "everything,"
> the new comer feels inclined to like the island without further question; nor
> is the impression removed upon a closer acquaintanceship.[36]

In Victoria, Frances' attention was drawn to a photography studio and
its fine views of the wild and beautiful Fraser River country. For half a
day she looked through the proprietor's albums.

"Like the Columbia the Fraser breaks through the Cascade range, and
has even a much longer passage amongst mountains," she observed. ". . .
The entrance to the river is not obstructed by a dangerous bar, nor exposed
to storms, as is the Columbia. Vessels drawing eighteen or twenty feet can
enter, with ordinary care."[37]

After passing the marshy land at the Fraser's mouth, one entered a vast
expanse of magnificent timber. Fifteen miles inland was New Westmin-
ster, population about 800, then the provincial capital.

"The river," Mrs. Victor continued, "is navigated by the Hudson Bay
Company's steamers as far as Fort Yale, about ninety miles above New West-
minster. A portion of the way the banks are heavily wooded, but another
portion of the country is an open, fertile prairie. Fifty miles brings the
traveler to the junction of the Harrison river — one of the routes to the
Cariboo mines. . . . From here the travel goes on up to Cariboo by a wagon
road, built at a very great expense, and for which the Colony is still, I
believe, in debt."[38]

She estimated that not more than 10,000 persons resided in British Columbia, 6,000 of whom were on Vancouver Island.

"Nor will the population materially increase until Great Britain makes them part and parcel of herself, or they decide to unite with the nearer life of the American people," Frances opined. "Their condition now [in 1870] reminds one of the condition of the Oregon colony before its adoption by the United States Government; the same pleading, and hoping, and waiting — the same patriotic clinging to their own institutions, with occasional secretly nourished schemes of 'independent action.'"[39]

Mrs. Victor also had the pleasure of meeting in Victoria with Sir James Douglas, governor of British Columbia and Vancouver Island, who was well known to early Oregonians as a result of his long connection with the Hudson's Bay Company.

"He spoke of his intimate and beloved friend Dr. [John] McLoughlin with much feeling, avowing that he had never known his equal for genuine goodness of heart, and forbearance under circumstances of great trial," Frances recalled.[40]

Mrs. Victor also enjoyed a ride with friends out along the headlands of Esquimalt Bay, and from a pretty nook they had a lovely view of the water and the Olympic Mountains.

After returning to Victoria, she immediately boarded a steamer for home. Although the trip was smooth, Frances was seasick — "through force of habit, I believe . . . I shall never be able to make friends with the sea nor with steamships," she added, "though there were positively no bad odors about the *California*, and I could not blame the little steamer for making me ill through the olfactory nerves. The passage to the [Columbia River] bar was made in little more than twenty-four hours, and to Portland in a dozen more, with good weather all the way."[41]

14

A Stage Ride in Oregon and California

On 8 October 1870 Mrs. Victor again left Portland, this time for a trip to California and the East. In order to examine southern Oregon more closely, she took a train to Salem and then rode a stagecoach to the railhead at Chico, California.

The night train ride to Salem was quick, which Frances liked because the countryside was "not very interesting, being too little cultivated and too monotonous."[1] It served, however, as a perfect backdrop for the glorious moonlight.

On the afternoon of the 10th, she boarded a coach of the Oregon and California Stage Company to begin the long overland journey to San Francisco. Four men and two ladies with infants were also there, and other passengers rode on top with the driver.

"One baby, as is customary with travelling babies, ate some sticky compound, which it dispersed about upon neighboring dresses liberally, alternating this innocent amusement with barbaric yells and imperious demands for impossible privileges," Mrs. Victor recalled. "The other baby was a miracle of sweetness, crowing and laughing with every one who noticed it. This conduct on the part of the little innocent interested a tipsy gentleman who occupied a seat opposite to the mother, and a subscription was started among the passengers to buy the good baby a new ribbon for its cap. Not succeeding in raising the amount demanded, our inebriated friend turned his attention to politics, avowing himself, little by lit[t]le, until he finally declared he was 'secesh'; after which he related his family history, and alternately avowed himself a New Jerseyman and a Virginian. His conduct and avowals being consistent, we were inclined to believe he might be either or both that he claimed to be — prudently refraining from criticising his statements."[2]

The road from Salem to Albany was dotted with fair-goers, who cheerfully greeted the coach's passengers. They also often traveled alongside gangs of railroad-building Chinamen, and past piers and trestlework of bridges soon to be completed for the iron track.

"It was a very pleasant afternoon drive," Mrs. Victor wrote, "such as lovely October weather, a pretty country, autumnal foliage, and diverting incidents conspire to furnish."[3]

Passengers ate a good supper in Albany, and preparations were made for the night ride to Eugene. Frances was now the only lady passenger; and she was glad when an acquaintance, who was riding up top, came inside the coach on account of the sharp air of a fall evening.

As the stagecoach picked up speed on the road south from town, Mrs. Victor could see "a faint star struggling with the waning daylight in the east, and a pink flush resting along the topmost peaks of the Coast Range to the west.

". . . Never was there a more beautiful night, a more star-spangled heaven, or brilliant moonlight," she wrote. "It was too enchanting to be given up to sleep."[4]

Frances settled herself in a corner, with a pillow to deaden the motion of the coach, and thought. She could not remember the substance of her musings, only that they were pleasant. After awhile, her acquaintance asked permission to share the back seat and, after making himself comfortable, began a discourse on the cosmos.

"How strangely comes upon us every great revelation of our lives!" Frances marveled. "In the tea-kettle singing on the hob, a steam-engine; in the philosopher's kite, the telegraph; love where we had not looked for it; death where we had not expected it; — the expounder of the mystery of creation in an Oregon stage coach! Does any one smile incredulously? [T]hen I say to them their incredulity is idle; for a philosopher is coming who will be able to fix their delighted attention, and they will be shown how worlds are made and dissolved by law, and not by fiat."[5]

It seemed to her that this "feast" was broken off in the middle when, at about 4 in the morning, the coach drew up at the hotel in Eugene, and "the greater than Newton or Humboldt" bade her a hasty farewell.[6]

Mrs. Victor paused to spend a day admiring the scenery of this little city at the head of the Willamette Valley. The foothills of the mountains closed in on three sides, and Spencer's Butte attracted attention with its pointed cone.

"I found little enough of business life in this portion of the valley, where neither steamboat nor railroad whistle break the quiet monotony, at present; water enough to carry boats to Eugene only existing in the rainy season," Frances observed. "In the future it must become a brisk, as it is now a beautiful town, when railroad communication brings the outside world a little nearer."[7]

It was a bright and cold morning on October 12 as the stagecoach left Eugene and headed up into the mountains. Mrs. Victor was the only passenger. She wanted to ride atop the coach for better views of the country, but resisted her inclinations and the polite invitation of the driver until the sun was well up. She snuggled under her blankets to ward off the chill, but at the first opportunity she clambered into the box beside the driver.

"We were in among the russet-colored hills, which bore green fringes of firs along their crests, and wreaths of green, gold and crimson about their feet," Frances recalled. "To the east, a delicate mist veiled in violet the tops of the Cascade Range, just visible through gaps in the hills nearest us; and on the west, the lower Coast Range broadly reflected the strengthening sunlight. Such brilliant scarlet leaves as the vine-maple flaunts in the autumn sun do not grow on any other shrub, and they glowed on every side where the road twisted in and out among the hills and along streams. In equal prodigality of color the soft-maple drooped its broad palms of gold, spotted with amber, in great masses of yellow, beside the way, while the rich browns and various greens toned down the excessive brilliancy of the redundant foliage to a pleasant relief for the eye."[8]

The stagecoach entered Calapooya Pass by the gorge of a stream known as Pass Creek, where the air was chill and damp even after the long drought of summer and the road rough and uneven.

It was a treat to get thus into the heart of a mountain, Mrs. Victor remarked, and discover the secrets of the wilderness in their hiding places.

"Such magnificent trees, such towering ferns, such deep shadows, such eloquent silence, broken only by the clatter and rumble of the lumbering stage, which waked the echoes in every rocky dell!" she wrote. "And then such a quiet talk as we had — the driver and I! The worlds in which we had lived had been so different; and we exchanged notes on their points of difference. He was as simple-minded as a child, and I not averse to hearing his views of life, nor unwilling to give him mine in return. So we chatted along the mountain canyon and out into the Umpqua Valley. Being of a sociable temper, I felt sure that he was disappointed when I signified my intention to stop over until the next day at Yo[n]calla, the residence of the Hon. Jesse Applegate, surnamed 'the Sage'; but he could not have been so disappointed as I was at not finding Mr. Applegate at home."[9]

The Umpqua Valley, Frances observed, was divided into still smaller valleys by countless spurs of mountains. It was excellent country for stock-raising and fruit-growing. Several apple trees were in blossom, and from one she gathered several apples of the second crop.

After a day of visiting the Applegates, Mrs. Victor continued on her way, not knowing where next to seek a respite from "the constant thumping and bumping of staging."[10] Neither the road nor the driving was bad, she wrote, "but the load was light through this portion of the country, which gave the vehicle too great latitude in swaying and pitching about."[11] But two or three way-passengers helped balance the coach, giving Frances more opportunity to observe the passing scenery.

"At a country post-office, somewhere along the road to Oakland, the driver threw down the mail-bag, which was taken and carried into the house by a slovenly-looking woman, while a three-year-old urchin, in a single blue check garment, followed, bellowing at her heels," Mrs. Victor related.[12]

While the outgoing mail was being readied, the stage driver watered the horses at a stream near the house.

"After a little waiting," Frances continued, "there appeared, staggering under the weight of the small mail-bag, the little three-year-old postmaster who had cried because his mother took in the mail. Seeing how it was, the driver went half way to meet him, when he made an effort to toss the bag as he had seen his elders do, and it fell short in the dust of the road. Hastily picking it up again, he gave it another toss, which brought it by a great effort, almost to the driver's feet, when he turned and fled, believing, no doubt, that he had done himself great credit in the service of the United States."[13]

The travelers went on to Oakland — a town, nicely situated on the Calapooya River, which seemed much busier than Eugene — where they had an excellent supper and changed stages for another night ride.

Frances thought Roseburg, eighteen miles further south, was a "very romantic looking place" framed by the Umpqua River and the rolling countryside. It had 500 residents, two churches, very good schools, a courthouse and a U.S. Land Office.[14]

The night was again beautiful, with stars winking in the distant firmament, and the light of a full moon distinctly illuminated the scenery. The road was generally good, although there was one bridge "which it took some twenty or thirty minutes to repair before the horses would go over it," Mrs. Victor wrote.

> Careful driving is required on these mountain roads, necessarily narrow in the most dangerous places, so that a few inches divergence from the single track would be a sure upset into ragged abysses of darkness below. But all through Oregon there was the best of driving, the professors of the whip being also polite, sober, and attentive.
>
> The stock on the road was excellent, seeming to know just what was required, and to be willing to do it.[15]

On October 14, Frances arrived in Canyonville, where awaited breakfast and a change of coaches. It was a cold morning, with a light fog that dissipated in the sun.

The road passed through Umpqua Canyon, which gained notoriety late in 1846 when a group of immigrants made their way through it in high water. A number of settlers abandoned their wagons before reaching the gorge; and at all the crossings, men and women alike had to wade sometimes breast deep through the cold, rushing water. There was a great loss of livestock and other property, but no deaths among the party directly attributable to the rigors of the passage.

"I found the cool morning air in those deep shadows sufficiently benumbing," Frances wrote, "and shuddered to think what those fearful struggles with a mountain torrent must have been."[16]

After leaving the canyon, the stagecoach entered the valley of Cow Creek, made famous by the Indian wars of the 1850s in southern Oregon.

Mrs. Victor averred she never before had seen such beauty of form and color in trees. The variety, too, was surprising.

"Fir, pine, cedar, live-oak, maple, laurel, alder, dogwood, elder, manzanit[a], with many shrubs and vines unknown to me, are here growing in a perfection of development, and charming grace of combination rare, even in this land of prodigal loveliness," Frances observed. "Nor did I

find the beauty of vegetable forms to excel the richness of vegetable coloring; both were perfect."[17]

The coach passed into Grave Creek Valley. "Mountains are everywhere
about us apparently thrown together in hopeless confusion," she commented.[18] She also saw on oak trees in the valley "a black hanging moss
of a most funereal aspect," as if its hue had adapted to the doleful name
of the region.[19]

The wild grape vine — "a stranger to more northern Oregon" — was
also visible, however; and, though of little worth for fruit, it provided
"a perfect garland of gorgeousness in the autumn," Mrs. Victor wrote.
"Growing in clumps upon the ground it was gay as a bed of tulips, or,
depending from the wayside trees, it flaunted its crimson and parti-colored
leaves in the rich sunlight, with a gai[e]ty that mocked at all sobriety."[20]

Frances added that "this carnival of color" extended all through
southern Oregon and northern California.[21]

In the region between the Umpqua and Siskiyou mountains, she could
see traces of mining operations in abandoned cabins, rockers, sluice-boxes,
sieves and other paraphernalia. Gold had been found in the area in the
early 1850s, and men hastened to take advantage of the new bonanza.
The claims had not been worked for several years by the time Mrs. Victor
saw them. In all, an estimated $18 million in precious ore was extracted
from southwestern Oregon mines between 1850-1870.

"Only these abandoned mining implements, and the torn and disfigured
surface of the ground, hinted at former life in these now quiet scenes,"
she wrote.[22]

The stage stopped in mid-afternoon in Rocky Point, a "neat little village" on the Rogue River, where passengers dined and rested briefly.[23]
The place was so clean, quiet and pleasant that Frances was tempted to
extend her stay. But the moon was waning, which meant less light for
the night ride over the Siskiyous, and she decided to continue.

There was a good, mostly level, road and plenty of dust enroute to Jacksonville. The travelers had the Rogue River in view an hour before reaching Rocky Point, but left it soon thereafter. It was "a handsome stream;
rapid, clear, blue, with beautiful banks," Mrs. Victor wrote, and she was
just as ecstatic about the Rogue River Valley.[24]

"Certainly the features of the country could not be improved: its produc-
tiveness in fruit and pasturage perhaps excels its grain capacity, but so
long as it has no railroad communication with markets, it is unnecessary
to raise more grain than is demanded for home consumption," Frances
wrote. "Its climate is that happy medium between the rains of Northern
Oregon and the drouths of California which is most desirable for agreeable residence. The spring is early, commencing in February. At this season the open woods are carpeted with flowers. The sweet-scented violet
which we call French, grows spontaneously here, and can be traced to
its sheltered nooks by its delicious odor. It is easy to imagine how much
sought after such a valley will sometime be, when communication with
it shall be made less difficult."[25]

On October 14, at about 8 p.m., the stage stopped in Jacksonville for an hour, before starting with a full load over the Siskiyou Mountains. It was a long, slow climb, Mrs. Victor recalled, "six miles up hill, and six down again — a fearful grade too."[26] Even by moonlight, she could discern the autumnal tints on the mountain sides. Nothing bigger than a gray squirrel appeared, larger animals having apparently gone deeper into the forest for food because of the drought.

The travelers breakfasted next morning at Cole's Station, on the California side, and drove over open and comparatively smooth country towards Yreka. Frances looked eagerly for Mt. Shasta, but the massive peak was shrouded in the morning mist and only its triple summit was dimly visible.

The stagecoach arrived about 11 a.m. in Yreka, but the town was full of revelers attending the county fair. Mrs. Victor had been on the move for 2½ days, and she wanted a respite from the close confinement — the thumping, bumping and clatter, and the swaying motion, of the vehicle.

The hotels were crowded, but the stage driver told Frances of a pleasant country place called "Forest Home" five miles beyond. There she stayed for a day in what to her was "a 'home' indeed, full of plenty and pleasantness."[27]

Mrs. Victor left her sylvan retreat at about noon on October 16. For a couple of hours the stagecoach crept, in dust and sunshine, up into the hills and down again, past piney slopes and bunches of autumn color.

The travelers entered Scott's Valley, a "long, narrow and pretty" area "quite enclosed by mountains."[28] At Fort Jones, a lady and a little girl entered the coach and shared Mrs. Victor's formerly exclusive back seat. The woman was "intelligent and communicative," and told Frances much about the region.[29]

"I found that there was a good deal of grain raised here," she wrote, "which was converted into flour . . . for home consumption, and market in the mines; and that lumber mills and stores did a good business."[30]

Scott's Mountain was considered the roughest of all those crossed by the stage line. Mrs. Victor conceded "it is the highest certainly, and very stony," but she could not say that the passage, made in the darkness of a clear and cold night, was any more difficult.[31]

"I had become used to jolting," she commented, "so that a bump, more or less, did not signify."[32]

The stagecoach followed the Trinity River, a foaming torrent, for several miles. Relieved passengers thawed themselves before a blazing fire at the Trinity Centre breakfast station.

"We had mountain trout for breakfast, cooked by a Chinaman, and served by a 'white man,'" Mrs. Victor related. "Indeed, I forgot to [mention] that I seldom saw a woman along the road — for our breakfasts were invariably as early as half-past five o'clock, before the families were astir; and the culinary department, everywhere, seemed given over to men."[33]

After crossing the river, the stagecoach traversed the last mountain on the route. It was a very nice drive on a smoothly graded road. Frances had a good view of the Salmon Range, which was considerably higher than the other mountains, and much more rocky and bold.

"We dined at a pleasant country inn, called the Tower House, supped at Shasta, a rough looking place, and travelled over a stony country to Red Bluffs, where we made the customary change of coaches for the night," she wrote. "The country near Red Bluffs, though rough for stage travel, is very pretty. The nut, or 'digger' pine, grows to splendid proportions about here; and the Coast Range makes a grand outline for the western horizon, over some peaks of which I saw the last sunset colors lingering."[34]

The morning of October 18 brought Frances at last to the railhead at Chico, where she boarded a train for San Francisco via Sacramento, a trip she considered as familiar enough not to need description.

"In spite of fatigue and some rough road, I enjoyed the journey thoroughly — a little less perhaps than if I had started with my own party of through passengers," she concluded. "It is the only way to get an idea of the country — of its extent or peculiarities; and instead of being appalled by the accomplished undertaking I should not be averse to repeating it."[35]

15

Tracking the Indian Wars

When Frances returned to Portland the following spring, she renewed her travels around the Pacific Northwest. A new book, entitled *All Over Oregon and Washington*, a revised and expanded version of her earlier unpublished observations, was in the offing.

By early November 1871, Mrs. Victor was again in San Francisco, supervising publication of her manuscript.

Six weeks later, Frances wrote Elwood Evans to ask him to speak favorably of the book among Washington citizens "and get them to send me two or three hundred dollars right off. I must have fifteen hundred at least for the first edition; and after that more to defray the expenses of getting it into the market in good shape."[1]

Mrs. Victor came briefly to Portland to arrange for the sale of her book, and then left for another visit with her mother and sisters in the East.

On 3 May 1872 she informed Judge Deady that, because the Bay area was "as green and flowery as Eden" and the weather akin to paradise, she almost regretted leaving, but would depart in a week.[2]

"I have not found that Oregon is much appreciated in the east — nor is it likely that I shall make a fortune out of my interest in it, literary or otherwise," Frances noted sadly in an October letter to the judge from her mother's Marysville, Ohio, home.[3] She asked if he could obtain the position of librarian at the Portland Library for her, or for a sister she was trying to persuade to join her.

"I could think of nothing else to attempt for her if we lived in Portland, as I would like to," she continued. "I have no home — never shall have as long as I am alone in the west — and it is a very ardent wish of mine to set up my lares and penates somewhere soon, as I observe the gray beginning to show among my auburn locks; and I prefer being carried from my own house to 'that bourne' etc.

"I am writing — trying to retrieve some of my quixotic errors by hard work," Frances added. "Have hope that if I live long enough I may die comfortable!"[4]

Judge Deady replied that the vacancy had already been filled, and he suggested that she might want to consider studying law in his office.

Frances returned to San Francisco in the spring of 1873 after her trip to the East, and found invitations from Jesse Applegate and his nephew Oliver C. Applegate to visit them in the Klamath country of southern Oregon and write a history of the recently concluded Modoc War. She was delighted to accept, and in a May 11 letter to Oliver Applegate also asked him to try to obtain as many official photographs as possible of historical and other significant points.

"Illustrations are absolutely necessary to the success of a book, and certainly add greatly to its interest with the reader," she explained.[5]

Mrs. Victor soon was in Portland, readying herself to go to Ashland to join the Applegate family members preparing to return to their homes in the Klamath basin.

In late June she started south via the Oregon & California Railroad, and was permitted by the train crew to ride with them on the locomotive through the most scenic portions of the route to the railhead at Roseburg, where the rigors of the journey began.

> At Roseburg we leave a comfortable car, and hasten to take a *not* very comfortable coach. As a tourist must grumble somewhere, I seize upon this opportunity. When one is about to commence a night ride, one wants three-quarters of an hour at the very least to prepare for it; but at Roseburg it is presumed that you can attend to your toilet, take supper, and get into your night wraps in fifteen minutes — all on account of the stage company's enthusiastic intention to make time, and deliver its passengers to the waiting train on the California end of the road at a stated moment. I left out the supper, having been fortified thereto by a private lunch on board the train. Stage-driving in Oregon is good — I find no fault with that. But the Stage Company probably could afford, if they thought of the sufferings of their passengers, to put in cushions that are a trifle less hard than a rock.[6]

She was astonished to have survived the night on the stagecoach "without being reduced to jelly," and felt much revived after an early breakfast.[7]

The nervous system and digestive organs, however, retaliated for being bounced and jarred so much; and after a dose of camphor-and-water, Mrs. Victor sought the "tonic" of the bright morning air. She clambered onto the seat next to the stage driver, with whom she chatted amiably until the coach reached the dinner stop at Rock Point.

"After the coach arrives, time is consumed getting dinner on the table, necessarily," she complained. "By the time we are seated and have *swallowed* half a meal, the word is given to start again. Of course the horses and driver have had their meal before-hand without hurry. The miserable passenger, whose only business is to pay his fare, is not consulted. On the contrary, he is compelled to consent to be regarded as fast freight; faster when at the stations than when on the road. But it all conduces to make us glad to come to our journey's end, as well as to vow we never will — no, never! take coach through Oregon again. But we shall — of course we shall — and the Stage Company knows it."[8]

In Ashland, Mrs. Victor was a guest at the home of Lindsay Applegate, a brother of Jesse.

She then joined a party enroute from Ashland across the Cascades to Linkville, sixty-two miles away.

The party, which also included Jesse Applegate, covered the distance in three days. They had an ambulance, a baggage-wagon and horses, and could ride or walk as they chose.

Mrs. Victor regretted that Palace cars and stagecoach cushions had caused her to become effeminate and awkward, and unable to ride a hard-trotting horse — "and to redeem my character from the charge of too great luxuriousness, I walked miles in the fragrant shadows of giant pines, conversing meanwhile with a companion of inexhaustible resources, and did not feel in the least punished by my self-imposed penance."[9]

The first night was spent in the valley of Jenny Creek, and the party enjoyed a trout dinner. Frances "had a good sleep, quite undisturbed by grizzlies, of which there were not a few in the mountains." But, not knowing any better, she left her shoes out in the dew, "of the effect of which I became unpleasantly aware" when she put them on in the morning.[10]

Later, as she and Jesse Applegate were walking together, reminiscing about the early days, Jesse told her about the road on which the party was traveling. It was called the Southern Immigrant Road when he and others laid it out in 1846 to allow American soldiers to enter Oregon and defend the settlers should the U.S. and Great Britain fight over the boundary question.

It was thought at the time that a southern passage would be safer than the Columbia River and Mt. Hood routes in the event of war.

Jesse also showed Mrs. Victor a tree, near the Klamath River crossing, where several men of Captain Fremont's exploring party carved their names in 1843.

Hunters killed a deer, and while they dressed it Frances went ahead. But she had gone only a short distance when "Cinnamon" — her term for a huge brown bear — darted across her path.

She presumed that the bear had heard the rifle and guessed what it meant. "The guns were behind, and we quietly watched his departure, thinking it was an escape on both sides," she recalled.[11]

That night the party camped at the summit of a mountain. They toasted venison on sticks over a blazing log fire, told stories and sang songs. Early next morning, Mrs. Victor was awakened by the "Sage of Yoncalla," who called upon her to observe the brightness of the morning star.

Bear-walks passed near the campsite, and Frances found it "pleasantly exciting to surmise the possibility of an ursine visitor in camp; and terribly disturbing also to be wakened at three o'clock in the morning to see Venus! — just as if Venus was not likely to last one's life-time, and to be evening and morning star at intervals during the whole of that period. I know of people so insane as to invite you to look at the moon — as if the moon were a novelty!"[12]

On July 3, the party arrived in Linkville, whose residents were preparing to celebrate the Fourth of July.

Mrs. Victor was invited to participate, and she happily joined in the festivities. Oliver's brother, Ivan D. Applegate, was orator for the occasion and, Frances wrote, his "discourse of our Nation's history from first to last [was] in a manner rather more original than anniversary orators are accustomed to do."[13]

A ball brought the day's activities to a close, Frances added, "and if any one is malicious enough to aver that [she] danced, I should state uncompromisingly that they told the truth."[14]

Linkville, she observed, was well located for travel and business in southeastern Oregon. The town lay at the base of the Cascade Mountains and at the foot of Upper Klamath Lake, just where Link River, which connected with the lower lake, ran out of it.* (Lower Klamath and Tule lakes were drained in a federal land reclamation project in the early 1900s.) "Hot springs and ashen soil attest the volcanic origin of its peculiar features," she wrote.[15]

Thirty-one miles north was the Klamath Agency and six miles beyond that lay Fort Klamath — "both handsomely located among pine groves of great beauty, and furnished with the most deliciously pure and cold water," Mrs. Victor noted.[16]

About twenty miles south of Linkville was Tule Lake — a place, she wrote,

> rendered forever historical, first by unprovoked murders of immigrants, and lastly by an unheard-of act of treachery on the part of the murderers toward a Commission which only dealt too leniently with them. The history of the events which led to the Modoc war will hardly be written in this generation; and the unwritten facts will be those possessing the intensest interest, even when something like a history shall be produced. It is not the fault of interviewers, be it understood, if no account of these things is furnished to the public in proper form. One of this uncanny tribe myself, I felt some compunctions of conscience when I beheld the rapacity of my kind. Be it known that Job's patience would scarcely have been sufficient to meet the exigencies of the q[u]izzing which the officers of the Agency, particularly, had to undergo. The courtesy and kindness extended to us is, and always will remain, a wonder to my mind.[17]

Frances noted that it was customary to berate Indian agents for a whole catalogue of sins: stealing, peculation, unfairness to the Indians, cruelty, lying, etc. She wondered how agents on the Klamath reservation could make anything out of their positions when appropriations were so small and so slowly remitted. In fact, funds were so scarce that necessary improvements could not be made, let alone carry out treaty stipulations.

"At this rate an Indian Agent may be looked upon as an underpaid and suffering rather than a money-making individual," she wrote. "The duties required of one are anything but agreeable, the servant of, rather than the master of his wards — attending to every want from a gun-lock to a baby's shroud. An Indian likes or dislikes, very much like any other ignorant and

---

*Almost twenty years later, on 19 March 1892, the Salem *Daily Oregon Statesman* carried this dispatch:

LINKVILLE, Or., March 18. — The name of Linkville postoffice is to be changed to Klamath Falls. The change goes into effect at the beginning of the next quarter.

narrow-minded person. Everybody knows how much more difficult to deal with is ignorance than intelligence. Add bad propensities and savage ideas to a total lack of all valuable knowledge and you have the character of many of the Indians with whom an Agent has to deal. But the Government ignores the wrongs of its employes, and in its surpassing sympathy for the Indian forgets to 'be just before being generous.' "[18]

Mrs. Victor expressed confidence that affairs at the Klamath Agency would survive the minutest scrutiny, and what she considered as the reckless charges being made by uninformed critics in Oregon and California. "Having an opportunity to observe the administration of the present Agent, and being acquainted with the man who formerly managed affairs on the Reservation, I feel competent to say that there was not only no ground of complaint against them, but that they seem to have acted with singular manhood and good faith towards the Indians and the [Indian] Department," she wrote.[19]

Frances spent six weeks in the Klamath country, most of it at Klamath Agency, where under the tutelage of young Oliver Applegate she learned about Indian life, customs and mythology. With him as guide, she attended the trial of the Modoc prisoners at Fort Klamath. She also visited Yainax, and explored focal points in the massacre of settlers and the war that followed — Clear Lake and the lava beds.

She made drawings of flowers in the Klamath basin, and later took them to botanists at the San Francisco Academy of Sciences for identification. Butterflies she collected proved to be the same as fluttered in similar localities in the Sierras, but a box of snail-shells and fresh-water shells from the Modoc lakes elicited some interest.

Frances regretted that it was impossible to procure a "not much mutilated specimen" of the gray rattlesnake that inhabited the lava beds, or one of "that queer little armadillo-looking creature" that she saw near Clear Lake.[20]

Traversing the country was no easy matter, Mrs. Victor found, and she warned potential female travelers of what to expect, and gave tips on how to minimize discomfort.

"Suffice it for the present that to travel in Eastern Oregon requires you to wear stout shoes, a linen duster, a dust-cap, an immense hat; to carry a field-glass and a carbine; to know how to make a hemlock bed, or sleep on a haystack, and to talk jargon," she wrote. "With these accoutrements and accomplishments, if you are a good and indefatigable rider, you will get along."[21]

The "crowning pleasure" of her visit was a trip to Crater Lake, then little known but soon to become famous.[22]

The Klamath Indians had long known of the lake's existence; but few dared to look upon it for fear that they would be devoured by water devils, called Llaos. Twelve prospectors foraging for food were the first white men to see the lake, on 12 June 1853. They named it Deep Blue Lake. It also was called Lake Mystery and Lake Majesty. More detailed exploration, however, revealed that the great rocky bowl containing these beautiful azure waters was an immense crater, egg-shaped in form and six-by-seven miles in extent, so the name Crater Lake came into general use.

A military road from Jacksonville to Fort Klamath ran within four miles
of the lake, and was the route usually taken by tourists. "But the approach
from the east side [was] much more easy, being a comfortable afternoon's
drive from the Agency to camp at the turning-off point," Mrs. Victor wrote.
"Our party found bear-tracks close to camp, and deer-tracks in the ashes
of our burnt-out fire when we arose from our mosquito tormented slumbers."[23]
Although their ambulance-wagon was driven to the summit, the party
had to walk most of the four miles to the rim because "the ground was
very lumpy with rocks and frozen snowdrifts which July suns had failed
to liquefy, and which, to them unaccountable, phenomenon kept our
mules in a greatly agitated state of nerves," she wrote.

> On arriving at the summit we found the earth light and ashen, diversified
> by patches of snow, and by other patches of alpine flowers, some of which
> were very pretty in form and color. The air was bright and mild; we had left
> the forest behind us; there was nothing anywhere about more elevated than
> our position, nor any living thing anywhere near us. We were apparently
> on the highest point of the earth, for there was nothing to look up to, and
> it would not have surprised me to have been whirled off into space. *The soli-
> tude of the situation was thrilling.*
>
> One cannot, owing to the sunken position of the lake, discover it until
> close upon its rim, and I say here, without exaggeration, that no pen can
> reproduce its image, no picture be painted to do it justice; nor can it, for
> obvious reasons, be satisfactorily photographed. At the first view a dead
> silence fell upon our party. A choking sensation arose in our throats, and
> tears flowed over our cheeks. I do not pretend to analyze the emotion, but,
> if I were to endeavor to compare it with anything I ever read, I should say
> it must be such a feeling which causes the Cherubim to veil their faces before
> God. To me it was a revelation.*
>
> The water of Crater Lake is of the loveliest blue imaginable in the sunlight,
> and a deep indigo in the shadows of the cliffs. It mirrors the walls encircling
> it accurately and minutely. It has no well-like appearance because it is too
> large to suggest it, yet a water-fowl on its surface could not be discovered
> by the naked eye, so far below us is it. It impresses one as having been made
> for the Creator's eye only, and we cannot associate it with our human affairs.
> It is a font of the gods, wherein our souls are baptized anew into their primal
> purity and peace.[24]

One evening, in the fiery hues of a summer sunset, Frances gingerly
made her way to the edge of a large overhanging stone parapet to get a
view of its reflection in the lake. In recognition of her feat, the place was
later officially designated Victor Rock.**

---

*This apparently was not an uncommon reaction to the first view of Crater Lake. Capt.
C.E. Dutton and a United States Geological Survey party spent five weeks, in July and August
1886, making a detailed study of the lake. In his report of the survey Dutton wrote: "It
was touching to see the worthy but untutored people who had ridden a hundred miles
in freight-wagons to behold it, vainly striving to keep back tears as they poured forth excla-
mations of wonder and joy akin to pain. Nor was it less so to see so cultivated and learned
a man as my companion hardly able to command himself to speak with his customary calm-
ness." *Quoted by Victor in Atlantis Arisen, pp. 180-181.*

**It is now the site of the Sinnott Memorial, dedicated in memory of Nicholas J. Sin-
nott, who represented Oregon's Second District in Congress from 1913-1928.

At the end of the visit, Oliver Applegate and his uncle escorted Mrs. Victor back to Ashland. She boarded a stagecoach to Roseburg, with railroad connections to Salem and Portland. On 27 August 1873 Frances wrote Oliver to update him on her travels.

> . . . After you saw me perched up beside the driver I continued to keep my lofty position all day and enjoyed the ride very well, but not well enough to keep me from feeling the bruises inflicted on unhappy shoulders. By night I felt as if half a dozen Sandwich Islanders had been practicing "lummi lummi" (is that the way it is spelled?) on me with something harder than their fists. However I survive[d] it. It is strange and edifying to remember how many things we do survive which we have only sworn we should succumb to! The day following my departure from Ashland found me at Mrs. Clarke's in Salem. . . . The house is very lively now, with so many girls going and coming, and frequent visits of their gentlemen friends. It reminded me of my girlish days when music and merriment sounded forever in a happy home which no other later home has ever equalled.*[25]

Mrs. Victor continued on to Portland to the home of a friend, D.W. Williams, a partner in the firm of Williams and Myers Commission Merchants on Front Street. Mrs. Williams was visiting in Hood River, so Frances "assumed charge of the house and am house-keeping this week for the first time in five years."[26]

Mrs. Victor expected to stay in Portland long enough to put her affairs in some order. A sister in Ohio, Martha F. Rayle, expected to come to San Francisco in mid-October and Frances wanted to be there to meet her.

During the time that Oliver and Frances were together, a warm bond of friendship and admiration grew between them. Both looked with disdain upon the conventions that then governed society and locked the sexes into preordained roles. Each had high regard for the other's talents, abilities and intellect. For Frances this was ecstasy. Such esteem for her personal worth was something she never before experienced, although she had a common interest and the respect of her peers in the history-writing field. The attentions of a man twenty years younger thus brought special pleasure to her hard, eventful, but often lonely, life.

When her letter arrived two weeks later in Oliver's "sylvan retreat" at Swan Lake, he responded at once:

> . . . The mountain Bliwas** ruffles his plumes with delight and taking a pen in his claw undertakes briefly to reply.

> "Thy symbol be the mountain bird
> Whose glistening quills I hold;

---

*This was Harriet T. Buckingham (1832-1890). Born in Norwalk, Ohio, she came to Oregon nineteen years later. In 1852 in Portland she married Samuel A. Clarke (1828-1909), who was born in Cuba and had been in Oregon for two years. S.A. Clarke promoted early railroad development in the state. He helped to incorporate the Oregon Central Railroad in 1866 and was secretary of the company for three years. Clarke became well known as a journalist, poet and historian, and for his interest in fruit-culture. During a long and varied career he edited the Portland *Morning Oregonian*; and the *Daily Oregon Statesman* and *Willamette Farmer*, both in Salem.

**The Klamath Indian word for "golden eagle."

> Thy home the ample air of hope
> And memory's sunset gold.''[27]

There was nothing new of importance, Oliver reported, although he expected to attend the execution of the four Modocs convicted of murdering the peace commissioners. Leroy S. Dyar, U.S. Indian sub-agent at Klamath, was east visiting his parents. His wife remained to help take care of the agency's paperwork.

"The Government has often commissioned less capable public servants than Mrs. D. would make," Applegate commented, "and I expect to live to see a day when merit shall be regarded as the chief qualification for office, and sex shall not debar any capable individual from mounting to any run[g] of the political ladder.''[28]

In a September 17 letter, Frances set out at length, among other matters, her feelings for "Bliwas," and philosophized about the nature of love in general. She wrote:

> As the regard in which I hold my "plumed" friend is quite different from the ordinary friendships of mortals without wings, I have, upon mature reflection adopted the above style of address which if not distasteful to him shall be adhered to in the future. . . . There are some minds, you know, which prefer to avoid the beaten track, even in so seemingly trifling a matter as naming a friend; and I choose a designation which by power of association brings before my mental vision many pleasant scenes and agreeable recollections.
>
> Perhaps you do not guess that it pleases me to invest you with a title, which might be written thiswise: "Oliver Applegate: Gentleman, by the grace of God and the nobility of his own nature." Here again the "poetical privilege" comes in with which the poetical sad soul of a too worldly-wise woman comforts itself. To endow with rare virtues a "Chance Acquaintance" of whom just so much may be known as not to destroy whatever pretty theories and fine imaginations said soul, being in want of cheer, charms itself with. At all events, it cannot be complained of by the recipient of these honors that they require anything of him except non-interference with the harmless pastime of adorning him as a lay figure with the fine raiment of a friendly imagination very much in want of something on which to hang its exuberant fancies. Nay, that last sentence seems to take the grace out of the compliment, by allowing a doubt to insinuate itself as to the verity of the qualities assigned. Hold it then unwritten; for my imaginations are not so very immaterial, I am sure, as to attach themselves to nothing. Being a poet, and your senior, I may without circumlocution say that I take great pleasure in liking you and esteeming you a number of degrees more than other chance acquaintances every day met with; and that I think it a privilege to cherish and enjoy the sentiment; holding it a gift of God when anything is sent us to which our faith can pin itself. These gifts have their "sweet uses" like adversity; or in the language of a true poet: —
>
> > "God sends us Love: Something to love he lends us;
> > But when love is grown to ripeness, that on
> > Which it throve falls off, and love is left alone."
>
> Very barren and unhappy is the soul in which none of the affections can grow to ripeness and exist independently of "that on which it throve;" poor and uncultivated is the mind in which love exists only as a passion of the blood;

and both unhappy, and barren and uncultivated the life of that person who cannot or does not sometimes own a sentiment above and apart from those ordained by conventionalities.

If I had not dubbed you "Gentleman by the grace of God" I might fear you would misconstrue what I have written to mean some silly and unbecoming sentimentality. But you will not; knowing I am perfectly a self-poised woman, whose appreciative regard is as pure and simple as it is sincerely avowed. There may happen times or events in your life when to know of this regard may be of some now un-guessed-of use to you; therefore is it here recorded.[29]

Mrs. Victor was dismayed that the editor of the *Overland Monthly*, John Carmany, did not use an article she had submitted. "I think Mr. C. is behaving very unhandsomely by me," she wrote Oliver, "since he gave me leave to choose my subjects, and the article I sent him was a good one for the time and place. I have written to him to find out the footing on which we stand."[30]

Frances lamented that although Mrs. Dyar could demonstrate efficiency in any task she was allowed to do, and was a very good woman in every way, "she does not know her powers — being used to 'serve and wait' upon the nobler sex."[31]

The first annual meeting of the Oregon State Woman Suffrage Association had taken place in Albany. Mrs. Victor evidently considered the event a noisy, sandlot affair, for she asked Oliver if he thought "any woman's convention would have been ashamed of the proceedings of the Albany Convention? What next, in the name of decency!"[32]

Frances thanked Oliver for his thoughtfulness in enclosing a packet of blue snapdragon seeds, which she was parceling out to friends and florists. She had already forwarded to New York for study a bottle of beetles and bugs she collected in southern Oregon.

She wrote that she knew the rumor of dissatisfaction among the Klamath Indians over the impending execution of the Modocs was untrue, "but how to stop systematized falsifying — that is the problem."[33]

Late October found Frances in Portland. She still expected her sister, Mrs. Rayle, to spend the winter with her in Alameda, California, and she was impatient to be off, but was detained by "one thing after another" — not the least of which was her work on Indian wars in Oregon.

"I have just now come from an interview with [Brig.] Gen. [Jefferson C.] Davis, who sent me word that he was at my service if I wished any assistance from his office in writing up the Modoc war," she wrote. "I explained to him that my intention was not to hurry a history of that matter before the public, but to include an account of it [in] a general history of the Indian Wars of Oregon — and accepted his offer very gratefully of course."[34]

Mrs. Victor noted that she would have to return to Portland, in any case, for the spring term of court, at which she hoped some important property rights would be established.

"All the legal business may and probably will prevent my going abroad," she wrote, "but if it makes me better able to go in the future I shall submit very amicably to the detention."[35]

By mid-November, Frances had abandoned all hope of getting down to San Francisco before spring 1874 or even later. She was hard at work on the Modoc War, and warned Oliver Applegate that he would be often called upon for information.

She was busily engaged in taking notes, "a somewhat lengthy task," from military documents at the headquarters of the Army's Department of the Columbia in Portland. "Gen. Davis is very kind, having given me an office . . . and access to all the Documents," she told Oliver.

"Every day some question arises in this investigation which makes me wish for you at my elbow — for this is the <u>military</u> side of the subject alone and I must needs get at the other to become a faithful historian.

". . . 'Facts are stubborn things' and not always easily obtained," she wrote. ". . . The labor of getting together all the material for a well written history is very considerable — the writing of it nothing, in comparison."[36]

Mrs. Victor then listed several detail questions that would require Applegate's "well practiced patience to answer," and she commiserated with him on the particular perversity of grizzly bears.[37] She regretted being unable to participate in a grizzly-hunt while in southern Oregon, and vowed that when again visiting such a region she would be more persevering in efforts to do so.

Frances wrote that it would be useless for Oliver to look for her Klamath article in the *Overland Monthly*, as she had asked Carmany to run it in the September issue or not at all.

"Mr. C. has never explained, nor acknowledged the receipt of the article," she wrote. "He was waiting, I presume, to do so in person; but I wrote him lately to not expect me in San Francisco this winter."[38]

By Christmas, Mrs. Victor had Oliver's "copious notes" in response to her earlier queries, and gave him more questions to answer.[39] Frances felt she had absorbed enough of the facts and "<u>animus</u>" of the intricate Indian question to dare call herself an historian.[40] She was, however, "making haste slowly" in order to write an unquestionable work.[41]

Mrs. Victor mentioned that she had a story running in *The New Northwest,* a weekly newspaper in Portland, published by Abigail Scott Duniway, leader of the woman's rights movement in Oregon.

The piece was a lengthy and realistic tale of frontier life, romance and adventure — entitled "Judith Miles; or What Shall Be Done With Her" — which was printed in twenty-three installments, beginning 5 December 1873.

"We have been having a little winter, sleighing and all," Mrs. Victor added. "But today [December 22] has been springlike and beautiful. Everybody is running about to find Christmas things — and Portland is quite gay."[42]

Frances was pleased to note that Carmany was now appealing to her for short stories for the *Overland Monthly.* She had been so bewildered by his ordering then declining articles for the previous year that she had just about decided not to submit any more. Fortunately, too, since she could not afford to refuse an offer, he also had hired an able editor from the San Francisco *Evening Bulletin,* Benjamin P. Avery, to conduct the magazine's affairs.

Mrs. Victor was ready to submit any kind of story the magazine required, but she reminded Avery that it would be difficult for a writer to afford to do good work at the pay offered — $4 a page.

Political life after the Civil War reflected changing economic conditions. The railroad linked farmers and stockmen to international markets. The outside interests, who controlled the railroads, charged what the traffic would bear. When stock and crop prices were low, as frequently happened in the 1870s, the farmers and ranchers blamed the railroads and grain elevator and steamship operators. The Oregon State Grange was formed in 1873 as part of a nationwide protest movement, but the early grange was more successful in alleviating rural loneliness and advocating the rights of women than in obtaining legislation to control large corporations. At the time, however, much hope was entertained for them.

Mrs. Victor, taking note of this phenomenon, asked O.C. Applegate if stockmen in his area had formed a grange, and what monopolies he disliked.

From what she knew of the grange movement, Frances wrote a month later, "in the states east of the Missouri they are opposing themselves to the R.R. monopolies, high rates, etc.; not to the roads a priori, but to the management of them. It is expected that they will build roads of their own; even one across the continent is talked of. They are liberal, progressive, and powerful; and ought to revolutionize politics to a considerable extent. . . . The New York Grange estimates that it takes ¾ of the wheat crop of the country to get the other ¼ to market; and it is to cure such evils that their organization was first formed. If the organization can keep itself out of the hands [of] politicians it will doubtless do a great deal of good, by at least causing laws regulating freight, to be passed, in the different states."[43]

After discussing some of the particulars of her investigations into the twists and turns of the relationship between the Klamath and Modoc tribes, Mrs. Victor told Applegate:

"I shall be glad of your views on any of the points bearing upon the success or non success of the war as, if I trust myself entirely to the military I shall perhaps be governed too much by them. I long since learned that there are two, if not more sides, to all cases, which demand our study before making up a dispassionate unprejudiced judgement."[44]

Frances was perplexed by Jesse Applegate's refusal to account for certain actions of the peace commission. "There are many things he could help me about, going back twenty-five or more years," she told his nephew, "but at present he is like the Sphinx — a (grim and) silent puzzle."[45]

The weather was no less frustrating. As she was writing her letter on 18 January 1874 the rain fell constantly, "at odd times changing to snow, which comes down so fast and furious as to make one dizzy looking at it; and last night the wind blew in quite boisterous style, from which I conjecture there was a rough time at sea."[46]

Frances spoke very glowingly of Rev. Thomas Condon's lectures on geology. Even though she had covered the same ground in reading, the Congregationalist minister's talks were a pleasant treat for her.

"Mr. Condon's warmth and earnestness win him great applause, especially upon those points where science is supposed by many to conflict with religion," she told Oliver. "He saves his religion — but he vindicates the truth of science nobly."[47]

Mrs. Victor admired the beauty of the silver gray fox skin she saw at Clear Lake — "with glossy black ears and black tail" — and suggested that several of the boys in Oliver's employ might think it worthwhile to trap four or five of the animals, whose skins she would buy to make a set of furs or a traveling jacket.[48]

On 13 February 1874 Congress defeated a bill to reimburse settlers in southern Oregon and northern California for losses incurred in the Modoc War, which lasted from November 1872 to June 1873. Legislators opposing the measure claimed that the military authorities did not try to negotiate an end to the conflict in good faith. They also asserted that granting relief to the settlers would establish "a very dangerous policy" — that the federal government is responsible for the reimbursement of citizens damaged by war, specifically the Civil War.[49] One congressman warned his colleagues that thousands of claimants "will come trooping in here if you pass this bill, . . . and you can only answer them by opening wide the doors of the Treasury and letting the last dollar be taken from it, and that before the winter is over."[50]

Public and editorial opinion in the two states, needless to say, was inflamed. "So the settlers must pocket their griefs and their losses together," she lamented to Oliver six days later. "It is the history of frontiers, from first to last."[51]

Frances also assured Oliver that she relied more on his views than those of military men, whose "connection with the Indian Department has been but brief and partial at the most."[52]

She regretted that the "weather manager" should be bearing down on Oliver at Swan Lake with such vehemence, and that "it never rains but it pours" had become a well-established adage.[53]

"There has been such a constant pouring upon me, for at least six years, that I sometimes am inclined to believe there will never be a rift in the clouds," Frances remarked. "Getting used to it is half the battle anyway, and I am well used to adverse luck by this time, and do not wish to be understood as complaining whatever happens. But I would like to see my friends succeed."[54]

She wrote that her Indian war history was progressing slowly, and that it was very difficult to get people to care about anything in which they did not have a financial interest.

"It will hurt nothing, however, to wait a little," she remarked. "It gives me more opportunity to pick up here and there a thread of the skein that otherwise might be overlooked and lost; and it gives me a chance to attend a little to the matter of bread and butter, which cannot be neglected with safety to the other plans — for the most intellectual of us must eat, drink, and wear, as well as the least."[55]

By early spring, candidates were readying themselves for Oregon's political wars, which would culminate in early June balloting for state and local offices.

On a late-March evening, cannon boomed in Portland, calling the people to hear Governor Lafayette Grover speak on his own behalf as a candidate for re-election.

"One thing he may count on — the women who want the suffrage will be against him, and will make him feel it too," Mrs. Victor told Oliver Applegate. "Some of you young men can begin now to fit yourselves for the suffrages of women. We want earnest, firm, temperate, right-minded men, with breadth of thought and purity of principle. We want such men in office as we can approach without scandal, and trust our public interests to, as we can our private reputations. The old stock of politicians would scarcely suit us, and if the places of honor are wanted, younger men and purer men will know how to get them."[56]

Frances tried to console Oliver, who felt badly about some personal losses, and misfortunes that had befallen other members of his family. His brother Ivan, for one, had broken a collarbone and was recuperating slowly.

"I hope you know of your own self how sorry I am for the hardships of which you say so little, — both for yourself and your friends," she wrote. ". . . I have always held, and never more strongly than now, that men and women of ability, genius, culture, sensibility and the like qualities, have no right to exile themselves from the society of their peers, and waste these qualities 'on the desert air.' That has been Jesse Applegate's mistake, irreparable now; and such, I fear, may be the error of O.C.A."[57]

Mrs. Victor lamented her financial insecurity. So much time and thought was wasted in writing "fugitive articles for present pay" that she could not get much done with any of her work — the Indian war history, a romance based on her Klamath travels, and a sequel to "Judith Miles."

"This horrible bread and butter business does so clog the fancy, and bind the wings of imagination, that I am often willing to cry quits with Fate, and give up the battle of life, disgusted with my ill success in being or doing anything I most desire," she confessed to Oliver. "But I shall never do it, I presume. That inexorable policeman Pride, backed by Necessity, will keep urging me to 'move on' to the end."[58]

The dismal winter rains left Portland about mid-month, she wrote, and the balls and parties had given way to outdoor recreation in the beautiful early spring weather.

"Gen. Davis and his staff have kept up the dancing pretty well all through the season," Frances added, "but owing to a lack of unmarried officers and ladies, the parties were said to be rather stiff. I only speak from hearsay, for I do not go to parties of this kind. I have a calling acquaintance with the wives of the military set, and like them for the most part, very much . . . because they have all been very kind to me."[59]

16

Woman's War on the "Web-Foot" Saloon

In March 1874, word reached Portland that a temperance movement had begun three months earlier in Ohio and was spreading across the nation. It seemed a novel and exciting idea for women to spread God's word, and convince saloonkeepers and their patrons to renounce liquor.

On March 6, Mrs. Duniway published an editorial threatening local saloons with the presence of disapproving women, who "will blockade sidewalks, interfere with municipal ordinances, [and] sing and pray in the most public places to be seen of men."[1]

Large numbers of women in the middle and western states had undertaken to visit saloons. It was hoped that Portland would match this turnout; but at most forty-three, and seldom more than twenty-five, took part on any one day.

The lack of volunteers was attributed to the transient and generally rough and reckless clientele at the saloons, who were unknown to the ladies either by sight or by name, and the fear of being insulted for entering places that men had set aside for their own vices. On March 28, a few days after the effort had begun, Frances wrote Oliver Applegate:

> . . . The Methodist Church building [on Taylor St.] stands open all day, and prayers are going up morning, noon and night for the success of the Crusaders. Every day bands of women go from saloon to saloon throughout the city praying, singing, exhorting, and with various effect. They are often rudely addressed, and yet more often treated respectfully. It remains to be seen whether they succeed in closing any saloons or liquor stores in Portland. But whether they do or not, they will have awakened a strong public sentiment on the side of reform, and vindicated woman's ability to engage in the most arduous work of progress. I regard it, and so do very many, as the best argument we have yet seen . . . for enfranchising women. Every day some man says to me, "If the women do not pray down this traffic, we shall have to give them the ballot and let them vote it down." This I think will be the end of it, and that it will be a Providence of God none will deny. The women seem everywhere to be lifted up out of themselves, their little vanities and sectarianisms, and to be moved with a very powerful influence.[2]

The work of ridding Portland of "demon rum" went ahead — slowly. A number of women offered to provide lunches at the Methodist Church so those involved in the crusade would not have to go home before the day's work was done. Anti-liquor pledges were sought from businesses and individuals. Efforts were underway to tell people about poisonous drugs, and in compounding so-called wines, brandies, and even whisky. Patronage declined at the saloons, and several of the main establishments offered free drinks to attract rude crowds to disrupt the ladies' reading, singing, exhorting and praying.

"Very exciting scenes sometimes took place," Mrs. Victor wrote, "and large assemblages of people gathered to witness them."[3]

Other booze-marts simply closed their doors against the women, who attracted even larger crowds of onlookers by holding their services in the street. Almost always, there was some man who saw the error of his ways and promised to lead a better life. Sometimes, too, the women were roughly handled — bringing over other men who were appalled by the brutalizing effects of drink.

One saloon was operated by two women, whom the crusaders thought were as hardened as any men in the business; they said several solemn and impressive prayers and then left. When the temperance women returned several days later, one of the proprietresses angrily slammed the door. There was a loud argument inside: one voice saying the ladies should *not* be admitted, the other that they *should*. A woman opened the door. She listened tearfully to the pleas and prayers of the temperance workers, and begged them for more tracts. She vowed to write her brother for money to take her back to friends in the East, where she hoped to live a different life.

"It is always doubtful, of course, whether these sudden resolutions are kept," Frances observed sadly, "for there is so much in the way of these repentant sinners to prevent their return to virtue; and so much apathy in the public mind, and in the Christian mind concerning whether they shall be saved or not; so little chance of help from any source except God alone! — and they have not yet learned to trust Him."[4]

In higher class establishments, the women freely conducted their services at the bar and in billiard rooms, and patrons were not allowed to imbibe during these visits. At one prominent place, the ladies tried to convince the proprietor to join them. The man wavered. He did not try to defend the business, and hoped his friends in the East would not learn of it. It *was* his business, however, and as decent as could be made; he was in debt and wanted to get out.

"The argument is all on your side, ladies," he would say, "but *money* is my object."[5]

The liquor interests in Portland were not taken by surprise, as those in Ohio and elsewhere had been. They were prepared and, as soon as they were convinced the temperance forces were serious, organized for defense and mutual support. Thus, wavering saloon operators were dissuaded from acting on their best impulses.

Although two or three taverns closed after the temperance movement began, the "Web-Foot Saloon," at the corner of First and Morrison streets, proved a constant irritant.

On the campaign's first day, March 23, two elderly temperance advocates entered the saloon. But before they could say a word the proprietor, Walter Moffett, seized each woman by an arm and thrust them back out into the street.

"Get out of this!" he exclaimed. "I keep a respectable house and don't want any d----d wh---s here."[6]

Mrs. J.H. Reid, one of the women to whom this vulgar remark was made, turned in surprise and looked up over the door to determine what sort of place, kept by what sort of man, this might be. She was horrified.

"Walter Moffett!" she exclaimed. "Can this be Walter Moffett? Why Walter Moffett, I used to know you; and I prayed with your wife for your safety when you were at sea years ago!"

"I don't want any of your d----d prayers," he retorted, "I want you to get out of this and stay out; that's all I want of you. I don't keep a wh--e house."[7]

Temperance workers soon revisited the tavern, and Moffett drew around them a crowd of people that disrupted traffic in the street. Police were summoned — to disperse the ladies, whom the proprietor said caused all the trouble. One officer not only ordered the women away but began to shove them about, bruising the shoulder of one against the post of the awning.

After some thought and discussion, the Women's Temperance Prayer League decided it should continue to visit the Web-Foot Saloon. If Moffett were allowed to prevail, members reasoned, then the other tavern owners would be free to use violence against them to achieve the same goal.

On Tuesday morning, April 7, at about 10:30, fifteen women belonging to the league began to pray and sing outside the Web-Foot. Several hundred spectators quickly gathered on the sidewalk and street.

Moffett blew a police-whistle to summon officers, several of whom responded. After pushing through the crowd, these minions of the law asked the ladies to stop. Just then, James H. Lappeus, Portland's chief of police, arrived on the scene. Lappeus, too, saw the potential for a disturbance, and made his way to the saloon's door.

The proprietor loudly demanded that the women be dispersed. He asserted that as a taxpayer he was entitled to the protection of the law. He had just that morning paid $100 for a license to sell liquor at the two saloons he owned, and did not want his business disrupted.

The police chief told the women that there was danger of a disturbance — and even bloodshed — if they persisted, and he "asked them . . . even implored of them" to go quietly home.[8] Several of the ladies replied that theirs was a holy cause, one they had a duty to perform. Lappeus made further entreaties, but to no avail. The crusaders told him they had a right to occupy the sidewalk and, for that and other reasons, would not leave.

The chief announced that he had no alternative but to take the ladies into custody, for what the arrest record described as "disorderly praying," and started with them in the direction of the police court.[9]

After walking a couple of blocks, the crusaders realized their escort had disappeared. They concluded it was not customary for arrested persons to find their own way to jail and turned back towards the saloon to resume their interrupted duty, but the chief reappeared.

Lappeus knew it was no use. The ladies were not afraid of imprisonment. He bore them off to the lock-up, "where they spent a couple of hours in prayer and song, to their own refreshment and the delight of the other prisoners." [10]

Police Judge Owen N. Denny wanted to postpone the matter until the next morning, court having adjourned for the day. But several hundred people interested in this "test" case, pro and con, were milling around outside the building.

The building's entrance was closed and locked, with a policeman stationed there to prevent the crowd from intruding on the court proceedings.

After hearing the complaint, Judge Denny ruled there was no ordinance under which the women could be held and that, in any case, the state and federal constitutions guaranteed every person the freedom to worship God according to the dictates of their own conscience.

As they left the building, each lady cordially shook the hand of Chief Lappeus, himself co-owner of the prosperous Oro Fino saloon on Stark Street, "and fervently invoked the blessings of Heaven on his head." [11] The women went to a prayer meeting in the Taylor Street church, and in the afternoon they prayed and sang at several other drinking houses.

"The arrest of the ladies created, of course, a strong feeling of indignation in the community among their friends, and rejoicing among their enemies," Mrs. Victor wrote. "It also increased the number of those who thought the ladies had not chosen the right way of making temperance converts; the idea of policemen and prisons being too terrible to contemplate." [12]

The temperance league also had to confront the inertia "of luke-warm Christians, and characterless good people." [13] In mid-April, while circulating a petition demanding city council action against the liquor traffic, the women found that many people refused to sign, even though they agreed that Portland had too many saloons.

"Tradesmen were reluctant to do so, for fear of losing the custom of the liquor men," Frances wrote. "Clerks and salaried men often refused through fear of their employers. Men frequently said they did not drink, themselves, but did not wish to have anything to do with this movement. Others had wines at home, and so could not consistently take any action against the free sale of liquors. These last generally advised the ladies to teach their sons to be temperate at home, and all would be well with them. They could see no inconsistency in teaching temperance, and practicing social drinking under the same roof. Many women professed 'to have no interest in the matter,' saying that *their* sons and husbands gave them no uneasiness, therefore they thought the ladies had better stay at home and attend to their households.'" [14]

Despite all obstacles, however, and within three or four days, more than 1,800 persons signed the petition, which was submitted for consideration by the city council.

The petitioners were so anxious that they importuned the councilmen constantly until assured that some action would be taken to limit licenses, if not impose absolute prohibition.

Moffett, a Republican, had recently completed a three-year term on the city council, including active service on its Health and Police committee. He was a man of wealth and respectable business stature. With these credentials, the women wondered why he needed to own two drinking houses, or consent to make himself notorious by ridiculing Christianity and insulting them for the sake of such an occupation.

The climax of the temperance "war" on the Web-Foot Saloon came on Thursday, 16 April 1874, at about 2 p.m., when sixteen women began to pray and sing in front of the building.

Supporters placed camp-stools at the sidewalk's outer edge for the women, who were encircled as a crowd of more than 1,000 persons pressed in along the sidewalk and from the street.

This time, Moffett was ready for the crusaders, with a pair of Chinese gongs and an "old wheezy hand organ."[15] He employed a half-witted German named "Tripe Fritz" to crank the organ, and two small boys to beat on the gongs. Moffett blew his police-whistle. Several other people banged on tin cans and a drum, and rang a bell. All this, added to the shouts and mutterings of the mob, made for a "hideous and distracting din" that lasted for several hours.[16] Passers-by added to the confusion by stopping in the street to learn what was transpiring in the center of the surging mass of humanity. Other citizens lined the upper floors and roofs of nearby buildings to get a better view of the spectacle.

The sixteen women remained calm and serene in their devotional exercises, even though they could not even hear themselves amidst all the chaos and noise. It was clear that something else would be needed to drive them away.

One of Moffett's bartenders, a young man named James F. Good, picked up a hose from a nearby hydrant and flooded the sidewalk with several inches of water. This caused many people to move, but the ladies did not flinch. Good then directed a stream of water into the awning over the sidewalk. It poured down on the women, thoroughly soaking them, but with no other visible effect.

Many friends, afraid that the ladies would be harmed, joined the already immense crowd. Good was now quite drunk. He stood on a chair, banging a gong and making obscene remarks to the crusaders. A one-time Portland city marshal, William Grooms, flattened the bartender with a violent punch between the eyes. The gong flew off into the crowd.

This incident uncorked the tension that had been building all afternoon under a hot sun; people scrambled to get out even as others were trying to get a "lick in." Guns and knives were drawn, furniture was tossed about, and windows broken. One of the crusaders was struck by a tumbler thrown out of the saloon, and another had a pistol held at her head by Moffett himself.

Police had no especial desire to interfere. Since this riot was of Moffett's creation, they felt it wiser to let the disturbance run its course as long as no serious injuries resulted. Now, however, as bloodshed and death appeared imminent, officers waded into the mob, and with great exertion pushed it back.

The sixteen crusaders did not move from their position in the center of this human cauldron, and still sat tranquil and composed.

By 6 o'clock, the noise had faded to an occasional rattle or bang, and people were drifting away. The ladies also took leave, exhausted by their ordeal. Many people were amazed that the women had withstood the abuse with such equaminity, enduring things that would ordinarily have driven them mad with fright, or to faint or go into convulsions.

The temperance league reappeared in front of the saloon the next morning to continue their work, after Mrs. Moffett pleaded in vain for them to desist, lest her husband commit some violent act which would cause him trouble. The women still felt Moffett was tormented by a guilty conscience, and that caused him to be so malevolent towards them.

Several hundred persons quickly gathered, expecting a repetition of the previous day's events, but they were disappointed. Mrs. Moffett, with one of her children, again appealed to the women to leave her husband to his own ways. One of the crusaders, whose father perished from drink and whose son, though carefully reared, was an alcoholic, issued an eloquent remonstrance. The ladies sat on camp-stools at the outer edge of the sidewalk and began to pray and sing, and to pass out tracts, this time without interruption.

The proprietor, finding it impossible to keep the sidewalk clear and rid himself of the annoying presence of the women, decided to again appeal to the law for redress of his grievances. An hour after the ladies arrived, Moffett filed a complaint with the authorities. At about 11:30 a.m., Chief Lappeus and half a dozen officers came to serve the warrant and escort the twenty-two ladies to jail.

The warrant alleged, specifically, that on April 16 six of the women "did wilfully and unlawfully conduct themselves in a disorderly and violent manner, on the corner of First and Morrison Streets, by making a loud noise and creating a disturbance, whereby the peace and quiet of [Portland] was disturbed," in violation of city ordinance.[17] The ladies were arraigned on the charge and released on their own recognizance. The trial was set to begin next day.

On Saturday morning, large numbers of people gathered in and around the police building. The courtroom itself "was literally jammed, almost to suffocation," wrote an observer.[18] The crush was so great that the defendants and their lady friends had to be admitted by a private door.

Defense attorneys asked Judge Denny to dismiss the complaint because the facts alleged were insufficient to constitute a crime, that the complaint stated conclusions not facts, and it was not prepared substantially in accordance with the state criminal code.

The motion was denied, and six ladies — Lizzie Fletcher, Josephine Ritter, G. Shindler, Helen Sparrow, Helen Stitzel and N.S. Swafford — were required to take seats on one side of the courtroom. The complaint was read; the ladies declared they were not guilty and asked that a jury be selected. Six jurors were empanelled, and the court recessed.

On Monday, April 20, the courtroom was again packed. Eighty women attended, as did a dense crowd of men both inside and outside the doors, which were guarded by police.

About 4:45 p.m., the case was submitted to the jury. Judge Denny reminded them that all they had to decide, on the basis of the evidence presented, was whether the women were guilty, as alleged in the complaint, of "wilfully and unlawfully making a loud noise, whereby the peace and quiet of the city was disturbed."[19] The jurymen also were told it was their duty to give the crusaders the benefit of any reasonable doubt.

Hundreds of persons stayed in the courtroom and outside the building to await the verdict. Many thought it would be a hung jury, that no decision would be agreed upon. As time passed, most of the people went home. Other than the lawyers, very few were present when a rap was heard on the jury-room door shortly before 7 p.m.

Court was immediately convened. The jurymen entered. "Gentlemen, have you agreed upon a verdict?" Judge Denny inquired.[20] The jurors nodded affirmatively and handed a piece of paper up to the bench; the judge read:

"We, the jury, find the defendants guilty as charged, and recommend them to the mercy of the Court."[21] (To save the ladies costs, however, they generously refunded the jury fees.)

Jurors were dismissed from any further consideration of the case, and a defense motion to defer sentencing of the five remaining defendants — Mrs. Ritter having been exonerated by testimony given at the trial — until next morning was granted.

At least 100 women were among the crowd at the police court Wednesday morning to hear the verdict. Proceedings were delayed more than an hour by another trial that occurred during the forenoon. All the ladies waited together in two adjoining rooms, engaged in cheerful conversation and prayer.

The five women awaiting sentence told friends that they would go to prison rather than pay any fines. The crusaders believed they would be able to spend the time profitably. There was as yet no ordinance against praying in prison, these five ladies said, and at intervals they thought they would do some neglected sewing.

Shortly after noon their case was called, and everybody filed into the judicial sanctum. Defense attorneys asked the court to suspend judgment, and they sought a new trial. Both requests were denied.

Judge Denny then said it was his unpleasant duty to punish the defendants. The five ladies went before the bench and in a statement read by Mrs. Sparrow reasserted their innocence, that the verdict contradicted the evidence and the judge's instructions to the jury. The women complained that the jury had been partly composed of liquor dealers, who "had already prejudged us."[22]

The women also asserted that many men died from alcoholism, and that many others were unable to fulfill their aspirations or the hopes others had for them.

. . . These evils, your Honor, are not in far-off lands, but at our own doors, as that wife can testify who a few months since went to a prominent saloon in this city and plead with the proprietor to sell her husband no more liquor, as her life was in danger whenever that husband came home under its influence, and she was coldly told: "O well, if I do not sell him liquor, some one else will." Or that other wife, whose twenty years' experience has deprived her of everything the heart holds dear "but her trust in God," whose husband can go and keep the books at this same saloon, and Saturday night take his pay in this cursed fire-water and go to his home to make it such a hell upon earth that the children must be sent from the house and the wife remain in terror of her life. Such instances are not rare, and it is in behalf of these suffering sisters that we act. We have not power to amend the laws; but since the day that woman was first at the sepulchre, it has been her conceded right to pray, and this right we claim as inalienably ours.

The jury have kindly recommended us to mercy; we ask no mercy — we demand JUSTICE.[23]

Judge Denny with evident embarrassment replied that the jury had been fairly and impartially selected according to law. He urged the ladies to abandon confrontations with the law in their war on alcohol, and to "go to the fountain head" — legislative bodies — which avenue was effectively closed since women lacked both the vote and representation.[24]

During the trial, the judge insisted, all safeguards and protections consistent with the law and the facts had shielded the women's rights. They had been ably defended and all evidence which could explain their conduct had been presented to the jury, which considered the facts and reached a verdict.

The court then imposed the lightest sentence possible: a fine of five dollars each, or one day in jail.

Several men indicated their willingness to pay the fines and set the women free, but Mrs. Sparrow arose and said:

"For this very kind and generous offer we tender our most heartfelt thanks to the gentlemen, but under all the circumstances we feel compelled to decline this offer. We think that it is best for us to go to jail."[25]

There was a considerable demonstration of affection by the ladies in the courtroom for their friends. Many tears were shed, and words of condolence and encouragement passed. The scene was a moving one to many spectators.

The five women were taken to the third-floor jail and shown to their common apartment. In accordance with the customs of the place, the crusaders surrendered to the officers their only weapon — a Bible — after first inscribing it with their names.

The ladies were thoroughly exhausted and wanted to rest for the remainder of the day. But the novelty of their situation made this impossible, and there was a steady flow of anxious visitors with plenty of food and conversation.

At about 8:30 Wednesday night, the women were donning their night clothes in preparation for bed. Several of them had their shoes unlaced and others were partly undressed when Police Chief Lappeus strode in and ordered curtly that they leave the jail.

The crusaders protested against this order being given so soon after their friends had left, and assured the officer that they were prepared and willing to stay for the full extent of the sentence imposed by law. Lappeus was unmoved. "I'm boss here; you leave!" he commanded.[26] The five women groped their way down stairs, and out into the street. They noticed that quite a crowd of men had gathered at the corner of the block. The crusaders retraced their steps to the police building and pondered what to do next. They were homeless for the night, it being impractical under the circumstances to separate and go to their own houses. The ladies decided to go together to the Methodist Church on Taylor Street, where they knew their supporters would be gathered, and asked a young gentleman, a stranger, to escort them.

The first hint friends at the church had of their liberation was when the five women walked down the aisle, and leaned over to speak to or kiss some surprised sister.

The church reverberated with cheers and bursts of enthusiasm that had not been heard since the end of the Civil War. A minister requested silence and decorum within the sacred edifice, but to no avail.

"There are times and occasions when the voice of the people is the voice of God and will be heard," an observer wrote, "and it was heard on that night."[27]

On the day after the crusaders were imprisoned, Mrs. Victor wrote another letter to Oliver Applegate to update him on events in Portland. Spring had arrived in the city — "warm, dry, and dusty," she wrote.[28] It was the season for women to come out in something bright and fresh, but this time Frances observed that there seemed to be less exhibition of finery than usual, which she attributed to the temperance crusade.

"Certainly I never saw so few ladies out shopping in such fine weather," she told Oliver, "and I for one have done little for two or three weeks except to attend meetings, circulate petitions, and edit the New Northwest in Mrs. Duniway's absence."[29]

(Mrs. Duniway spent almost two months, between mid-March and mid-May 1874, as a guest lecturer in California under the auspices of that state's Woman Suffrage Association. She also attended the organization's annual meeting as a delegate representing the O.S.W.S.A.)

Mrs. Victor noted that although the papers carried much news of the temperance crusade, they could not give distant readers a sense of the strong feeling that existed in Portland over the issue.

"I stand by the 'Crusaders,' but I do not regard their work as effectual and permanent," Frances told Oliver. ". . . The arrest and trial of the Crusaders was extremely sensational. I was three days in the Police Court — my first experience of this sort of thing. But it was very interesting, as was shown by the crowds that stood patiently for hours every day to hear the evidence and pleading. I made up my mind I did not want to be a lawyer, since I should be bound to plead equally hard on either side of a case; and one could not be always on the right side."[30]

On April 24, temperance league members were back on the streets. Liquor dealers met the night before to devise ways to protect themselves.

In the morning the ladies found saloon doors closed, and they "were met with universal coldness and hardness."[31]

The league adopted resolutions of love and kindness towards the liquor dealers, and reiterated its disapproval of retaliation or revenge.

"We are sure the only way to reach these men is with *our* hearts filled with the love of Christ," the ladies said.[32]

It was cold and rainy on the 25th, only nine women being in the party which visited saloons that day.

"Some of us felt a depression of spirits because the representatives of Jesus in this work were so few in number," read a disheartened note in the league's records. "But the work is the Lord's, and he can carry it on by the few or by the many, as shall please him best."[33]

Although the crusaders encountered steady opposition from liquor dealers, only Walter Moffett engaged in "profanity, obscenity and abuse of every description."[34]

On several occasions, Moffett burned an "ill-smelling and peppery compound" in the faces of the ladies, two of whom became quite ill, as they prayed and sang in front of his saloons — the Web-Foot and the Tom Thumb.

"So alert was this anti-Crusader that he seldom failed to know when the ladies were at either place," Mrs. Victor remarked. "Not content with setting off fire-crackers, with throwing water, with burning villainous compounds, blowing police-whistles, beating gongs, drums, tin-cans, and the like, and with forcing the ladies into the street, and then ordering an express backed up right among them; he even became so energetic as to lift a lady off her knees while praying upon the public sidewalk."[35]

The ladies always refused to allow their friends to defend them. They wanted to spread a gospel of love; and feared if men took up the quarrel that Moffett meant to start, then the resulting blows and wounds would accomplish nothing.

Moffett's malevolence was becoming unendurable, however, and he was twice cited into court — on May 20 and 22 — for insulting and burning noxious substances in front of the ladies.

On both occasions the jury found Moffett innocent, much to the disgust of the crusaders who felt the evidence was clearly in their favor. The ladies were even more incensed by the remarks of Moffett's attorney, Eugene A. Cronin, who called them "as debased and corrupt in heart *as any women in this town, no matter what their calling or character!*"[36]

Temperance league members continued to visit the saloons; and also the city and county jails, where they found that most inmates had been sentenced on liquor-related charges.

"The moods and tempers of the saloon men varied with circumstances," Mrs. Victor wrote. "Each day furnished its incidents, some serious, some ludicrous, but all instructive."[37]

It was often argued that this was not women's work, but men were shouted down on those rare occasions when they tried to convince saloon operators and patrons of the evils of drink.

"The liquor men feel that all men . . . are in some sense guilty with themselves; else why have they so long held silence, thereby consenting to the monstrous growth of this iniquity?'' Mrs. Victor explained. ''Men have had the power to make and enforce laws, while women have not. Men have known just what the evil was, and women have not. Men have lent their countenance to it, and women have not. Men have brought about the evil, while women have suffered by it; suffered in their persons, their affections and their fortunes. Every man in the liquor business, who is able to think or feel, is in some dim way conscious of this. Therefore, when women reason with him, unless he is a brute, he feels compelled to listen with such respect as his avarice will let him, to these helpless victims of the united wrongs of his sex. But to men he will not listen.''[38]

In the two months before the June elections, temperance sentiment had so grown that the gubernatorial candidates were everywhere asked to define their position on the issue.

The State Temperance Convention had already put out a ticket composed of the least objectionable men from each of Oregon's three political parties — Democrats, Republicans and Independents.

The convention reasoned that voters were not ready for a purely temperance party, and the most that could be done was to help elect the best men of all parties.

The crusaders did not yet believe that women needed the vote or would ask for it. These women did not want to get involved in political action because it would convey the impression that they favored suffrage. Prayer was their weapon against the liquor trade.

But there were other women, equally zealous on the side of temperance, who believed that laws were needed to keep men on their best behavior. They sympathized with the crusaders, but were anxious to secure a lasting result for their labors by means of the ballot in men's hands, if not their own.

These ladies pleaded with their male counterparts to run a straight temperance ticket, to no avail. Chastened but not convinced, they went to work for candidates who did not represent them.

After the 1 June 1874 election, when Oregonians voted for their one member of the U.S. House of Representatives, and state and county officers, the result was as expected — to give this or that party unexpected majorities in the various races, but to leave the temperance people without any reliable representative.

''We *hope* we have helped to elect some men who are friendly to our cause,'' Mrs. Victor observed plaintively, ''but we are aware that not one of them is pledged to anything.''[39]

It had been predicted that the ladies would be treated rudely if they appeared election day on the streets of Portland. The crusaders went out as usual and were received courteously. There was an all-day prayer meeting at the Taylor Street church, and a lunch was served for all women who chose to partake.

''There was never a quieter election in Portland — never a day when there was so little drinking,'' Frances marveled. ''. . . It was very evident from that one day's experience that a healthy public sentiment had been created.''[40]

The liquor dealers, however, were exasperated, and they prepared for further contests.

The petition, which two months before had been signed by more than 1,800 citizens demanding strict control or abolition of the liquor trade, was still before the city council. Its advocates were still using all their influence to obtain a favorable hearing. In time it became generally understood that a majority of the council favored a stricter ordinance, which alarmed the Liquor Association and guaranteed a hotly contested city election.

In the two weeks between elections, the women argued constantly for a straight-out temperance ticket, "on which a strictly Temperance party could be founded; and were willing to run the risk of defeat in an open fight for their principles," Mrs. Victor explained. "They wished the same at the State election; but as men still insist upon regarding women as minors, their wishes had no weight with the Nominating Committees at either election."[41]

The temperance men demurred, feeling the best course in the city election would be to elect Republicans.

So the Temperance Committee awaited the Republican Committee's choices, Frances wrote, "to see whether or not they could avail themselves of the same men, and thereby perhaps secure the election of candidates who possibly might fail if put up purely as Temperance men."[42]

The Republicans knew the temperance vote carried weight at the state election, and they wanted to put that vote to use in Portland.

Three candidates were nominated, to whom temperance advocates could not reasonably object. This was on a Friday. The election was Monday, June 15.

On Saturday, the Republican Temperance nominee for the First Ward city council seat, John R. Foster, withdrew. Some devious manipulations seemed afoot. The liquor interests were ready to wage an all-out fight for city council seats and now, when it was too late to canvass for temperance candidates, it was discovered that they were needed.

"Men were busy all day Saturday endeavoring to find an influential, sound man in the First Ward who would stand without fear or favor for the Temperance vote," Mrs. Victor wrote. "Such a man may exist within those limits, but he was not to be met with on that momentous Saturday."[43]

That afternoon, in the Methodist Church, half a dozen ladies and a few gentlemen sat, discussing the dismal prospects.

One man had spoken well at the nightly meetings and was considered a staunch temperance supporter. Moreover, he was known as an easy writer and acquainted with politics. To the ladies, of whom Mrs. Victor was one, this man revealed that he had written a circular for election day which would tell powerfully for temperance and against the liquor interests. He took the draft from his pocket and read it in an ordinary tone.*

"I, for one, gave not much heed to it," Frances wrote, "presuming that, as men were accustomed to that sort of electioneering, the gentleman knew what he was about."[44]

---

*See pp. 250-251 for the document's full text.

After a brief discussion as to "ways and means," the ladies agreed informally to print the circular and Mrs. Victor, who was enroute downtown with a friend, offered to leave it at a printing office.

The liquor dealers were indignant at this "scurrilous" attack on their characters. They protested! They scowled! They grimaced! They swore! They condemned those women and those ministers who had authorized such a publication!

All this was a revelation to the innocent-minded citizens who saw only the truth the circular contained. It did not occur to them that those who lived by the ruin of other people had sensibilities, too.

The liquor men went to the polls, complaining to voters, who once might have been weak enough to be seen with temperance ballots in their hands, that it was a crying shame and an insult to all decent men that those failing to vote for the Republican Temperance ticket should be called such names as these. With much bluster and gusto they persuaded voters to repudiate "those low-minded Temperance people — the Crusaders especially!"[45]

There was a "wild invasion" of the Taylor Street church, where it was demanded of the ladies present who was responsible for the evil flyer.[46] No explanation could be given because very few persons knew about the matter.

The leaders of the temperance movement in Portland tried to disavow any connection with the circular. A message was drafted at once and signed by Mrs. M.A. Mitchell, president of the Women's Temperance Prayer League; George Abernethy, chairman of the Temperance Committee; and Revs. George H. Atkinson, George W. Izer and Thomas F. Royal. The disclaimer was printed up and posted around the polling places. It read:

"We, . . . and those we represent, take this method of informing the citizens of Portland that [the circular] was prepared and published without our knowledge; and we most emphatically disapprove it."[47]

But the scare created by the liquor interests was too good a thing to let fade, and they took care that it did not. Although the ladies were received courteously when they went to the polls to disabuse voters' minds on the subject, it was too late. The Republican Temperance ticket lost by 549 votes, the largest margin of defeat then given in a city election. The opposition People's Party swept the three council seats being contested.

There was another reason for the defeat. The patent manipulation of the anti-liquor faction by the Republicans alienated many temperance voters. "It was considered a prostitution of the temperance cause to base purposes," one editor commented.[48]

Mrs. Victor admitted that once she saw the circular in print she considered it "unnecessarily irritating, and in some portions unjust; but I think I may say with certainty, that zeal and not malice prompted it."[49]

Frances had no doubt of the propriety in saying or doing anything to defend "that valiant little band" of crusaders, as she proclaimed in a letter to the *Morning Oregonian* soon after issuance of the infamous circular,

> but a fear of the expediency makes me tremble, because of the cunning of their enemies in turning everything, even the efforts of their friends against them; and I hope I am a friend of theirs — certainly I should feel it an honor to be allowed to kiss their hands.

. . . The crusaders had nothing to do with the conception or the publication of the "Voters Book of Remembrance." Nor would it probably have been written (certainly not so carelessly adopted) had not everything been thrown into confusion at the last moment, primarily by the neglect to put out a temperance ticket as the ladies desired, and secondarily by the withdrawal of Mr. Foster. The ladies, so much of whose toilsome effort has been counteracted by this blunder, and it is hoped all good temperance people, can learn a lesson from last Monday's experience.

Wars, for principles, are always more bitter, longer and harder to fight than wars for empire only. If women are to fight this temperance battle, the necessity for which was brought upon them by men, it becomes every man worthy to be called such, to smooth the way for them as much as possible; and it becomes all women not actively engaged in it, to lend their sympathy and assistance, and that, too, without presuming to dictate to those who give their time and labor freely, how they shall work.[50]

On June 17, the city council finally took action to tighten controls on the liquor trade in Portland. The ordinance doubled license fees, to $100 per quarter, and required $1,000 bonds to keep orderly houses. All females were to be denied licenses, and saloonkeepers were not permitted to have women entertainers or bartenders. In addition, the ordinance prohibited the dispensing of liquor at all outlets during voting hours at any general or city election, and prescribed various penalties for violation of its provisions.

About the same time, an "Alliance" was formed by ladies who disapproved of saloon visiting but still wanted to help the temperance movement in a general way.

The Liquor Association took a rather dim view of the city council's action, and members in various ways made known their displeasure to the crusaders.

"To have raised their licenses when business was good would have been irritating enough," Mrs. Victor observed, "but to raise it when some of the saloons were unable to pay even fifty dollars, was indeed a grievance."[51]

At one saloon, a woman who was unaware of the bitterness, or that the proprietor forbade women to come near his premises, sat on the doorstep to rest. She was ordered away, but not feeling able to stand this woman went round the corner of the building and sat in a little recess.

The enraged proprietor grabbed the lady's arms and pulled her up. He ordered her to leave but she refused, feeling that she was in nobody's way.

"What is your name?" he demanded. The lady did not answer, so he gave his name and asked if she was ashamed of hers.

"Certainly not," the woman replied, identifying herself.

"Ah," the proprietor said, "I will see that your husband keeps you at home after this!" He called a policeman to arrest the "obstinate woman."[52]

The lady inquired if she was where she had no right to be. No, the officer said, but the proprietor was a "bad and violent" man, and urged her to sit on the edge of the sidewalk to avoid trouble, which she did.[53]

The lady's husband was warned to take her off the street, or suffer the loss of his business through the enmity of the Liquor Association.

"Very well," he replied. "It took a higher power than I to place her on the street, and it will require one higher to remove her. If you want to ruin my trade you can try it; I will certainly fight yours as long as I live."[54]

On June 24 there came before the city council a petition signed by 143 persons, fifty-six of whom sold liquor, asking for reinstatement of the original fees. The petition was referred to the Committee on Ways and Means for study.

When the new councilmen took their seats, they found that the new liquor ordinance would take effect July 1. An effort was made that very day to restore the original fees, but on July 3 the mayor vetoed the proposed amendments and the council fell one vote short of the two-thirds needed to override. One of the new councilmen sided with three of the old ones to oppose the lowered fees; five councilmen voted in favor of them.

More amendments to the new liquor ordinance were proposed, but were laid over until the next council meeting. The mayor warned temperance advocates that the council might not be able to withstand the pressure unless there was a counter-petition.

One circulated, and was signed by 130 of the heaviest taxpayers in the city who were not liquor dealers.

Both petitions went before the council on Wednesday, July 15. That same evening an ordinance was passed, and signed by the mayor two days later, restoring the fifty-dollar quarterly license fee for drinking houses.

"It would seem as if men would rather part with their 'life, liberty and happiness' — with all that our fathers fought for — than with whisky!" Mrs. Victor exclaimed bitterly. "There is no patriotism equal to the power of whisky."[55]

Of course, she noted, the city could not afford to do without the income from licenses. But then it had to pay that money, and as much more, to care for the drunkards made under the licenses.

> . . . There is altogether too much *political economy* about this way of doing business to have it productive of the general good, for which laws are presumed to be made.
> . . . Not that the City Fathers of Portland are wickedly conniving at drunkenness. They are not. They are between two fires in respect to the license system. Prohibition they dare not attempt; and amelioration is such a treacherous ground to stand upon. You cannot pull out one foot so fast as the other sinks in; and finally restrictive laws dissolve into veriest license.[56]

The women of the crusading band felt called upon to do a higher good in their efforts to stop the liquor traffic in Portland. The compelling nature of their task added a new dimension to the humble and modest stations these ladies occupied in life; though interesting, their work was not sensational.

"It did not seek to bring a crowd of excited converts into this church or that," Mrs. Victor explained. "But it sought to save men from their sins, in Christ's name. It consecrated every interest — including woman's tenderest one, her good name — to the work of uprooting the greatest moral evil of the times."*[57]

Mrs. Victor published a pamphlet — entitled *Women's War with Whisky; or, Crusading in Portland* — describing the abortive attempt to control or eliminate the city's liquor traffic.

Abigail Duniway, writing in *The New Northwest* on September 11, denounced Frances' 60-page effort, calling it "a remarkably one-sided affair" for not faithfully portraying "some of the proscriptive and intolerant acts of a few of the crusaders and their self-righteous leaders against the Woman Movement."[58]

Particularly distressing to Mrs. Duniway was "to see so graceful a writer as our amiable and gifted friend, engaged in any sort of connivance at or sympathy with the few proscriptive bigots who have been and are yet vainly trying to carry on the war against whisky, without consenting that rational appeal be made in their meetings to the *voters* of the nation to empower women to work as law-makers where they can now only work as outlaws."[59]

Mrs. Duniway professed to support the good and conscientious work of the crusaders — and to be as true and sincere a friend to them as Mrs. Victor — but she complained that

> some of them have done much that merits the condemnation of all sincere temperance workers. And we know also that the faithful historian is expected to publish both sides of a question in hand, and this our friend has signally failed to do in the work before us.
>
> . . . We assure her . . . that she utterly mistakes the public sentiment to which she tries to cater, and that she will learn the same by sad experience before she is done with the sale of her pamphlet.[60]

Mrs. Duniway claimed that by ignoring women's rights, and applying the gag law to its earnest advocates in the temperance movement, the crusaders had crippled themselves and caused the loss of public faith in their sincerity, as well as the declining attendance at their meetings.

"We see nothing in the pamphlet which we can recommend to suffragists as an aid in breaking the political fetters that hold women subject to the power of the law-making rabble who vote regularly in the whisky interests," she concluded.[61]

Mrs. Victor also discovered about this time that her book *All Over Oregon and Washington* was not producing any profits, its sale being limited to the Pacific coast.

Frances traveled to Salem in an effort to get the Oregon legislature to support her literary endeavors. In 1874, legislation died in committee that would have given her $1,500 to publish her book "in a successful manner in the East."[62]

---

*If prayer was unable to exorcise demon rum, then sometimes progress could. In Moffett's case the crusaders had the satisfaction of reading this item in the Friday, 23 June 1876, edition of *The New Northwest*: "The Webfoot saloon, of 'crusade' memory, is demolished. A new brick edifice will soon take its place."

Lawmakers had soldiers' bounties to pay and would spend no money to advertise the state. Mrs. Victor found, too, that she was opposed by Mrs. Duniway for not being radical enough on the suffrage question.

Frances felt this to be more than " 'a rose-leaf on the beaker's brim' " because of the large amount of unpaid material she had contributed to *The New Northwest* in support of the cause.*[63]

On September 22-23, she attended a meeting of the Oregon State Woman Suffrage Association at Reed's Opera House in Salem. The conference sent to the legislature a bill accompanied by a petition signed by about 1,500 persons, both asking the vote for women.

Mrs. Victor was an outspoken advocate of woman's rights and suffrage. But she felt strongly that women should first learn how to best use the vote, and so wrote in a paper that was read to the convention.

Mrs. Duniway was displeased, and in various ways made her feelings known. Frances endured the unpleasantness in silence, but in an October 8 letter to Oliver Applegate complained of the treatment she received.

> I went up as a delegate to the Woman's Suffrage Convention — or rather as one invited to make an address. As I do not speak in public, I was under the necessity of asking Mrs. Belle Cooke to read my address. The Convention passed off pleasantly and since that time the Bill, with petition asking for the privilege of voting, has been presented to the House and rejected — I did not expect a different result, but Mrs. Duniway did. She was much annoyed because I said in my address that I was in no hurry about it, though I claimed the right to vote as being as much my right as my father's, brother's or husband's; but because women were so unaccustomed to act for themselves I felt some preparation to be necessary, and did not care to have the ballot thrust upon those who would repudiate it, instead of comprehending its best uses. She gives me some of her characteristic little stabs in her paper, and did all she could to weaken my influence in the Convention, and by leaving my name out of the proceedings as much as possible — even substituting her own on one of the committees where mine should have been! It is a great pity she has not better taste in these matters. Although she does not understand it, she retards the cause by appearing as its leader in Oregon.[64]

Mrs. Victor told Oliver that a planned overland journey to California would not materialize, and that she had allowed his last letter to sit on the table a month while she decided what to do.

"I find all plans so mutable with me that I hereby declare myself as irresponsible as thistle-down," she confessed, "and simply resign myself to float with every wind of fate."[65]

Frances reported that there had been a very interesting temperance meeting in Salem to prepare the state legislature for a local option and civil damage bill, and she was pleased to note "one of our Portland ladies made a very good speech in the House."[66]

---

*Despite their differences, Frances later testified that when she came to write up the history of Oregon and Washington (see Chapter 23), she gave Mrs. Duniway "the credits she deserved for her work in the field of woman's rights." *Victor autobiographical sketch,* p. 2 c. 3.

50 Years

of

Pictures

of

People and Places

from

Our Past

THE BETTMANN ARCHIVE

Wall Street facing Trinity Church, New York City, 1850.

THE BETTMANN ARCHIVE

View of Culebra or the Summit, the terminus of the Panama Railroad in December 1854, sketched from Nature by F.N. Otis, M.D., surgeon in U.S.M. Steamship Co.'s service. The line reached Panama in 1855, making it the first Atlantic to Pacific railroad.

Lawyer, Hal-hal-teostsot, head chief of the Nez Perce tribe, sketched by Gustavus Sohon 25 May 1855.

WASHINGTON STATE HISTORICAL SOCIETY

THE BETTMANN ARCHIVE

Broadway in New York City in 1863, looking up from Barnum's Museum with the Astor House. At the left is the site of the present Woolworth Building and on the right is a Civil War recruiting stand and refreshment booth (beer at 3 cents a glass).

THE BETTMANN ARCHIVE

New York Harbor in the early 1860s.

IDAHO STATE HISTORICAL SOCIETY #2711

Lewiston, Idaho Territory, 1863.

SAN FRANCISCO PUBLIC LIBRARY #810

View of Market Street, San Francisco, California, in 1865. From T.E. Hecht's collection.

OREGON HISTORICAL SOCIETY #6807

The "Brother Jonathan," a wooden paddlewheel steamer of 1,181 tons, was built in Williamsburg, New York, and launched on 2 November 1850, at a cost of $190,000. The ship was 220 feet long, 36 feet wide and 14 feet deep, with room for 350 passengers. She plied the San Francisco — Central America route from July 1852 to November 1857, then was sold and carried passengers and freight between the Bay Area and the Pacific Northwest. The vessel underwent a thorough overhaul in San Francisco in 1861 and returned to service, but sank on 30 July 1865 after striking a sunken rock off Point St. George, northwest of Crescent City, California. Only 19 of 232 passengers survived the disaster.

PROVINCIAL ARCHIVES OF BRITISH COLUMBIA #7973

Victoria, B.C., harbor from Songhees Reserve, ca. 1865-1870.

Matthew Paul Deady (1824-1893), ca. 1865. A native of Easton, Maryland, Deady lived in Virginia and Ohio before moving to Oregon in 1849. He taught school and did part-time legal work. He served in the legislature and in 1853 was appointed to the territorial supreme court. He was president of the state constitutional convention in 1857. After Oregon became a state in 1859, Deady was named a federal judge and served 33 years. President of the Portland Library Association since 1868, Deady also helped establish the University of Oregon in 1876, serving thereafter as president of its board of regents.

OREGON HISTORICAL SOCIETY #9506

SOUTHERN OREGON HISTORICAL SOCIETY #2375-A

Jacksonville, Oregon, in the 1860s.

OREGON HISTORICAL SOCIETY #57514

Astoria, Oregon, in 1866.

OREGON HISTORICAL SOCIETY #50700

Main Street, Olympia, Washington Territory, in 1866.

OREGON HISTORICAL SOCIETY #63081

The Cascades of the Columbia. Sometimes — and not always successfully — daring steamboat captains would run these dangerous rapids to bring vessels to the lower Columbia River, often attracting large crowds of spectators.

OREGON HISTORICAL SOCIETY #21109

C.E. Watkins photo of portage railway and steamship landing at the Upper Cascades, 1867. A blockhouse built in 1855-1856 to protect settlers from Indians appears at the upper left. At right: the steamer "Oneonta," on which Mrs. Victor had a pleasant voyage up the Columbia River in 1865.

OREGON HISTORICAL SOCIETY #5344

The Dalles, Oregon, 1867, showing U.S. Army fort viewed across the Columbia River behind the town. Carleton E. Watkins photo.

OREGON HISTORICAL SOCIETY #21585

Portage railroad on the Columbia River at Cape Horn near Celilo, Oregon, 1867. This and some of the other pictures used here were taken by Carleton E. Watkins (1829-1916), widely regarded as the best wet-plate photographer of the American West.

CALIFORNIA STATE LIBRARY #23,030

Portland, Oregon, in 1868. Carleton E. Watkins stereograph.

OREGON HISTORICAL SOCIETY #52294

Reed's Opera House, seen here shortly after its completion, was built in 1869-1870 by Cyrus A. Reed, and is still part of downtown Salem activity.

WASHINGTON STATE HISTORICAL SOCIETY

Seattle, Washington Territory, from Marion Street to Union, in 1870.

THE BANCROFT LIBRARY

The Grand Hotel, San Francisco, California, 1870. T.E. Hecht photo.

CALIFORNIA STATE LIBRARY #9283

Francis Bret Harte (1836-1902), pictured here about 1870, was born in Albany, New York. His father, a professor of Greek at Albany College, died when Harte was still young. He attended the public schools before, at age 17, accompanying his mother to California, where he worked as a teacher, miner, printer and express-messenger, and contributed serials to the press. When the *Overland Monthly,* the first notable literary magazine on the Pacific coast, was established in 1868, Harte became its editor; and his articles and poems began to attract wide attention in the eastern states and Europe. It was he who strongly influenced Mrs. Victor — by encouraging her to write history instead of fiction. Partly in recognition of his writing, Harte was made secretary of the U.S. Mint at San Francisco and held office from 1864-1870. He was an early master of the short story, and between 1868-1898 he published 44 books. After a year as a professor at the University of California, Harte lived in New York City from 1871-1878. He then became the U.S. consul at Crefeld, Germany, from 1878-1880; and Glasgow, Scotland, from 1880-1885. He later went to London to write. Harte died in Camberley, England.

OREGON HISTORICAL SOCIETY #38311

Portland harbor and the Willamette River, 1872; Oregon & California
Railroad docks and ferry, right, at the foot of Oregon Street on the east side.

OREGON HISTORICAL SOCIETY #72108

Corvallis, Oregon, in 1873.

SOUTHERN OREGON HISTORICAL SOCIETY #740-A

Crater Lake in 1874, with Wizard Island at right. This photo, by Peter Britt of Jacksonville (1819-1905), a prominent southern Oregon photographer, was the first taken of the lake. The lake formed after a volcanic eruption shattered ancient Mt. Mazama thousands of years ago and left a crater. The area became a national park in 1902.

Portland's new police building in 1874, with the jail on the third floor, at the time of the women's crusade against saloons.

OREGON HISTORICAL SOCIETY #5626

OREGON HISTORICAL SOCIETY #26698

Joseph L. Meek (1810-1875), having entered the fur hunting service, found it dangerous. An estimated 20-25 percent of the trappers were killed by Indians, or succumbed to accident, illness or exposure, each year. Meek spent 11 years in the mountains without suffering serious injury. His fine physique, good temper and ready wit made him popular among comrades and employers, and helped in dealing with friendly Indian tribes. In winter the beaver could not be taken, because of the cold, and in hot weather its fur was worth little. It was during these semi-annual vacations in camp that Meek used some of the time to learn to read; few of his companions were really illiterate, most having been educated for lives quite different from the ones they were leading. Meek also met parties of English noblemen, painters or naturalists, who for greater safety traveled with the trappers' caravans, and picked up much additional information. By 1839, the beaver population had been seriously depleted and several trapping companies were disbanded. Meek took his family to the Willamette Valley in Oregon. He farmed near Hillsboro, but in 1843 he played a leading role in forming a temporary provisional government. In 1848 Meek was entrusted with important messages for Washington, D.C. He traveled for three months, arriving at the end of May. His cousin, Knox Walker, was President James Polk's private secretary; and Meek stayed at the White House as a guest of the president until August 14 when Congress made Oregon a U.S. territory. Meek returned home as U.S. Marshal for Oregon. Afterwards he lived quietly on his farm, but often rode around the valley telling stories of his life and what early Oregon was like. "He entertained for me a profound respect and affection, as refined and loyal as one could wish for from the most cultured of men," Mrs. Victor recalled. "When his eyes were blind with approaching death he called upon my name; but I, in San Francisco, was ignorant of his dying wish to bid me farewell."

EASTERN WASHINGTON STATE HISTORICAL SOCIETY

Main Street, Walla Walla, Washington Territory, in 1877.

THE BANCROFT LIBRARY

The Bancroft Library, at 1538 Valencia Street, San Francisco, California, in 1881.

OREGON HISTORICAL SOCIETY #54417

Hubert Howe Bancroft in 1882. A noted literary entrepreneur, he died on 2 March 1918, at the age of 85, after being struck by a streetcar in San Francisco. The University of California had acquired his library in 1906, and it is still an important resource.

OREGON STATE LIBRARY

Frances Fuller Victor in 1883. Photograph by Bushong, of San Francisco, California.

CALIFORNIA STATE LIBRARY #6401

MERGING TRAFFIC: Horse-drawn streetcars, wagons and pedestrians, ca. 1885, looking east on Market Street from Third Street, San Francisco, California. The second building at right is the Palace Hotel, constructed in 1875, one of the city's leading hotels. I.W. Taber photo.

This view down Montgomery Street ca. 1885 shows the Palace Hotel at the far end. Another leading hotel, the Lick House, at the corner of Montgomery and Sutter streets, is visible through the row of ornate street lamps. Photo by I.W. Taber, San Francisco.

CALIFORNIA STATE LIBRARY #1381

Oliver Cromwell Applegate (1845-1938) occupies a prominent place in southern Oregon history as an early settler and explorer, Indian agent, cavalry scout and newspaper editor. He also was a delegate to the 1912 Republican National Convention in Chicago. Studio portrait by Peter Britt, ca. 1886.

SOUTHERN OREGON HISTORICAL SOCIETY #1237

EASTERN WASHINGTON STATE HISTORICAL SOCIETY

Spokane, Washington, in May 1889, Riverside Avenue looking east from Post Street.

OREGON HISTORICAL SOCIETY #38878

Elwood Evans (1828-1898) was born in Philadelphia, Pennsylvania, and as a young man was appointed deputy clerk to the U.S. revenue collector for Puget Sound. Evans returned to Philadelphia in 1852, but came west again the following year as private secretary to Isaac Stevens, the first governor of Washington Territory. Evans was a careful observer and recorded the progress of events, in which he took great personal interest. By profession a lawyer, he was one of the three men designated to revise, digest and codify the statute laws of the territory. Their report was submitted to the legislature in 1869. Evans was speaker of the territorial house of representatives during the 1875 session. He married Elzira Z. Gove of Olympia, formerly of Bath, Maine, on 1 January 1856. Evans resided in Olympia from 1851-1879, and then moved to Tacoma.

WASHINGTON STATE HISTORICAL SOCIETY

Street scene, Seattle, Washington, ca. 1890.

OREGON HISTORICAL SOCIETY #67558

Mt. St. Helens and Portland from Riverview Cemetery, 1894.

OREGON HISTORICAL SOCIETY #38559

Frederic George Young (1858-1929).

OREGON HISTORICAL SOCIETY #4199

Eugene, Oregon, looking south from Skinner's Butte (rear of Dr. T.W. Shelton residence in foreground), 1890s.

THE BANCROFT LIBRARY

Looking north on Powell Street, San Francisco, California, in the 1890s, showing cable cars and, top center, the Nob Hill mansions of Mark Hopkins (left) and Leland Stanford. The men made large fortunes in the railroad business, and exercised much economic and political power in the state.

WASHINGTON STATE HISTORICAL SOCIETY

Frances Fuller Victor in 1900. Photograph taken from *Souvenir of Western Women* (1905), edited by Mary Osborn Douthit.

Responding to Oliver's query about Addie L. Ballou, a Salem woman active in the feminist movement, Mrs. Victor said that lady had achieved considerable renown.

> . . . She makes a <u>pretty</u> speech — often a good point. But she is not a woman of culture — speaks and writes ungrammatically — and is not just the kind of woman I should like to see at the head of any reform. , . . She is rather pretty; and is that style of woman that men very often seem greatly to admire, yet who with her own sex is not popular. I think the explanation of this difference of judgement lies in the fact that these women themselves hold their own sex at a distance, and prefer the friendship of men, because as men they can assist them more effectually, or defer to them more flatteringly. I have heard Mrs. Ballou several times, and like her very well; while I have at the same time a conviction that there is no real basis of congeniality between us. Mrs. Duniway has been courting her a good deal because she thought she could use her popularity with the men to influence the vote on the Suffrage bill. In this expectation she has been mistaken, as the final vote shows. We have now a couple of years more to wait, at all events, and in that time there is room for a change of sentiment, and for a better understanding of the merits of the cause.[67]

Frances looked in the *Pacific Christian Advocate* for an account of a visit by a party from Klamath Agency to Crater Lake, and she was disappointed to learn they found it not to be very deep. "I <u>did</u> wish to imagine the depth of the water to be in proportion to the height of the walls of the lake," she told Oliver, and asked him to let her know of any new discoveries.[68]

She wrote that a group of people with whom she had planned to spend the summer in the southern Oregon mountains were all still so occupied with business that they could not leave town for more than a week at a time.

"What a pity it is that just when we have discovered a source of pure and satisfying bliss, so simple and innocent as a summer party in the mountains — the dreadful spectre of 'business' should rise to threaten and destroy," Frances lamented. "For my own part, I have had so much of toil and turmoil that to be at rest, if only with a pine tree for shelter, within the sound of pleasant voices of friends, would be most utter and delicious satisfaction. I ask nothing more of fate than simply repose — not only from the discordant anxieties of life, but from its passions and emotions of every kind: — to sit aside and see the play go on, without one movement of responsive interest, love, fear, or ambition. Do you think <u>that</u> a sort of death-in-life condition of being? Perhaps so. But when life has been too hard for us, we over-estimate the relief that comes from the burial of our interests in it. If I could be placed back years-and-years with time before me to recover myself in, there might come a reaction."[69]

She was glad to learn that Oliver was not yet compelled to live alone on his ranch near Linkville, and advised that with all his resources it was not good for him to do so.

"Idiosyncracies, and one-sided views of things come from too much isolation," Frances warned, and although she had utmost confidence in

Oliver's ability to keep his "temper sweet, and mind clear, the tendency of inaction in any direction is to weaken and waste.

"You know already my opinion of you," she confided, "and with such an opinion I could not but have a strong personal interest — almost a pride — to have you attain to your highest, in every sense. I hope — in connection with this last remark — that my outspoken assurances of such interest are not offensive. If you truly understand me, I think you could not be offended, though sometimes I have fancied you doubted of my right to criticize favorably or unfavorably. Be assured then that I have too much experience of the world to attempt such a freedom with any but those most worthy of regard — those whom I regard most highly — and that would be about once in a thousand acquaintances. To the average man, who has but one construction to put upon a woman's kindly interest in himself, I have nothing to say — and for him very little regard. — But here I am talking 'under the pines' still!'"[70]

Two Essays on Women

Mrs. Victor's thoughts that winter also turned to the question of "woman's rights," in which she was perennially interested. She was not content simply to blame men for the inferiority of women; she also scorned women who passively accepted that status and, what was worse, then allied themselves with men to oppose rational efforts to bring about change.

"By a singular and most illogical mode of reasoning, a woman is womanly in proportion as she forsakes all allegiance to her own sex, and devotes herself to the other," Frances wrote in a paper that on 13 February 1874 was read before the second annual meeting of the Oregon State Woman Suffrage Association in Portland. "Not so men. Men support and strengthen each other. A man of brains is a prince among his peers. A woman of brains is, among women, a crow, to be pecked at. If she gets recognition at all, it must first come from men. Women have no coherency about them. Each one is for herself, in some man — uncharitable, unappreciative, merciless — notwithstanding she knows that by a turn of Fortune's wheel she may herself be brought to occupy the same lonely, aimless and joyless condition for which she has such a contempt in others. . . .

"What wonder that when a woman is placed, either by choice of duty or by circumstances, between the upper and nether millstones of this false social system, her voice becomes hoarse, her disposition fierce and unwomanly? The habit of repressing tears, and forcing back sobs is not mellowing to the voice. The constant endurance of cruel injustice, not from men only, but from sister women, is not sweetening to the disposition, The face that is never smiled on, soon forgets to smile."[1]

Mrs. Victor defined a "lone woman" as lacking legal rights to the protection and support of any man.

> A man marries or not, as pleases him. If his wife dies, or is in any way separated from him, his life, to all appearances, goes on quite the same. If he is rich, he remains rich. If he is popular or famous, he remains popular or famous. The woman with whom he was once connected was only an incident of his free, untrammeled life. But a woman! Why, a woman *must* marry, albeit she

has to wait to be asked. Not to marry, is to be held in contempt. She takes her *rank* from her husband. Of herself she is nothing. And should her husband die, her position in society then depends upon how much of his own personal *prestige* he is able to leave with her, in the shape of fortune or title. If these perish with him, then her life, or all there is of it, worth considering, perishes too. She has hardly any excuse for continuing to cumber the earth, since the entity from which she derived all that she was, and all that she had been permitted to enjoy, has become a nonentity, and *she* has become that disreputable thing, a "lone woman" — a "*relict*."

How can she now expect to regain riches, or enjoy titles? It may be necessary to labor, but her toil must be menial; at the very best she may be thankful to get some of the lower grades of men's work, at half their pay. To aspire to an honorable or lucrative position is to bring upon herself the charge of being *unwomanly*. To go into the world's mart of business with the intent to find something congenial or profitable to do, is to justify men in being rude to her. No sort of personal freedom is allowed to her; all public places are forbidden to be entered alone. The "protection" of even a bad man is preferred to the scandal of being alone.[2]

What, Frances asked, by going outside her "sphere" made a woman less charming and refined in appearance?

. . . Mind is the same, whether it resides in a man's form, or a woman's. All the laws of the mind, the soul, the affections, are the same in men and women, so far as observation or science can determine. What affects the one affects the other, and in exactly the same way. What makes the woman who has to do battle with the world — as earning one's own money in one's own way, is called — more awkward, or cold, or less lovely than her sister? What cut the consciousness, chilling her blood and paining every nerve in her sensitive organization, that she is bringing herself under censure, however unjust, rousing opposition, however thoughtless? And whether she has undertaken to do battle solely for the sake of truth; or whether "unmerciful disaster" has forced her into the world's broad arena to struggle for the poor privilege of a joyless existence — she suffers the same. Oh, what heroism there often is under the plain, sad face of the woman who toilsomely earns the right to endure, not to enjoy, her life.

. . .

Will the time ever come when this shall be different? When a woman may earn honors and emoluments, and not be thought less pure or less womanly for desiring them? . . . Will the time ever come when women will work together intelligently, freely, and effectually, as men do? How long could men withhold woman's share in the benefits of life, if woman should unanimously agree to claim them?[3]

Frances urged women to study history and learn why men became the dominant sex.

"It did not come from the hand of God — He made all things free," she asserted. "It began in barbarism, when rude physical struggle governed. Being first enslaved by brute force, the subsequent elevation of the ruling class only widened and deepened the valley of humiliation between them. And it was all the worse that the dependent class was also the favorite class, for they were indulged in just that amount of knowledge, and corrupted by just that degree of vice, which made them agreeable to their masters.

"Let women investigate for themselves the means by which men, in Church and State, have for ages hindered their advancement in mental and moral culture," Mrs. Victor concluded. "The world is ruled by precedent. A precedent established centuries ago, keeps women in chains, even in this age of refinement and culture. Let there be once established the precedent of an intelligent, independent womanhood, and the ages to come will abide by that, until the words 'slavery' and 'equality' will have become obsolete in their relation to woman's legal or intellectual estate."[4]

In a subsequent article for *The New Northwest*, Mrs. Victor argued it was time to begin a religious movement favoring suffrage for women. Very few ladies, she noted, could be persuaded to work for anything for which they could not pray; and men, artfully or conscientiously, often made them feel that something in the liberty of the ballot was essentially defiling to the purer womanly nature.

"Now, the very principle upon which Republican government is based is the intelligent consent of the governed," Frances explained. "That thought was made the central idea of American institutions scarcely a hundred years ago. But many things have been discovered, and many new conditions evolved in a hundred years. During this period, men have demonstrated to the satisfaction of the world that arbitrary government is not good for them. Gradually the injustice of involuntary subjection for themselves has come to shock their sense of right and justice.

"And now has come a new departure. The peculiar position of woman in society, half of equality and half of bondage — or rather half of *social* equality and *wholly* of political bondage — the intricate complications of her relations to society have prevented even herself from including herself in the class of persons who were entitled by the spirit of the age to the right of self-government. Every woman, theoretically, was a part of some man, and as such was supposed to be free, as he was free. But with the increasing intelligence of the age, with greatly enlarged opportunities for comparing the facts of the case, it at last became apparent to women that being theoretically free, because men were free, was a very different thing from being free because they were *unfettered*.

"When the idea became plain to them," Mrs. Victor continued, "it was easy to discover to how many of their material interests this freedom by proxy was injurious, and how sure it was of being abused. But it was a matter of more serious study to discover all the ways in which women are and have been injured, mentally and morally, by the conditions of their parasitic existence."[5]

Frances asserted that "men's household words, their literature, their preaching, their law-making" all subordinated woman's interests to themselves rather than to God.[6] While it was true that men no longer demanded absolute obedience from women, she wrote that "the spirit of their teachings remains the same."[7]

It was 1,800 years since Christ taught freedom and equality in all spiritual matters, Mrs. Victor noted, and a century since the American government was founded on the rights of conscience.

"Women begin, very justly, to question whether their Creator meant them to be mere helpless instruments in the hands of men, for the carrying out of their selfish purposes and desires; and whether they have not done wrong in so long yielding up all individual moral responsibility to men," she wrote.

"*If* it is right for women to yield themselves unquestioningly to men, it is right that men should answer to God for the sins and failures of women. But has God in His laws made any provision for such substitution? If it is true that each soul stands or falls for itself, are not women accumulating a terrible burden through their complicity in sins not originating in themselves, but at the same time not resisted as sinful both in themselves and others?

"How can a woman be honest who knows her husband is wronging a neighbor, yet will not warn that neighbor?" Frances asked. "To be sure, the law can not touch *her.* But if I had anything to do with making laws, I would see that they should hold the wife who conspired in her husband's wrong-doing as accountable as he, legally as well as morally. How can a woman be pure and yet allow her husband to keep vile company? The only excuse for her is, that her forbearing self-sacrifice more than equals her sense of propriety, or her self-respect."[8]

Pure and honest women, however, did spend their lives with impure and dishonest men — because of ignorance, fear, aversion to pecuniary loss, or social disruption. But often as not, Mrs. Victor observed, "it was a feeling that in some way she, the wife, might carry the sin of the husband to Christ; and He to the Father; and so by a circle of vicarious atonements, all might come right at last."[9]

Frances contended men lied by advising that women could do or say nothing about the right and wrong of things.

> We *have* a right to say that we will not associate with uncleanness. We *have* a right to say that we will not give truth for untruth. We *have* a right to hold a nice sense of honor, and to keep the highest principles of our religious natures untarnished by contact with evil. We have a right to hold men accountable to us, as we have ever been held accountable to them.
>
> The woman movement, like the temperance movement, began by lectures upon its merits as a matter of social and political economy, and by attempts at legislation. Now, there is nothing better established than that you cannot legislate convictions into anybody's head or heart. And what we require at this particular point of our progress, is earnest conviction of our duty in this matter — sober, religious conviction.
>
> If we have made up our minds that it is wrong for us to go on silently or openly abetting any and every form of evil in the world that by our resistance could be diminished, then we must commence our own reform in that direction, and refuse to remain any longer silent and passive. If it is necessary to have the ballot, the ballot we must demand until we get it. If it is necessary to overturn some prejudices that are obstinate, and ought to be obsolete, let us overturn them — doing nothing rashly, or petulantly, or unreasonably — but everything with a pure and elevated sense of the responsibility imposed upon us.[10]

Mrs. Victor remarked that she had little desire to quarrel with the conservatism of the pulpit. "There must be conservatism somewhere," she wrote, "and nowhere more properly than here."[11]

Frances urged women to show that their hearts and consciences are in the work, as well as their wills. "If, in short, they can feel to *pray* for political and moral freedom, as for other right and good things, their wish will be accomplished," she commented.[12]

This spirit, Frances added, would compel the ministry to consider the justice of women's demands, and to side with them. The opposition of the pulpit she regarded as "the most powerful and hurtful," and felt the battle would be won if ministers stood for the rights of women.[13]

"It will then have become a comparatively easy task to show the world through the most acceptable channels of moral instruction that 'what subsists to-day by violence, continues to-morrow by acquiescence, and is perpetuated by tradition, until at last the hoary abuse shakes the gray hairs of antiquity at us, and gives itself out as the wisdom of the ages,'" she wrote.[14]

18

"Dorothy D."

On Saturday morning, 21 November 1874, Frances embarked on the steamer *Ajax* for San Francisco. She planned to spend the winter with her sister Mrs. Rayle, from Ohio, who had secured a teaching position in Alameda.

Mrs. Victor had formed a strong attachment to San Francisco during her first years as a writer on the Pacific coast. She made a practice of going there often, "as being a better point for my sort of work than Portland."[1]

But there also was a chemistry; a tolerance of ideas, people and lifestyles. And a level of culture and sophistication unmatched elsewhere in the West, superimposed on and yet made possible by the excesses of the Gold Rush days, blended with those more primitive attitudes to give the city its color and charm.

"Probably you could not conceive of a greater contrast to your quiet way of living than that of San Francisco during the winter just past," Frances wrote Oliver Applegate on 9 February 1875. "The excitement in mining stocks would be a great amusement to you if you did not catch the fever. I own that I have had it, but my inability to invest for want of spare cash saved me from making some thousands of dollars! Those who were satisfied with making 400 per cent were wise enough to sell out in time — but those who were waiting to make twice that, held their stocks too long, and had them go down on their hands. The crowd on California Street during the sessions of the board is something wonderful to look at — not exactly an army with banners, but a full sized regiment of hustling, crowding, eager, restless, excited men in black clothes instead of blue or gray. The spectacle is something to moralize over, certainly.

". . . We are having lovely weather," she added. "The almond trees across the bay are in blossom and choice flowers beginning to awaken from their winter rest."[2]

Mrs. Victor soon found employment on the *Morning Call*, a newspaper known for bright, lively writing. Its contributors also included her friend Bret Harte and a coterie of female chirographers.

Writing under the pen name of "Dorothy D.," Frances contributed a wide variety of social commentary.

No sight, she wrote, was more "pitifully suggestive" than the frequent glimpses she got of the harassed lives of women who had various degrees of culture but no money.

"Educated to the idea that labor is degrading, and that marriage only is honorable, these women lead secretly the most tormenting lives," Mrs. Victor opined.

". . . No woman of culture and family will train her daughter, as she does her son, for any money-getting trade or profession. It would be, she feels, that daughter's social excommunication, and her mother's heart is not hard enough for the office. She would prefer risking her child's future in the hands of some yet unknown, and possibly wholly worthless man — would even prefer she should be poor, in company with a husband picked up by chance, than to have her known as a self-sustaining, independent woman."[3]

Providence concerned itself little with "these moneyless, tradeless, professionless and thoroughly helpless women," Mrs. Victor continued. "The marvel is how so many of them keep out of lives of shame, since men control the money of the world, and women are bred to consider themselves merchantable articles. We talk soundingly of bribery and corruption among men, of the dishonor of selling votes and bartering influence; but our lips are closed to the infamy of subjecting woman's moral nature to the pressure of absolute want."[4]

Some impecunious educated women, she realized, *did* manage to survive outside marriage. The question was not necessarily how few opportunities there were for women not physically strong and with the breeding of a lady, but how little they were "permitted" to do.

"Foremost of all, there is teaching," Frances observed, "but late revelations have shown through what mire she must wade to secure even a poorly-paid place in the public schools; and of private teachers there are more than can find employment. Rarely a woman finds a place as bookkeeper, or telegraph operator, or copyist. Then comes sewing, from which we drop to kitchen service. In manufacturing towns the cheapest work of factories is given to women."[5]

Most families, Mrs. Victor wrote, had one or more dependent women, who without particular duties within that sphere clung to it "like a fungus."[6] The men were burdened with the need to support so many persons. But the women themselves, lacking "any positive motive for being in the world at all, often emphatically wish they never had been born."[7]

The more cultured a woman, the greater her sense of abject dependence; and yet there persisted an unwillingness to be known as a worker.

"Men, as well as women, look down upon a woman-worker," Frances commented. "While a man would be commended for industry and money-making — and while his actual standing in society depends upon his energy and success in business — a woman's attempt to gain both a competency and a position in society by the same means is frowned down. Women despise the business woman; men half contemptuously patronize her, and totally set her aside when looking for a woman to marry, as being 'out of her sphere.' As if a woman's sphere was to be a beggar!"[8]

There were hundreds, and even thousands, of women in San Francisco alone, Mrs. Victor asserted, who, if freed from their shackles and "feeling that they had something to do, and could do it, would become useful and enterprising citizens; and those who have considered themselves too lady-like to work would head the list. . . . But just so long as women content themselves to be parasites, no matter how graceful or beautiful in their dependence, so long will they degrade the idea of work for their less fortunate sisters, make more thorny the path of the honestly struggling of their sex, reduce the wages that woman receives for her work, and perpetuate their own moral enslavement."[9]

The advertising columns in any city paper would reveal the real market for woman's work, Frances wrote. A long list of servants desire places, which she thought they would get readily enough; then a widow wanting to be a housekeeper in a bachelor establishment.

"Poor thing! she has found out that unencumbered men are her only chances of even a temporary home; and tired, perhaps, of a fruitless struggle with fate, has determined to take the hazard of an always equivocal position," Mrs. Victor explained.[10]

Then followed a " 'lady' " who had been " 'thrown on her own resources' — as if that were not where every healthy human being ought to be thrown — desires to make some arrangement by which some man may be willing to take care of her. Several really willing and hopeful ladies advertise to teach something or other, which will probably just keep their weary souls in their frail bodies," Frances added. "This is being ladylike."[11]

A business proposal by a woman, backed by a statement she understands what she is doing, almost never appears in a newspaper, Mrs. Victor observed, and it was still less likely to hear of a woman investing her fortune in business.

"Yet how often could the rich lady, by entering upon business and employing the poor lady, not only benefit herself, but by so doing perform the noblest beneficence for her sex," she commented, "removing by her example the conventional disgrace that attaches to active money-getting pursuits."[12]

As women became more educated and cultivated, they joined an ever-increasing number of poor ladies. Frances contended that something must be done for so many intelligent human beings barely able to obtain food and shelter for themselves.

"Every day men grow richer, more selfish, less home-loving," Mrs. Victor argued. "Hence, in a great measure, woman's occupation of ministering to man, the provider, is failing her. She is being left to starve alone by the wayside of life, while man strides on to selfish aggrandizement and unrestrained luxuriousness. He lives in first-class hotels, fares sumptuously, drives fast horses, does business in a palatial edifice, buys himself anything and everything that he desires; while woman, possessing equal or superior culture, drags out a joyless existence in the cheapest places, patching everlastingly at her cheap finery, rather than go at any honest, active work in the face of the opposition of a society that does not regard her real happiness in the least. Is not the cost of being a poor lady greater than the benefits?"[13]

One big question in women's affairs, Frances wrote, was how and in what direction "the girl of the period" should be educated.[14] Young ladies were thought to be shallow and pretentious — a poor contrast to their grandmothers many years ago.

> . . . Our mothers' mothers are the models on which our characters are to be formed. At the first utterance of the overwhelming charge that we are in every way inferior to somebody we never knew much about, we are inclined to admit our guilt without attempting its refutation; for how can we deny it, not knowing whether it is true or not? A little investigation goes a good way toward curing us of this submissive modesty.
>
> We find upon inquiry, by reading and from the study of pictures, that in the one matter of dress, about which so much is all the time said, the girl of the period is far more intelligent, sensible and reasonable than the girls who married our grandfathers, and are now held up as models to us. To be sure, when we knew them they were very sober old ladies — spectacles on nose and 'kerchief crossed on bosom, who sat quietly in their favorite corner by the fire, knitting and snuffing. But then they had been girls in their time, who wore, instead of that sober garb, a dress that left very little to the imagination, so scant was the skirt and so low the bodice. That which we call "full dress" now, because it is almost no dress at all, was the every-day costume of those paragons — our grandmothers. For our high-heeled boots they had only the low slipper, with heels far more insecure than ours; for bonnets, perfect frights of straw-sheds, with immense bows, and feathers two feet in length. And as to the laws of health, they used to lace themselves into hysterics as a common thing. Fainting, that used to be so fashionable in the novels of that period, has almost disappeared from ours, because it has disappeared from among us.
>
> But, we are told they were industrious and pious and everything that was good and proper. Well, being their grand[d]aughters, we trust they were; though if we may credit the annals of those times, there was about the same per cent of social irregularities then as now — only there were fewer newspapers to publish the[m] to a disgusted world. As to industry, probably there was a more general application to certain domestic affairs than there is to-day, and for several good reasons. In the first place, very little time was given to the acquisition of any branches of book knowledge. Libraries were rare, and belonged only to the rich. The same was true of musical instruments. Therefore, all the time that a girl now devotes to these things, must have been given to something else, because absolute idleness did not exist among women then, any more than now. This superfluous time was needed, too, in the carrying on of domestic manufactures. A girl could not be married until she had spun and woven both [woolen] and linen goods enough to furnish her house. Therefore, it became her to become industrious; and as girls then, the same as now, wished each to excel the other in a wedding outfit, they had the greatest incentive to industry.
>
> The houses of our grandmothers were built on the top of the ground, and had no superfluous rooms but the one sacred "spare-room," so seldom used as seldom to need cleaning. The rest were common to family and guests, were simply furnished and easily taken care of. As to food, that was of the plainest description, and baking-days, like washing-days, finished up that sort of work for the week. All sewing having to be done by hand, the garments of the family were plainly made; and being of strong material, lasted a long time. Taking all in all, our grandmothers, while undoubtedly they practised industry and economy from the very necessities of the times in which they

lived, and in some cases overworked themselves, to the injury of their unborn daughters and granddaughters, had quite as easy a time as the present generation of women, who are impelled to the ceaseless hurry and worry of a money-spending, refined, and too luxurious age.[15]

Popular education of the time demanded that children be taught natural philosophy, chemistry, physiology, botany, astronomy, geology, mathematics, mechanics, word analysis, logic, rhetoric, mental philosophy, criticism, history, languages, literature, art and music.

"The sudden greed for education is like the greed for money, and is equally aimless, except as a mere matter of personal aggrandizement," she asserted. "Children are taught to get learning, for learning's sake, and not for any use it can be put to. Every father and mother, with means to dress their boys and girls well enough for the public schools, is ambitious that they should obtain a 'good education' — too often without the least idea of what that thing is. Not being able to judge properly of the attainments of either teacher or pupil, and satisfied that their children know so much more than they did at the same age, they fail to discover that the much-desired education is the merest smattering of several branches of learning, the attainment of which fits them for nothing under the sun, but to be taken care of by their parents, instead of fitting them to relieve their parents of the growing burdens of life, as in the course of nature they should."[16]

The growth of the manufacturing and selling trades freed the young lady of the 1870s from many of the toilsome duties that burdened her ancestors, and she naturally turned to other pursuits.

Mrs. Victor contended that girls, coming out of school at the age of eighteen, possessed mere rudiments of subjects which would be called learning if pursued to some end, but by themselves were worse than useless.

"Why worse than useless? . . . Because the first eighteen years of a human being's life should be spent in gaining that bent of mind and habit which is to continue and become fixed, with some purpose of being serviceable in the attainment of whatever that individual may be in need of," Frances explained. "If at eighteen the girl has spent all her time in acquiring that which she cannot utilize except by teaching it in her turn to others — and provided she does not teach — is not her education a failure?"[17]

All knowledge in any degree may be good for an individual, she conceded, but "still the lack of practical knowledge and skill makes a failure of the life of the individual whose only resources are in his or her theoretical acquirements. Nor is the evil only relative — it is positive; for the habits of eighteen years are not easily changed; and it is with real difficulty that a girl who has done nothing else all her life but follow a certain routine of school duties, under the stimulus of rule, example, and the desire of promotion, can determine upon doing anything independently and of her own will. She may remain at home, as a kind of upper servant . . . The only escape . . . is to be looked for in marriage; not that she is any more fit for superintending her own house, or a household of her own, than for undertaking any other business, but simply because the natural impulses of youth and the experience of all time indicates to her that in all probability she will marry. And as the duties and cares which marriage brings are of such a nature that they cannot be escaped, they thereby resemble the school she has but recently quit, and she feels more willing to undertake them than to assume the responsibility of mapping out a course for herself. Hence, hasty marriages."[18]

Previous generations were not superior to the one of the 1870s; they just did what was required. Many changes occurred with the passage of time, Mrs. Victor wrote, and each generation had to be evaluated in light of different circumstances.

If young ladies did not choose to follow the callings of their mothers and grandmothers, Frances added, then other avocations should be made available.

"It is in vain ... to fit the girls to the situation," she advised.

> The real attempt should be to fit the situation to the girls, the latter being of more importance to the progress of human affairs than the former. Let the kind of education they receive be more practical. Discountenance superfluous studies and trashy reading. Discourage accomplishments that are undertaken with no other view than to fill up a certain programme, and are not meant to be continued through life. . . .
>
> There is nothing more certain than that the women who succeed best in taking care of themselves are of two classes — those bred to work, and those bred to that high degree of culture that can turn itself to use in art or literature. Between these two classes there are thousands struggling with the will, but not the way, by which to attain independence and position in society. To browbeat or discourage such, is to betray either great ignorance of the causes which have brought such an effect, or great brutality, or both . . . The only way known to form a useful and independent character is to place the individual in circumstances where action is possible and free, as well as necessary.
>
> The fact that with such enervating conditions there is still strength enough left in the girl of the period to demand something to do in the world besides that which Ah You can do as well, proves at least the possession of traits that may have some resemblance to those of her grandmother.[19]

Mrs. Victor also discussed the popular notion that culture was "a real and existent condition" of the feminine mind.[20] Of all the women Frances met in her life, she thought only half a dozen were really entitled to be called cultivated. The minds of most cultivated women, she thought, resembled an untended garden of beautiful or choice plants which were only alive enough to be known by their already perishing foliage.

Very few women, Mrs. Victor asserted, could afford to devote their lives to study; and few indeed wanted to do so, because popular sentiment was always against learned women.

"The very smallest number have the genius for study that would justify the devotion of a lifetime to the pursuit of knowledge for its own sake; and thus far, in the world's history, women, as teachers of higher learning, have seldom been called for," Frances wrote. "Nor do I imagine will they ever be in so general demand as men, for the reason that . . . such study requires the devotion of a life; and men always inculcate the notion, and put it forward to prevent this devotion of women to intellectual pursuits, that it is every woman's duty to give her life to rearing children."[21]

No provision had been made, she observed, for the thousands of single women, many of whom had been educated only for marriage and were left as disappointed maidens.

"It is just here that women are between two fires," Mrs. Victor wrote. "On the one hand, popular opinion demands that they shall plant out their intellectual garden; on the other, the same high authority decrees that they shall not carry its cultivation further than the planting, lest its necessary care should interfere with the one common duty of all women."[22]

Logically, Frances commented, popular opinion also would compel every man to have at least one wife, and provide everything she desires, but is not permitted to get for herself, while she provides the world with children.

She suspected, however, that there was little logic in "this extensively respected autocrat, P.O.," and that compulsory education would be the rule; although, for men at least, compulsory marriages were still in doubt.[23] She condemned the Mormon practice of polygamy, the abolition of which was a condition of Utah's admittance as a state in 1896.

"In Utah, P.O. compels women to marry one-fourth or one-fifteenth of a husband rather than to idle away their lives in childlessness, and compels men to fractionize themselves matrimonially in the same cause; but then Utah is still a little peculiar, though the land of prophets," Frances wrote. "Rome, too, in its wisdom took cognizance of these matters, and enforced marriage upon man, or in lieu of this, taxes — all of which was, under the social law, eminently proper."[24]

Roman law, Mrs. Victor conceded, would not work in the United States, where women, unmarried and without children, had to be put to some other use. Every woman yearns for and expects a position in her "proper sphere," Frances asserted, but meantime wastes the education she has received, reasoning that:

"'I shall probably marry. If I do marry, I shall be asked somewhere between the ages of fifteen and thirty — more probably before twenty. When I marry I shall have all I can attend to without undertaking to follow up study, or without practising any kind of industry except that required of me in my own home. I may be married next year, or the year following; why bother my brain about things that may never be put to any use in my future life?'"[25]

Mrs. Victor reiterated that education should be pursued as a means to an end, as a lever to move the world.

"The girl would be just as intelligent from whose catalogue should be dropped half the studies she is now required to take in an ordinary high school course — provided, always, that the essential things remained," Frances proposed. "The time saved might be much better employed in gymnastic exercises and out-of-door sports that would develop the physical frame perfectly, and secure strength for future usefulness, either as house- and home-keepers, or as workers in any other department of life."[26]

Mrs. Victor felt it was unwise to emphasize the mental aspect of education over physical training. If the proper balance was maintained, people would think it equally disgraceful to be physically puny and helpless as to be ignorant of school books.

"A thoroughly healthy man or woman is capable of being thoroughly educated; and just as fast as means are taken to make girls as strong as boys, just so fast, and no faster, will they be made able to endure continued hard mental effort," Frances wrote. "Good physical health is properly a part of true culture, and the teacher who neglects that, imperils all the rest."[27]

Even those capable of the mental effort needed to acquire a thorough education would find that, because of the need to earn a living, their schooling had to suit their occupation. To give men a general education before determining its relevance, Frances suggested, was perhaps "beginning at the wrong end."[28] Self-made men, she continued, had gotten an education after they found a need for it — "hence an education that was eminently practical and adapted to their uses."[29]

The then popular practice of giving each boy and girl the same kind and amount of learning, she contended, produced extensive mediocrity "in every literary or learned profession, but no high mountains of originality and learning together."[30]

Once the United States had been a sort of paradise, Mrs. Victor wrote, "when it was easy for everybody to live, and when women were deemed entitled to be cared for in somebody's household, whether owning a niche in it or not."[31]

But the Civil War, which "carried off so large a number of men in the prime of life, and the high rates of living that have held ever since that time, have entered as factors into the new state of things," she wrote. "Together with these is our system of education, taking up . . . the whole of girlhood, not leaving even time to acquire proper physical stature and strength. It is quite evident that here is an unfitness and discrepancy. The capacity for self-helpfulness has not come with the need of it and the circumstances that demand it. Nor will any kind of self-dependence spring from such a hot-house method. We shall be forced into something more practical, and the sooner the better."[32]

Mrs. Victor hoped that someday women would follow the example of the lady who, without neglecting a single duty of her house, devoted some time every day to reading books of the highest character for wisdom and learning.

One need not be familiar with the entire range of science and literature to be called cultivated, Frances wrote. "Yet this knowing a little of everything, and knowing thoroughly nothing of anything, is what is so often mistaken for culture."[33] Knowing something thoroughly, she added, could provide "a centre around which other knowledge would gather by mere force of attraction."[34]

She wondered if there was a better way to create intellectually cultivated women, to whom knowledge of science and history could be imparted in brief but practical form.

> . . . Is there no way of directing girls in the paths of literature so that the acquisition of the cream of good authors may be rendered simple, easy, and of permanent benefit? Cannot habits of study be grafted upon a stock of useful industry? It would be folly to deny that there must be and is. There should be found a reasonable mean between the devoted scholar and the educated

know-nothing. There ought to arise a race of women who could inquire of you without an affected simper of complacency whether you had read the last book by a celebrated author, whose title they have learned from the book reviews. The inquiry is not made, as it should be, in order to introduce a critical discussion of the author's topic or mode of treating it, but merely that you may know that this kind of cultivated woman has found out that such a book has been printed, which fact she is desirous of advertising.[35]

Women were carefully excluded from science academies, literary clubs or other places where men discussed great questions of the day, Frances wrote, "because of their childish ignorance, and want of ideas."[36] Women who brought worthwhile ideas to these forums would be welcome, but the "silliness of the many prevents the more thoughtful few from gaining entrance into the intellectual arena," she added.

"The woman who cares for women, and desires their elevation, will not hesitate to lay bare the flimsiness of the foundations on which our pretensions to culture are built, if by so doing she can stimulate any to essay a little real cultivation, independently of set rules laid down for us by school directors. The main thing is to make sure of knowing something well — after that as many things well as we can afford to; always bearing in mind that we cannot afford to waste time on that which will never be made useful, either in the business or in the adornment of our lives. It is the business of scholars to pursue knowledge simply for its own sake; it is ours to absorb, as the plant does, that which adds to our growth and strength."[37]

19

Love Letters

Mrs. Victor dissected the nature and philosophy of love letters, to which men and women alike ascribed the writer's true and actual sentiment — more so than if spoken in enthusiasm and passion aroused by the person's presence.

If affectionate words pass directly between a man and woman, the avowal might be considered premature or unwittingly elicited by the individuals involved, "but in the case of the letter, we reason that the writer understood himself; that he must have reflected before he wrote; that he expects, and by his candor deserves, a candid reply from us. And if his letter has been beautifully worded, full of fine sentiment, strong in protestations, and every way a charming and satisfactory one, we are much more influenced by it than anything the writer would have been likely to utter in the agitation of a verbal confession of love," Frances observed.

"If our hearts respond to the call how we dote on the precious missive. What happy smiles and blushes brighten our faces while we devour over and over again every word, until they are fixed indelibly in our memory."[1]

For all the shallowness of love letters, Mrs. Victor confessed that she felt sorry for the girl who never kissed or carried on her person "the deceitful things," which still remained "the most exquisite ideal enjoyment of 'love's young dream.' "[2]

She recalled how delightful it was to answer suitors' letters, "to choose and pick your words to make them tell enough and not too much; to exhaust expression in the effort to do justice to the delicacy, yet the warmth of the subject."[3]

Still, Frances commented, most love letters were worthless, because they were written by "callow poets and idle young people with a literary turn." These people, she added, "are in love because they are not in business; and who, having laid down the last new novel, take up a pen and put a climax to the pleasant excitement by putting into words of as much meaning as they can command, the often purely imaginary passion evoked by sentimental reading."[4]

There were, she conceded, a few cases of strong characters moved by real and absorbing love. Otherwise, the literature of love letters was "the most heartless in existence, and the most deceiving," she wrote. "Not intentionally deceiving, perhaps, but recklessly, carelessly so."[5]

A genuine love letter, Frances stated, is unmistakable for its lack of style. The affectionate notes between husbands and wives, set apart by circumstances, are known to be truthful because they are so natural. Letters without one affectionate phrase, she felt, were written by lovers because they contained hints of the interest that stems from love.

"These were written by sensitive and reticent persons, who do not have credit with the world for the tenderness that is in them," she wrote, "and who, by reason of their secretiveness, never inspire as much love as they feel."[6]

Mrs. Victor wrote that girls in their teens are not very good judges of character, or discerning critics of style. A man must lack serious work, she reasoned, when he has time to sit and write an elegantly worded letter of six or eight pages telling a girl of his feelings for her and his hope of reciprocity.

"If he were really as much in earnest as his letter would make us believe, the more natural course would be to treat the subject briefly and diffidently," Frances observed. "A modest doubt of having made the desired impression is more reliable proof of devotion than folios of pretty and poetical composition. But then we cannot see these tiresome truths without having first experienced them."[7]

Absurdly sentimental letters had been introduced as evidence in nearly all public cases of breaches of promise, criminal and scandalous love affairs, and divorces. Such letters, she added, were quite likely to figure in any love affair; the difference in the absurdity indicated the difference in character.

"Ten to one, the most purely absurd are sincerest — the most labored and elegant of the least worth, though the circumstances and culture of the writers must be taken into account, as well as the style," Frances observed.[8]

A girl often explained her unwise choice of a husband with the phrase: "But he wrote such beautiful letters."[9] Mrs. Victor related the story of a lady she knew who was taken by the letters of a clergyman, and discovered that he was a "lifeless, impractical, and in every way unsuccessful husband."[10]

The young woman had not considered that the man's profession was a literary one, and being unoccupied just out of college he felt inspired to demonstrate his talent at composition.

"His letters secured him a wife," Frances wrote, "but his sermons have hardly secured him bread since his marriage."[11]

She also knew an army officer's wife whose life had been painful and disappointing, and could not forget her facial expression and tone of her voice when talking of letters.

"My husband courted me with letters, which he has the gift of writing," this lady told Mrs. Victor. "I have hundreds of them, seemingly inspired by the highest sentiments and the greatest tenderness. But men, I find, may differ from their written sentiments."[12]

The officer was then a young lieutenant on a frontier post, with nothing to amuse him but letter-writing and learning how to drink whisky.

This kind of deception was not exactly willful, Frances thought. The man was probably trying to sustain himself, by his letters, in the views to which he was educated; but in the process he also misled the lady to whom they were written.

Women most often seemed to crowd all their intellect and passion into love letters. They had no other outlet for their creativity and, as Mrs. Victor put it, were "not always particular as to the qualities of the earthly god to whom their written devotions are offered."[13]

Foolish or reckless sentiments made known in love letters were liable to be used against their authors by unscrupulous persons, with sorrow and humiliation the result. Frances warned, therefore, that no woman should risk placing such letters in the hands of any man before marriage.

Even married couples, Mrs. Victor added, "sometimes may keep alive an unusually vivid impression of each other" through extravagant love letters, but she professed not to know of any marriage based on "real well-grounded, abiding love" that needed or ever had this stimulus.[14]

"Never put on record in the shape of letters those feelings or those facts that are not proper for discussion in confidential conversation," she admonished her readers. "If your feelings are not fit to be talked about, they are not fit to be harbored, and you had better make up your mind to dismiss them altogether."[15]

20

A Warning About Popular Literature

Mrs. Victor noted with alarm that there was a growing taste among young people for trashy literature — "the more trashy, the more widely read."[1]

People who knew how to take care of themselves could, by carefully watching what they ate, pretty much control their physical development.

If equal status was accorded to mental development — whether one viewed the matter religiously, or scientifically and physiologically — its importance would remain, Frances asserted.

The concept of "a sound mind in a sound body," she wrote, was a much rarer combination than most people realized, since it was often prevented by accident, ignorance and inherited infirmities.[2] But individuals had the ability to control the quality and quantity of their mental development.

On certain days and evenings, Mrs. Victor observed, libraries in San Francisco and other cities were crowded with boys and girls — "girls especially." Boys preferred adventure stories — "stories of peril by land and sea, and fascinating descriptions of impossible scenes," she wrote. "That is not so bad as it might be, yet it is bad enough, as being so often false, while it stimulates the boyish imagination until it is exalted above any of the actualities of life, and can see nothing desirable in the hum-drum pleasures of the ordinary people about him. . . . It is not that boys should not need books that gratify their taste in this direction, but it is the fact that they are allowed to select without let or hindrance any and all books of the character called adventurous, and allowed to read them to the exclusion of other matter, during the age of from ten to fifteen."[3]

Girls, on the other hand, were encouraged to read books which Mrs. Victor described as "a cross between a religious tract and a fifth-rate novel."[4] She accused Sunday schools and public libraries of fostering the desire for this kind of literature, although young women outgrew it and joined boys in completing their education with books "of the most sensational or sickly-sentimental character."[5]

A boy might vary his routine with an occasional book on travel, she added, but "the girl, being of a less enterprising turn of mind, keeps to the study of social and emotional subjects."[6]

Frances argued that five years were almost entirely wasted in reading these books instead of acquiring useful knowledge. If parents or guardians took an active interest in what their children read, the latter might have become thoroughly familiar with the discovery and history of the Western Hemisphere, while experiencing the same enjoyment they found in works of fiction.

What could provide more fascinating reading for boys and girls of California families "than the narratives of the old Spanish discoverers, the conquest of Mexico and Peru, the voyages along the Pacific Coast, the founding of the Catholic missions and their subsequent history, with the manners and habits of the native Californians?" she asked. "Here is real adventure, real daring, real courage and heroic endurance; and here all the accessories of the wildest adventure joined to truth, and the lessons that truth always teaches. What a pleasure for any one to be able to run over in his or her mind the history of a place seen for the first time. Take, for instance, the Isthmus and town of Panama. . . . If one seeks for a record of perilous daring, high courage, and glorious success, let him read how the Pacific was discovered at Panama. If they want to hear of wonderful deeds, let them read how, when De Soto had discovered the Mississippi River, and had died and his body been buried in its waters, and the natives had dispersed his forces, a company of three or four men made their way through to the Coast of Mexico, occupying several years in the journey. Read the stories these men related to the Spanish Viceroy in that country and the expeditions that were set on foot in consequence. Read the voyages of Sir Francis Drake, if you want to know what real privateering or buccaneering is."[7]

How many California children, Mrs. Victor inquired further, having visited Acapulco and been delighted by its unique sights, knew that 200 years ago it was the chief commercial port of the Pacific, from which Spanish galleons sailed to the Philippine Islands and returned with precious cargoes — at least those that eluded their English pursuers, or that weren't victims of bad weather or mutinous crews? And did youngsters also know the history of the old town of Monterey, or even the facts of California's conquest by Americans before the Gold Rush?

"Yet all of this, and much more, reads like a romance, and ought to be placed on [library] shelves now filled with doubtful fiction," Frances contended.[8]

Novels did have their uses, she conceded, particularly for those seeking relaxation from mental effort or business cares.

"And novels often furnish interesting studies of character, or convey useful lessons of life," Mrs. Victor wrote. "They are the dessert after meals — the comedy after the heavy drama of real events."[9]

The problem was that young minds were constantly focusing on the more pleasurable aspects, she asserted,

> and that on such pabulum as this no great mental structure is ever going to be built up. Not only this, but the effect of reading, year after year, when the character is forming, stories written with more or less art, and claiming to represent certain phases of real life, must be to warp the judgment and pervert the conscience. Even if there were nothing more objectionable to be

mentioned than the fact that they are all love-stories, that alone is a sufficient reason for their condemnation. The age at which these stories are most eagerly devoured, is the age at which the imagination is taken up with love-fancies. It is the pairing-time of life when, if ever, all influences ought to be brought to bear upon young minds to make them see clearly the vital importance of choosing wisely. What indiscriminate novel-reading does, is to cloud the perception and influence the fancy, besides furnishing excuses for erratic choice. Novels, being usually located in a rank of life superior to that of the ordinary girl and boy, man and woman, while they may cultivate the taste in some directions profitably, have a tendency to make the habitual reader dissatisfied with his or her actual surroundings; and if they cannot be lords and ladies, they can at least make a highly romantic marriage, all for love, and coming to their senses afterward, be picturesquely miserable all their lives. This is the effect of what might be called the second- and third-rate novel. Of the lower grades, much worse consequences might be indicated — such as a corruption of the morals and actual leadings into vice.[10]

Specifically exempted from this trenchant analysis were the works of such celebrated English and American authors as Charles Dickens, William Makepeace Thackeray, Nathaniel Hawthorne, James Fenimore Cooper and Charles Reade. But with the exception of Cooper and Reade, Mrs. Victor asserted, "these novels are too philosophical to recommend themselves to the very young, who read for the narrative, and not for the character-painting."[11]

Frances charged that the weekly newspapers and monthly magazines were equally guilty with libraries in catering to public demand for "worse than useless" reading material.

"Such is the demand at present for stories, that writers of serials for such papers as the New York *Ledger* and New York *Weekly* get higher pay than almost any other class of writers," she commented. "Finding that this growing taste must be deferred to, even the religious newspapers have fallen in, and give their highly-colored serial stories. Thus there is no check anywhere. The young people have *carte blanche,* and the publishers and writers are doing all they can to gratify them."[12]

While "Young America" was "very sharp and intelligent" collectively, Mrs. Victor reiterated her belief that they were unable to select without help writings that would benefit their growing minds.[13] She felt this was a matter that should concern philanthropists, and suggested that an Inspector of Public Libraries be appointed.

"You desire your children to know a good deal in this knowing age," Frances told the parents among her readers. "You pay taxes, with more or less cheerfulness, to have them taught all manner of 'ologies and 'osophies in the public schools, and you subscribe to a scientific journal which they never open. Ten to one you do not more than open it yourself, and never get your children to read it to you, or talk over with them any readable thing there may be in it. Then, how are they to presume that it would or could interest them? But you do furnish them with tickets at the Mercantile Library; and doing this, consider your duty discharged. There are a very large number of books in the Library — some very rare ones; many very excellent ones. It is true that there your children might acquire a vast amount of knowledge, and you have given them the key to it; but they do not go there for knowledge. They are forgetting all they ever learned at school in the absorption of silly romances — actually cultivating away their memories; for when one reads a great deal without the effort to remember, the habit of not remembering grows upon him; and if he does not succeed in 'forgetting himself to stand,' he does at least find himself unable at last to retain his intellectual grasp of things worth holding."[14]

Although freedom of the press was one of America's founding principles, Mrs. Victor warned that "we have to take care that [it] is not our ruin — not by plain speaking in politics, but by sapping the very foundations of sound morals, on which must rest any sound political superstructure."[15]

She termed it "a frightful commentary" on American free culture that many indecent publications were allowed to exist, to be read by young men "who hang around street corners, with nothing to do except to annoy passers-by."[16]

It saddened Frances to realize that although these youths could read, "yet in this free country to which all nations come for work and the reward of labor, cannot or do not earn an honest livelihood."[17] She thought it would have been better to teach them some useful skill than to permit them to learn about every sort of crime through reading the public prints.

"'Knowledge is power' just as much for the ruffian as the philosopher," Mrs. Victor remarked, "and intelligence wrongly directed is worse than ignorance."[18]

The first step to encourage good literature must be made by parents and guardians, who should examine books given their children from Sunday school onwards.

"If young people do not know how to select books of the right kind, let them ask somebody who does," Frances urged. "Even the librarian might be appealed to in most cases with profit, though he could hardly be expected to give his time to selecting books for general readers."[19]

21

Plain Talk About Men and Women

In the July 1875 issue of *Scribner's*, a writer ridiculed the middle-aged woman as commonplace. "The mists of dawn are far behind her; she has not yet reached the shadows of evening. The softness and blushes, and shy sparkling glances of the girl she was, have long been absorbed into muddy, thick skin, sodden outlines, rational eyes. There are crow's feet at either temple, and yellowish blotches on the flesh below the soggy under jaw," this man commented.

"The middle-aged woman expects nothing . . . She [carries] a basket of undarned stockings. Her talk is of butter and cures for [colds], and if she adverts to roses, it is to tell you the secret of her success in raising them, and the manure which they prefer."[1]

Mrs. Victor retorted in the *Morning Call* that commonplaceness was a virtue — a tendency to stay on "the beaten track of social prejudices" — was eminently conservative and therefore respectable and desirable in women.[2] The way to a man's heart was through his stomach, she noted, hence the talk of butter and like matters. Woman's function as a nurse would account for her concern with cold remedies, as would her love for flowers turn on the best nutrients to grow them.

It made no sense to waste time darning fabrics which were made cheaply, she added, but societal prejudices remained in favor of such work. Ten-year-old girls were spending "hours upon hours bending over [in] ugly and senseless labor" sewing patchwork quilts, which were deemed certificates of character, instead of participating in activities that would ensure their healthy physical and mental development.[3]

Domestic skills did not account for the sin of commonplaceness, Mrs. Victor insisted, rather it lay in a woman's haggard appearance and her lack of grace, vivacity and intelligence.

"It is not enough that a woman should be simply one of the three types selected by our author — 'domestic machine, fool, saint' — or rather she should refuse to be [any] of these, to the exclusion of her right to be a thinking, observing, reasoning creature, with an individuality of her own," Frances wrote. "Persons of strong individuality may escape the leading tendency of monotonous and unintellectual pursuits; the average mass of humanity cannot, without an effort."[4]

Men had no right to criticize women for having the qualities expected of them; ladies who demonstrated culture and intelligence were denigrated, too. Women had long been spoken to and of as if they had no feelings, but it was not good to ignore criticism that might be beneficial.

"We have not inquired whether it was best for us or for them that we should practise this subserviency — we have simply yielded without question," Frances wrote. "*They* have told us it was unbecoming in us to oppose our opinions to theirs, and therefore we have not done it. . . . Our reward has been a public sentiment to the effect that our virtue was in proportion to our willingness to be thought brainless on the one hand, and an undisguised private contempt on the other. Nowadays, however, the contempt is more open, and suggests the inquiry in our minds as to whether it is not deserved."[5]

The *Scribner's* writer related that young ladies may lack beauty and wit, but that there was charm in their untainted homeliness and the ardor of their foolishness.

"They pour forth their thoughts in silly school essays, and they run no deeper than roses and moonlight and eternal friendships," this man wrote. "They talk all day long about their lovers and pretty finery, and we listen with delight to it all, and do not ask for common sense any more than we would in the chatter of the swallows building their nests."[6]

Mrs. Victor argued that under this reasoning all that was considered sweet and charming in young womanhood would be destroyed if ladies thought about more serious and relevant matters. It put obedience above intelligent thinking, and household affairs above all other knowledge for women.

Men were commonplace in a different way, she observed. Businessmen were in contact with real events and a variety of people; they had to be informed about current events, politics and government.

"In short, he is continually pushed forward and forced to know something," Frances wrote. "Besides, the necessity of acting and deciding for himself gives him a facility and promptness that those accustomed to wait for orders cannot have."[7]

Women became old the day they ceased to be young. They lacked the foresight to provide a supply of charms to replace those of mere youth.

"If we had the common sense to do this," Mrs. Victor averred, "we should hear less about being old, and nothing at all about being commonplace."[8]

The monotony of women's lives need not bar their taking an active part in life, seeking knowledge or the graces of body and mind. Taking into account individual circumstances, Frances believed it was simply a matter of will for a woman to become a domestic machine or an attractive member of society.

The active, intelligent woman, she felt, would make a better mother because she would impart some of her vitality to her children, as well as understand their physical needs, although not present to give them constant care.

"We shall never know to what an extent the race has suffered through the want of intellectual culture in women — suffered congenitally and accidentally," Mrs. Victor wrote. "It is altogether too late in the world's history . . . for women . . . tamely to submit to be openly caricatured by those who have so grudgingly yielded the demands of the age for them. At the same time, it becomes us to take under consideration all such hints that we might and ought to do something that we are not. If men have come at last openly to confess that we do not satisfy them intellectually, we have the same incentive to violate the old traditions that we formerly had to obey them."[9]

Traditions mattered not to men. However, everything which might become profitable to them had to be proved. Every step men took, Frances added, left women further behind.

"As long as the little country girl crooks her soft young bones over patchwork and the little city girl is made the victim of flounces, furbelows, frizzes, and improper hours and diet, and so long as neither of them are taught any real useful knowledge, but only the imperative duty of following the last absurd fashion and the disgrace of not being married in their teens — just so long shall we continue to resemble . . . the picture of the middle-aged woman quoted above," she wrote.

"As long as we are content to make no remonstrance, the increasing arts of civilization will continue to augment our cares instead of lessening them."[10]

If women were able to prevent increases in the luxury of living, Frances asserted, they might give a direction to science and the arts in which women could claim their share. She wondered if a Greek type of beauty, in good health, would be better — insisting on elegant simplicity in appliances, furniture and dress while focusing on the acquisition of learning and knowledge.

Men at first might call such women "strong-minded," but even so they need not lose self-respect or the regard of their critics. Every woman, Frances added, should struggle against becoming commonplace, "even to the extent of sacrificing that day's indigestible dessert, or one row of exquisitely fine 'knife plaiting.'"[11]

Western life, Mrs. Victor wrote, was unique in that it gave "an opportunity for native talent and inborn grit to come to the surface and achieve something."[12]

This had become impossible in the rest of the country, where birth and antecedents were relied upon to gauge an individual's fitness for any endeavor.

"But in that generous West . . . antecedents are not very much inquired into," Frances observed. "Here is room for the development, and here the circumstances that promote the development of whatever character or genius there is in an individual!"[13]

The chief danger to children of newly successful arrivals, Mrs. Victor asserted, lay in being overprotected by their parents.

The father, remembering how the hard work of his youth made him clumsy, awkward and shy, may grant "too perfect immunity from physical exertion" to his son; and, not yet fully realizing the importance of education, also condone a good many failures in the way of school tasks.

> . . . He may be weak enough, too, remembering the awe *he* used to have of rich men's sons, to permit his boy to ape the vices of some of these, if only to show that there is no difference between them. He has been just far enough inducted into the mysteries of city society to have discovered that a great many people sneer at good, old-fashioned, plain morality as not high-bred; and not far enough inducted to have learned that the highest breeding is to have a stainless character.
>
> His girls will have their mother's healthy physical beauty, toned down by the altered circumstances of her present way of life into something sweeter and gentler than hers was when she married him. So precious and so fair will these young creatures seem to him that he will wonder at his fatherhood to them, inclining to look upon them as happy accidents in his life, as he looked upon his money when it first came to him. Therefore he will indulge them foolishly in every youthful extravagance. The mother, too, thinking back to the time when every coveted luxury cost her so dear, reflects that there is "time enough for her daughters to become acquainted with care," and has not the courage to cross them in their smallest wishes; forgetting that the best preparation for life's responsibilities is that which comes like our daily lessons, in slight instalments every day from our childhood up.[14]

The firm application of good sense, however, should be enough to save their children from the worst effects of over-indulgence, "leaving them to discover in their own way, as their parents did before them, the road to a higher level in society," Mrs. Victor wrote.

"It is not for men, or women either, to settle down in San Francisco to reproduce Boston or New York or New Orleans. Here are the individuals, here the new circumstances and fresh material."[15]

If a miner strikes it rich, and is equally fortunate in his choice of a wife, it can and will "lay the foundation of business schemes grander than those New York and Boston have known, and families as 'good' as either have produced, what may not be predicated of the civilization of this glorious California?" Mrs. Victor asked. "We start with a hundred years of headway in this race, which shall be run all the more quickly for not being retarded by well-worn grooves or ingenious fetters of effete conventionalities."[16]

Earlier that summer, a San Francisco woman published in the *Morning Call* a poetic invitation to "Dorothy D." to join her for tea. Mrs. Victor accepted in an equally playful, satirical verse. But before the tête-à-tête was arranged, many people indicated their desire to attend.*

Frances professed to be a quiet and modest person, but all the letters she received placed her in danger of being spoiled by conceit.

"If you were all to come, who propose to make my acquaintance," she told her readers on August 1, "the 'tea party' would assume the nature of a public reception, and my native timorousness forbids me to consent to such a proposition at once, and without due consideration."[17]

*See pp. 225-227.

Mrs. Victor preferred to remain "modestly unknown" even to her friends. She agreed, however, to respond to criticisms made in several of the letters.[18]

Answering an assertion that she criticized men more than necessary, Frances said that she had no quarrel with men as men and in fact was a "warm advocate" of the nobility of manly men.

"I respect them even more than the average of my own sex, because both their virtues and their vices, alas! are on a grander scale. No; my quarrel, if I have one, is with the selfishness, the vices, the meanness of individuals, or classes of individuals. In the same way I design to make war on individual women and classes of women," she wrote.[19]

"Men stick together, sustain one another, encourage one another. They can be generous even to an enemy if that enemy does a deserving thing. They are independent, and stand by their opinions. They have opinions. I like them for that, and I respect them. On the contrary, women have no cohesion about them. They will not hang together; they betray one another, and do not know how to be generous to one of their own sex. They are spiteful, and ready to believe evil where there is none. For this I despise them. But I will not let a man say such things about them as I say myself."[20]

Mrs. Victor felt the "mean . . . vices" of women — cowardice, lying, deceit, jealousy, envy, treachery — were attributable more to their inferior position in society, rather than to their natures.[21] The opposite traits — courage, truth, fidelity, magnaminity — were outgrowths of intellectual liberty "properly restrained of course; for liberty is not license."[22]

Women, she noted, were starting in the nineteenth century to leave their imprint on the literature and manners of the period. She thought the prevailing coarseness of old English authors, great as they were, provided an example of purely masculine literature; and as women began to read — and write — obscenity found neither publishers nor readers in polite society.

"I refer to this only as an example and proof of that intellectual, and consequently moral, subjection which has placed [women] in an inferior position; for . . . when women first began to read they read only men's ideas, and received as gospel the maxims laid down in men's books, not having any other to compare with them," Frances commented. "Wherever these teachings went against nature, yet were accepted as true, there arose a conflict in the minds of women which ended usually by their being true to their teachings but false to themselves. It is easy to see how this sort of conformity to enslaving opinions must act deleteriously upon character."[23]

This state of affairs was a part of human growth and development. "The average mass of men and women always conform to existing circumstances; the exceptional man or woman endeavors to mould circumstances to suit the ideas he or she thinks worth the trouble of maintaining," Mrs. Victor wrote. "Thus in all ages there have been individuals who saw clearly truths that it took ages more to make popular. Ideas grow slowly, but are indestructable. . . . Nobody need ever be afraid of ideas perishing out;

they may be uprooted in one place, but they have scattered their seeds in another."[24]

Frances reiterated that her criticism of men for being selfish in certain ways, or having other faults, was meant to illuminate facts with which women had to contend and find remedies for. She averred that blame would rest "upon those who continue the evil after it has been pointed out to them."[25]

Mrs. Victor admitted that she did not like women's parties, because women needed men to keep them in check as men needed women.

"Come, and be welcome, to any party with which I have anything to do," Frances told her male readers. "And you may make pretty speeches to Jennie B., if you like, who I suspect enjoys 'a little nonsense now and then,' in spite of her threat to 'pick you to pieces with barbs of steel.' I can tell quite readily when a girl is putting on airs of that sort; and between ourselves and the door-post, Jennie is one of them. And just for that reason I fancy she is very nice and piquant. She will affect to have a great detestation for all mankind, and be making *beaux yeux* at you all the time. But she cannot help either the affectation [or] the *beaux yeux*. They are the half unconscious signs of the interest that she feels in gaining your good opinion, as your animated glances in her direction indicate the pleasure of that hardly acknowledged expectancy of something on your part. It is that involuntary obedience of natures to the great universal law of attraction between the sexes, and constitutes the grace and the charm of life. Mind, I do not mean to encourage downright *flirting*, that is another thing; but I give you *carte blanche* to admire and amuse each other as much as you can; and if it should turn out that a tender sentiment should grow out of it, and a happy marriage should result, do not forget to invite me to the wedding."[26]

Mrs. Victor hoped that if the tea-party came off, it would contribute to better understanding between the sexes. And she ridiculed a suggestion that she take a leading role in the battle to reform women's dress.

She related that she had a friend who was an advocate and exemplar of the cause. This "gifted and cultivated woman" wore convenient, inexpensive and healthful clothing. Frances conceded its good points, ease and lightness, but told her it was the "ugliest contrivance" imaginable.[27]

"If you *will* wear it short and loose, pray do trim it up a little, and make it look pretty," she advised.

"*Trim* her dresses! cut up cloth into little bits and strips, and sew them together again to no purpose! Not she, indeed! Waste her precious time that way? Humph! she did think I had more sense than to advise such folly as that!" this lady replied in substance.

"My dear, the world wasn't made in a day," Frances said, laughing. "If you think you and I, by making ourselves conspicuous in this age of flummery by the entire absence of it, can revolutionize dress, you make a great mistake."[28]

Even if they both threw themselves behind dress reform, she added, at best only San Francisco would follow them, and then "the great world outside" would laugh at the city.[29]

Her friend retorted that *"of course* nothing can be done while such women as *I* set so bad an example" — a statement Mrs. Victor took as combining a compliment and a criticism.[30]

Frances slyly asked if her friend was an evolutionist, and after receiving an affirmative reply she told a fable.

"Well, suppose that when men were monkeys, some simia[n], wiser than the race, should have addressed himself to his tribe somewhat in this wise: '0, you miserable apes! are you not ashamed to have tails? Bite off your tails, I say, and be men.' At which, of course, the tribe only laughed and replied: 'What do we know about men? that is something we never heard of. All respectable monkeys have tails — always have had, and always will have — for, you see, they know nothing about evolution, and believed that apes were made apes at the beginning. That old fellow has always some hobby to ride; let him bite off his tail if he wants to. When he can no longer swing himself by it, he will be sorry he has made such a guy of himself to no purpose.'"[31]

The stern visage of Mrs. Victor's friend dissolved in laughter, saving Frances the trouble of having to explain the moral of the story: "monkeys cannot make men of themselves, nor the present type of womankind project themselves far into the future and be something that they have not yet grown up to."[32]

Mrs. Victor decided that she was too concerned with her own comfort to make changes in her apparel, and she liked pretty things too much to willingly forego them.

"Nature paints and crimps, ruffles and stripes her flowers, dresses her birds in gorgeous plumage, gilds the butterfly's wings, makes pearls and gems, and every form of beauty — then where do I get license to despise it?" she asked.[33]

Dress reforms, Frances believed, would occur when women loved intellectual attainments more than flimsy. They needed something to exercise their brains; even ruffles and fancy work, she conceded, had saved many a woman from insanity.

A dress of rich fabric, Frances admitted, could be made to look elegant with just lace and ribbons, otherwise it must be trimmed considerably to give the requisite air of fashion. She did not blame women of limited means for spending time and effort sprucing up their wardrobes, and she felt that those who failed to do so lacked self-respect or good taste.

"At the same time I deprecate . . . the evil of too great devotion to dress. It is a waste of time, of talent, and often of money. Nevertheless it is an outgrowth of our republicanism, and at this stage of our political history cannot be prevented any more than the naturalization of foreigners can be prevented," she wrote.

"But we are at liberty to dispense with our rights if we choose, and to rebel against our privileges. The question is, Is it wise to do so? There are ways and ways of compromising with fashion without giving up your independence entirely."[34]

Mrs. Victor was convinced a better knowledge of physiology and the laws of life would work beneficially in the matter of dress, but this infor-

mation was just starting to be disseminated and half the theories were put
forth by quacks and imposters.

"There is nothing for us to do . . . but to do as well as we can, and
wait," Frances counseled. She urged reformers to use their influence in
their own social circles in an effort to achieve some results.[35]

"The second anniversary of our Centennial may bring to it women with
fewer furbelows, and better furnished brains than will be present at the
first," Mrs. Victor predicted. "But when you reflect how few generations
there are in a century, it is being very sanguine to hope for much improve-
ment in a hundred years."[36]

The plight of women in San Francisco also came to her attention; and
she described the annoyance and insult to which they were exposed daily
by men in businesses, and on the streets and public conveyances.

Mrs. Victor recited the case of a lady who boarded a typical fully loaded
streetcar. A gentleman rose and offered his seat. She declined, not wish-
ing to pose an inconvenience. A young woman nearby took in the scene.
An elderly man sitting beside her commented on the circumstances.

"The matter has been canvassed so much that we prefer standing to
accepting a favor," the woman explained.

"Well, in these days of woman's rights, women have the right to stand,
and I want 'em to use it," the old man retorted.

"Most of us are quite willing to," the lady assured him, her cheeks
flushed slightly in embarrassment.

"They have my permission, sure," was his parting comment.[37]

The elderly gentleman "wished it to be distinctly understood that before
the question of woman's political rights was agitated he . . . used to be
the pink of chivalry; but that woman, by claiming to have any other rights
than those granted by man's courtesy, had lost all claim to the courtesy
rights," Mrs. Victor explained. ". . . We have always accepted the polite
attentions of men in exchange for legal rights — not on the ground, as
we had supposed, of our inability to endure the same fatigue at all times
that man can, or that might be endured by us at some times. Men, we
had fondly believed, took into consideration the fact that Nature required
of us, in the interest of the race, sacrifices of comfort much greater than
any they could possibly make in trying to save for us our small reserve
of strength, or in promoting our comfort in the numberless small ways
that the true gentleman finds out. It is a shock to our womanly faith to
have the matter put forward in the light in which O.M. puts it."[38]

Frances thought it should be illegal for streetcars to carry more passengers than could be seated comfortably and decently. Men also should
be prevented from crowding against women in ways that would not be
tolerated elsewhere — "laying their arms upon ladies' shoulders under
the pretense of holding open a newspaper that does not need to be held
open; or of leaning over on a lady's lap to get their hands in their pockets
for change."[39]

The legal right to regulate such transgressions, she believed, would sur-
pass "the pleasure of accepting a seat that is given to us as a favor after
we have paid for one that we fail to find."[40]

Mrs. Victor contended that no lady wanted to deprive anyone of a seat, and would especially dislike it if offered one by an elderly gentleman. The courtesy, she added, was often accepted because men insisted upon it, and because more inconvenience was caused by women standing in a streetcar than men.

"These considerations, joined to the thought that the courtesy is *customary*, and therefore that ladies are *expected* to sit, even at the expense of a gentleman's comfort, govern most intelligent women in taking what is, strictly speaking, not their own," Frances wrote.[41]

Women had nothing to do with ordering the circumstances in which they found themselves, and submitted with "tolerable grace" — even silently enduring rude treatment from men.[42] Yet, women were threatened with the loss of their privileges if they even talked of having legal rights.

"If O.M. represented all the men of America, and should make the proposition to me to exchange the uncertain privileges for the certain rights, I would take him up on the spot," Mrs. Victor asserted. "And so would anybody that appreciates a good bargain. Then he should have his seat in the cars unmolested, and I should have mine without having to blush at close yet unavoidable contact with total strangers, who use more freedom in their contiguity than my own brother would."[43]

Men also liked to form lines for two or more blocks outside theatre entrances and stare at ladies returning home after attending a matinee.

"As if there were not women enough always in sight in San Francisco who might be seen without resorting to so odious a plan as this of making them run the gauntlet," Frances complained. "Does any one say that we have suffered no harm in being looked at? That depends on circumstances. If we were really objects of curiosity — say we had just arrived from the moon — or if, as in the early days of California, even an old sun-bonnet that a woman had worn was regarded with interest, as reminding the men of 'the girls they left behind them' in the States, it might be considered pardonable for a crowd of men to form lines along the streets where we must pass to get a look at the rare spectacle. But in California to-day, and in the city of San Francisco, whose streets blossom every day with women in handsome toilet[te]s, there exists no motive for turning an assemblage of ladies into a show to be gaped at, but the one of overbearing impertinence. A man may be just as insulting with his eyes, as with his hands or feet or arms. It is a matter of indelicate and unwarranted freedom."[44]

A woman on window-shopping strolls in the city often found that when she paused to look at things some man would also immediately stop beside her, causing her to move on. This process would be repeated several times until the man was satisfied that the lady was not going to talk to him at all, but simply mind her own business. Mrs. Victor listed some of the remarks that had been made for her own ears or those of a lady companion:

"I would rather own such a woman as that than a thousand-dollar horse!"

"That's one of them!"

"She's a married woman!"[45]

Such comments were rarely so pungent as to make a man liable to arrest. Their sole intent was to annoy and demean a woman, and make her uncomfortable.

> . . . O, my friends, it is a fearful and wonderful thing to be "womanly!" To deserve this heavenly title, you have to *be* the most despicable creature alive, and try to believe yourself the most angelic. Does anybody believe that there is really so little true *manhood* in a woman that she feels no impulse to avenge an insult, such as being told she is more desirable than a thousand-dollar horse? — and that on the street, by a perfect stranger. Some men will say, and a few will perhaps think, that a woman is not spoken to in that way who is modest and quiet in her demeanor; but I can assure them, from actual knowledge, that they are . . . I have myself, when passing along the streets of this city, especially in that part of town north of Pine street, been repeatedly spoken to, or spoken about, in a manner to attract my attention.[46]

Mrs. Victor related that she had just talked to a young woman who complained of advances made by a gray-haired gentleman when she was trying to mail a package at the post office. This man followed and persisted in offering his services to the lady as she was looking for the proper place to leave her parcel.

Hoping to escape her tormentor more readily, the young woman volunteered what she was looking for, but the man only seized her arm to lead her on. She jerked herself free and hurried off, but as she was depositing the box the gentleman leaned over her shoulder to say that it "gave him infinite pleasure to serve pretty young ladies!"[47] The man so harassed the woman that her only recourse was to run away from him. She was so frightened by the experience that she dreaded having to go to the post office again.

Frances appealed to the "manly men," whom she presumed ran San Francisco, to see that women were protected from abuse in the city.

"The disrespect and discourtesy of men make a woman's lot intolerable, because its own peculiar ills are all that we are able to endure with resignation," she wrote.

". . . It must be taken into account that a constant demoralization is going on in society through the accumulation of such influences. Men are indifferent. We, ourselves, finding how impotent we are, cultivate a feeling of indifference in preference to bearing the full burden on our hearts. Children, if not born with a moral obliquity past all remedy, are constantly exposed to contact with influences that warp them more and more in the wrong direction. Street talk, some of the public prints, the examples of their elders, are all educating them to disregard principles of purity, honor, decency. All this is a positive evil to every member of society; but the heaviest curse falls upon women, who must suffer the penalty of their own short-comings and the sorrow of every sinner in the family, husband, son, or daughter, besides."[48]

Women's interests required an increase of social purity, and women should be regarded as pure everywhere and under all circumstances in which they have not shown themselves impure. But this was not the case in San Francisco.

"You feel that you are suspected until opportunity has been given you to prove yourself," Frances commented. "The degradation of such a position is intolerable to womanly pride and delicacy. No lady but wishes to walk the earth as if vice did not exist in it; and she should be protected in doing so. It is an injury only to suggest the existence of evil except for the purpose of abating it."[49]

Mrs. Victor believed the manners of bad men were known in a general way, but that good men weren't aware of the many ways in which lesser types annoyed women. She cited the remark of a beautiful and talented young lady, who because of a reversal of fortune had to take in sewing for the furnishing stores: "I am becoming so used to being insulted that I do not mind it, but just shut my ears and look the other way."[50]

It was an experience like this that took the bloom off a woman very quickly, Frances lamented, and society lost by the process.

22

Opportunity Knocks

"LOSS OF THE STR. PACIFIC!" screamed the headline of the Portland *Morning Oregonian* on Tuesday, 9 November 1875. The Pacific Mail Company vessel sailed from Victoria, B.C., enroute to San Francisco, five days before, but had foundered in a heavy gale about forty miles off Cape Flattery on the northern Washington coast. She was a wooden side-wheel steamer of 900 tons built in New York in 1851, and was almost completely overhauled in San Francisco in 1873.

Among the estimated 236 persons who perished in the disaster was Frances' husband, Henry Clay Victor, a resident of Tacoma, Washington Territory. In September he had announced plans to build a fishery nearby — "on quite a large scale," a newspaper said. "Besides putting up fish and making oil, he intends to make isinglass and glue."[1]

Mrs. Victor was living in Portland when news of the sinking reached the city. Anxious citizens scanned the list to learn the fate of relatives and friends. For Frances, the shock was cushioned by distance and time. Seven years before, she and Henry agreed to separate, after unsound business ventures and speculations he made left the couple deeply in debt.

Frances continued to support herself, albeit marginally, by writing fiction, poetry and historical vignettes for the press. As she renewed her travels around the Pacific Northwest, making observations in preparation for another book, her deep concern for the status of women now led her to take a more active and prominent role in such matters.

Soon after her return from San Francisco, Mrs. Victor became corresponding secretary of the Oregon State Woman Suffrage Association, in which position she did what she could to promote women's rights through her letters, leaflets and articles, and also by advocating concepts and courses of action she thought the organization should follow to best achieve the same goal.

Despite frequent appearances in one publication or another, Frances always found that there was barely enough money coming in to meet her essential needs, and she was constantly on the lookout for some more remunerative occupation to which her skills could be applied.

Through her friend Judge Deady, who was instrumental in its found-ing, Mrs. Victor learned that faculty members were needed at the newly established University of Oregon in Eugene.

She promptly made application. But "certain parties," apparently act-ing without Judge Deady's consent, met in caucus to elect a set of teachers.[2] A sister of Reuben P. Boise, an Oregon Supreme Court judge, got the position Frances wanted.

"All these failures of mine seem to point one way, and that way is out of Oregon, into a country where there is a larger sphere of operation, and better pay for services rendered," she remarked, in a sad letter to Oliver Applegate on 22 April 1876. "I do not know how soon my exit will be, but it cannot be a great ways off. All I wait for is to have my property rights determined one way or another."[3]

Mrs. Victor served on the Committee on Resolutions during the O.S.W.S.A.'s fourth annual convention, in February 1876, at Reed's Opera House in Salem. She was named recording secretary and a member of the organization's executive committee.*

Somewhere between working for the O.S.W.S.A., and on her various literary endeavors, Frances found sufficient leisure time to develop her talents as a painter; and in September, the press reported, she exhibited "a fine picture of Mt. Hood recently finished, to her many friends."[4]

Mrs. Victor was in Astoria, at the mouth of the Columbia River, when the fifth annual convention of the suffrage association was held in mid-February 1877 at the Linn County courthouse in Albany.

Frances sent a letter, "freighted with a great weight of sympathy," regret-ting her inability to attend the meeting in person.[5] She had thought, however, of "the thousand and one things" that she felt the women ought to discuss.[6]

She reiterated a point made in her earlier writings — that women must first prepare themselves to participate at all levels in the conduct of human affairs, and then *doing* it.

"I still insist that if we fit ourselves and show our fitness the world is sure to want us. The rights of women, physically weak, unarmed, and anti-belligerent, secured without bloodshed or strife, is to mark the tri-umph of modern and Christian civilization. Nobody really doubts it now-a-days, though the final achievement of the ballot is delayed by the force of ancient customs retarding men's judgments. It behooves us, then, to be educating the boys and girls of this generation in different sentiments, as it behooves us also to put ourselves in training for a wider sphere of duties," Frances wrote.

"Where are the women's clubs for the study and practice of political questions and forms that we all agreed were a necessity? Is it such a great matter to give an afternoon or evening once a week or fortnight to such a duty as this? Perhaps if you had given yourselves to this work, you might

---

*"When it comes to a matter of *rights* between men and women, I would simply ask to know how men acquired the authority to either grant or withhold rights from us," Frances wrote in an essay that was read to the convention.

have been able by this time to have solved the electoral muddle of this Centennial year," she chided her readers. "At all events, let us try to prevent such a thing occurring by the next Centennial!*

"I do not by any means think that the obtaining of the ballot is the chief end of our associations. I think women have a thousand other interests to study far more precious to them than the privileges of political equality; but as it is only through political equality that we are ever to force the recognition of our dearest wants and most urgent needs, let us work manfully to secure the means."[7]

Mrs. Victor believed that women had "the ability, the courage and coolness for any great work," but that their heroic deeds attracted little notice and then only as a passing wonder.

"Men do not reflect that it requires more courage to dare motherhood than to face an enemy; more heroic patience to bear with children and invalids, and to endure the never-abated cares of domestic life, than to essay the most difficult undertakings in which they engage. But we shall educate them up to it after a while," Frances wrote.

". . . It certainly needs to be impressed upon the minds and hearts of all men, and women, too; for women in order to become good mothers must also begin the child's education in themselves."[8]

By early 1877, Mrs. Victor's book, *The New Penelope*, was ready for publication. It was an anthology of short stories that she had written about western life, plus selections from her poetry.

Frances told O.C. Applegate in a March 18th letter that she was living, as usual, on a little cash and much hope; and that, since it was the chief enjoyment of life, she would continue believing in the future, to the end.

"I must make a <u>success</u> of my new book," she wrote. "Further, my friends must help me where they can, without too much effort. I cannot afford on a two dollar book, to employ agents at a commission. Here, and in all the places I can reach, I shall do my own canvassing: but where the communities are small and distant this will be impracticable; and I hope my friends will send in their names — if they desire the book — and any additional ones they can . . . obtain for me. I do not mean to print more than I am sure of selling."[9]

Mrs. Victor wistfully remarked on how nice it would be to follow the seasons like a migratory bird.

"But wings or steam engines are necessary to convey us from clime to clime with ease enough to make migration practicable," she wrote.[10] Fortunately, spring that year in Portland was so alluring that travel was unnecessary; and she added:

"Fruit-trees in blossom; dandelions starring the lawns; shrubbery in gay colors of red and yellow according to its kind; the delicate weeping willows hanging out their long yellow-green trailing or drooping branches; the air mild and balmy! — one might fancy one's self in California, or any other most favored country."[11]

*See p. 252.

Three months later, however, she reported that arrangements for her book were still incomplete.

"It is a hard time to deal with publishers," Mrs. Victor wrote, "but I shall know in a few days."[12]

She congratulated Oliver on his accession to the "editorial quill" of the Ashland (Oreg.) *Tidings.*

"The office is one of no great profit, nor much honor in this country," Frances wrote. But she noted that in southern Oregon people and events received more attention than in Portland, where there were "so many contestants for public favor."[13]

She expressed confidence that Applegate would make the *Tidings* acceptable reading all around.

"There is so much that you know better than others about the history and scenery of the state, that you could not fail to have plenty of resources," she told Oliver. ". . . And whatever of a literary nature you write will go to embellish the rest."[14]

Frances said she would try to write some prose sketches for the paper, but her head was "full of all sorts of work."[15] She was leaving for Puget Sound, on an extended tour, and planned to run a series of historical articles in *The West Shore*, a monthly magazine in Portland, during the year. She also had been working on some poetry.

Mrs. Victor asked Oliver to furnish her with a systematic mythology of the Klamath Indians. She thought it would be "very interesting to know their religious ideas in all their developments," and wanted to familiarize herself with the subject.

"I wish you were not so far off — but we cannot always combine our helps as we could wish," she told him. "It is a comfort to know you are somewhere."[16]

Never one to sit back and wait patiently for life's offerings — she could not afford to and, besides, it wasn't in her character — Mrs. Victor decided to reissue *All Over Oregon and Washington*, published just five years before.

Such were the changes in the Pacific Northwest brought about in that brief interval by new arrivals and increased commerce and industry, that Frances felt a revised and updated version of her book was necessary. The original volume described the botany, climate, geology, mineralogy, resources, scenery and soil. It also contained an outline of the region's early history, and provided tips to immigrants and travelers.

In late May, the press reported that she planned to begin gathering information that summer for a new edition of *All Over Oregon and Washington*, and soon would visit eastern Oregon in the interest of the work.

In the summer of 1877, *The New Penelope* was published to favorable reviews. The book was not stereotyped and only 1,000 copies were printed. These sold readily, netting for Mrs. Victor a small profit.

So now Frances had a dual purpose in traveling around the Pacific Northwest: she could gather material for the revision of one book while selling the other.

Still, despite all her other work, Mrs. Victor made it a point to stay active in the woman's rights movement; and on August 17 the feminist newspaper

The New Northwest announced that she would provide specific information to "active, energetic and capable young ladies" seeking "remunerative employment."[17]

Frances continued her Pacific Northwest travels, and on 26 April 1878 a newspaper reported that she had prolonged a visit to eastern Washington to canvass the towns of that region for *The New Penelope*. This book had been printed by H. H. Bancroft & Company, a San Francisco firm, which shortly thereafter announced plans to publish a series of Pacific coast histories.

23

The Bancroft Years

Hubert Howe Bancroft was born 5 May 1832 in Granville, Ohio, a descendant of old New England families through both paternal and maternal lines. He found schoolwork difficult; and his mother, convinced he was not being fairly treated, all but removed him from class.

At the age of fifteen, Bancroft was given the choice of preparing for college or working at a bookstore in Buffalo, New York, owned by George H. Derby, a brother-in-law.

Bancroft became discouraged after a year's study, and entered Derby's employ in August 1848. After six months, the young man returned to Ohio as a sales agent for his brother-in-law, and was so successful that he was invited to become a clerk in the Buffalo bookstore.

His father had been drawn to California by the gold excitement; and, together with George L. Kenny, his closest friend, Bancroft was sent hither by Derby in February 1852.

The pair decided to locate in Sacramento, and young Bancroft worked in the mines until arrangements could be made to start a bookselling operation, but Derby's death ended the plan.

Bancroft went north in 1853 to the new mining town of Crescent City, where he worked as a bookkeeper and bookseller. He made $6,000-$8,000 there, most of which he subsequently lost in property investments.

He visited his sister in the East two years later, and in return for helping to recover Derby's California investment she gave him the sum, amounting to $5,500, with which to begin business.

Bancroft obtained credit in New York, and shipped a $10,000 stock of goods to San Francisco where, with Kenny, he organized the firm of H.H. Bancroft and Company about 1 December 1856.

From the start he had a taste for publishing, but it was not until 1859 that the idea for a history project was conceived.

Bancroft decided to keep for future reference books that had been used in the preparation of an almanac. To these original seventy-five volumes dealing with the region he added, gradually, works acquired locally from second-hand stores and from bookstores in New York, Boston and

Philadelphia. He had 1,000 volumes by 1862; and four years later, after a tour of Europe, the collection grew tenfold. By 1869, after Bancroft started gathering Mexican works and to purchase private libraries in the United States, his holdings totaled 16,000 volumes.

A number of people were arranging and cataloging the material in the library which housed it. At first the library occupied part of one floor, but so grew that it filled an entire building specially constructed for the purpose. Several writers were already preparing manuscript for the project.

After several years of discussion, suggestion and revision, Bancroft and his colleagues decided to shift the entire plan of work. Instead of a Pacific coast encyclopedia, they would publish a series of history books about the region — commencing at the Isthmus of Panama, with the Spaniards' first appearance, and then taking up successively the regions to the north as their history began.

Bancroft corresponded with the heads of governments of countries within the scope of his research. The presidents of the Mexican and Central American republics and the governors of the western states accorded him every facility. Especially favorable letters were received in 1874 from the presidents of El Salvador, Guatemala and Nicaragua, the last appointing a special commissioner to secure and ship documents.

"Mr. Bancroft, as founder of the library and organizer of the history, has rendered a real and lasting service to historical literature," an observer concluded.[1]

". . . At no other time and in no other land has there been carried to completion a work of like character and magnitude. There had previously been written a few histories . . . designed chiefly to give a treatment of a certain institution or political subject, but so far as the thorough working up of the whole ground was concerned, a virgin field presented itself."[2]

Henry L. Oak, Bancroft's chief assistant for the history project, devised an indexing system which speeded the retrieval of information in the library, and made life far easier for the writers by transferring certain tedious chores incident in their work to other personnel.

In addition to a card index as a sort of subject catalog, Oak simply had the library staff read each book and manuscript. Notes and references were extracted and written on half sheets of legal paper, with blank lines separating each item to facilitate the later, purely mechanical, cutting up and arrangement.

The pieces of paper were deposited in paper bags labeled according to the subject matter they contained. Thus, writers had only to consult an alphabetical and chronological arrangement of bags, each containing between twelve and 1,000 notations on a desired topic, and proceed at once to a critical examination of their sources and determine what additional information was needed.

The process was later refined to permit new staff members to so prepare rough material that the writers could produce manuscript more quickly.

The history series began with five volumes on the *Native Races*, a compilation of what was then known about the Indians of the Pacific slope, published at three-month intervals between 1 October 1874 and Christmas 1875.

As fast as the library staff completed work on the *Native Races*, their attention turned to organizing the great mass of information on California, which was considered the starting point for the history of several other states as well — including Arizona, Nevada and Utah. Bancroft and company hit the road to gather additional information, culling a variety of official and private records along the way.

In what was called "the greatest single effort" ever made in connection with the history project, Thomas F. Savage, the Bancroft Library's chief Spanish interpreter, directed twelve men for the year it took them to copy extracts from official records of Spanish California, consisting of 400-500 volumes in the possession of the United States Surveyor-General in San Francisco.[3]

Savage and three assistants copied in a month the mission records held by the Archbishop of San Francisco. Other Bancroft agents and employees copied records at missions all over the state.

Bancroft and Oak sailed to San Diego early in 1874 and returned overland to San Francisco, visiting depositories of records enroute.

The collection of California material, at first so vast as to be awesome, was now well in hand and Bancroft's attention shifted to the Pacific Northwest.

In May and June of 1878, he toured British Columbia, Oregon, and Washington Territory. Official records were opened to him, and he interviewed early settlers and prominent people. Others gave him their personal papers, including several who had planned to write a history of the region.

Among those Bancroft most wanted to see in Portland was Frances Fuller Victor, whose writings on Oregon he considered "by far the best extant."[4] But she was on the southern coast gathering information for the revision of her book, *All Over Oregon and Washington*.

After returning to San Francisco in early July, Bancroft wrote to offer her "an engagement" in his library.[5]

Frances hesitated. She had been gathering information since 1865 for her own history of Oregon, and did not want to sacrifice it.

"As I had prepared by a long study of my subject to write a history of Oregon which should be standard, I felt a good deal cut up by having my field invaded by another, not so well prepared, but who had a plump exchequer and an army of assistants," she later remarked. "It was useless to compete with such superior forces, and . . . rather than have my previous work lost I consented to join his corps of writers, taking as my division Oregon history."[6]

In a letter on 1 August 1878 Bancroft told Mrs. Victor how he intended to conduct the work of the library, and promised only to acknowledge his assistants' help by printing biographical notices of them in a summing-up volume at the end. He explained:

> When all the material I have is gone over and notes taken according to the general plan, I shall give one person one thing or one part to write, and another person another part.
>
> The work is wholly mine. I do what I can myself, and pay for what I have done over that; but I father the whole of it and it goes out only under my name. All who work in the library do so simply as my assistants. Their work

is mine to print, scratch, or throw in the fire. I have no secrets; yet I do not tell everybody just what each does. I do not pretend to do all the work myself, that is, to prepare for the printer all that goes out under my name. I have three or four now who can write for the printer after a fashion; none of them can suit me as well as I can suit myself. One or two only will write with very little change from me. All the rest require sometimes almost rewriting.[7]

These terms did not bother Frances at the time. In 1878, it was estimated the history proper would comprise fourteen volumes at most. No one knew that it would ultimately almost triple in size.

On October 20, anticipating the challenge of finally getting her Oregon history into print, Mrs. Victor left Portland aboard the steamship *Great Republic* for San Francisco, where in the next few years she would perform the crowning work of her life.

Three days later Frances arrived at the Golden Gate, and soon was at work on the fifth floor of the Market Street building that housed Bancroft's publishing establishment. The large amount of historical material she brought from Oregon was added to the Bancroft Library collection.

Bancroft often stood at his desk writing for eleven or twelve hours each day, but he did not expect Mrs. Victor to stand and furnished her with a private study.

As Frances began to sift the information available in the library, she encountered many problems. On 8 December 1878 she wrote her friend Judge Deady, upon whom she relied heavily to supplement material in the Bancroft collection:

I have not yet seen your dictation to Mr. Bancroft — there is such a mass of matter here that it will take a long time to wade through it. A good deal, however, is comparatively useless and not to the point. There are two things that I particularly want done. 1$\underline{st}$ Somebody to take the Oregon archives from the beginning to the formation of the state government, and go through them with comments on the acts of the legislature, that is where an act was of sufficient importance to deserve comment. Of course I can see the act, but I cannot know the motive or the circumstances that prompted it. Who could do this for me?

2$\underline{d}$ I want biographies of all the men of any mark, in early times and later. How am I to get them? . . . Will the Digest of Oregon Laws help me in the history of legislation? . . .

I should be glad of pen pictures of the first Territorial officers. How is the Statesman for clear facts? It is so hard to steer a way between two partisan papers like the Statesman and Oregonian, and do everybody evenhanded justice. Write to me of these things. Of course this is Mr. Bancroft's history, but I am getting everything in shape as he never could — not being so familiar with the ground — and if we agree about it when I am ready to begin, I shall probably write it. In any case it is my conscientious desire to do my work faithfully.

"By the way," Frances added sadly, for the debate was raging over whether or not to call the Willamette River by its original Indian name and she and Judge Deady favored the latter, "Mr. B. will not allow Wallamet — says custom rules. It cuts me to the quick to write <u>Will</u> + <u>ette</u>, but I have to do it."[8]

Mrs. Victor became so immersed in her subject that, she admitted later, she gave little thought to who would actually receive credit for her work.

A few months after her job began, Bancroft told her that he expected to "father everything" produced in his library.[9]

Frances was taken aback. She was the only writer on Bancroft's staff who had a literary reputation before entering his service and was accustomed to being known as the author of her writings.

"Why, Mr. Bancroft," she asked, "do you not intend to give the names of your helpers on the title pages?"[10]

"That is just what I wish to avoid," he replied. Bancroft said that he planned to publish at the end of the series a volume entitled *Literary Industries* in which he would give each writer "a mention with my estimate of them."[11]

Mrs. Victor later remarked that Bancroft's intention "troubled me considerably. I did not know him well enough to judge how much or how little justice we should receive at his hands, nor could I learn until the work had been all done."[12]

Bancroft never promised explicitly to acknowledge his writers' work, nor did the writers consent to remain silent about their rights to recognition. But it was understood that they could keep their jobs only if they allowed Bancroft to claim their work as his own.

"This bread and butter argument for silence proved effective in all cases," a friend of Mrs. Victor later wrote.[13]

In 1879, Frances' letters revealed the progress she had made toward a clarified knowledge of Oregon history after a year's study of the materials available to her. To a friend, the historian Elwood Evans in Olympia, Washington Territory, Mrs. Victor wrote in December:

"I should be glad if you could go over some of my Oregon chapters — and you would be delighted. I have entirely and completely unravelled the tangles that troubled you (and me) in 1870. The whole story is plain as A.B.C. You would enjoy the unfolding."[14]

Mrs. Victor used as much of her own material as possible while preparing Bancroft's volumes on the Pacific Northwest. She enjoyed her work, but found it quite detailed, intricate and time consuming.

"Only those who have done such work can estimate the labor that goes into the writing of original history," she recalled. "I had no example before me of a complete history of Oregon. I had a mass of undigested material of all kinds — books of early travel and adventure, newspaper clippings, letters from pioneers, dictations hurriedly taken and 'recollections' of men and women who had been 'from the beginning' in the Oregon country. Some of this was undoubtedly authority, but some had to be proven. I had constantly to correspond with people whom I knew or did not know; and it did not take me long to find out that memory, like the human heart, was 'deceitful' if not 'desperately wicked.'"[15]

In a letter to Elwood Evans early in 1880, Frances more specifically described her work in the library and vented some of the frustration that she felt:

... I doubt if you would have the patience to work as one of Mr. Bancroft's assistants. Last year I wrote or worked fifty-one weeks every day except Sundays from 8 o'clock in the morning until 6 in the evening, with one hour at noon for exercise and luncheon. This year I am doing the same . . . I often wish to do something for myself . . . but have not the strength left. But I find time to write letters that concern my work — I write a good many to find out things, and put a good deal of material into the history that would otherwise not be there; in short, work just as conscientiously as if I were doing it for my own glory, and put into Mr. B's hands and under his name all the results of my long preparation for this particular work. Do I seem to grudge it? Well, sometimes I do — because it was my stock in trade which I cannot use over again, and I get nothing for it — only my very moderate monthly salary. However if I die before I've had a chance to do something for my own reputation, I hope a friend or two will give me a decent obituary![16]

Bancroft appreciated her dedication, and in *Literary Industries* he wrote: "I have found . . . Frances Fuller Victor, during her arduous labors for a period of ten years in my library, a lady of cultivated mind, of ability and singular application; likewise her physical endurance was remarkable."[17]

Inspired by the view she had in 1877 of wild scarlet poppies growing in a dry riverbed near the ruins of the Whitman Mission, Frances had also half finished work on a 1,000-line poem about the tragic events that occurred there thirty years before.

Mrs. Victor told Elwood Evans that she did not know what would become of the poem once it was completed.

"There is no market for such things," she confided, "and the interest in the theme would be chiefly local. I really do not know when it will be finished either — but if it were finished, printed and set afloat in a pretty little book it would not pay its expenses. Oh dear! that our inspirations should wait upon publishers."[18]

Frances sent several books requested by Evans, including her last copy of *All Over Oregon and Washington* published eight years before.

"I wanted to revise this book," she lamented, "but there is no money in it and I am in debt now for trying to do impossible things."[19]

For all the help Mrs. Victor had from note-takers, indexers and other staff in the library — and despite her own familiarity with the subject matter — she longed to meet the people involved, as she did in earlier days, and so reduce the chance for misunderstandings.

"Occasionally when I am writing up something I come to a point on which I am not quite clear, and wish I were doing my work in Oregon instead of California," she told Judge Deady in April.[20]

By early 1880, Frances had written most of the first of two volumes on Oregon history.

Spanning the fifteen years between 1832-1847, when Americans began to settle in the region prior to its coming under federal jurisdiction as a territory, the volume was Mrs. Victor's most thorough study. The *History of Oregon I* was also the first of the state histories written in the Bancroft Library, and in it Frances helped set the pattern for the others. It was she who made a point of including biographical footnotes of all the pioneers possible and a list of each year's immigration.

While collecting information for her history of Oregon, Frances was assisted by such well-known and influential pioneer families as the Applegates and McBrides, as well as Judge Deady and Elwood Evans. Valuable material concerning the Hudson's Bay Company domination of the early Oregon Country was provided by George B. Roberts, for many years head clerk of the company in Vancouver, with whom Mrs. Victor corresponded for several years.

The Bancroft Library included an extensive file of papers from the Sandwich (Hawaiian) Islands, and Frances gleaned much information that was useful in her study of Oregon history. Many years later she recalled:

> . . . I have no doubt if the proper records were searched we should find a good deal of our unwritten history shadowed forth in brief paragraphs under the head of "shipping news" in newspapers both foreign and domestic . . . The Sandwich Island Gazette in the '40s . . . was a considerable aid to me, seeing that all the vessels to the Columbia touched at the Islands in those days. All the whaling vessels also, and the China traders left some mention of themselves to be chronicled in the shipping news of the Gazette.[21]

Frances had to use more matter than she wanted from the Bancroft Library and newspaper files while preparing manuscript for *History of Oregon II*, which dealt with people, events and developments in the period 1848-1888.

She relied more than before upon her friends in Oregon and Washington for original data, as well as for clarification and resolution of discrepancies in the material directly available to her.

"Do not let me trespass on your time and patience," she admonished Judge Deady in a letter on 17 June 1880. "I know you give all the aid possible — and I am busy enough myself to understand the difficulty of doing extra work."[22]

As Mrs. Victor's knowledge of Pacific Northwest history deepened and expanded, her standards for judging evidence became ever more exacting.

"The course of my studies for several years has been such that I have disenchanted myself of many groundless impressions; and my love of ideality is changed to a reverence for truth, pure and simple," she explained to Elwood Evans in February 1881. "Whatever cannot stand the test is worthless."[23]

It was about then that Hubert Howe Bancroft decided to begin publication of the histories in 1882. Henry L. Oak, who had direct charge of operations in the library, argued for a postponement so that there might be no haste in locating and digesting facts. But the publisher — restless at the prospect of a deferred return on his large financial investment and fearful also that through some calamity the work would never be completed — was adamant.

Mrs. Victor saw that data was lacking on Oregon's institutional history, and she wanted to return to the state to make further collections, but Bancroft would not allow the additional time and expense.

Frances was especially disturbed that an emissary was not sent to gather material for a chapter she wanted to write on the Oregon Steam Navigation Company.

Soon after its founding in 1860, the O.S.N. Co. monopolized passenger and cargo traffic on the Columbia and Willamette rivers. By the time it was absorbed in 1879 by Henry Villard's transportation empire — which aggregated ocean, river and rail routes — the company had acquired increased and diverse interests, and was rightly considered by Mrs. Victor as an important factor in Oregon's development as a state.

Meanwhile, Bancroft had persuaded the elders of the Mormon Church that he was not prejudiced against them and asked Orson B. Pratt, the church's official historian, for material the publisher needed for a prospective volume on the history of Utah.

John Taylor, president of the church, called a council of its twelve apostles, who agreed to comply with the request; and in 1880 Franklin D. Richards came to San Francisco, as Professor Pratt's personal representative, to furnish the Bancroft Library with any desired information.

The original intention was for Mrs. Victor to write the volume on Utah because, during her years on the plains, she had made a study of early Mormon history through coming in contact with some refugees from Nauvoo, Illinois.

"The story of Utah . . . was in the first place assigned to me," Frances recalled, "and, as Mr. Richards can testify, when he came to San Francisco, bringing with him the archives of the Mormon Church, I had almost daily interviews with him and Mrs. Richards for about a fortnight."[24]

Mrs. Victor "was at that time engaged on the history of Oregon." But before she "reached a point where I could have taken up Utah" she had been given too much other work, and so the task befell Alfred Bates, "a scholarly and serious minded man," another staff writer in the library.[25]

"There were certain things in the story of Utah that I shrunk from contemplating," Frances added, "but which I should have been forced to tell, with or without extenuating circumstances."[26]

For protection against fire, the library, on 9 October 1881, was moved from its perch on the fifth, and topmost, floor of Bancroft's Market Street publishing firm to what he described as "a substantial two story and basement brick building, forty by sixty feet," that had been specially constructed for the purpose.[27]

On the ground floor were arranged 16,000 volumes encompassing voyages and travels, documents and periodicals, public papers of the federal government and states and territories of the West, laws, briefs and legal reports, scrapbooks, almanacs, directories, bound collections of pamphlets, cumbersome folios, and other miscellany.

Three high double-tiered shelves, loaded with 500 bulky files of Pacific states' newspapers, extended across the room from north to south.

There also was a large case, with drawers for maps geographically arranged. Other cases housed the card index, and the alphabetic and chronological file of paper bags containing notes and references, which enabled the library's writers to quickly evaluate their sources and decide if additional information was needed.

The second story, containing the main library and workroom, was reached via a central staircase. A dozen writers and library aides were seated at tables, working at their special tasks.

On the west side of the room, opposite Bancroft's private study, were the offices of Henry L. Oak — who still acted as librarian, business agent during most of the intercourse with the publishing house, and reviser of the final proofs of all the volumes — William Nemos, a talented writer who now also exercised day-to-day supervision over the library staff; and Mrs. Victor.

Shelving nine tiers high lined the walls. Most of this space was occupied by the working library — books alphabetically arranged and numbered consecutively from one to 12,000. A master catalog was prepared, indicating "the shelf position of every book in the library," Bancroft noted, "and the plan admits of additions almost limitless without breaking the alphabetic order."[28]

Also on the second floor were about 400 rare books, "set apart by reason of their great value, not merely pecuniary, . . . but literary value, representing standard authorities, bibliographic curiosities, specimens of early printing, and rare linguistics."[29]

Manuscripts aggregating 1,200 volumes in three subdivisions — Mexico and Central America, California, and the Northwest Coast (Oregon and the interior, British Columbia and Alaska) — were there, too, as well as 450 reference and bibliographic works.

Bancroft estimated that his library contained 35,000 volumes in 1881. There were almost 50,000 by the time the history project neared completion nine years later.*

"Regular business hours were kept in the library," Bancroft wrote, ". . . from eight to twelve, and from one to six. Smoking was freely allowed. Certain assistants desired to work evenings and draw extra pay. This was permitted in some instances, but always under protest."[30]

Eventually such work was banned altogether — on grounds that nine hours of literary labor each day was tiring enough, and that efficiency did not noticeably increase thereafter.

---

*Years afterward, when it was suggested that Oregonians might raise enough money to purchase the library, Frances was asked for advice on how to approach Bancroft. He had already offered it to the State of California for $500,000 in 1887; then there was talk that eastern investors would buy it for $300,000; and finally the Chicago Library offered $150,000. But none of these offers were satisfactory, and Mrs. Victor suggested that Bancroft be asked the lowest figure he would take and that would be acceptable for a memorial library.

"As to the *value* of the books I should think he would be justified in asking $250,000, as such collections go," Frances wrote in January 1902. "But there are a good many books of no great worth, purchased on the chance of finding something in them — and they swelled the list. . . . Mr. B. claimed that his catalogue contained 30,000 authorities. Many of these were no more than leaflets, yet as valuable to the writer as a costly volume of several hundred pages. What they cost him is one thing — what they are worth another. He had to pay agents for collecting, as well as to pay for the books." *Victor to Young, 2 January 1902.*

On the day after the Bancroft Library was transferred to the Valencia Street repository, the printers began work on the first volume of the history series — *Central America I* — which was immediately followed by *Mexico I.*

Bancroft sent to press whatever was available, so that frequently parts of several volumes were in type at one time. When printing began, manuscript totaling fifteen volumes was ready — *Mexico, Central America, California, Oregon, Alaska, Literary Industries* and *Northwest Coast.* He estimated at this time that notes had been taken for three-fourths of the works still to be written.

"I suppose you have seen the frequent notices of the Bancroft history," Mrs. Victor remarked sardonically in a 1 November 1882 letter to her friend Judge Deady. "There will be a fortune spent in advertising."[31]

In May 1883, Bancroft sent Judge Deady and a few other Oregon men who knew the state's history the proofs of *Oregon I* for criticism.

A month later, Frances wrote the judge that she was glad he was reading the proofs and hoped he would get the second volume also, for in *that* volume there would be even more reason to make corrections. Then she added some comments on Bancroft's editing of her work:

> I find that Mr. B. is given to making disparaging remarks not really necessary to the truth of history of some of the most prominent men of early times, such as Pratt and Lane.* Whenever he alters anything I have written it is usually to put in a paragraph of that kind. He made particular war on Pratt, using such words as "infamous" and "disgusting," and where I had given Pratt some just praise, cut it out entirely. It is a piece of personal malice, because Pratt would contribute nothing to the history. On the other hand he was well pleased with Thornton because he was anxious to furnish as much material as possible, with the object of being immortalized. I happened to know Thornton well enough to weigh his evidence carefully, or whatever he said about being author of the land law, and other misstatements would have gone in more as he desired. What I am getting at is to put you on your watch for these passages, and that you may criticize them when the proofs go to you. Mr. B. will regard your remarks, knowing that he is under obligations to you, besides having a high opinion of your knowledge and attainments. I should have said further about the Pratt business that I used your name to get him to take out some of the most obnoxious expressions. He calls Lane an "Indian butcher" and the like, which is not, as I tell him, historically true, but Lane is dead, and will never buy a set of the histories.[32]

By August 1884, Mrs. Victor had almost completed the second volume of Oregon history. Nevada, Colorado and Wyoming were in prospect. Bancroft was gathering material there and wrote Frances on September 11, instructing her to familiarize herself with the region's history.

The *History of Nevada, Colorado and Wyoming* received more attention than earlier works because it was written under Bancroft's immediate supervision, and he himself collected and forwarded material from the field as required. That Bancroft also wanted the work done in the least

*For biographies, see pp. 242-243.

possible time with the least possible cost is abundantly clear in his letters
to Mrs. Victor on how he wanted the volume prepared.

"I am rusticating my wits among the sage-brush of Nevada just now
— on paper, of course — and expect soon to take up Colorado," she
informed Judge Deady seven months later.[33]

In October 1885, Nemos was told to count the number of pages Mrs.
Victor had written since entering the library. Frances resented this proce-
dure, because she considered it an unjust basis for evaluating her historical work.

On the 20th, Bancroft asked her to bring the draft "at first writing within
the requisite compass so as not to make it so terribly costly."[34] About two
weeks later he stated that if she were to write three volumes more, the
history project could be finished in three years instead of six. Frances had
a very different view of the situation. Having already worked out many
of the problems in Oregon history before joining Bancroft's staff, she was
able to write those two volumes with dispatch. But now that she was entering a new field she found she needed more time. That Bancroft did not
allow for this was shown in a letter he wrote Mrs. Victor in mid-November.
He was not dissatisfied with her work, nor had anyone even faintly criticized it; he just wanted to complete the project before he was dead or
failed in business. He went on:

> I do not know when the present volume will be finished ready for the
> printer. But six years have already passed, and, calling this volume done, it
> would be two years to a volume. About fifteen hundred of your pages make
> a volume, I believe, and counting three hundred days to the year, would be
> two and a half pages a day. When you first came, you started off with ten
> pages, which we all thought rapid, but the outcome makes it exceedingly small.
> This, with what other work has been done on your volumes, would make
> every page of your manuscript ready for the printer cost me considerably
> over two dollars a page.[35]

After denying that this was a complaint about the past, Bancroft told Frances:

> Go on and do the best you can. I have written equivalent to six volumes
> during the last six years besides devoting my time to revising and outside mat-
> ters. But I don't expect any one to work as I do. I am not satisfied with old
> hands now, however, who do not give me say, four or five pages a day all
> ready for the printer.[36]

The writing of the Nevada, Colorado and Wyoming volume, so far as
the available material permitted, was finished at the end of 1885. Despite
all the care that had been taken, however, the Colorado portion had to
be condensed by one-third — a simple matter of using small type and printing the text as footnotes — to make it fit the space allowed.

Early Oregon history, which was Mrs. Victor's specialty, took in Washington and much of Idaho and Montana, as did her writings.

By 1886, Frances had completed most of the work she did for Bancroft.
Her contribution to his histories is even more significant when one con-
siders that the original manuscripts of *Oregon I* and *II*, and the section
on Washington, were all much longer than their printed versions.

In a "confidential" letter to Elwood Evans, she made some interesting comments about Bancroft's editing of her draft on Washington history:

> . . . It was my wish, and judgement, that Washington should have a volume to herself. Mr. B. however, finding that his work was going to be so extensive, decided to cut it down (after it was written) and put it into the vol with Idaho and Montana. Still as the earlier hist. of Wash. is contained in that of Or. it is pretty full as it is. But I was disappointed, thinking that you, Swan, and others would be so, because Mr. B. took out of Wash. the chapter on the San Juan difficulty, and, also a chapter on the Puget Sound Agric. Association, to make room, and put them in other vols of the Northwest Coast. He also cut down to nothing, almost, the account of the Stevens and Wool war which I had written out fully.* He changed my estimate of Stevens, apparently without any good reason — about the only important change of coloring given anywhere.[37]

Although written six years earlier, not until October 1886 did *Oregon I* appear in its designated place in the sequence of the histories. A fearful calamity had threatened publication even then, for an April 30th fire gutted the Bancroft publishing house on Market Street, causing an estimated $500,000 damage that insurance would not cover.

Twenty volumes had been issued by then. The publisher was still $200,000 behind on the history project, but gaining.

"Suddenly, office, stock, papers, correspondence, printing-presses, type and plates, and the vast book-bindery, filled with sheets and books in every stage of binding, were blotted out, as if seized by Satan and hurled into the jaws of hell," Bancroft wrote. "There was not a book left; there was not a volume of history saved; nine volumes of history plates were destroyed, besides a dozen other volumes of plates; two car loads of history paper had just come in, and 12,000 bound volumes were devoured by the flames. There was the enterprise left, and a dozen volumes of the history plates in the library basement, and that was all."**[38]

The account books had been saved from the burning building, however, and operations were reorganized to more efficiently carry on the publisher's various enterprises. The firm of Bancroft and Company supervised the business aspects. The literary work, which had been a department of the general book concern, was now managed by The History Company, a corporation Bancroft organized for the purpose.

Both the manuscript and plates for *Oregon I* were lost in the blaze, but by good fortune two of the first copies of the book off the press had been taken to the library on Valencia Street. The type was reset from them.

*See p. 253.

**Henry L. Oak, who retired in 1887 after eighteen years in the library, recalled in 1893 that "in those years Mr. Bancroft's prospective wealth was considered by all, and represented by himself, as exceedingly problematic; and after the fire all my hopes could have been cashed at a very low rate. But his financial recovery was remarkably rapid . . . and he is now by far a richer man than ever before — several times a millionaire by his own estimate." Henry L. Oak, *"Literary Industries" in a New Light*, p. 65.

In reply to a congratulatory note from Judge Deady on the publication of her work, Mrs. Victor made additional observations on Bancroft's editorial methods:

> As far as I could, I made note of each immigration as it came, giving names. I had done this down to 1852, but after '48 they were cut out for want of room — and then Mr. Bancroft decided to add at the end of each vol. in the manner you complain of, everybody who subscribes! It is poor taste, but he thinks it necessary to financial success. The plan I followed was to include everybody in the immigrations and whoever made himself notable afterwards was duly mentioned in the place where he did something to signalize himself. . . .
>
> I labored under the disadvantage of having my ms reduced by another — Mr. B. performing this editorial work. As he did not always take in the value of certain matter, and as my ms overran terribly, he slashed in the wrong places often, and I knew nothing of it until it came before me in the galleys and could be changed but slightly afterwards. But considering all things, I do believe the history is more nearly correct than any original history you can point to before the Bancroft series was begun, and I am glad to have your favorable judgement upon it.[39]

In May 1887, Bancroft was planning to publish at the end of the history series a biographical work to present in detail the lives of wealthy or influential men who had gained prominence in the western states. These individuals were charged $1,000-$10,000, for between three and thirty pages of print plus a portrait engraved on steel.

The biographies, originally called *Chronicles of the Kings*, were published under the title *Chronicles of the Builders of the Commonwealth*.

When it became known afterwards that Bancroft accepted money for the notices, he lost the regard of the Pacific coast press. Grave doubts were expressed about his objectivity as a historian, and many bitter — sometimes utterly false — statements damaged the reputation built on the patient literary labor he had sponsored and nourished for almost twenty years.

By 1888, Bancroft's promotion scheme was making Frances restless. She disapproved of a money-making project where men paid large fees to be included, especially since the publisher did not increase her salary.

"I am not fairly treated by the History Company, which sends all of the most difficult work to my desk and never advances my pay," Mrs. Victor complained to Judge Deady.[40]

"Mr. Bancroft has never paid for my services more than $100 per month, less than a copyist in the City Hall would be paid," she wrote from San Francisco. "I have asked several times for an increase of pay, without receiving any, but he has very artfully so contrived that I have not been able to release myself [from his service]. Of course the longer I remain the harder it will be for me to start afresh."[41]

Frances explained that when the plan was first discussed, she understood Bancroft to say that if she remained on his staff she would have the literary work on the *Chronicles* at better pay. But when she returned from a trip to the East, she found that various parts were already being written, and she was given transportation and railroads to do.

"When . . . the subject of pay came up he excused himself to Mr. Nemos (the manager in the Library) by saying that I had gone east to endeavor to get a better situation, and failed, and he would not do more than he had done," she told Judge Deady in December. "I was sick when I came home, having been laid up at Los Angeles of fever, and my funds were exhausted, so there was nothing for it but to do the first thing at hand when I was sufficiently recovered to resume work. Besides I had left some of the California history incomplete, and felt a sort of obligation to finish it."[42]

When biographical material for the *Chronicles* started arriving at the library, Mrs. Victor wrote a few at the request of Bancroft's sales agents — and they "were perfectly satisfied and successful with them." She saw that "bushels of money" were to be made in this undertaking, and decided not to do any more until she received proper compensation for her efforts.

"This raised a tempest when Mr. B. came to hear of it especially as the other gentlemen were all on my side," she wrote. "Mr. B. went so far as to order all communication with me cut off; but not the less I have been kept informed. He . . . came into my room and removed all the new dictations, in order to remove the plea for better pay, and left me the transportation work to do, which will occupy me for a few months longer."[43]

Mrs. Victor wrote over 400 pages of manuscript on transportation, which with relatively minor editing by Bancroft was published in the *Chronicles of the Builders* as chapters eight and nine of volume V and chapters one, three, four, six, seven, eight, nine and fourteen of volume VI.

"Transportation section including railroads and biographies of men connected with them will complete all the work I have in hand or shall ever attempt — I would not for the world have anything interfere with your finishing that work," Bancroft assured her.[44] But she noted wryly that he continued to solicit business, using one of her biographies as an example of the work he would do.

In April 1889, Bancroft was in Colorado "drumming up Kings," as Mrs. Victor put it.[45] She had not seen him for two months, but had already declined an invitation to work on another of his projects at the same salary and hours as before ("No" was how she described her reaction in a letter to Judge Deady), and she looked forward to being on her own again in a few weeks. "I rather long to see my name in print once more," she confided.[46]

Deady was angry about a carelessly handled biographical sketch of him in the *Chronicles*, and he blamed Mrs. Victor for not correcting it even though she had no connection with the work.

"It would be a loss to me to forfeit your good opinion, as the broadminded intelligence, and cultivation of taste met with in you was for several years of a painful and arid life one of my enjoyments," she reassured him in one of several letters that passed between them on the subject.[47]

Although pleased with the encouragement given by friends and correspondents who knew of her labors, the general lack of recognition that her work received still rankled Frances.

"I do not want for myself the credit due to my assistants," Bancroft reiterated in a note to her soon after *Oregon I* was published. "At the same time, I do not deem it necessary to explain to the public just what part of the work was done by each. Everybody knows that you have been at work on Oregon, and that is all right, although I have done considerable work on your manuscript for better or worse, or at all events to make it conform to the general plan."[48]

Mrs. Victor believed that the publisher's condensation, by deleting some of her material and placing other parts in different volumes, did not affect her claims to authorship.

"[S]ometimes . . . he altered what I had said to make it suit some opinion of his own, or for some other reason . . . [and] if he was displeased with a certain man for a purely personal reason, he [punished] him by leaving him out of history or by making him obnoxious," she recalled.[49]

Frances said that although future readers of her work would not know of these discrepancies, "still I regret their existence."[50]

Bancroft's technique involved selecting "certain parts for omission — much as if an artist should reduce the size of a painting by cutting out a rock here and a tree there," according to Henry L. Oak, for eighteen years librarian, superintendent of the history project and himself author of ten volumes.[51]

"If you have seen the several eastern reviews which generally persist in giving Bancroft the sole credit of the histories written in his library and under his name," Mrs. Victor told Elwood Evans, "you will understand that here, on our own coast, I am anxious to receive more justice than simply to be mentioned in the last of the series as one of the several who have done nobody knows what."[52]

She asked if Evans — "without disparaging Mr. Bancroft's ability, enterprise, ambition, or deserts" — would write a review of Oregon I and mention her "as having had an important place in the corps of writers on Mr. B's works, and particularly, on Oregon and all the Northwest . . . This should be done in justice to my long continued study of, and labor for this region; and to give me a position whereby I may secure other work if necessary."[53]

Mrs. Victor had expected her work in the library to end sometime late in 1886. She was considered especially good as a political writer, however, and helped prepare the American portion of the History of California. During the next two years, according to her own estimate, Frances wrote 234 pages on politics for volume VI (chapters three, four, five, twelve, thirteen, twenty-three and twenty-four) and 489 pages on politics and railroads for volume VII (chapters nine to twenty-one inclusive and twenty-five). A complete history of the Modoc Indian War of 1872-1873 in southern Oregon, written by Mrs. Victor from notes she obtained on the ground, took up all but ten pages of "Some Indian Episodes," a chapter in California Inter Pocula.

"She had the enviable faculty of putting life into her writings," a friend commented, "and it was partially on account of her graceful style that Mr. Bancroft sought her services, for his eye was always attracted by good literary work. But the volumes written by Mrs. Victor were of a far different stamp from the popular literary history. . . . All who were acquainted with her personally recognized the fact that she placed the truth as she conceived it before all else. The leading opponents of the stand she took on disputed questions freely recognized the fact that she had striven to do conscientious, painstaking work. Given to speaking what she believed was the whole truth, even when it was contrary to her immediate interest to do so, she was the last of all persons whom a regard for literary effect would swerve from the path of historical accuracy."[54]

In 1893, four volumes written by Mrs. Victor for the Bancroft history series were exhibited in San Francisco and at the World's Columbian Exposition in Chicago. Her name had been placed on the back of each book, and in a special preface she explained why.*

This action, she observed later, won approval from "gentlemen in the historical service."[55] One of them was Henry Oak, chief assistant to Bancroft for the history project, who wrote that for her to claim credit for such volumes as she had written was "entirely justifiable and proper."[56]

"As a whole I am willing to let my work stand, though I had not always had my way about it," Frances stated.

"If I had been able to place my name where it properly belongs on these . . . volumes I should have made an international reputation."[57]

Bancroft steadfastly denied that Mrs. Victor "wrote any finished work" for him.[58] But he did concede that she "furnished . . . much valuable raw material in a crude form, which I put into suitable condition for publication, according to my general plan."[59]

Frances expressed pleasure that her contribution of material was

> at least admitted. It was material, too, that I had spent years in collecting, and for which I received no compensation. Perhaps that was my own fault. But I am not good at bargaining, and no compensation was ever offered. I can truthfully say that whatever knowledge of Oregon history Mr. Bancroft possesses, he obtained from me. I do not mention that fact as a conspicuous defect in his education, for there was not much known on the subject 25 years ago, and at best, not every one can be a historian, but because I am fond of my work and am grieved that through too much editing it has failed somewhat of my purpose in performing a long and serious labor.[60]

---

*It is well known, Mr. Bancroft having set it forth in his *Literary Industries*, that the series of Pacific Coast Histories employed the talents and labors of a number of writers besides himself. As one of those writers whose individual work is not acknowledged, being called upon to state what literary work I have done for the Pacific Coast, it seems not only just but necessary to affix my name to at least four volumes of the *History of the Pacific States*, although this does not cover all the work done on the *History* by myself. The four volumes referred to comprise the states of Oregon, Washington, Idaho, Montana, Colorado, Wyoming and Nevada. My name is therefore placed on the backs of these volumes, without displacing that of Mr. Bancroft.

Frances Fuller Victor.

24

A Court Case

On 22 March 1883 attorneys for Mrs. Victor and Mary Edwards V. Sampson, a daughter and only child of her husband by previous marriage, filed papers in Columbia County Circuit Court to oppose a suit seeking review of a federal court decision that made the women part owners of the townsite of St. Helens and several hundred acres of land in Columbia and Multnomah counties.

In November 1865, Frances' husband purchased the townsite of St. Helens, on the Columbia River in northwestern Oregon, with prize money he had received from the federal government for helping to capture a British steamer trying to run a Union blockade of the port of Charleston, South Carolina. In April of the following year, he entered into joint ownership, with Frank A. Davis, of property in Columbia and Multnomah counties.

Henry Clay Victor's last will, admitted to probate after his death in a steamboat accident in 1875, named his wife as executrix; and to her and Mrs. Sampson he bequeathed his share of the land.

On 4 December 1877 Mrs. Victor, and her stepdaughter in Ohio, asked the U.S. District Court in Portland to enforce their claim, against Frank A. Davis and his brother Walter. The law firm of Addison C. Gibbs acted as solicitors for the women in the case. It was Gibbs who, as governor of Oregon thirteen years before, piqued Frances' interest in the history of the state by suggesting she write a book about it to correct false impressions in the East.

"To enable . . . H.C. Victor and . . . Frank A. Davis to sell and convey [the] property without delay or hindrance the deeds for [the] property were taken in the name of . . . H.C. Victor alone and that he held the legal title to said lands by deeds absolute on their face but in fact he was a trustee for . . . Davis of the undivided one half of the lands so owned by them," Mesdames Victor and Sampson alleged in their complaint.[1]

Before 15 May 1867, the two women claimed, Henry Clay Victor and Frank A. Davis jointly owned, in equal shares, the entire townsite known as the "St. Helens Land Claim" and 680 acres of "coal land" in Columbia County, six miles west of St. Helens; also two-thirds of 441 acres of property in Multnomah County. On that date the two men agreed, for business reasons, the legal title should stand in Davis's name alone and that he should hold an undivided one-half of the property, with a value thought to exceed $5,000, in trust for Victor.

The women further alleged that Frank A. Davis, by transferring the deed to his brother on 4 May 1870, had intended to defraud H.C. Victor of his property or those claiming under him their rights to the land.

The defendants, in California, did not contest the matter, despite extended publication of notice and efforts to serve subpoenas, and after seven months Judge Matthew P. Deady decided that the statements made by Mesdames Victor and Sampson in their complaint would be taken as true.

When the judge finally announced his ruling, on 7 October 1878, he decreed that Mrs. Victor and her stepdaughter owned in fee simple an undivided two-thirds of the contested real estate, but required Frank A. Davis and Walter S. Davis to convey title to the undivided one-half of the property which the ladies claimed to own.

A year or so later, when Frances finally got the documents to compare, she was horrified to discover that Judge Deady's order left out forty acres which the complaint said was hers. She tried repeatedly to have her attorneys correct the decree, but without success.

"They took their fee, and they do not propose to finish their work," Frances complained to a friend. "The land I wish to sell, but cannot until it is in proper shape."[2]

Mrs. Victor also was concerned about the status of tide land, in front of her St. Helens property, on which the Columbia River rose and fell, and wondered if people could legally claim it.

"The pirates are getting it all away from me," she stated, "and I have written to the Commissioners about it, and made application myself for what is left; but I wish to know if the land is really open to such seizure. If so, it is abominable. If I could have gotten any satisfaction out of my feed attorneys I would have remained discreetly silent, but that seems impossible any longer."[3]

One of her own attorneys even deeded to himself some land which Frances managed to redeem from tax sale. This was just one of the many annoyances she had to endure, and that were "not mentionable" in a private letter.[4]

In the Columbia County suit, Frances and Mrs. Sampson asked the circuit court to affirm the federal decree that they owned one-half the disputed property, a quarter share each, and that Walter S. Davis owned one-sixth and his attorney Columbia Lancaster one-third. The women also wanted the court to appoint referees to so partition the land, and apportion all costs and expenses according to law and equity.

Davis countered that the proceedings in U.S. District Court, from which he said all claims and rights of the women to the land were derived, were invalid.

For one thing, he contended, Judge Deady erred in crediting Mesdames Victor and Sampson with two-thirds of the property, when they claimed to own only a half interest. Davis alleged that the federal court's order was not published, nor was the affidavit of publication made, according to law. Then, too, the U.S. District Court lacked jurisdiction because the defendants did not live in Oregon, "nor were they or either of them found in said district nor did they or either of them voluntarily appear in said suit."[5] The federal court did not make reasonable efforts to have one of the defendants appear and respond to the suit, Davis said, and had also failed to show that no one seemed to be in charge or possession of at least some part of the property. None of these individuals had been served with the court's order, he added.

"This Deft avers that at the time said order was made + ever since persons were + have been in possession of portions of the property . . . holding under + through the Defts in said suit," the brief filed with the circuit court read.[6]

Columbia Lancaster, reputedly the long-time attorney for Frank A. Davis, held a one-third share through Walter S. Davis who said he purchased the land from his brother in 1870. At the time of the U.S. District Court suit Lancaster was said to have been residing nearby, in Washington Territory. Walter S. Davis purportedly was in Los Angeles. Both men insisted they had no knowledge of the suit or its outcome until more than a year after Judge Deady issued his ruling.

Davis revealed that on 16 May 1867 his brother agreed to convey a half interest in the Columbia and Multnomah properties if Mrs. Victor's husband would pay $6,000 within two years. Apparently, no part of the money was ever paid; and on 16 June 1868, in San Francisco, Henry C. Victor acknowledged receipt of $1,000 in U.S. gold coin from Frank A. Davis for a release from all conditions of the agreement made thirteen months before. The document was verified by the signatures of two witnesses.

The Columbia County Circuit Court was asked to declare the federal court decree void and of no effect, to deny the plaintiffs' request for partition, to grant Davis ownership of the disputed property, and award "such other further or different relief as to the court may seem meet with equity and good conscience, and that the defendant have from the plaintiffs his costs and disbursements."[7]

On Tuesday, 15 April 1884, in St. Helens, the matter came before Circuit Judge A.S. Bennett for trial. Judge Bennett agreed that the federal court lacked jurisdiction, and ruled in favor of the defendants. Lawyers for Frances Fuller Victor and Mary E.V. Sampson on September 6 served notice of intent to appeal to the Oregon Supreme Court. Records of the case were prepared, and filed with the court early in December.

"The defendant shows no excuse for waiting five years before bringing his suit," one of the attorneys asserted. "His delay is unreasonable, and his case is one where courts of equity will refuse relief."[8]

The two women and D.W. Williams, a Portland merchant and long-time friend of Mrs. Victor, promised to pay all damages, costs and disbursements, to the extent of $250, that might be awarded against them on the appeal.

Attorneys for the two parties argued the case before the Oregon Supreme Court on 29 January 1885 in Salem. The justices next day decided there was "not error as alleged," that the circuit court judgment "be in all things affirmed," and that Walter S. Davis and Columbia Lancaster were entitled to recover their surety.[9] Frances was bitterly disappointed by the court's decision. "You know, of course, that I have lost my case, my property, and all the hard-earned money I ventured in the attempt to save it," she remarked in a letter to Judge Deady on April 25. "Had Gibbs in the first place attended to his duty properly the point on which the decision turned could not have been made; and had Lancaster not laid a plot to work himself into my place through that error the case would have remained where it came from your court. Such is a woman's chance in this man's world. I am dreadfully vexed, and I must add dreadfully discouraged, also."[10]

25

"Atlantis Arisen"

Mrs. Victor resigned from The History Company in May 1889, and with a niece she spent several quiet weeks at Santa Cruz in the bright, bracing ocean air. Bancroft's selfishness had caused her to sever connection with the work "except on my own terms, which I do not expect to get."[1] She returned to San Francisco towards the end of July.

Frances kept many of the historical documents as well as other correspondence she had collected over the years, and by 1890 she was back in Oregon researching a new book.

She often was urged to revise and republish *All Over Oregon and Washington*, but almost twenty years had intervened and that book was "not only out of print, but out of date," due to the enormous changes brought about by the railroads.[2] She spent the spring and early summer months traveling in the region to gather updated information and observations, and not surprisingly found that practically a new book would be needed, although she utilized passages from her earlier writings to do justice to her subject.

To a newspaper reporter who interviewed her in Spokane in early June, about five weeks after she began her northern swing through Washington, Frances remarked that she hoped to have her manuscript ready for publication in the fall. "I have been delayed so long on the trip," she said. "There is so much to see, so many changes to note, that I find it impossible to get through and move on as rapidly as I had proposed when I first started out."[3]

In August 1890, Mrs. Victor wrote Judge Deady about the book she envisioned — about 400 pages long with a dozen or so illustrations; general in nature, descriptive, gossippy, historical, enough statistics to impress readers "with the possibilities and actualities" of the Pacific Northwest "and with enough about what is to be <u>seen</u> to attract tourists," she commented. ". . . It has cost me considerable effort, time and money so far, and now in order to get the work where it will do good — that is into print — will require more of all these, and certainly more money."[4]

Frances already had contacted several state officials and Chamber of Commerce members for funds to help her complete the work, but all told her no money was available. She felt that men who had money and interests in Oregon should create a fund "for this special book."[5] She contended a similar work, Charles Nordhoff's *California,* settled half that state and prompted tourists to visit.

"I want $500 just now to go at once to eastern publishers with the book and see it through the press," she told Deady. "It ought to be twice that amount, but perhaps I could manage with that, and argument. I do not know how to approach business men, or who to select to approach. Could not you aid [me] in this matter? Would not some of your friends among rich business men see the point? I put this request in writing because I am not sure of an opportunity to talk it over even should I call in person."[6]

On September 5th, she wrote the judge to acknowledge receipt of $200 in checks. A week later she and her manuscript were gone, by way of San Francisco, to the J.B. Lippincott Company of Philadelphia.

Mrs. Victor had received so little compensation for her work on the Bancroft history series, or from her writing in general, that she was forced to rely somewhat on the generosity and good-will of her many friends and acquaintances in the Pacific Northwest — although she insisted wherever possible upon paying her own way.

Frances filed for a pension under Act of Congress dated 27 June 1890, providing for widows and dependents of veterans of the nation's wars. Listed among her assets was a small amount of land in the town of St. Helens, and an unimproved lot on Central Avenue in Alameda, California. According to a statement she gave to the clerk of the U.S. District Court in Portland, and subsequently filed with the U.S. Pension Office in Washington, D.C.:

> . . . It is possible that one thousand dollars might be obtained for everything owned by her. No income is derived from any of it. Her support has depended on literary work, which is difficult to secure, and ill-paid on this coast. The income from this source barely suffices to maintain her from year to year, as the small amount saved in sixteen years would go to show. There is no regularity about it: it might be twelve hundred one year and four hundred another; or it might be almost nothing. One thing only is certain, that no provision for old age has been made, or could be made out of it.[7]

Harvey W. Scott, influential editor of the *Morning Oregonian*, took note of Mrs. Victor's financial plight. The editorial page of his paper helped to rally public support for her latest endeavor — "not as a gratuity, or personal favor," but because the Pacific Northwest had benefited from her literary work:

> . . . She has been writing on subjects pertaining to this region for nearly twenty years, has been repeatedly, and again recently, all over Oregon and the Northwest, and has a national reputation as an able and entertaining writer.
> . . . The interests of Oregon in so influential and permanent an advertisement ought to be fully represented, and it is but just that publication of the book should be properly encouraged and assisted here.[8]

Canvassers for J.K. Gill & Co., a well-known bookseller in the city, gathered names of subscribers; and the money was deposited in the First National Bank of Portland, to be drawn on by Mrs. Victor for the publishers.

After Frances returned from the East, and was waiting for her volume to be printed, she was stricken with malarial fever and confined to bed for several weeks at the home of Edward H. Kilham, a bookseller and long-time friend, 19th and "L" streets in East Portland, where she was staying. But as her condition improved she got restless and wanted to write again.

At hand was a genealogy of her family that occupied her at intervals over the years. On 2 October 1891 she asked Deady to return reference material he had borrowed, and that she now needed. She was disappointed to learn that "the book" seemed somehow to have vanished, but told the judge not to worry if it could not be found even though her "'patent of nobility'" went with it, "'and I do regret its loss.'"[9]

Copies of *Atlantis Arisen* were arriving in Portland by this time, and the *Morning Oregonian* issued a glowing review:

> . . . Mrs. Victor possesses not only elegance of style in description, a perfect ease in narration, but also rare discernment of the valuable and interesting, coupled with a full knowledge and familiarity with every scrap of history and legend pertaining to the two great Northwestern states of which she has written. . . . Although it purports to be a tourist's story of a land traversed, rather than a history, yet it contains so much of the latter that the library of no Oregon bibliophile can be called complete without it. It is at once comprehensive, entertaining, accurate and valuable.
>
> Whoever reads the book will readily discover that the author is no hasty observer. It shows marks of study from many points of view, and while the work will probably be better appreciated here at home where its real merit will be known at a glance and thoroughly appreciated for truth's sake, yet it will do most yeoman service at the firesides of Eastern readers — who seek books of travel with great avidity in these modern days. The want of knowledge in the East of this northwest corner of the United States is greatly to be regretted, and no publication can do more to remove ignorance, and perhaps prejudice, than this instructive volume, showing the immense strides in improvement made by two great commonwealths since the era of railroads.
> . . .
> The book is a perfect storehouse of such interesting descriptions of the origin of places and names, many of which are by no means generally known. . . . The author should receive recognition and substantial encouragement through subscriptions to the volume, for which an active canvass will be made. . . . It is a duty our people owe to her intelligent and painstaking effort in behalf of the Northwest.[10]

Two days later, on November 9th, Frances wrote Judge Deady again, this time from 73 First Street, where she had moved since her last letter. She promised to send him a complimentary copy when her new book arrived in quantity, and she was expecting them any day.

"Please do not supply the Library until the town has been canvassed," she requested. "I want every subscriber I can get — and need it too. I cannot even venture to take proper measures for restoration to health until I know that money is coming in to meet expenses. What is a thousand years of noble lineage to the poor author? Money is King."[11]

26

"The Early Indian Wars of Oregon"

HOUSE CONCURRENT RESOLUTION 22

Resolved, That the secretary of state . . . is . . . instructed to [compile, tabulate and publish], as far as is possible from the material in his possession, a complete record of the early Indian wars of Oregon, including the wars of 1855 and 1856, and a brief sketch of the pioneer history preceding such wars and connected therewith, and that he be instructed to expend not to exceed the sum of fifteen hundred dollars, out of any moneys not otherwise appropriated, for the compilation and tabulation of such historical record, and such other information as will preserve the names and incidents connected with the Indian wars of Oregon, such historical work to be compiled under his direction.[1]

A companion measure — House Bill 305 — which authorized the project, was filed 21 February 1891 with the secretary of state. George W. McBride, whose responsibility it was to carry out the legislative mandate, knew that Frances Fuller Victor was best qualified to do the historical work.

Indeed, before the resolution was amended to give the secretary of state discretion in the matter, its sponsors provided that Mrs. Victor be named. And the McBrides had been among the pioneer families who helped her gather material on Pacific Northwest history.

Between March and June of 1892, the grand commander of the Indian war veterans, Thomas C. Shaw, made a record of those who served in the conflicts half a century earlier. And about the middle of that year Frances began to write her account from the thousands of pages of archival material in the secretary of state's possession. It was a task for which she was admirably fitted by her earlier experiences.

Frances tried to let "nothing extenuate, nor set down aught in malice," but took a philosophical view of the events she was writing about "because fiction and sentimentalism on one hand, and vengeful hatred on the other, have perverted the truth of history."[2]

The work proceeded smoothly. In his biennial report to the legislature at year's end Secretary McBride said the final roster of Indian war vete-

rans would be ready in a few days, and that Mrs. Victor's historical sketch
was also well along.

On 11 February 1894 a Salem newspaper announced that the state
printer's office was busy on *The Early Indian Wars of Oregon*, and
predicted after a look at advance proofsheets that the book would be a
valuable addition to the state's literature.

After the history was published, some people charged that Mrs. Victor's work was "not entitled to the patronage or sanction of the state"
because she did not include accounts by veterans of their experiences,
even though many were readily available for interviews.[3]

In a letter to the *Daily Oregon Statesman*, Frances replied that she did
try to learn the veterans' opinions and get narratives from them. But from
the whole extended correspondence she gleaned nothing "more than a
few disconnected incidents as they remembered them" which she included
in her account only when they were confirmed by documentary evidence.

> I contend that I have faithfully and conscientiously executed the intent of
> the resolution, which purposely bars out the story-tellers, and keeps the
> author to the facts as found in the archives of the state. This is the only his-
> tory which is of any value. Everyone with ordinary observation knows that
> of a dozen witnesses in court, testifying upon oath to the same fact, no two
> tell the particulars in the same way, but quite diversely. Add to this differ-
> ence of sight or understanding, the lapses of memory that have occurred in
> from thirty-eight to forty-seven years, with the personal motives governing
> most of the narrators, and it will be found that the historian depending upon
> such evidence has launched his craft on a most uncertain sea.[4]

Thirteen hundred copies of the book were printed, and in order to
recover expenses Harrison R. Kincaid, who in January 1895 succeeded
McBride as secretary of state, decided to charge three dollars each. Some
people felt this price was too high, and that it would keep the book from
being widely read.

Mrs. Victor subsequently explained that the 200 pages of muster rolls
added to the volume's bulk, and the printers were paid double rates for
setting this fine-typed, columned and closely spaced data. "The rolls cost
probably one-half more to put in type" than her 500 pages of historical
narrative.

> Me, as author of the book, the secretary has permitted to have one copy,
> though he transcended his authority in granting me this boon. I could not
> have a few more copies to give the newspapers for review to help the sale
> — since it must be sold. If the veterans could have their say about it, I fancy
> it would be different, and that they would recognize the fact that no one
> has ever more earnestly maintained the character of the Oregon pioneer for
> courage and patriotism than the writer of the "Early Indian Wars."[5]

27

The Battle of Life (cont.)

During the previous winter Frances had been named to an advisory council preparing for a Woman's Congress. Every question pertaining to the education, employment and advancement of women would be discussed, with particular reference to the Pacific coast. Those desiring to address the conference, or to submit papers to be read before it, were urged to contact her.

Mrs. Victor received her final payment from the state on 24 April 1894 for completing the Indian war history, and went to San Francisco as one of three Oregon delegates to the week-long congress that began on the 30th.*

Her essay — "The Physical Evolution of Woman" — was read the next day in Golden Gate Hall. A newspaper considered it "a careful study of great depth" and she "very justly received many compliments upon the able manner in which she handled her subject."[1]

Frances remained in the Bay Area to recuperate, said the press afterwards, "from the effects of her long work of nearly 30 years with the pen."[2]

Her "absence almost continuous" from Oregon lasted nearly six years.[3] But while she regained strength, there was the constant worry about how to make money and support herself.

Writing from San Jose on August 18 to Ellen M. White, a sister-in-law living in Salem, Mrs. Victor revealed that $600 she was expecting to get in San Francisco — presumably from the sale of a lot she owned in Alameda — was a total loss.

Frances confessed she was having "great difficulty" deciding what to do next. "Perhaps I may give up trying to earn money by writing though that would be [a] very unwelcome necessity."[4]

Mrs. Victor alluded to "some small schemes" she had in mind, including selling women's notions door-to-door, and asked her sister-in-law to consider helping. "Would you like to make a little money out of the vanity

*In all, according to official records, Mrs. Victor was paid $1,306.13 by the state for her work on *The Early Indian Wars of Oregon*.

of our sex?'' Frances asked. ''Men are doing that all the time — why not
we?''⁵ She continued:

> I have been revelling in fruit this summer: apricots, figs, peaches, plums
> etc., since the berry season has passed. We have fine peaches in the garden,
> and on the table every meal. I spent one week recently with an old friend
> in the Santa Cruz mountains, among the most beautiful scenery, and enjoy-
> ing fruit and flowers in abundance. Of course I drive about, and have a good
> time generally, but I do not feel contented anywhere with my affairs in so
> unsatisfactory a state.⁶

As her condition slowly improved, Frances got involved in women's
congresses and the Pacific Coast Women's Press Association (which she
joined while still in Oregon).

''My health is better than when you saw me last, though I do not expect
ever to be strong again physically,'' she told Oliver Applegate, a long-time
friend in southern Oregon. ''I managed to read a page or two about Crater
Lake before the P.C.W.P.A. the other day, but the effort gave me the sharp-
est pains in my back. But that is so much better than the hysterical condition into which any excitement or nervous strain threw me a year ago,
that I feel encouraged. When I have had papers to read before the congresses, etc., I have had a reader to deliver them.''⁷

These activities called for a good deal of work, which Frances enjoyed
even though there was no money in it — and she needed money to survive.

''If I could get enough of it to enable me to settle down to the enjoyment of life for the remaining years allot[t]ed to me I should feel satisfied
not to move much more,'' she wrote.⁸

During the eighteen months Mrs. Victor had been ''fighting the battle
of life'' in California, she got ''plenty of blood and dust, without much
gain,'' but was grateful to still be alive.⁹

The small rewards Frances received for her labors over the years,
however, could not assuage the frustration she sometimes felt.

''I have sunk more money in getting books before the public than ever
I got out of them,'' she declared in 1895, ''therefore it was not avarice
that prompted me, but love of my theme.''¹⁰

And when Mrs. Victor was in one of her down moods, a friend reminded
her that: ''You are authority on Pacific Coast history; and if I were authority on anything, I should not call myself a failure.''¹¹

Indeed, Frances was pleased to note that Californians were beginning
to call her a ''historian.'' On 7 July 1895, two months before she renewed
her contact with Oliver Applegate, the San Francisco *Call* carried a lengthy
article about her life and career.

Although there were many women writers, the *Call* reporter observed,
the woman historian was a ''rara avis'' in the literary field.

> . . . Her sisters in the inky craft, as a rule, prefer flights of fancy to the
> ferreting of facts, and . . . when they distinguish themselves at the point of
> the pen, it is in the beaten path of fiction rather than the less frequented
> byways of historical research.¹²

The *Call* recognized that Frances had "a genuine affinity for statistics . . . with a faculty for removing the mantle of tradition from skeletons of the past, giving to the world the interesting results of her discoveries."[13]

Mrs. Victor did not crave publicity, and was content to live quietly — accessible to her friends but reserved with strangers. She did not readily grant interviews to the press and, in the *Call*'s words, remained "undisturbed by the noise of less gifted workers clamoring at the gates of fame."[14]

The years Frances spent in Bancroft's library not only impaired her health but made her name unfamiliar to a whole generation of writers who came to maturity in those years and gradually replaced earlier journalists who knew of her work.

"The way has not been easy for her," the *Call* noted, "but her book-making days are far from being over, and she is now engaged in accumulating material for ultimate publication. One who, like Frances Fuller Victor, ranks her art above the greed of money-getting, deserves praise. Few among us, in passing, will leave work of so enduring a quality behind."[15]

In 1896 Mrs. Victor corresponded with Hiram Martin Chittenden, of St. Louis, who was working on a book about the fur trade.

To help her answer some of his questions, Frances relied upon her friend, Oliver Applegate, who lived near Klamath Falls.

She noted approvingly that Chittenden was trying "to get at the true history of the early fur traders and explorers."[16] He wrote her several times for information and to explain his differing views about some minor matters.

Chittenden considered Mrs. Victor's 1870 work — *The River of the West* — an invaluable reference, and he told her: "The careful reading I have given it has shown its worth to me in a more forcible light than ever. It will always stand, not only as a pioneer, but as one of the ablest examples in historical work of the fur trading era."[17]

Frances confided to Oliver Applegate that she was thinking about revising and re-issuing *The River of the West* because it would be more popular than in earlier years. "Hence, not only to settle some points which Chittenden disputes, but to make my revision final, I need all the help I can get."[18]

Oliver forwarded several newspaper articles about Crater Lake. For Frances the clippings evoked pleasant memories of her visit there twenty-three years earlier. She was especially gratified to see that there was still a Victor Rock, so named one summer evening in honor of her venturing to peer over the edge at its image and the sunset colors reflected in the azure waters below.

"Like Helen Hunt Jackson, I should like to be buried with a rock for my monument, beside the lovely and awe inspiring Crater Lake, as she was in her favorite 'Garden of the Gods.'"*[19]

Frances had been the librarian for the Pacific Coast Women's Press Association in San Francisco; but about two weeks before her 16 September 1896 letter to Applegate, she was named the organization's treasurer.

*For biography, see p. 243.

Neither was a salaried position. She was pleased to report, however, that her health was "very much improved."[20]

Mrs. Victor continued to write poetry and historical sketches for the press. But despite that and her involvement in P.C.W.P.A. activities, Frances became interested in plans for an Oregon Historical Society.* During the next several years, she often exchanged letters with Frederic George Young, a history professor at the University of Oregon in Eugene, who became the society's first secretary. On 20 September 1897 she gave him a frank appraisal of her situation as well as some thoughts on historical research:

> . . . I do not quite know how I can aid the enterprise to any considerable extent. If I could do so financially, I know of nothing to which I should more willingly apply whatever funds were needed — but hard-working authors seldom have money to spare, and of these none have more completely lost sight of their own pecuniary interests than I have done — my work and not my income having been always first in my mind. That this is unfortunate — and therefore unwise — must be admitted. But it is now too late to change my course. The years begin to suggest the want of time for recovery, and there is still work unfinished and pressing.
>
> . . . As to counsel, the thought that first occurs to me is to warn you against gathering a mass of correspondence from persons who only remember events. There should be always contemporaneous recorded history. It is my experience that little value attaches to any other evidence, and that confusion results from admitting hearsay testimony. My whole effort has been to weed out worthless authorities, and to stamp out prejudices.
>
> The method you are pursuing is the only correct one. No one can gainsay to any extent a plain statement, made at the time and on the spot, by a sensible witness.[21]

Frances took pride in the thoroughness of her historical writings which — though arousing opposition in some quarters — she considered better than most original histories. "In particular, I endeavored to rescue from oblivion, if only by the merest mention, the names of the Oregon pioneers," she told Professor Young in December 1898. ". . . If any were left out it was because I had no knowledge of them, or means of procuring that knowledge."[22]

She was delighted to learn that the Native Sons Publishing Company in Portland would put out a historical magazine. William Gladstone Steel, a well-known naturalist and mountaineer, was named editor.

Mrs. Victor wrote Steel in February 1899 to say that while she had been certain a historical magazine would someday be a reality, "I am equally sure that it will be a struggle to maintain it. Still I am glad it is to be ventured."[23] She went on to caution her friend about what all too often passed for truth in historical writing:

---

*The Oregon Historical Society was incorporated 17 Dec. 1898 and has published its *Quarterly*, with a wide range of Pacific Northwest topics, continuously since March 1900. The society also has a large and diverse collection of documents, correspondence, photographs, maps and artifacts pertinent to the region's life and history. Its museum and archives are located at 1230 SW Park Avenue in Portland.

... Do not rely too much on what the <u>old</u> pioneers tell you. I have proven how little the recollections of fifty years ago are to be trusted. Again the descendants of these men who were children forty or fifty years ago, have imperfect recollections, and are besides prejudiced in some way concerning early events by the stories they have heard. I make it a rule to prove things by contemporary written or printed records. If I publish anything on hearsay, I make it known that it <u>is</u> hearsay. If you do this you will doubtless provoke discussion, but you will get . . . facts as nearly as possible and possibly find the key to the truth.[24]

Unfortunately, Steel's background and good intentions did not equip him for the project he had undertaken, and he was unable to judge or criticize the contributions sent to him.

"The mischief of it is," she lamented to Professor Young in August 1899, "not that the average reader may be made to believe what is false, but that the conscientious searcher after truth may be deceived by a statement published in a magazine calling itself historical, if the editor accepts it without question."[25]

Young hoped to gain access to the Bancroft Library in San Francisco to do research. Frances doubted this would be possible, since even those who had written the histories were no longer allowed in the Valencia Street repository, but promised to get Bancroft's address if the professor wanted to try and obtain permission. "There is a volume or two of my own in the Library which I am unable to get, much to my grief," she added.[26]

Mrs. Victor also wanted to write an article on one of early Oregon's most influential men, Dr. John McLoughlin, for an eastern magazine.* But although Frances reckoned that she had more of his papers than anyone, she was handicapped by the lack of illustrations.

"I wrote to the McLoughlin <u>heirs</u> who felt too poor to get a few photographs taken for the purpose!" she explained.

"Pray, do not set me down for a grumbler, but when one does the harder part of an unpaid work, as I am constantly doing, it is lawful to feel slightly cross."[27]

About this time, however, Mrs. Victor was doing some "pot-boiler" writing — routine work of no especial significance to her, but that would help pay the bills — for a book about the campaign in the Philippines.

Frances was greatly cheered when Professor Young proposed to make her an honorary member of the Oregon Historical Society.

"I thank you sincerely for the compliment, and the more that it is the first public recognition won by twenty-five years of painstaking work on Oregon historical and otherwise. I shall be happy to give what aid I can to your society in the future as I have done in the past to all efforts to bring out the facts — the truth I mean — of history."[28]

As the century's end drew near, Mrs. Victor began to revise *The River of the West*. Her spirits were buoyed by the prospect of a visit the following summer to Yellowstone Park in Montana to look at camping sites used by early fur traders.

*For biography, see pp. 243-244.

"My health is still the same as you have seen it these last years, and never can be any better, since the addition of a decade now and then increases the natural burden as well," she wrote Oliver Applegate on 21 November 1899. "But I keep on doing — that is the only way to enjoy life — is to use it. The end will come, of course, but it need not be met half way."[29]

28

The Whitman Myth

Perhaps more than her labors for Bancroft, Frances won recognition — primarily from historians in the East — for her efforts to put in proper perspective the role played by Dr. Marcus Whitman in Oregon history, especially in the immigration of 1843 which was a key event leading to U.S. jurisdiction over the Oregon Territory five years later.

Whitman, a medical doctor, came to the Oregon Country in 1836 and established a Presbyterian mission at Waiilatpu, near Walla Walla. Another mission was set up at Lapwai, about twelve miles east of Lewiston.*

But the Cayuse and Nez Perce Indians remained hostile or indifferent. Mrs. Victor wrote that Whitman had found them "selfish, thieving, given to lying, haughty and ungrateful. From their standpoint he was a trespasser on their lands, making money out of their country and them, without any sufficient exchange of benefits."[1]

After six years, the parent organization, the American Board of Commissioners for Foreign Missions in Boston, decided to abandon the two missions as the cost of maintaining them outweighed the good they did among the Indians. Most of their staffs were to go northeast to Spokane, where the Indians were quiet although likewise indifferent to religious instruction.

This order was received in September 1842, and Dr. Whitman decided to go east to consult with the A.B.C.F.M., and arrange some other matters to his satisfaction.

The Oregon Country had been under joint Anglo-American occupation since 1818. But Congress wanted to assert the U.S. title and was considering legislation to encourage immigration and settlement, as well as for the year's notice required to abrogate the joint occupation agreement. An exploring party was in the Rocky Mountains selecting locations for a chain of forts to protect future immigrants.

---

*A small press, the first in the Pacific Northwest, was set up here in 1839. During the next six years the Mission Press, as it was called, produced nine books in the Nez Perce and Spokane Indian dialects. Several were bibles, others were primers for reading.

Knowing all this, Whitman may have wanted to obtain some office under the United States government for the area in which he resided. But he was well aware that he could not be both a missionary and a government officeholder, and was unprepared to give up the one unless he was assured of the other.

Dr. Whitman told contradictory stories to several people about why he was going east. His associates from Spokane felt he should obey the board. Whitman promised not to leave until October 5, in order to take their letters and reports. But he decided not to wait, and on the 3rd he rode off with two companions. At least part of the journey was cold and stormy. The party may have suffered from frost, but they pushed on.

On 30 March 1843, Whitman arrived in Boston. The A.B.C.F.M. criticized him for leaving his post. Board members felt that the Waiilatpu and Lapwai missions should become self-supporting. Thinking of all the new settlers who would soon be coming to the Oregon Country, Dr. Whitman alertly suggested that these missions be used as trading posts for immigrants and Indians alike — and the board agreed. In this way, he avoided the unpleasant choice of going to Spokane or resigning.

Whitman also visited Washington, D.C., and his former home in Wheeler, New York. Then he called on his sister in Quincy, Illinois. Afterward, he traveled to the Shawnee mission near Westport, Missouri, and about June 1 he left to overtake the pioneer wagon train on the Platte River.

"A great many cattle are going, but no sheep," Whitman wrote his brother-in-law.[2] The missionary — thinking of his section, the great bunchgrass region — considered sheep indispensable for Oregon.

"I mean to impress it on the secretary of war that sheep are more important to Oregon interests than soldiers. We want to get sheep and stock from government for Indians, instead of money, for their lands. I have written him on the main interests of the Indian country, *but I mean still to write him a private letter touching some particular interests.*"[3]

He traveled west across the plains with the head of the pioneer column. At Fort Hall, near Pocatello, the missionary learned that Indians had burned his mill and grain and tried to abuse his wife. Narcissa Whitman fled to The Dalles and waited most of the time in western Oregon until her husband returned.

With a few impatient spirits who longed for the glory of being first to reach the goal, Dr. Whitman hurried ahead of the main body. These leaders, assisted by several Indian guides, searched for the best route whenever compelled to leave the trail. At Grand Ronde, Whitman received a message that his professional services were required at Lapwai, and he turned north.*

In the fall of 1865, Rev. Henry Harmon Spalding published in *The Pacific*, a San Francisco religious paper, a heroic account of Dr. Whitman's eastern ride. A strikingly similar story, written by William H. Gray, another former colleague of Whitman's in the Oregon mission, appeared in the *Astoria Marine Gazette* in July and August 1866.

---

*See Chapter 12 for account of Whitman's death.

Both men claimed that Whitman went east specifically to raise an emigration of about 1,000 persons, and bring them back with wagons to show that Oregon could be settled overland from the United States. Spalding and Gray also asserted that Dr. Whitman successfully lobbied President John Tyler to prevent Secretary of State Daniel Webster's trading the Oregon Country to Great Britain for fishing privileges off Newfoundland.

Mrs. Victor in her first writings on Oregon generally accepted the Spalding-Gray version of Whitman's activities, but she expressed doubt that he had any real influence in Washington, D.C., or helped much in starting the emigration of 1843.

Frances later discovered that she had been misled, particularly about Whitman's acts and motives. After entering the Bancroft Library, she published a repudiation of the Whitman legend, using evidence gathered while writing the *History of Oregon.*

Mrs. Victor's article in *The Californian* in September 1880 triggered a veritable Niagra of opposition from believers of the Spalding-Gray account of Dr. Whitman's adventures.* She was variously denounced as an enemy of missions, a tool of the Jesuits and a secularist — no small criticism at a time when interfaith rivalries were especially strong.

Elwood Evans, a noted Pacific Northwest historian and lawyer, likewise accepted at first the popular version of the Whitman ride. But Mrs. Victor, an old friend, gradually convinced him that it was a fabrication, and he joined in her battle against the opposition.

The debate was long and voluminous, especially in 1884-1885. Editors groaned under its weight, but were generally patient in carrying the load and they took care to air *all* sides.

On 6 November 1884 the Portland *Morning Oregonian* published a very scholarly article by Mrs. Victor, in which she still more completely demolished the Spalding-Gray story. The article covered almost an entire page, with two columns of footnotes in even finer type, and was appropriately subtitled "An Exhaustive Examination . . . of all the Points in the So-called Whitman Controversy."

Frances' investigation convinced her that some person or persons used "falsehood and deceit" in describing Dr. Whitman's activities.[4] His associates knew that he went east on a political errand, Mrs. Victor wrote, but "concealed that motive from the public from a fear of disgracing the missionary cause . . . and also from a fear of alarming the Hudson Bay Company," the dominant British presence in the region.[5]

But Whitman himself contributed to the bewilderment of his colleagues by being so vague and contradictory about his intentions. Frances speculated it was the "greed of gain" that had disgraced his undertaking.

"Was it then that Whitman was planning to enrich himself at the expense of his missionary character, that he practiced so much strategy?" Mrs. Victor asked. "To me this seems to be the solution of the puzzle. But he failed.

The Californian was published from 1880-1882 in San Francisco by the publishers of the *Overland Monthly,* which ceased publication in 1875 but was revived in 1883.

Neither the board nor the secretary of war were induced to enter into his plans."[6]

Despite all efforts to bring to public notice the true story of Dr. Whitman's ride, the mid-1880s marked the real spread of the legend and its acceptance — at least for a time — by reputable scholars.

Frances was exasperated by the resiliency of the Spalding-Gray tale. "A lie well stuck to is as good as the truth," she lamented in the press.[7]

The argument flared again after publication of Bancroft's *Oregon* in 1886. But this time Matthew P. Deady, a federal court judge and long-time Portland resident, came to the aid of Evans and Victor.

"I am aware that some persons fancy that because I earnestly adhere to what I am convinced, on evidence, is the truth, that I intentionally affront the memory of Dr. Whitman," Mrs. Victor wrote the *Morning Oregonian* in March 1891. "Dr. Whitman does not enter into this controversy. He never pretended to have done these things."[*][8]

The only avenue left unexplored was the true authorship of the Spalding-Gray story, though Frances promised that would be a matter for future explanation. The legend, she noted, however, did not appear until eighteen years after Dr. Whitman's death in 1847.

"It had never been heard of before the attempt by Mr. Spalding to induce congress to bestow upon him a mile-square of land in the Lapwai valley, which had not been complied with, the mission having been abandoned, and that the narrative of Gray is founded on the document presented to congress, at that time. Whether it was the production of one or both remains to be found out. Spalding failed to get the land.

"[I]f Mr. Gray had read a good deal more, and asserted a great deal less," she added, "there would not be so much for subsequent historians to take back."[**][9]

As the years passed, and the Whitman legend ballooned to national proportions, Frances concluded that she would have to write a book to answer her critics and hopefully stop the apparently endless debate — even though it "serves to keep alive an interest in historical matters."[10]

By the end of 1898, Mrs. Victor had completed what she considered to be a definitive account, and was submitting the manuscript — "a considerable volume" — for publication.

---

*So bitter was the feeling aroused by this issue that Secretary Young told an OHS meeting in December 1902, five weeks after her death:

> . . . It may not be advisable for this society to attempt at this time an expression of its tribute to the memory and services of Mrs. Victor to Oregon history, owing to traces of a spirit of division that was unfortunately engendered from an honest difference of conclusions on an important question in Oregon's past in which Mrs. Victor was prominently identified with one side, yet we cannot be unmindful of the fact that hers was the largest and ablest part in recording the development of the Pacific Northwest. *Portland Morning Oregonian, Monday, 22 December 1902, p. 14 c. 5.*

**See Senate Executive Document 37, Forty-First Congress, third session, in *U.S. Serial Set*, Vol. 1440.

"I have spared no pains to get at all the facts of the story," she told a friend. "I give a history of the missions — which the missionaries themselves never have done — and I settle forever the question as to motive and deed of Dr. Whitman in his journey East."[11]

Elliott Coues, a litterateur and historian in Washington, D.C., to whom Mrs. Victor had sent her work, praised the manuscript and was trying to have it published when he died in December 1899.*

Frances was bitterly disappointed to learn of his passing. The subject, she told an acquaintance a month later, was still a sore one with her.

"I inquire as so many have done before me, 'why he and not some useless man must be taken?' To me he was as kind as a brother. His large heart and brain found room for all who were striving to do something for the world."[12]

Mrs. Victor was still trying to sell her manuscript in December 1900 when she wrote the *American Historical Review* to offer an article on the Whitman legend. She was rather upset to learn that Professor Edward Gaylord Bourne of Yale University would read a paper on the subject at the annual meeting of the American Historical Association that month, and that the *Review* would publish it in January 1901.

"I think you will be greatly pleased with his article," J. Franklin Jameson, managing editor of the *Review* and a historian, told Frances. "He speaks of your labors in the most handsome way and agrees substantially with you in the main contention."[13]

Professor Bourne was concerned because professional historians, and many school textbooks and general-interest publications, were unduly crediting the Whitman legend.

In his article, Bourne recognized the work of Evans and Victor in promoting the true story.

"The picture of the grapple of criticism with a legend in its earlier growth, and of the survival if not victory of the fiction in spite of crushing attack in an age which flatters itself on its intelligence, would be full of sobering instruction for the historical student," Bourne wrote.[14]

In a footnote, the professor complimented Frances for her meticulous labors:

> . . . After such a critical examination of the sources as I have made in this study . . . it is not a common experience to find in any general history, constructed directly from the raw material, so faithful and trustworthy a presentation of the contents of those sources as in the parts of the first volume of Bancroft's *Oregon* that I have subjected to this test. . . . To Mrs. Frances Fuller Victor as the avowed author of Bancroft's *Oregon*, working under his editorial supervision, every student of Oregon history is under great obligations for her scholarly and honest presentation of the facts derived from the unparalleled collection of materials gathered by Mr. Bancroft.[15]

Frances was disturbed that a number of professional historians had "brought themselves into prominence by using the facts" that she unearthed, "without giving any credits whatever."[16]

---

*For biography, see pp. 244-245.

No one contradicted the Whitman myth — at least in print — until after Mrs. Victor denounced it in 1880 and the discussion that followed had drawn public notice all over the Pacific Northwest.*

"Now, when people are writing books and essays, leaning to one side or the other, each new historian talks as if he had made an original discovery," she wrote angrily to a friend.[17]

Although Frances considered the American Historical Association's repudiation of the legend "a victory for, or vindication of" her position, she was displeased that "the gentlemen who spoke for it, every one of whom received his information directly or indirectly from me failed to mention that his 'attention had been called to it' . . . There is quite too much human nature in people, a fact which bodes ill for the 20th century."[18]

As for the legend itself, Mrs. Victor noticed in November 1901 that proponents were modifying its more mythical elements and admitting that mistakes had been made. "But that will not save the legend at last," she contended, "for the more they declare it the less they make out of it."[19]

After Professor Bourne's article on Whitman was published, Frances rewrote her book, completing it in March 1902. She spent all of Easter Sunday reviewing the manuscript "preparatory to sending it off — somewhere."[20]

---

*"Mrs. Victor appears to have been the first to issue a contradiction to the Whitman-Saved-Oregon story," wrote historian Clifford M. Drury on page 451 of his *Marcus Whitman, M.D., Pioneer and Martyr* published in 1937.

29

The End: "All work and no pay."

Frances Fuller Victor returned to Portland in June 1900, after an absence of almost six years. The visit was apparently inspired in large measure by her interest in the Oregon Historical Society and its newly launched *Quarterly,* first published just three months before.

Mrs. Victor felt that publication of several volumes on the Pacific Northwest at her own risk, her labors for Bancroft, as well as writing much material for magazines and newspapers, should entitle her "to some profit, and to some privileges above the ordinary."[1]

Frances estimated that $100 was all she ever received from Oregon newspapers in thirty years of writing about the state. "This ignoring of my value as a writer naturally forced me towards California, where I could get pay," she remarked, but "the marked decline in literary values has made it very difficult to earn a living by the pen."[*2]

She had written more or less for the Portland *Morning Oregonian* on historical subjects since 1870, "and never received one dollar for it."[3] Now that she needed help, Frances asked if the paper would employ her in some capacity, with a weekly salary, but was denied — this despite the paper's ample resources and its editorials in earlier years urging public support for her literary endeavors.

---

*Answering a question posed by a reporter from the Portland (Oreg.) *Evening Telegram,* Frances said:

> Do I consider the general standard in literary work advanced since beginning to write? The average literary work at that period was more carefully done than it is now. The enormous expansion of utilitarian ideas has led to a lowering of literary taste and expression. It is true that more people are educated up to a certain level, but the level is not high enough. You cannot have intelligent, good morals without a certain amount of culture; neither can you have the best intellectual product without good morals. I think there is danger in excessive intellectuality without morality, and that there is also a narrowing in excessive morality. There is a point at which virtue may become almost a vice. So few are likely to reach this point, however, that my ethical views are not likely to disturb society. *"Talk with a Woman Who Writes Poems," Portland Evening Telegram, 11 September 1900, p. 8 c. 2.*

Another source of discouragement was the feeling among pioneers that they were better historians "than the most painstaking student of history."[4] It was for this reason, Mrs. Victor believed, that the early Oregonians, "naturally controversial" and suspecting "every one who has anything to say of having an interested motive . . . they still, according to their several leanings watch for an opportunity to throw discredit upon the conclusions to which I have arrived by the conscientious labor of years."[5]

While her experiences might have made Mrs. Victor reluctant to contribute to a new literary enterprise, she hastened to assure Professor Young of her interest in the *Oregon Historical Quarterly*, as she considered it "a dignified means of teaching the history of the country and its lessons."[6] She also hoped that he would be able to mold "a more liberal and just public sentiment" by it.[7]

The *Morning Oregonian* hailed Frances' return to Portland, calling her the "Mother of Oregon History."[8] The press reported that she felt much stronger than five or six years ago, and was ready to begin new labors with her pen. On 13 September 1900 she wrote to Frederic George Young:

> . . . As I have intimated to you before, I cannot, with justice to myself, keep on working and giving out to Oregon without some return — for I must live before I can work. I want to hit upon some plan to bring myself into a position where I can do good work easily and where I can afford to give worthy effort to unpaid work. . . .
>
> I will tell you — but under the seal of secrecy at present — that I have thought of trying to secure a pension from the state legislature for the remainder of my intelligent and generous consideration, for the future, of our kind of work. The state had better pay its brain workers more, and its politicians less. And they have got to be educated up to it.[9]

At this time, Frances published at her own expense a small volume, entitled simply *Poems*, a selection of the best metrical compositions that she had written for various periodicals over the previous sixty years.

But while the modest proceeds from this poetry book allowed her to concentrate on more extensive historical work, Mrs. Victor expressed concern that "pot-boiler" projects were taking up "too much valuable time" and that it gave her "an unpleasant feeling of sacrifice to put my verse to this purpose."[10]

She also spent much time reading Capt. Chittenden's manuscript, *The American Fur Trade of the Far West* — subsequently published in three volumes — and taking notes throughout.

"This I did as a favor, though it was a tremendous task," she told Professor Young. "He gave me leave to use any of my notes in my own work, and many were useful in the revision of my River of the West, a part of his work covering the same ground, and being very thoroughly worked up."[11]

Frances was confined that fall, on account of poor health, to her residence at 624 Salmon Street. It was the home of Joseph Gaston, with whose family she boarded soon after her return to Portland.* But on December 10 she expected to go downtown for the first time in seven weeks.

---

*For biography, see pp. 245-246.

Meanwhile, she found that an honorary member of the Oregon Historical Society didn't necessarily get considerate treatment. The oversights seemed small, and were probably unintentional, but they irritated Mrs. Victor a lot.

She had written for a copy of the *Quarterly*, but received no answer. Mr. Gaston got a notice of the Society's annual meeting, but she did not. Nor did her name appear in the list of members that was printed in the papers.

"You will no doubt set me down as a constitutional grumbler, since it is certain I do a good deal of fault finding," she wrote exasperatedly to F.G. Young on the 16th. ". . . Am I to consider myself unworthy of these attentions? . . . Wet blankets seem to be the raiment in which Oregonians delight to drape the presumptuous mortal who dares to suggest fair play or courtesy. It is very likely to promote emigration I should think."[12]

In January 1901, Frances was kept indoors by the flu and did not expect to get outside much until spring. Revising *The River of the West* remained her primary concern.

Besides her literary labors, Mrs. Victor provided Professor Young and the Oregon Historical Society with ideas for basic planning of the Lewis and Clark Exposition. She also contacted prominent historians in the East to enlist their aid for a history building.

"I should be pleased to devote the remainder of my life to carrying forward the historical idea which I am sure I may claim to have done more to develop than any other writer," she told Professor Young. "My only reluctance would arise from a fear that my physical disabilities would hamper my usefulness too much to give scope to my abilities. However, if I can be assured of financial support, removing a serious waste of energy, my efficiency may be retained or increased. At any rate you may be assured of my cordial support and cooperation."[13]

Her frail health imposed additional burdens, and although still unable to spend much time outdoors Frances felt she was "overcoming some of the most troublesome symptoms" and hoped to be more active in 1902. "I should like to be strong enough to take an active part in the Lewis + Clark Centennial," she wrote on November 9th.[14]

A week earlier, Capt. H.M. Chittenden stopped in Portland on his way home from San Francisco. He spent the day with Mrs. Victor, who thought it "a very pleasant and entertaining visit."[15] She had already read most of the proofs of his book and wrote a review for the *Morning Oregonian*. A more extended one was contemplated for the *Oregon Historical Quarterly*.

As the last year of her life began, Frances continued to have money woes even as she was busy on some new work. "Nothing is bringing anything my way at present," she lamented.

"I think I must quit Oregon, unless it appears that I can find my services worth something to somebody; and this must be decided in the course of a few weeks."[16]

Frances added that if she did stay, she would move further downtown — "nearer car lines so that I can go out more. I am getting too unworldly here. One cannot live on green trees, and snow peaks — not even a poet."[17]

Mrs. Victor remarked sardonically that she would have to "go to writing bear stories for children" unless Professor Young could persuade "the moneyed members" of society to support the *Quarterly* and planning for the Lewis and Clark Centennial Exposition.

"Debt is an intellectual incubus too wearing (even if one's credit is assured) to be accepted as a condition of one's existence," she wrote. ". . . I shall feel it throwing away my labor and time to follow up the lines projected."[18]

Recent magazine articles by other Oregon authors discussing notable literary people in the state either ignored her or gave only a passing mention.*

"There are some people in Oregon who have a private opinion, no doubt, on this subject, which might be as flattering as I could wish; but they <u>keep</u> it <u>private</u>, and they are not generally of the moneyed class," she wrote bitterly. "No one in this state in any proper way has acknowledged my services, in many ways, to the state. Occasionally I receive by letter, or by the good will of a country editor, a word of commendation. That is gratifying as far as it goes, but it is not the real thing due me."[19]

Frances asserted that what standing she had in Oregon was derived from her influence with literary people in the East, and that it should be increased by any means available to be more useful to her or them. She asked if Professor Young could arrange for her to receive a small stipend for her labors.

> At this moment there lies before me all this:
> 1 Chittenden's book to be reviewed in extenso.
> 2 Notes for the article on the Astoria etc.
> 3 References for the article on the Oregon Question (English).
> 4 Material for a novel — half done.
> 5 A half written book on the Whitman Legend.
> 6 Material for an article on Oregon Literature.
> 7 Notes on books for Newberry Library — and many
>   incidentals, correspondence etc. And nothing to
>   show for it! "All work and no <u>pay</u>."[20]

Professor Young finally agreed to pay Mrs. Victor for some of her articles in the *Quarterly*. Others in Oregon and California were helping in various ways to sustain her — some out of friendship, some in recognition of her contributions to Oregon history. For twelve years, she also had been receiving an $8 monthly federal pension, based on her late husband's service in the Navy during the Civil War. Congressional action in March 1902 increased it to $20, because age and feeble health prevented her from earning a living. Several of her friends tried to gain for her "recognition as a useful citizen!" as she described it, but apparently without success.[21]

Frances believed that the study of history needed much encouragement. So when a fellow boarder, a young high school teacher named William Alfred Morris (later a professor at the University of California), who had

---

*See, for example: Eva Emery Dye, "Oregon Writers," *The Pacific Monthly*, Vol. 4 No. 6 (Portland: The Pacific Monthly Publishing Co., October 1900), pp. 253-257.

just graduated from Stanford, asked her how and where to begin studying Pacific Northwest history, she put aside her other work to offer suggestions and talk with him.

Mrs. Victor thought to start him on the most recent books and then gradually work backward in time. "This may seem to be inverting the usual method, as it is," she wrote, "but I think the love of history would be fostered by this practice."[22]

Seeing that the young man was a Yamhill County native, Mrs. Victor asked if he might like to make an article out of an old letter she had about McMinnville and McMinnville (now Linfield) College. Although little if any pay would be involved, Morris seemed "pleased with the idea" and he showed Frances "a handsome gold medal" he won in a debate on French history.[23]

By the end of March, Frances had cleared her desk of major work and her "next anxiety is to get things in shape so that I can perform all that is expected of me, or all I have undertaken."[24]

One long-time resident had written to compliment Mrs. Victor for several of her articles in the *Quarterly*, which he said showed there was more to Oregon history than Dr. McLoughlin and Dr. Whitman.

Frances, still anxious about her finances, asked Professor Young to be more specific about a promise as to when she would be paid.

"I am sorry to seem too urgent for your convenience — but knowing what to expect may enable me to arrange my accounts so as to escape annoyance," she wrote. "If I could feel settled in my mind as to income I could please myself, and you probably, much better than when disturbed by uncertainty. As matters have been for some time, I have not had time, and mental repose enough to do as good work as I ought — I cannot afford to polish. Of course you understand this."[25]

A month later, Mrs. Victor thanked the professor for sending $25 and hoped that if he could not pay her every month, at least "arrange it to suit the conditions, and I will try hereafter to conform to them."[26] This was easier now that her pension had been increased, and she expected eventually to accumulate a small emergency fund.

In September 1902, Frances moved her possessions for the last time in her long and unsettled life. She left her quarters on Salmon Street for a pleasant, comfortable room in the boarding-house of Mrs. Emma M. Gilmore at 501 Yamhill Street. During the move she suffered two or three breakdowns. On November 10 she wrote Professor Young a brief last letter to say that she could not send him that month a manuscript on steam transportation (part of a history she was writing on the Oregon Steam Navigation Company) because she had been "seriously ill again, and am still unfit to take up my pen."[27] Still, she expressed a willingness to work "'by hook or by crook'" if he could take advantage of any delay in press work to give her time.[28]

At 3 a.m. on Friday, 14 November 1902, with Mrs. Gilmore at her bedside, Frances Fuller Victor died peacefully from the effects of old age. Although she hadn't been feeling well for two or three weeks, and took meals in her room, the end was not thought to be so near.

Funeral services were conducted November 17 at the First Unitarian Church in Portland. Despite extremely stormy weather, many of Mrs. Victor's faithful Oregon friends were present but only one relative, James B. Wilson, a cousin from Walla Walla, Washington. Her only surviving sister, Celia F. Van Pearse, lived in Ohio and could not come. Frances was buried in Riverview Cemetery in Portland.*

The Portland *Sunday Oregonian* stated:

> The life of Frances Fuller Victor is in itself a history. It touched at many vital points the life of a wide section still too new to civilization for its full and permanent history to be written. Those who knew her in the earlier as well as in the later years know that she was always a struggler in the ranks of labor, though never an obtrusive one. Disappointment rather than success followed many of her endeavors, but she kept through all a gentle courage ... Among the wide circle of acquaintances formed ... during the long years of her active literary labors she left many friends who recognized the value of her work and admired the sterling qualities of her character. The voices of her critics, never harsh, will now take on gentler tones or cease to be heard, and Frances Fuller Victor will take her place among those who did what they could for those that are to come after them. ... [29]

---

*A marker at her burial site was dedicated on 1 Oct. 1947 by the Daughters of the American Revolution, of which Mrs. Victor had been a member. The action came after newspaper reports that the noted historian lay in a nameless grave. See, in particular, Ben Maxwell, "Oregon Forgot History Writer," Portland *Sunday Oregon Journal*, 10 Mar. 1946, Pacific Parade Magazine, page 3.

Appendix

MONTHLY HESPERIAN AND ODD-FELLOWS' LITERARY MAGAZINE
(Detroit, Michigan, Vol. II No. 8, pages 87-88)

LETTER FROM MISS FULLER.

Ashland, Close of a Spring-day.

Mr. Ingersoll — Arrived at Ashland, find myself thinking I would like to know how fares the *Hesperian*, and you, its sire; and being moreover in a letter-writing humor, have come to the determination to write you a letter. Not a sentimental letter — oh, no! do not fear it; only a roving, rambling sort of an epistle, which shall be a pretty fair exposition of my thoughts, and a map of my travels. After landing at Sandusky, from that pet of knowing travelers, the *Arrow*, of course you lost sight of me in your mind's eye; for farther than here you were not advised of my intended course; nor was I aware what I should decide upon. But taking the Mansfield and Sandusky Railroad, I started for the interior. By the way — being compelled to endure the distress of a ride over this same miserable, shabby and dangerous road, makes one intensely sensible of the comfort, ease and speed of our own Central Railroad. We are exceedingly fortunate to accomplish fourteen miles an hour on the Sandusky and Mansfield road; and our usual rate, including the daily number of delays from causes foreign to the business of the road, makes the average speed of travel, ten miles an hour, though often not more than seven! — and all on account of the condition of the road, which, most of it flat rail, is rougher than the primitive railways made of logs, in the days of our forefathers. But the other day, the locomotive ran away from us, and left us to come gradually to a stop, which lasted until the engineer got back to us with his flighty iron horse, and re-coupled the train to its powerful body. Of all the accidents of traveling, I am most amused by this, of the running away of a locomotive. There is something so very ludicrous in our position, as we sit helplessly, in patience or impatience, awaiting the apparent will of the snorting monster, which scorning us from its heels, has fled away untrammelled, while we remain abandoned perhaps in the midst of a wilderness, with only the prospect of agueish-looking gutters of water on either side to divert the eye, and relieve the suspense.

But, leaving railroads, (which after all are too modern to be romantic,) for the old-fashioned stage-coach, which takes us up at Mansfield, let us go on. Surely, the country never looked so beautiful to me in the spring-time as it does now. I had the *blues*, yes, actually a severe fit of these delightful spirits, when I left Mansfield; but a mile into the country sufficed to remove the shadow from my soul, and I went on my way rejoicing. Lend me your eyes for a view from the top of this hill! Enchanting! Were the wheat-fields ever of so lovely a green? — and bordered round with rows of flowering peach-trees, whose pink bloom looks so lovely on the bright emerald landscape. Then the gardens, with their clusters of white-blossomed cherry trees, and little beds of early flowers — tulips and hya-cinths and violets. The meadows too are quite green, and the woods are of every shade of forest hue. The red of the maple-blossoms, the light green of the buckeye, the green and brown of the oak; and the color of the rougher trunks still showing through the just budding foliage, making up with [a] hundred other shades of hue a most diversified landscape to which the rich brown of the just ploughed fields adds not a little of effect.

One wishes to be the little bird that perches so saucily on the road-side fence, calling out to us in its most daring tones, and singing us a burst of its sweetest song; then showing us its speed, darts away to swing a moment on the topmost branch of some tall cherry-tree, until our com-ing up excites it to haste again, and on it goes, and stands wetting its little feet in the meadow brook, by the time we reach the valley, when away it flies to tell its mate of what clumsy mortals we are; and we sigh, alas, for its graceful freedom.

How many familiar objects I met in riding through the country, that had been as way-marks to me on my path of life, which, in absence and distance, and the ever increasing turmoil of existence, had been forgot-ten! but now brought back long trains of recollections richly freighted with the flowers and fruits of soul-life. Starting up from many a woody recess, seemed visions of long separated friends, uttering with their pale and shadowy lips the sentences which have made the place remembered, and the recollection of which can never wholly die. By an old farm-house, in a corner of the garden, is a tall lilac-tree, the sight of which brought back vividly a little romantic era in girlhood, when life was all *couleur de rose*; and a vision of a tall, dark-eyed boy, with black silken ringlets and smiling lips, riding proudly along, bringing in his arms a whole wealth of those fragrant lilac-blossoms. He had "found out a gift for his fair," and I was the pleased recipient of his armful of flowers, from this same old lilac-tree. I looked sadly at the old tree as I passed it; for I saw that by its many dead branches it would not long remind me of that blissful time. As surely as aurora's rose colored drapery fades away at sunrise, so surely the onward course of our being leaves behind these delicate tints, and our existence merges into the heat and noon-day of feeling and suffering.

Since I have been in A., I have only idled away my time; doing nothing and thinking nothing; but choosing rather to let the hours go by so far that when I come back I shall have a good chase to come up with them. I like vigorous work, if I work at all. I stagnate in a measured-out, regular, every-day-alike kind of an existence; hence my idleness now, and my willingness to work at intervals. I am going out into the country next week to live a little while amid the freshness of ever-renewing nature; and with a pleasant book to alternate the enjoyment, intend to dream away a week in solitude.

I have been reading "Reveries of a Bachelor," by 'Ik. Marvel.' Get it and read it, if in Detroit, and give your readers a "Flake" about it. You will like it; for it is a heart-book, imparting to its readers the delight of reverie without that idleness of habit which is necessary to produce it.

The Spring is still capricious; but I hope these slate colored clouds will soon give place to sunshine. I shall follow my letter soon; in the meantime, *adieu*!

F.A.F.

Coggeshall, William T. *The Poets and Poetry of the West: with Biographical and Critical Notices.* Columbus, Ohio: Follett, Foster and Company, 1860. Page 512.

FRANCES F. BARRITT.   [1850-60.

SONG OF THE AGE.

MEN talk of the iron age —
    Of the golden age they prate,
And with sigh on lips so sage
    Discourse of our fallen state.
They tell of the stalwart frames
    Our gallant grandsires bore;
But, honor to their good names,
    This century asks for more:
It asks for men with the toiling brains,
Whose words can undo the captive's chains,
    For men of right and men of might,
Whose heads, not hands, decide the fight!

And a mighty band they come,
    More strong than the hosts of old;
Nor by clarion blast nor drum
    Is their onward march foretold.
But with firm and silent tread,
    And with true hearts heaving high,
On, on where the wrong hath led —
    They will vanquish it or die!
And they beard the lion in his den,
With the fearless souls of honest men,
    Like men of right and men of might,
Whose heads, not hands, decide the fight.

Tell not of the ages past,
    There is darkness on their brow;
For truth has only come at last,
    And the only time is now!
Away with your empty love,
    And your cant of other times,
For mind is the spell of power —
    Ye will learn its might betimes!
For this is the age of toiling brains,
Of liberties won, and broken chains,
    Of men of right and men of might,
Whose heads, not hands, decide the fight.

Coggeshall, William T. *The Poets and Poetry of the West: with Biographical and Critical Notices.* Columbus, Ohio: Follett, Foster and Company, 1860. Page 515.

1850-60.]   FRANCES F. BARRITT.

_____

CHILDHOOD.

A CHILD of scarcely seven years —
  Light-haired, and fair as any lily;
With pure eyes ready in their tears
  At chiding words or glances chilly:
And sudden smiles as inly bright
  As lamps through alabaster shining,
With ready mirth and fancies light,
    Dashed with strange dreams of child-
      divining:
A child in all infantile grace,
Yet with the angel lingering in her face.

A curious, eager, questioning child,
  Whose logic leads to naive conclusions
Her little knowledge reconciled
  To truth, amid some odd confusions:
Yet credulous, and loving much,
  The problems hardest for her reason;
Placing her lovely faith on such,
  And deeming disbelief a treason; —
Doubting that which she can disprove,
And wisely trusting all the rest to love.

Such graces dwell beside your hearth,
  And bless you in a priceless pleasure;
Leaving no sweeter spot on earth
  Than that which holds your household
    treasure.
No entertainment ever yet
  Had half the exquisite completeness —
The gladness without one regret,
  You gather from your darling's sweet-
    ness:
An angel sits beside the hearth,
  Where'er an innocent child is found on
    earth.

SUNSET AT THE MOUTH OF THE COLUMBIA.

There sinks the sun; like cavalier of old,
    Servant of crafty Spain,
He flaunts his banner, barred with blood and gold,
    Wide o'er the western main;
A thousand spear heads glint beyond the trees
    In columns bright and long,
While kindling fancy hears upon the breeze
    The swell of shout and song.

And yet not here Spain's gay, adventurous host
    Dipped sword or planted cross;
The treasures guarded by this rock-bound coast
    Counted them gain nor loss.
The blue Columbia, sired by the eternal hills
    And wedded with the sea,
O'er golden sands, tithes from a thousand rills,
    Rolled in lone majesty —

Through deep ravine, through burning, barren plain,
    Through wild and rocky strait,
Through forest dark, and mountain rent in twain
    Toward the sunset gate;
While curious eyes, keen with the lust of gold,
    Caught not the informing gleam,
These mighty breakers age on age have rolled
    To meet this mighty stream.

Age after age these noble hills have kept,
    The same majestic lines;
Age after age the horizon's edge been swept
    By fringe of pointed pines.
Summers and Winters circling came and went,
    Bringing no change of scene;
Unresting, and unhasting, and unspent,
    Dwelt Nature here serene!

Till God's own time to plant of Freedom's seed,
    In this selected soil;
Denied forever unto blood and greed,
    But blest to honest toil.
There sinks the sun; Gay cavalier no more!
    His banners trail the sea,
And all his legions shining on the shore
    Fade into mystery.

The swelling tide laps on the shingly beach,
  Like any starving thing;
And hungry breakers, white with wrath, upreach,
  In a vain clamoring.
The shadows fall; just level with mine eye
  Sweet Hesper stands and shines,
And shines beneath an arc of golden sky,
  Pinked round with pointed pines.

A noble scene! all breadth, deep tone, and power,
  Suggesting glorious themes;
Shaming the idler who would fill the hour
  With unsubstantial dreams.
Be mine the dreams prophetic, shadowing forth
  The things that yet shall be,
When through this gate the treasures of the North
  Flow outward to the sea.

Astoria, Or., 1865.

The (East Portland, Oreg.) *Democratic Era,* Friday, 26 May 1871, page 2
columns 4-6

"The Woman Question."

———

EDITOR DEMOCRATIC ERA:

Once the most momentous question a woman had to answer was —
"Will you marry me?" The answer to it however was often very quickly
rendered, having been cut and dried, like the replies to a popular toast
at a diplomatic dinner. But when now-a-days, that other question — "Are
you a Woman['s] Rights Woman?" is plumped at one at unexpected times
and in inappropriate places our answer is not always ready.

The aggressive manner, the "Stand and deliver your opinion" air with
which one is assaulted, makes the greater portion of the difficulty. And
yet the question itself is one not at all easy to answer in a definite manner. We have been asked a good many times, and never yet had our answer
ready. Somebody once asked us if we had ever *lectured?* and somebody
else, if we had not practiced medicine! Now all these queries are likely
sometimes to help us to an opinion on the Woman Question at large: for
there are certainly suggestions of possibilities in the inquiries — hints that
there are certain desirable privileges which we do not enjoy, and of latent
abilities which we had never thought of employing.

Perhaps it is right that people should demand from us, and reasonable
that we should be compelled to give a perfect opinion of a vastly important moral and social question. But the subject is so large, so long, and
so broad, in its many points of view, that it would be a liberal education
to have canvassed it thoroughly; involving as it does all the interests of
humanity, religious, moral, social and political. We do not yet feel prepared to say whether we shall insist upon our "rights" or not.

It does, we confess, seem absurd to attach gender to the question of
human rights. Absolutely and without prejudice, one human being can
have no rights which do not belong equally to all other human beings,
circumstances being equal. Circumstances! Aye, there's the rub. Expediency
or inexpediency, after all, must ever govern the question of rights; for,
morally speaking, the moment that we discover a thing to be inexpedient
we lose our right to do it. The Suffrage is the one great right for which
women are now contending, and whether they are justified in demanding it or not depends upon its expediency, and that alone. We have then
only that to consider in determining the propriety of Woman Suffrage.

Evidently every intelligent creature has a right to seek the highest
development and most perfect happiness possible to him or to her. He
or she has a right to remove from the road to happiness, usefulness, perfection, all obstacles to it, the removal of which does not imply the neglect
of some duty to others, the commission of some crime against humanity,
or the breach of some moral law. In other words, we have the right to
do "anything in reason and religion" which advances our happiness and
prosperity. If political suffrage will increase the comfort and the useful-

ness of women it cannot be denied to them, because there is no earthly power potent enough successfully to oppose the most powerful principle of intellectual life, which is progress, growth, expansion. Once the slightest rootlet of a great and true principle gets hold amongst the rocks of custom or prejudice, and soon its silent growth splits the solid stone, toppling it over fatal precipices into the sea of its final entombment. Feeling this, we have rested in the conviction that the "Woman Question" would make its way according to the innate vitality and the truth it possesses. If this conviction has made us seem indifferent or false to the best interests of woman, we regret it profoundly, being at heart deeply interested in the true welfare of our sex.

A man of the world once remarked in our hearing that "women had a talent for unhappiness." The astute remark set us to thinking. All unhappiness which is not the result of bereavement of the affections comes from unsatisfied or disappointed aspirations. Granted that women suffer more through their affections than men do, there is still a large amount of their discontent to be attributed to fruitless aspiration. To aspire, in the one sex, is thought to be noble and praiseworthy. But for woman to aspire has been, if it is not still, almost a crime. Not only the vain desire for a higher estate, but the consciousness of being thought guilty for having the desire, has given woman her "talent for unhappiness."

Few persons would feel justified in asserting that any class of men ought to be restricted to a certain round of occupations which should be denominated *duties* and be made binding upon them to the exclusion of everything else, no allowance being made for differences of taste, inclination or capacity. No one would deny that such exclusion was a species of slavery, mental as well as social and physical, nor that it would in the long run surely dwarf the capacities of the class so enslaved. If, slowly and by degrees, they battled successfully with the tyranny which held them in bondage, and rose little by little to freedom and full development, great would be their award of praise. But not while they were in the struggle would they receive commendation. Men are slow to praise anything whose success is not warranted.

The present desire of women for political rights is founded in their conviction that without the franchise they have no individual existence; and that without an individual existence it is in vain to attempt the accomplishment of any worthy object. The antagonism which exists in the minds of men towards projects initiated by women must ever defeat their usefulness in any but the pr[e]scribed field, so long as men only hold the voting privilege. It is perfectly useless to define the causes of this antagonism: the fact of its existence is patent and cannot be ignored. If, then, women, having found out that there is work for them, good paying work in which both inclination and profit are united, wish to be made politically alive (whereas before they have, politically, never been born), we do not know of any good and sufficient reason why they should not begin to exist in this new sense.

We say we do not know of any sufficient reason. Now that commits us to the affirmative side of the Woman's Rights question, does it not?

But then there is the other side: We are trying to find the reasons why they *should* vote, which after all is the main object of discussion. If enfranchisement will secure to them any important good, such as higher education, better social positions, larger pay for competent work, more full and perfect home influence and greater happiness, then there is ground enough for their demand. If men could be convinced of this, we think they would withdraw their opposition, notwithstanding they lost their positions as masters of the world's affairs and were compelled to accept partners in its management. For, after all, it is only a misunderstanding which prevents the agreement of men and women on this or any other question.

There appears to be in the minds of men a strong dislike to having women become like themselves. Uncomplimentary as this feeling is to themselves, it is evidently underlaid by a chivalric sentiment towards women which does credit to men as the friends of women. They are aware that they have "left undone the things which they ought to have done; and done those things which they ought to have left undone, and that there is no health in them," and they fear to contaminate women by having them brought into the knowledge of these things. But we think that they underrate themselves when they indulge this unworthy apprehension. If men are good enough to be the fathers, brothers and husbands of good women, there is no fear that they are not good enough to be their associates in other relations of life, including business and politics. If they are sincere in thinking themselves unfit for such contact, the deepest wrong they can do to women they do when they propose to them so intimate a relationship as marriage. If women married to bad men escape contamination, why shall it be feared for them that they shall be injured by buying and selling, or by voting in their company?

The truth is, no doubt, that men would relinquish those practices which they fear to have made known to women whenever the custom of association in business or politics should be established. In the family, in the church, and in the social circle the presence of women ensures good order and chaste conversation. It is a poor compliment to men to apprehend that they may behave differently in any circumstances; and it is a worse one to believe that they are so wedded to certain vices that they resolve not to give them up, and banish women from public places in order that they may indulge them unrestrained. Probably women are as safe to vote at an election as they are to attend a Fourth of July celebration.

Still this not touching the question of expediency for women. It cannot be denied by the thinking mind that as the population of the world increases do women become, as they are sure to and under the present ruling, more numerous than men, they either must take upon themselves some of the active work of the world, and become producers of capital, or they must sink into mere servile consumers of the capital of men. Where men are in the majority or in equal numbers with women, the position of political and financial nothingness is not felt severely, because the services of women are so much needed, and are in a manner paid for by the protection afforded by men. But when women greatly outnumber men, as in Great Britain and New England, the question becomes a grave one of how they are to live at all, with so few occupations open to them, so many disabilities upon them, and no "career" possible to be entered upon.

Undoubtedly women must enter more freely into the business of the world. But how do it while politically minors, and with the general sentiment of society against them? If it is hard for a man to succeed in life without capital, friends, or public approbation, how is the feebler and more sensitive woman to make her way in the world? Could women be found who are brave enough to attempt the acquisition of a thorough business education and to enter upon the pursuit of wealth as men do, we believe it would prove an infinite benefit to their sex at large, and to the world as well. Women capitalists would be more easily approached by other women needing a start in life or assistance in business than men are. Women dislike going to men for assistance for several reasons, not the least of which is their superior air and the polite doubt of the applicant's knowledge of her own intentions, which they are apt to express by look or tone, unconsciously or otherwise. This dread of meeting men on business grounds keeps many an ambitious and secretly aspiring woman always poor and sorrowful. If women can learn to assist each other, becoming each other's employers and bankers, is it really inexpedient? Would men prefer to have them dependent and wretched? If so, what could be their motive?

The motive commonly alleged is a fear lest women should neglect those peculiar labors which Providence has assigned them in the bearing and rearing of children. And here indeed we see for ourselves a great apparent disqualification for those pursuits which are most profitable and honorable. Not that we fear women who may have children should neglect them, or turn monsters of unnatural indifference to domestic affection generally. But there is a very proper fear that they should overtask themselves through the desire to do the best for their children and themselves. Women generally are more unsparing of themselves than men; and could they see an opportunity of gaining money or any other good by the complete sacrifice of themselves they would be liable to this species of self-immolation.

And yet would not the right to make laws, if conferred upon women, be the surest method of correcting any evils that might grow out of the new order of things? Certainly women must see for themselves the dangers that might beset them, and be the first to avert the peril by enacting laws having in view their own preservation and that of their offspring. If in the family, the school-room and the church, the advice and co-operation of women has been useful, why not equally so in affairs of every kind in which the mutual interests of men and women are involved?

Men too often talk as if what women wished in obtaining the right of suffrage was notoriety merely. We believe them to be unjust in this estimate of the Suffragists. Women naturally and by custom dislike notoriety. There certainly are exceptions to the rule, but the rule remains. As they leave, by universal consent, the rougher and more public contests of everyday life to men, very gladly, so they will leave those political questions, and national concerns of which men may prove the wisest judges to them.

We believe they desire only to have a voice in those things which effect their own and their children's welfare, and which give character and coloring to the morals of the world. If there are some who are ambitious simply for ambition's sake, they find few sympathizers among their own sex; and would find little encouragement were they to offer themselves for public positions which they are unfitted to fill.

Women, too, are great conservatives, as the opposition they make among themselves to the "woman movement" goes to show. They will "make haste slowly" in taking upon themselves unconsidered obligations or in disturbing the existing order of things, except in such cases as evidently demand some action on their part. The privilege of voting, if they have it, will not always be made available any more than it now is by many men. It will only be when society is threatened in some way that women will be eager to vote. Such is our belief. And still the expediency of the ballot for women can only be proven by testing it practically. If it does not accomplish for them what they hope for in certain amendments of their personal condition, they will abandon it themselves. If it does, there is little danger that men will any longer oppose it.

Geology reveals the fact that certain creations have passed entirely away and been succeeded by others which in their turn have also passed away, and that each succeeding one was more excellent than the others. So history teaches us that ideas and customs may become fossilized. Whether the idea of gender in human rights is doomed to be overlaid by a new stratum of liberal thought this century will prove. If the woman question goes by the board to be exhumed centuries hence as a curiosity, we shall say "Amen," because we have such faith in the eternal fitness of things.

Have we committed ourself on the question? If we have, we do not know it, but like the ostrich with its head in a bush, imagine ourself hidden. If too doubting or too uninformed to have an opinion, we know that we would not lay a straw in the way of any woman striving to reach higher toward an earthly or heavenly good.

MRS. F.F. VICTOR.

THE NEW NORTHWEST, Friday, 25 August 1871, page 1 columns 1-2

ALL ABOUT LOOKING-GLASSES.

By Mrs. F.F. Victor.

Why do people, I wonder, buy such hideous looking-glasses as they do. I arise sometimes tired enough and hurried enough, in travelling, to see things a little crooked at the best. The bewilderment and haste are not lessened on consulting a square of wavy, defective glass with a sheeting of quicksilver on the reverse. It is like looking into water in motion; — it makes one seasick. Then of how much use is a mirror which reflects one's face of a quarter more than its real breadth or length; or worse still, as if distorted by the grip of a desperate paralysis. It would be safer to trust to the sense of touch for evidence of effect in dressing, than to so false a reflection.

And yet how many house-keepers seem not to know that one mirror is better or worse than another? If they have a looking-glass stuck against a wall somewhere — anywhere — they think it enough. But that is all a mistake. A mirror, to fulfill its real mission, must be some general proportion to the object to be reflected. The human face, generally, is of greater length than bread[t]h. So should the mirror be in which it is intended the face only should be see[n]; by that I mean small ones. Full length mirrors must be, of necessity, in [t]hat proportion. Those intended for man[t]les being long in the other direction, are seldom pleasant to look in. But that depends again a great deal on the qual[i]ty of the glass. To determine the qual[i]ty, put the edge of your thumb nail against the glass and observe the thickness, which will appear between the nail and its reflection. Try the glass all over in that way. If the glass is an eighth of an inch thick, and even, it is all right in that respect. Then place your mirror in a good light, and place some white object before it. If the reflection is the least tinged with green, do not take that glass; for you will not wish to look jaundiced every time you see yourself in your mirror.

When your mirror is purchased let it be hung *between* two good lights — not opposite to them, nor to any; for in that case it would reflect the light direct, and give you a very poor chance of appearing well in your own eyes. You will look far better, and far more like yourself, if you give the mirror an opportunity of reflecting only so much of the light as shines upon your face. Don't be inveigled, either, into buying the handsomest dressing-bureau before testing the qualities of the mirror. It is just as easy to have a good article as a poor one if you are quite determined not to have the latter.

It is somewhat curious to note the value attached to mirrors in all ages. From Eve's time to our own they have been [e]steemed of great importance. Probably Eve tried on her fig-leaves by the side of some quiet pool, the manufactures not having advanced much at that date. But we hear that in a few generations there were "artificers in brass and iron," and have reason to conclude that the uses of polished surfaces had been some time discovered. The belles of ancient Egypt were not without these important accessories of the toilet; and from Egypt came the first knowledge of luxury to the inhabitants of Europe.

But it was in Venice, the city of the sea, that the art of making glass mirrors was discovered. So precious were they in that age, that great fortunes were made by their manufacture; and royalty spared no expense in embellishing the glass in which it beheld itself reflected, loading the frames of the royal mirrors with the costliest jewels. Later, France borrowed the art, and continues now to manufacture very superior plate glass mirrors. Some firms in the United States produce a good article of the same; but the French have the highest reputation. Whoever it is, is guilty of palming off upon the people these wretched, distorting, dizzying things, in cheap mahogany frames, ought to be discountenanced by every intelligent house-keeper in the country.

Talking about mirrors, and their value to all classes, reminds me of some amusing scenes I once witnessed in an Indian country, where a new town had sprung up like a mushroom in a night. Almost daily my merriment was excited by seeing one or two young "braves" strutting about the streets, their lordly brows crowned with wreaths of artificial flowers, a lady's parasol in one hand, and a small hand-mirror in the other! When a buffalo robe composed the toga of these noble chiefs, the effect was irresistibly comic. But their admiration of themselves was supreme, as one could tell by the frequent references to the hand glasses.

One day I was sitting with open door, reading in silent absorption some interesting book, when I was startled out of my composure by hearing a very slight stir just behind me. Glancing around in alarm, for I had believed myself to be alone, I beheld a tall Omaha "warrior" posturing before the parlor mirror, and evidently delighted with the effect of a wreath of pink roses around his head. Amusing as the spectacle was, I had been so shocked by the discovery, that I cried out *pock-a-chee,* with much sternness; and saw my light-footed visitor depart, carrying upon his bronzed features the most affected smirk conceivable. So fond of finery were those dignified "lords of creation" that it was their practice to place the principal part of the money paid them by the U.S. Agent in the hands of their squaws for safe-keeping, lest they should have nothing left for the purchase of more necessary articles.

Looking-glasses are supposed to imply personal vanity; and that man or woman who most often consults one is sure to be stigmatized as "vain." This view of the subject is no doubt a prejudiced one. It is quite as often the timid and doubtful person who refers to his or her mirror for an opinion, as the fop or the coquette. The mirror comes nearer than anything else, perhaps, to furnishing that "giftie" which Robert Burns prayed for, — "to see oursels as ithers see us;" and no doubt does from "many a blunder free us, an' foolish notion." If we have been particular to select a true one for our private chamber, we need not go into society ignorant of our defects, or unconscious of our excellencies of appearance.

And this brings us to the moral side of our subject. How are we to be supplied with moral and intellectual looking-glasses? If we seek for them in the opinions of our associates we shall find our images most often distorted — occasionally flattered — as we sometimes say a real looking-glass flatters our faces. When choosing a mirror for our toilet we take one that neither makes us long, nor broad, nor green-visaged, nor crooked, but one that simply shows us up with clearness, altering nothing that we have reason to know of our appearance, we judge we have selected the best; so when among our friends we find one who neither depreciates nor flatters, but accepts us for what we are conscious of being, making no effort to deceive or disparage us, we feel that we have discovered a safe moral mirror.

It is not the province of a mirror to improve anybody. Its whole duty is to show us where we may improve ourselves. If we consult the opinions of our true friends we have this opportunity of finding out where we need improving, and what our excellencies are. And it is quite as needful to know the latter as the former. I, for one, never had any patience with that class of moralists who think it necessary to hide from people the fact that they possess charming or excellent qualities. They are the crooked mirrors, and the sight of one makes me sick. Just as the bashful person would be teetotally discouraged by the sight of his image in a distorting mirror, so the man or woman lacking in self-esteem, and never being told of any meritorious qualities, would be certain to fancy the opposite. These convictions are often enough the result of some unkind or thoughtless reticence in those whose opinions are most valued by us. The harm they do cannot be estimated by the amount of suffering to the individual; it is best estimated by the consideration of the power it has to suppress hopeful effort.

The fear of encouraging vanity in others is a mean fear. Vanity does far less real injury in the world than silent detraction. Vanity is above-board, and so patent as to be easily avoided; while doubt and humility often wear the garb of pride and defiance — which are the wrinkles on the face of the mirror. There is no better polishing powder for our moral mirrors than sweet charity. Its price is above gold dust.

I need not say that even the best of moral looking-glasses need adventitious aids — like having itself placed in a favorable light. A little tact is a very good thing in every relation of life. Overpraise, like too powerful a light on the mirror, brings into derisive notice whatever defect there may be. A true mirror in the house, and one in the heart, are, beyond cavil, very good things to have. Put out the crooked ones, by all means.

Victor, Frances Fuller. *All Over Oregon and Washington.* San Francisco: John H. Carmany & Co., 1872. Pages 37-38.

. . . [D]irectly — very opportunely — we are confronted with the lighthouse keeper, who offers to show us his tower and light [on Cape Disappointment near the mouth of the Columbia River]. Clambering up and up, at last we stand within the great lantern, with its intense reflections; and hear all about the life of its keeper — how he scours and polishes by day, and tends the burning oil by night. When we ask him if the storm-winds do not threaten his tower, he shakes his head and smiles, and says, it is an "eerie" place up there when the sou'westers are blowing. But, somehow, he likes it; he would not like to leave his place for another.

Then we climb a little higher, going out upon the iron balcony, where the keeper stands to do his outside polishing of the glass. The view is grand; but what charms us most, is a miniature landscape reflected in one of the facets of the lantern. It is a complete copy of the north-western shore of the cape, a hundred times more perfect and beautiful than a painter could make it, with the features of a score of rods concentrated into a picture of a dozen inches in diameter, with the real life, and motion, and atmosphere of Nature in it. While you gaze enchanted, the surf creeps up the sandy beach, the sea-birds circle about the rocks, the giant firs move gently in the breeze, shadows flit over the sea, a cloud moves in the sky; in short, it is the loveliest picture your eyes ever rested on.

The friendly keeper explains to you, as you turn to look up the coast, that the beach north of the cape extends, in one unbroken level, about twenty miles; and that it is a long, narrow neck, divided from the mainland by an arm of Shoalwater Bay, extending almost down to the lighthouse. A splendid drive down from the bay! It is in the sandy marshes up along this arm of Shoalwater Bay, too, that we may go to find cranberries.

When we ask, "What does he do when the thick fogs hang over the coast?" he shows us a great bell, which, when the machinery is wound up, tolls, tolls, tolls, solemnly in the darkness, to warn vessels off the coast. "But," he says, "it is not large enough, and can not be heard any great distance. Vessels usually keep out to sea in a fog, and ring their own bells to keep off other vessels."

Then he shows us, at our request, Peacock Spit, where the United States vessel of that name was wrecked, in 1841; and the South Spit, nearly two miles outside the cape, where the *Shark,* another United States vessel, was lost in 1846. The bones of many a gallant sailor, and many a noble ship, are laid on the sands, not half a dozen miles from the spot where we now stand and look at a tranquil ocean. Nor was it in storms that these shipping disasters happened. It was the treacherous *calm* that met them on the bar, when the current or the tide carried them upon the sands, where they lay helpless until the flood-tide met the current, and the ship was broken up in the breakers. Pilotage and steam have done away with shipwrecks on the bar.

Victor, Frances Fuller. *All Over Oregon and Washington*. San Francisco: John H. Carmany & Co., 1872. Pages 53-54.

. . . [W]e listen to a legend, or tradition, which the Nehalem Indians relate of a vessel once cast ashore near the mouth of their river, the crew of which were saved, together with their private property, and a box which they carried ashore, and buried on Mount Neah-car-ny, with much care, leaving two swords placed on it in the form of a cross.

Another version is, that one of their own number was slain, and his bones laid on top of the box when it was buried. This, were it true, would more effectually keep away the Indians than all the swords in Spain.

The story sounds very well, and is firmly believed by the Indians, who can not be induced to go near the spot, because their ancestors were told by those who buried the box, that, should they ever go near it, they would provoke the wrath of the Great Spirit. The tale corresponds with that told by the Indians of the upper Columbia, who say that some shipwrecked men, one of whom was called Soto, lived two or three years with their tribe, and then left them to try to reach the Spanish countries overland. It is probable enough that a Spanish galleon may have gone ashore near the mouth of the Columbia, and it agrees with the character of the early explorers of that nation, that they should undertake to reach Mexico by land. That they never did, we feel sure, and give a sigh to their memory.

Some treasure-seekers have endeavored to find the hidden box, but without result. One enthusiast expressed it as his opinion, that he could go right to the spot where it is hidden; but why he did not do so, he failed to explain. Like the treasure of Captain Kidd, it would probably cost as much as it is worth to find it.

Victor, Frances Fuller. *All Over Oregon and Washington*. San Francisco: John H. Carmany & Co., 1872. Page 180.

. . . It is . . . claimed for Long Tom, that it originated the term "Web-foot," which is so universally applied to Oregonians by their California neighbors. The story runs as follows: A young couple from Missouri settled upon a land-claim on the banks of this river, and in due course of time a son and heir was born to them. A California "commercial traveler" chancing to stop with the happy parents overnight, made some joking remarks upon the subject, warning them not to let the baby get drowned in the rather unusually extensive mud-puddle by which the premises were disfigured, when the father replied that they had looked out for that; and, uncovering the baby's feet, astonished the joker by showing him that they were *webbed*. The *sobriquet* of Webfoot having thus been attached to Oregon-born babies, has continued to be a favorite appellative ever since.

SAN FRANCISCO MORNING CALL, Sunday, 6 June 1875, page 1 columns 7-8
[Written for the Morning Call.]

WANTED, A DIVORCE.

The Adventures of Mrs. Flibertigibbet in Search of One.

Dorothy D. Gives Her Some Good Advice.

Which May be of Service to Other Women Similarly Situated.

My friend Belle Flibertigibbet came to me the other day, and, with tears in her eyes, informed me that she had made up her mind to have a divorce. When I reminded her that this was not the first time she had come to a similar determination without finally doing anything, she burst out crying, and sobbed after her own passionate fashion. When this preliminary shower was over — which, by the way, I made no attempt to interrupt — her face softened and brightened, and I thought it a very good time to have a talk with her. By way of initiative, I very quietly asked her if she had seen a lawyer on the subject of a separation from her husband. She replied that she had. Of course I then asked her what he said.

"He did not say anything particular," answered Belle. "He asked me a great many questions — how old I was, how long I had been married, if I had children, what my ground of complaint was, and all that sort of thing."

"Have you any objection to telling me your story just as you told it to him? Perhaps I might be able to suggest something," I said.

"Well," said Belle, "you know I was married very young to Mr. Flibertigibbet, who was a great deal older than I — fully twice as old then. I was only a child in years or experience; an adopted daughter, whom my guardians were glad to be rid of; and silly and ignorant as I could be. Actually, Dorothy, I did not know enough to say 'no' to an offer of marriage, because I thought for a girl to marry was like a young man's going in business, and it was a sort of feather in my cap to set up in life so young. I wasn't in love — I've never been in love in my life — just think of that, Dorothy!"

"You have certainly missed an experience, then," I said; "but whether sad or happy nobody can say until they have had it."

"Well, anyway, it must be natural, and I do not see how a woman can know much about herself who has never been really in love," replied Belle, with a touch of bitterness in her tones. "But that is neither here nor there, in the story. I got along pretty well until I was twenty, and had my third baby; for I was so young and so engrossed with the care of children, that there was no opportunity for pausing to look back or forward either. But I grew better able to think after I was twenty, and I dared to have some wishes of my own in the matter of society. Mr. Flibertigibbet, you know, does not care at all for going out, from one year's end to another, except to go down town and collect his rents. But the world was new to me, and I am naturally fond of meeting people, and love to see something going on that is cheerful and amusing. At first I never did go anywhere, because I thought I couldn't; but afterwards I found I could, by having proper help, get away from the four walls that imprisoned me. And I did so. I went to evening parties once in a while, and to picnics, and boating parties, and the like, but always with several ladies and gentlemen, so as to have it look perfectly proper. But that is just exactly what Mr. Flibertigibbet does not like me to do. He is always crosser than two sticks, and scolds and rants around the house for a day or two after I have been out anywhere for a little recreation. He is jealous, too, and says the most abominable things; and one evening, when I had a few friends at home, and we were pretty lively, and a gentleman had just snatched a photograph or something from me that I was trying to recover, he came in abruptly, and began abusing me and this gentleman at a terrible rate, so that the party broke up immediately. You can imagine how agreeable it must be to be watched, and scolded, and charged with indecencies, when all you have been guilty of is a little frolic, that came on, you hardly know how, but innocently enough. Of course, the more he acts this way, the more lonely and forlorn I feel in the house alone, and the more I prize or need society. He says I neglect my house and children. Well, I do not know what other mothers do. I know my children are well fed and dressed, and go to Sunday School as soon as they are old enough; and the house is clean and orderly. But I'll confess I don't like to stay in it any longer — and if this goes on I shall hate it by and by. In fact, I hate it now, and *I won't stay in it*!''

Whereupon the little lady's countenance threatened another thunderstorm — that was, however, happily averted by Dorothy's adroitly remarking,

''But you *have* stayed in it, and *do* stay in it, without compulsion, which is no way to proceed about a divorce. People cannot be divorced who are living under the same roof, and guilty of no criminality nor breach of contract.''

''Oh, yes, they can,'' replied Belle; ''haven't you seen those advertisements of the Divorce Bureau? — 'No publicity; quick and cheap'?''

''But you certainly would not employ that sort of legal help?'' I said, rather astonished at Belle's familiarity with this equivocal means of obtaining freedom from domestic tyranny.

''Why not?'' she asked. ''It is the divorce I am concerned about, and not the means by which it is obtained. They offer to secure the decree before taking any fee whatever; but the other lawyers might bother you a long time, and want a pile of money, besides.''

''Have you consulted with any of these anonymous attorneys?'' I inquired.

''No; to tell the truth I have not. You know I told you nearly a year ago that I meant to do this, if I could not have a more peaceful and happy home than I have had. Not long after I told you about it, Mr. Flibertigibbet became so exasperating that I started one day to go and see a lawyer; but just as I reached my own gate, there was my husband being brought home seriously hurt by a fall he got clambering over an unfinished building. I could not have the heart, you know, to go trying to get a divorce when he was suffering and might die; so I just set to work and nursed him up as tenderly as I would a baby. And, strange to say, while he was helpless, and I was tied to his dressing-gown string every moment, he was as good as could be, and actually made me quite pretty compliments every once in a while. But just as soon as he was able to be around again, it was the same old story; and after a while I got tired of it, and started the second time to see a lawyer. But on the way I learned the scarlet fever was in town, and remembering that little Rudolph had not seemed well in the morning, I became alarmed, and hurried back home just in time to see that the doctor was needed; and so was confined closely to the house again for weeks by the illness of all the children. While I could not stir out of doors, my jailer was quite gracious, and never once got up a scene in which he played the jealous husband. When the children could play outside again, I began to feel as if a little fresh air and amusement would be good for me, and went with a party over to see a boat race on the bay. This was enough to start a new purgatory, which I endured as long as I could, and then once more set out to learn what I was to do. And, would you believe it? I sprained my ankle before I got to the corner of the second block away! I was taken home and laid up for weeks and weeks, so that I was forced to be a prisoner. And, just as usual, Mr. Flibertigibbet was so glad to keep me home that he never minded my being no end of trouble, and carried me up and down stairs with the greatest cheerfulness, waiting upon the children as patiently as I could have done. I believe that man would be perfectly willing I should be lame all my life if he could only keep me shut up in a closet. But I got well, you see, and it is the old story; and to-day I really have seen a lawyer."

Dorothy D., though a sage and sensible person enough, was a good deal moved to laughter by the conclusion of this story, that had in it the elements of the tragic and the comic, and would have made a very pretty drama. After indulging herself in a half-smothered fit of mirthfulness, she asked Mrs. Flibertigibbet what she expected would happen to her now.

"Of course, I half looked to be run over on the street, or something of that sort," she answered; "but I didn't much care, only on account of the children."

"But you have not yet told me how your interview with your lawyer ended?" I remarked.

At this, Belle blushed, and fidgeted with her parasol, but finally came out with it, as if with a desperate sense of the hopeless depravity of the whole world.

"He told me it was a very aggravated case, and that I was too sweet and pretty to be scolded. He ended by making a movement to kiss me, when I struck at him with my parasol, and ran away."

"So *that* is what happened to you this time?" I remarked, with a smile. "That is quite as bad as any of the other accidents; isn't it?"

"Yes, it is," said Belle desperately. "It is the first time in my life a man ever treated me so lightly, and I felt furious and ashamed altogether. A man, old enough to be my father, too! I suppose I'll not have courage now to see anybody else for months; and in the meantime, what am I going to do? I've a mind to try the Divorce Bureau."

"You'll find them a worse lot," I said, quietly. "Honorable men do not have to disguise their acts — nor honorable women, either. Take *my* advice, Belle, dear, and rest on this last interruption for a while. Or just go home and tell Mr. Flibertigibbet what you have told me, without any passion or tears. Let him see how you feel, and for what reasons; and let him know what you have done, and how you were received — withholding the name of the attorney whom you saw. This course will show him that he can trust you, and that he has not been so considerate of your happiness as he ought. Show him that your health of body and mind depends on having some free and unrestricted enjoyment of the ordinary pleasures of life, of which probably in his youth he had his fill, so that he does not care about them now. If, after time to digest these facts, he continues to be jealous, and disagreeable, it will be time enough to take other measures. I think he loves you, and you both love the children, who ought to have your mutual care. You would find it as hard to live separately with this little family between you, as it now is to bear with his inconsiderateness and rudeness; but it seems to me there is no necessity for either."

A dreary sort of smile passed over Belle's face. "What is to be will be, I suppose," she said with a sigh. "I might try your plans. If it does not work well, it will at last bring matters to a crisis, and remove from me the shadow of a doubt about the propriety of what I meant to do, and should certainly feel easier in my mind after that. But you cannot think how hard it is for me."

Poor Belle! it was hard for her, I had not a doubt, to humble her womanly pride before selfishness and injustice. My heart ached for her, when I remembered her saying she had never known what it was to love, what possibilities the future held for her, whose mind and soul were only just now blossoming out, having been stunted in her girlhood by too early wifehood and maternity. Turn the case over whichever way one would, there was no escape from the penalty of this fatal error. "Love is of man's life a thing apart. 'Tis woman's whole existence," wrote Byron; and thus most women feel, either from education or from nature. To be yoked for life to one whom we could never really love is hardly worse than being so situated only to find when too late that we have a strong capacity for love which we dare not use. So, however circumstances bent the current of my friend's life, her chances for happiness were poor indeed — the seeming only safety being in the chance that she might never discover what she had missed — a hardly possible chance, indeed, but strengthened most by the fact of having children to anchor her affections to.

But what about these divorce bureaus, lying in wait for unhappy young wives or unprincipled husbands? Do any good women patronize them, we wonder? Some do, perhaps, influenced thereto by dread of the remarks of society upon divorces. But let every blameless woman who has determined to sever an intolerable or a degrading bond, do so openly, declaring the facts in the case. If she has separated from her husband, she has thus declared that she repudiates allegiance to him, and established the fact that there must be a reason. In justice to herself, if she determines to be divorced, she should make her reason known as justification of the step to be taken. Any attempt at secrecy suggests at least the presumption of unfairness in the complaint — a presumption that a pure and proud woman should not be willing to allow. A bad husband is a misfortune; and it is true that society has little tolerance for the unfortunate; yet most people do respect those unlucky ones who have the courage to own themselves worsted in the greatest ventures of their lives, and who frankly avow their determination to undo as far as possible what has been done wrong. Therefore, to all good women, with causes more legally serious than our friend Belle has to present, we say, Do not go near any secret divorce agencies, but state the matter candidly to a respectable and responsible lawyer. Generally speaking, the profession is not given to such indelicate flattery as Mrs. Flibertigibbet was fated to encounter. But if any of them should so far forget themselves, you can resort to that lady's expedient with the parasol.

Dorothy D. wishes that young women, and young men as well, could give a reason for marrying above instinct or caprice. Until they can, and until both parties are educated to *think* on the subject, there will be plenty of cases like Belle's, and plenty more like those that have filled the newspapers with scandal from month to month — with desertion and murder cases — or with life-long suffering and bitter disappointment, in the endurance of which all that is best in man or woman is warped or wasted.

DOROTHY D.

[Written for the Sunday Call.]

TO "DOROTHY D."

Dear Dorothy D.,
    Are you fond of tea?
Oolong, or Souchong, or Old Bohea?
    One or the other —
    Or all together —
May I invite you to take with me?

    I wear caps
    And take short naps
Over my knitting, like all good dames;
    "Old fashioned" and "queer"
    They call me, my dear;
But, la! I mind neither them [n]or their names.

    Are you a "blue?" *
    And is it true
You wear your hair parted on one side;
    Write for the press —
    Ape men in dress,
And always have some hobby to ride?

    I know, of course,
    Your idea of divorce;
I read all about it in THE CALL:
    And your friend Belle
    For once did well,
To give you a chance to overhaul.

    I'd like to know
    If you've a "beau,"
And whether you chose him for his brains;
    I'm certain sure
    You couldn't endure
To marry a man for temporal gains.

    "Old School" or "New" —
    Which pleases you
When one's body or soul is out of tune?
    Have you your "Rights,"
    Or would you delight
To stand at the polls and vote men down?

---

*In London, England, about the year 1750, women began to meet for literary conversation and discussion, instead of the usual card games and gossip, at the home of Elizabeth Montagu, who wanted to introduce into society a healthier and more serious tone. Ladies visiting her house on Hill Street wore blue stockings as an emblem of the society Mrs. Montagu wished to form. So it was that "bluestocking," a derisive term for women having intellectual or literary interests, came into existence.

So now my dear
It seems quite clear
You must come and have a chat with me;
If you're agreed,
Why all you need
To do is to answer old   CHARITY C.

SAN FRANCISCO MORNING CALL, Sunday, 11 July 1875, page 8 column 3
[Written for the Sunday Call.]

REPLY TO CHARITY C.

————

DEAR [CHARITY] C. — You will please pardon me
For not answering sooner your "invite" to tea;
But the truth of the same is, that I'm not to blame;
I was absent from home when your kind letter came.

But now that I'm here, at your service, my dear,
We'll to tea and to gossip, without any fear,
But that we shall find we're of mutual mind,
Whatever the topics to which you're inclined.

All the same, since you ask, not to take me to task —
I don't see the motive for wearing a mask —
I will answer you true — I'm a bit of a "blue,"
But I don't part my hair on one side — do you?

And as for men's dress, bless your heart, I confess
To liking our fripperies not a whit less,
Though I know they're a weight on our forms and our fate,
And keep us from being anything that is great.

I've no time for a "beau" — they are idlers, you know;
And a hobby for me would be surely "no go;"
For, dear Charity C., I do love to be free,
And hobby's a strong-bitted horse — don't you see?

No; I like to keep clear from all "isms," my dear,
And from people that seem to me anyways queer;
And yet if I found any good, solid ground
That these people had taken, I'd say it was sound.

As to "voting" and "rights," and "old school" or "new lights,"
Their advocates mostly are "luneys" or frights;
But I'd give them their due, and so, dear, would you;
In a bushel of chaff may be one grain that's true.

And now as to the invitation to tea,
You've my thanks; I should relish a dish of Bohea,
If you're satisfied we in our cups should agree,
And that you should be happy with   DOROTHY D.

SAN FRANCISCO MORNING CALL, Sunday, 11 July 1875, page 8 column 3

[Written for the Morning Call.]

TO DOROTHY D. AND CHARITY C.

———

Dear Dorothy D. and Charity C.,
Please, may I come to your tea party?
  Though not given to naps, or wearing of caps,
I'll quickly don one if you grant my plea.
  And down and up, as we nod over our cup,
We'll flutter the white frills merrily.

Tea, there should be three, dear D. and C. —
There's luck in odd numbers, you all will agree;
  And so, don't you see, there surely must be
One to listen, and you will needs have me,
  Tho' the beaux may flout and tear their eyes out
With rage, don't have them at our tea party.

Ye impertinent fops, prized only at hops,
  Whose genius is all in your nimble heel;
Ye of waxed mustaches and heads like mops,
  I warn you but gently with you we'll deal,
As down and up, we nod o'er the cup,
  And pick you to pieces with barbs of steel.

To our sisters so meek, deluded and weak,
  Whom men, your brothers, have made to believe
You were made for no more than to serve and adore
  Themselves, and nothing else, or wish to receive,
For you we'll complain, while the teapot we drain,
  And eat up the pie — we will tearfully grieve.

So Dorothy D. and Charity C.,
  I pray you in all humility,
To grant me a seat when together you meet
  To belabor the masculinity,
And a cup of tea — very sweet for me,
If you please, begs your admiring friend,

JENNIE B.

SAN FRANCISCO MORNING CALL, Sunday, 15 August 1875, page 8 columns 6-7

[Written for the Sunday Call.]

DOROTHY D.

———

A Brief Discussion of the Girl of the Period.

———

Characteristics of the Variety as She Exists in San Francisco.

———

With a Glance at the Beauties Indigenous in the Country.

———

Every once in a while somebody says, "I wish I could see a real old-fashioned girl once more" — as if girls were gone out of fashion! "Old-fashioned girls" may have gone out; and they would speedily be banished to the attic if they had not; but girls — real live ones — there is no lack of in this country, if it is peculiarly a man's country. They are the sweetest things in life, too; there is no denying that, though, happily, they do not look like the pictures in an old annual, nor sit on moonlit balconies, with eyes cast up toward heaven, in the style of sentimental Juliet. This "wonderful Californy climate," as Joaquin Miller's Sierra Judge hath it, does not permit that sort of languishing. It may be very good for fruit and cereals, but it is a miserable climate to be sentimental in. That is one of the first observations Dorothy D. made on forming its acquaintance — "What a wretched climate for lovers and poets!" For, who ever heard of making love early in the morning, notwithstanding the adage, "It is the early bird that catches the worm"? And if you do not improve the sunny morning hours, when will you ever — in San Francisco particularly — find Nature in harmony with tender avowals? You cannot take an afternoon stroll, on account of the wind, nor an evening moonlight ramble, on account of the fog; and I hold it to be totally against all precedent for young things to sit down to love-making in a gas-lighted drawing-room. It may do for their *blasé* elders, but not for them. It is possible, even easy, to be sentimental in the cheerful firelight that throws its weird shadows through those homelike parlors of old New England houses, where some of the best poetry of the times has had its inception, and love-making comes naturally. More naturally and irresistably it comes of Summer nights "under the lindens," or in the rose-scented walks of the silent, moonlit garden. All these things are foreign to the "glorious climate of California," and so I wonder how their loss is borne by lovers and poets, though I know, theoretically at least, with what facility Nature adapts herself to conditions.

To their conditions the California girls are adapted, without doubt, more or less; and that is why the California girl with equal vivacity, has something less of softness in her disposition than the girl fostered in the more humid climate of the Atlantic States. Do you laugh? Well, it is no laughing matter, but one of those driest of dry things — a fact. Some people pretend to blame the girl's parentage; but was not her parentage of the same blood and bone as Miss Dulce's of Boston? You know it was. I could pile up facts mountain high, if I chose, to prove that character as well as physique is affected by climate.

And, consistently with "the eternal fitness of things," softness is not wanted where the circumstances of the case seem rather to prohibit it. There would be no end of ridicule heaped upon our girls should they put on a "melting into total deliquium" air, and go meandering about, quoting poetry and apostrophizing the winds, the flowers, the stars. For, you observe, a San Francisco wind is not one of the "gales of Araby" that the poet mentions, but a good strong muscle-trying, temper-provoking blast from the sea, suggestive of anything but dalliance and rhymes. The girls that can breast this bracing ocean wind are full of strength, vivacity and *verve*. They are ready for play or for work, as the situation demands, but not very readily susceptible to the approaches of the tender passion — or if they are, do not care to have it known.

There are girls and girls, of course; but not any of them excel your thoroughbred San Franciscan in piquancy and nerve, nor in real girlish frolicsomeness. Behold her! She attitudinizes before her mirror with the utmost frankness, studying, as an artist might, proper and becoming poses. Do you tell her she is beautiful, she asks you to "give her some news." Your best-turned compliments she criticises, nor ever loses her head one particle when you utter your compliments with the greatest *empressment*. "O, yes, so I am often told; but what does it amount to?" She sings love songs for you, looking over her shoulder with the most provoking rogueishness, or waltzes with you as if you were her brother. And all the time she is ravishingly beautiful, and she knows it. Not a point but has been studied; and after all she has only done what you would have required of her — made the best of her advantages. If she makes a mistake at all, it is in not giving you credit for being as much struck with her as you are. She is amusing herself, and so, she thinks, may you be.

Yet I do not see that there is anything in this mischievous play, if she be a girl of any brain or breeding, that need alarm you about her qualities as a woman in the future. It is the play of the kitten — pretty, graceful, wild, but quite harmless — less dangerous, in point of fact, than the seductive charms of sentimental young-ladyhood. And as a rule, this style of girl better appreciates what is before her in actual life than the sentimentalist, and enters upon her duties with a mind more made up to them. Therefore she falls off less in looks and spirits when she comes to be confronted with the verities of wedlock.

Some critics find fault with what they call the "flirtishness" of California girls, more especially the San Franciscans. Talking of flirting, commend me to the belle of a country village — an Eastern country village in particular. What, with some beauty, a trifle of accomplishments, a great deal of sentiment, and plenty of novel reading, she is furnished out for the profession of flirting. Her thirst for adulation is unsatiable, as her capacity for humbugging herself and others is boundless. It is not unusual for this sort of girl to be engaged to two or three men at once, nor for her to become an old maid after all, because she cannot determine among the number of those who are perishing for love of her who it is she loves most. I have known one of these town flirts who destroyed the peace of mind of several young men within two years — one of them a clergyman of fair talents, who was notwithstanding fool enough to want to marry her, knowing all about it, and because at the last she would not have him, had to give up his profession and leave the country. Probably this highly romantic *denouement* pleased that young lady exceedingly as a proof of her fatal power for conquest. She was very composed and proper over it — not the least bit flirtish or wild; her religious notions were orthodox; her father a banker; her standing excellent — and doubtless every one of these circumstances helped to delude her several victims — but her profession was that of a heart-smasher, and she gloried in it. I hope she had her proper and only fitting reward — a lonely and loveless life after she was found out.

But, coming back to California girls, if you do not like a San Franciscan, there is your country beauty, with a complexion darkened by the sun, and teeth as white as milk; who rides with her hands behind her if she chooses, and isn't afraid of a cow. She is rather more shy and reticent than her sister of the city, and gives you the cold shoulder, as you think, without reason; yet she believes more what you tell her than the other, and doesn't know what "a flirtation" means. Unless you are quite serious it is best to keep your distance from her, as otherwise you might have to listen to an unflattering opinion of yourself. She is not a girl to shirk any responsibility, for endurance is bred in her, "bone of her bone and flesh of her flesh." Her parents were of those who toiled across the continent with ox-teams. Perhaps her father died upon the way, and her mother arrived in a strange land with no other means than her worn-out cattle, her few house-keeping things, and her thin brown hands. But she contrived to live, and to rear her babies, this girl among the rest. Girls of this stock are not triflers, and the man who fools them should be held beneath contempt.

If you object to the ga[i]ety of city girls, and the solid practicality of country girls, there is at least one strongly marked type between, and that is the girl of the provincial town. After all, I incline to think she combines all the best attractions of all the classes. She is not coarse either from inheritance or association, nor of that super refinement that unfits her for practical duties; nor too full of pranks to listen seriously to your wooing. Let me draw her portrait for you. She is smooth-browed and brown-eyed, with quiet womanly ways, and an air of exquisite purity. Without being learned, she inspires you with admiration for her cleverness; and her talk is piquant and graceful without pedantry. Her father has a turn for science; has been a professor of something or other, and having a good brain herself, and not being distracted by frivolities, she has studied with him more or less all her life; so that what she knows she knows; and the knowledge having come easily and naturally, it sits easily and naturally upon her. Very likely if you ask her to sing she does not know an opera air; but she will give you a well-chosen song, rendered with expression. If you ask her to dance, she may decline, for dancing has not been a part of her education; but she is pleased to look on graciously while her city cousins whirl through the, to her, incomprehensible mazes of a german. This sort of girl attracts wherever she goes, but never by design. Her head not being occupied with plans of conquest, she fails to see how often she might conquer if she would. More often than otherwise she makes a fortunate marriage, for the reason that whatever she does she does with a womanly thoughtfulness that wards off the approaches of unworthy or inferior men. There is no position in life that she would fail to fill with distinction; for, being thoroughly a lady at heart, her well-furnished brain will enable her, even under new and embarrassing circumstances, to choose the proper course — the happy mean between too much self-assertion and too little.

Here are three distinct types of modern girls, with an infinite variety of shades between. But your grumbler wants to see a "real old-fashioned girl." Some people have these antediluvian fancies. They came into the world too late, and have no business in the same age with railroads, telegraphs, geology and evolution. They are like those frontiersmen who having always kept ahead of the westward march of emigration, on the event of the irruption of thousands of civilized people on the Pacific Coast, have been driven to turn back eastward and hide themselves in the fastnesses of the Rocky Mountains. The world has no longer any use for them, and they, unfortunately, have no use for the world. The paleontologist, a thousand years from now, may be interested in their fossil remains, digged from some "recent" deposit; but with things as they are, they can have no living sympathy. I suppose so felt the "missing link" between the Simian race and the race of men, when there was no longer any use for him; and the reason he has never been discovered is, that in his rage and disgust he retreated to the mountains, that afterwards fell upon him and buried him forever from scientific research. To avoid this impending destiny, it would be well for the present generation of men to accept the situation, and accept the girls of the latter half of the nineteenth century as being as much a part and product of the times, as themselves. In behalf of California girls — and boys too — this advice is modestly offered by Dorothy D., who has been accused of slighting the interests of the latter.

But there is a class of girls for whom I have little love, and almost less charity. I do not know that their type is a new one; on the contrary, I have reason to think it is a very old one, not improved by descent. These are the girls who deceive their mothers to get an opportunity to go out of an evening with young men, who think more of having a "beau" than of sustaining the dignity and delicacy of maidenly character, who take presents from their acquaintances — even who sometimes, it is said, lay plans to make men give them articles of dress. It is hard to think that any young lady — she would want to be thought a *lady*, no doubt — could be guilty of so indelicate a course; but truth compels me to own that I know of a few such. And I know of some girls, living in boarding houses, who allow young men to intercept them on the landings or in the hallways, and to keep them there talking half-hours at a time, to the scandal and amusement of the whole house. I always supposed that in such a case the girl was ignorant of the light in which she appeared to lookers-on, or she would never have yielded to such weakness.

Take my word for it, girls, that young man is not worth encouragement who is afraid to court you openly and with your mother's knowledge; and judged by the same rules, people will say of the girl who suffers herself to be courted on the stairs and in corners, that she is not a girl to be trusted. There is no better trait in a young man who desires to win your affections than frankness; and there is no trait in a girl so admirable as modest self-respect. If you sacrifice that for any man, you may reasonably expect that he exact[s] other sacrifices, and that if you marry him your life will be a sacrifice altogether. Girlhood is too lovely and womanhood too sacred to be thrown away on men of that stamp. Men who are true and manly are willing to take a little trouble to win their wives, and like a girl all the better for making them take it.

You are the light of the world, girls; but you are not to hold yourselves *lightly* for all that.

DOROTHY D.

Victor, Frances Fuller. *Atlantis Arisen; or, Talks of a Tourist About Oregon and Washington.* Philadelphia: J. B. Lippincott Company, 1891. Pages 42-43.

The fishing season begins in May, and ends in August. The manner of taking salmon in the Columbia is usually by driftnets, from twenty to a hundred fathoms long. The boats used by the fishermen are similar to the Whitehall boat. According to laws of their own, the men engaged in taking the fish, where the drift is large, allow each boat a stated time to go back and forth along the drift to hook up the salmon. The meshes of the nets are just of a size to catch the fish by the gills, when attempting to pass through; and their misfortune is betrayed to the watchful eye of the fisherman by the bobbing of the corks on the surface of the river.

When brought to the fishery, they are piled up on long tables which project out over the water. Here stand Chinamen, two at each table, armed with long, sharp knives, who, with great celerity and skill, disembowel and behead the fresh arrivals, pushing the offal over the brink into the river at the same time. After cleaning, the fish are thrown into brine vats, where they remain from one to two days to undergo the necessary shrinkage, which is nearly one-half. They are then taken out, washed thoroughly, and packed down in barrels, with the proper quantity of salt. That they may keep perfectly well, it is necessary to heap them up in the barrels, and force them down with a screw-press.

The canning process, which was kept secret for one or two seasons, is a much more elaborate one, requiring a large outlay, many hands, and much skill and precision, for its success. Such was the profit derived from this business that canneries multiplied rapidly until 1880, when it reached its height, since which time there has been a decrease in the output, owing to over-fishing. The legislature has come to the protection of salmon with a law confining fishing to a period from the first of April to the first of August. A hatchery is also in operation on the Clackamas River, a branch of the Wallamet, where spawn is cared for and developed, the young fish being placed in the river at a proper stage of growth. With these precautions, it is hoped to save this industry from further loss, and even to excel its former yield.

There are nineteen canneries at Astoria, in which are invested two million dollars, and almost as many more which are tributary to it, the capital operating them being furnished by Astoria. Shipments are made direct to foreign countries, as well as to domestic ports. In 1889 one cargo of salmon which was cleared for Liverpool was valued at three hundred and fourteen thousand three hundred and three dollars, the largest cargo, with one exception, ever cleared direct, by sail, for a foreign port from the Pacific coast. Astoria is the greatest salmon-fishing station in the world, the canneries using between four hundred thousand and five hundred thousand salmon annually, and Astoria sends out larger cargoes by sailing-vessels than San Francisco of fish and wheat.

Victor, Frances Fuller. *Atlantis Arisen; or, Talks of a Tourist About Oregon and Washington.* Philadelphia: J. B. Lippincott Company, 1891. Pages 228-231.

The most formidable of the bear family is the grizzly, which inhabits less the thick forests of the north than the manzanita thickets and the scrub-oak coverts of Southern Oregon. The color of this bear is a silvery gray, its bulk immense, sometimes weighing two thousand pounds, and its habits herbivorous chiefly, though it will, on sufficient provocation, kill and eat other animals, and even man. It subsists in Southern Oregon upon the berries of the manzanita, of which it is very fond, and will feed upon any berries or fruits within its reach, — occasionally, as a relish, digging up a wasps'-nest for the sake of the honey, not being able, like the black bear, to climb in search of bees'-nests.

In seasons when drought has destroyed its customary food in the mountains of California, it has been known to descend into the valleys and dig up gophers for food. If it scents fresh venison or beef, it will steal it if possible, and has been known to take the hunter's provisions out from under his head while sleeping. In such a case it is better to pretend to be sound asleep during the stealing, even if very wide awake, as is most likely to be the case, for any movement will be certain to bring down the bear's paw with force upon the hunter's head, — "a consummation most devoutly to be" avoided.

This trick of the grizzly — striking a man on the head, or "boxing his ears" — is a dangerous one. It is not at all rare to find men in the mountains and valleys where the grizzly ranges who have had their skulls broken by the blow of its immense paw. It is much to be dreaded in a personal encounter, and by no means easy to kill unless hit in the vulnerable spot behind the ear. Those who fancy lion-hunting in the jungles of Africa might find equally good sport in hunting grizzlies in California, Oregon, and in some parts of the Rocky Mountains.

During the summer months they retire to the mountains; but, as the berries ripen, they seek the foot-hills and river-banks, to feed upon their favorite fruits. If a cavern is not at hand when winter comes on in the cold regions, they make a bed for themselves in some thicket, or sometimes dig a hole below the surface, in which they pass the winter sucking their paws. It would seem that where the winters are as mild as in the Coast Mountains of California, they do not hibernate, as they are met with all through the winter season, and kill, and are killed, more than ever at that time, on account of the scarcity of berries.

There are several curious facts in the natural history of this bear, one of the most singular of which is, that the period of gestation is entirely unknown, even to the most observant and experienced mountain men. No one has ever killed a female carrying young, at any time of the year, though they are often discovered with their cubs evidently but a few weeks old. Where they hide themselves during this period, or how long it lasts, no hunter has ever been able to observe, though there are men who have spent half their lives in the mountains, and killed, in desperate encounter, many a grizzly, and at all times of the year, even when hibernating.

The grizzly seems to be "a man of many minds," with regard to attack. Usually, unless in charge of cubs, it quietly avoids a meeting with the hunter, and at times even seems timid and easily alarmed. But because one grizzly has given you room, you must not depend upon the next one doing the same. It is quite as likely that he will challenge you as you pass; and, unless well prepared to take up the glove, you had better "take up" the first tree you come to. It is not a pleasant sight to see one of these monsters on his hind-quarters, with his fore-paws ready for action; and when it comes to running, he can run as fast as you can.

The brown, or cinnamon, bear is also a savage creature, with many of the traits of the grizzly, but inferior in size. He inhabits the same regions with the latter, and also is found in the thick forests of Northern Oregon and Washington.

The black bear is common to every part of these countries, living in the mountains in summer, and visiting the low hills and small valleys, or the banks of rivers, in autumn. When the acorn crop is good in the foothills, bears haunt the groves which furnish their favorite food. If they can find a stray porker engaged in foraging, they embrace him a little too tightly for his health, — in short, "squeeze the breath out of him," — after which affectionate observance they eat him. But, unless exasperated, they never attack the human family, and are not regarded as dangerous under ordinary circumstances.

An animal which is ferocious, and not unfrequently met with in the mountains, is the cougar, — an animal of the cat species, with a skin something like a leopard's, and a long, ringed tail, but a head with a lion-like breadth. It is variously called the California lion and American panther. We saw one large specimen, which was lying dead by the roadside on the Calapooya Mountain, which measured seven feet from tip to tip. This animal seldom attacks a man, but is very destructive to calves and colts in the vicinity of the mountains, especially in the newly-settled parts.

There are three species of the wolf in Oregon and Washington, of which the black is the largest and most ferocious. It stands two and a half or three feet high, and is five to six feet from tip to tip. Such was its destructiveness in the earliest settlement of the country that special means were resorted to for its extermination, until now it is rarely ever met with. It attacks young cattle and colts . . .

The white or gray wolf is another enemy to the stock-raiser, though it is satisfied with smaller game than the black wolf, contenting itself with full-grown sheep; and, being more powerful than a dog, is a great destroyer of flocks in some localities, and so sagacious that it is very difficult to poison. The coyote, or barking wolf, is also a depredator, taking young pigs and lambs. One of these little animals has the voice of several, and can imitate the barking of a whole pack. It is almost too contemptible to be considered game, and is given over to strychnine.

There are two or three species of lynx, or wild-cat, also troublesome to settlers near the forest, carrying off young pigs and such small farm stock. When not stealing from the farmer they subsist upon young fawns, hares, squirrels, and game birds. These pests are numerous in the woods of the Lower Columbia. We have seen numerous good specimens depending from the limbs of trees, where they had been hung after shooting.

Of foxes there are the red, silver-gray, black, and gray varieties. It is thought that the black fox is a distinct species; as is also the gray, which is smaller. But the silver-gray is said by the Indians to be the male of the red species, the female only being of a reddish color. This species, in all its varieties, is very common on the eastern side of the Cascades, and the smaller gray is most abundant in Southeastern Oregon. Their skins, though not as handsome as the silver-gray, are still very fine. The gray is the "medicine fox" of the Indians, a meeting with which brings misfortune.

Elk are found both in the Cascade and Coast Mountains, but are most abundant in the latter, especially in the Olympic Range. In summer they keep pretty high up, but when snow falls in the mountains descend to the plains and river-bottoms. They travel in well-beaten trails and in large droves, which make them easy game. When quite wild they show considerable curiosity, stopping to look at the hunter, thus offering a fair shot. When wounded and in close quarters they are formidable antagonists, from their great size, heavy head, and large antlers. The immense size of their antlers would appear to be an obstacle to their escape when running in the forest, but by throwing back their heads they drop them over their shoulders so well out of the way as to enable them to pass through the thick woods without difficulty. There still are immense herds of them in the mountains near the mouth of the Columbia, and may be hunted in summer by parties sufficiently hardy for overcoming the obstacles of the forest. But autumn and winter are better seasons for hunting elk, as they then come down to more open ground. Elk-steaks are no rarity in Astoria, and occasionally they are to be met with in the Portland markets. It is estimated that not less than one thousand elk were killed in one year in Coos County alone, for the skins only.

Victor, Frances Fuller. *Atlantis Arisen; or, Talks of a Tourist About Oregon and Washington.* Philadelphia: J. B. Lippincott Company, 1891. Pages 255-257.

One of my excursions from Hoquiam was to a logging-camp several miles from town, the journey being performed in a small boat propelled by oars in the hands of the owner of the camp, who treated our party most politely, and by his exploits showed himself a thorough lumberman. Our boating ended, we walked a mile or more through the woods, over a very rough trail, really performing a portage around the dam constructed for "chuting" logs into the stream below. Having been refreshed with an excellent dinner in a comfortable mess-house, we were taken to where the woodmen were felling trees, standing on tiny platforms made by inserting a short board in a cut in the tree, five, ten, or fifteen feet from the ground. I had supposed that this was necessary, either on account of the size of some trees at the butt, or because of the pitch contained in them; but our host assured me the great height at which some of the choppers or sawyers stood was simply an exhibition of bravado — the common ambition to excel one's neighbor in skill or daring.

In felling a tree the foreman takes pains to direct its fall so as not to injure any other valuable tree in its descent, and they do this to a nicety by inserting wedges on the side opposite to the direction in which it is to fall which give it the necessary tilt, — for so straight are these great firs and cedars that, frequently, they will stand erect after they have been cut to the centre all round, and wait for a breeze to sway them to a fall.

It was evident there was an immense waste, ten or twenty feet of a tree at the thickest part, and then the reckless destruction of all that are unfit for the finest lumber. I was regretting this to our host. "The timber grows as fast or faster than it is consumed," was the reply. Admitting that this is true where young timber is left undisturbed, the forest lands when cleared by axe and fire are put under cultivation, except on the mountains, and thus the amount must be rapidly lessening.

Having seen a few trees fall, we were shown the manner of hauling them to the stream, six or eight yokes of oxen being hitched to a single log. The lower side of the log has been peeled before being placed on the skid, which is well greased. The oxen are then driven by experienced men, who receive better wages than any but the foreman and *cook.* This latter exception made me smile, but I find that cooks are important personages in camps everywhere. These western lumbermen do not feed their men, as the Michigan lumbermen do, but give them a variety of fresh and canned foods.

Having watched the hauling of logs, and their skillful management to prevent them from slipping forward on the cattle, and their descent into the basin above the dam with a deep dive, or a splash and a glide, we walked down to the dam to witness a "shoot" of the chute when the gate was raised. This operation requires quickness and nerve, and was superintended by our host. The water rushing out of the basin carries with it a great weight of logs, which must not be allowed to make a "jam" against the dam. The men are on the logs with pikes directing them so as to head them for the opening and send them endwise down the slide below the dam, when they take a header into the stream with a mighty splash, and go floating tumultuously down the agitated water to be arrested by a boom at the creek's mouth, and made into a raft for Gray's Harbor.

The wages paid to men in this camp is from forty dollars to sixty dollars, the foreman getting one hundred and forty. The price of logs is three dollars and fifty cents per thousand feet in the water. The price paid to the owner of the land is fifty cents per thousand. The average per acre is fifty thousand feet of fir and spruce. The cost of putting in a dam is from three thousand dollars to ten thousand dollars; the skidded road costs one thousand dollars per mile; the teams for hauling, one thousand dollars; the mess-house and dormitory, two hundred dollars or three hundred dollars. Nine or ten men at the wages named above, with their board, cost per month about six hundred dollars, and the supplies for the oxen eighty dollars. These figures make this camp cost for its first outfit, being very conveniently located, about five thousand dollars, and its expenses for a season of six months five thousand dollars more. Its profits depend, of course, on the amount gotten into the water ready for the mills. A good deal of money is disbursed in the towns of Washington, every winter, by loggers.

OLYMPIC, Saturday, 31 July 1897.

> Humpty Dumpty sat on a wheel;
> Said Dimple, soon after, "Well, how do you feel?"
> And Dumpty responded, "I feel as if Mars
> Had shot me to earth in a shower of stars."

> "Alas," whimpered Dimple, "not all the king's men
> Can make of poor Dumpty a whole man again;
> He has biked his last bike — his speed has been sped,
> In attempting too promptly to stand on his head."

> Now the moral of Dumpty is never to trust
> To a biking machine that is likely to bust,
> But to purchase a wheel that's as strong as it's neat
> And learn to land cat-wise, all right, on your feet.

Victor, Frances Fuller. *Poems.* Author's Edition: 1900. Page 63.

ON SAN FRANCISCO BAY.

> O perfect day, O sunlit Bay,
>   Whene'er our souls are called to sail
> The sunless strait where shadows wait,
>   May we emerge into a vale
> Where Angel Islands guard the gate!

San Francisco, September 1896.

Biographies

Metta & Orville J. Victor

In all, Metta produced more than 20 volumes of fiction and humor before her death on 26 June 1885, at the age of 54, in Hohokus, N.J. In July 1856, she married Orville James Victor, editor of the Sandusky (Ohio) *Daily Register* and a brother of Henry Clay Victor, Frances' husband. Two years later, Orville and Metta moved to New York City. Orville J. Victor gained prominence as a biographer and historian, and as editor of various publications, during a career that spanned more than half a century in the metropolis. He, too, died at Hohokus, N.J., on 14 Mar. 1910, at the age of 83.

Albert Bierstadt

Albert Bierstadt, an American landscape painter, was born 7 Jan. 1830 in Solingen, Westphalia, Germany, and taken to the United States when about a year old. Bierstadt returned to his native land to study painting at Dusseldorf from 1853-1856. His portraits of the American West, particularly the Rocky Mountains, made him widely popular. He received many German and Austrian decorations, and was a chevalier of the French Legion of Honor. Bierstadt's panoramic views demonstrated a certain ability, but critics considered his work more topographically correct and impressive than artistic in conception and execution. He died 18 Feb. 1902 in New York City.

John Ross Browne

John Ross Browne was christened 23 Jan. 1821 near Dublin, Ireland. His father, who edited a political paper called the *Comet*, emigrated with the family to America in 1833 and settled near Cincinnati, Ohio. In 1839 Browne started, in Louisville, Ky., the writing career that quite literally would take him around the world. Two years later Browne went to Washington, D.C., to help his father transcribe Congress' proceedings for the *Congressional Globe*; and mastered shorthand, a valuable and necessary skill. But he grew restless and in 1842 joined the crew of a whaling vessel on a 17-month cruise. Browne got as far as Zanzibar, an island in the Indian Ocean off the east-central coast of Africa. He returned to the capital 28 Nov. 1843, and about a year later married Lucy Anna Mitchell, daughter of a local physician. Browne worked four years in the Treasury Department, then was appointed to the revenue service and sailed for California to take up his post. On arriving in San Francisco, however, Browne learned that the service had been reduced and his own position eliminated. Fortunately, he met William M. Gwinn, an old acquaintance, one of 48 delegates to the constitutional convention preparing California's admission as a state. Browne transcribed the proceedings and was paid $10,000; he published his notes as a book in the East and obtained additional income. Now he could better provide for his growing family. In March 1851 the Brownes and their three children left for Europe. While the others remained in Florence, Browne toured northern Italy, Austria, Germany, Greece, Egypt and the Middle East. A daughter was added to the menage on Sept. 1. After the family returned to Washington, D.C., in the fall of 1852, Browne toured the South. He returned to California in the late spring of 1854, followed by his family a year later. From 1854-1859, Browne served as inspector of Indian reservations. In September 1859 Mrs. Browne and the six children returned to Washington, D.C., while her husband tried unsuccessfully to sell their house in Oakland. By July 1860 the family was reunited and settled in Frankfurt-am-Main, Germany, which Browne called home between tours of Europe, North Africa and Russia. After an unsuccessful lecture tour of the eastern U.S. in 1862-1863, Browne and his family returned to Oakland. He spent several months in Arizona, and in 1864-1865 he began receiving large commissions from eastern investors to draw pictures of mines and write reports. He visited Washington, D.C., in the spring of 1868, and by September the family was in Peking. Browne had been named U.S. Minister to China. He served only ten months, until July 1869, but not until 1872 did Congress pay him $2,164 that was in arrears. Meanwhile, Browne sold his house in Oakland, to satisfy various obligations, and in 1870 he began construction of a new residence, "Pagoda Hill." The last five years of his life, Browne mainly traveled between London, Washington, D.C., and Oakland. In all, he wrote eleven books and many shorter articles. He died on the night of 9 Dec. 1875 after a sudden and acute illness. Although the family lived in the house only a few years more, "Pagoda Hill" stood, deserted and vacant, well into the 20th century.

Albert D. Richardson

A.D. Richardson was born 6 Oct. 1833 in Medway, Mass., and worked for several years as a journalist in Ohio. He then moved to Kansas and was active in political affairs before a "roving disposition" brought him to Denver. In 1859 he first met Horace Greeley, who was on a trip to California, and accompanied the famed New York *Tribune* editor as far as Colorado. The two men became fast friends and Richardson agreed to contribute articles to the paper from Denver. Shortly before the Civil War began, Richardson went east to join the *Tribune* staff. He was sent into the South to write about the gathering storm from that quarter, and later became a war correspondent. On the night of 3 May 1863 Confederate batteries sank a Union vessel trying to run the gauntlet at Vicksburg, Miss., and Richardson was among those captured. He remained in prison until 18 Dec. 1864 when he escaped from Salisbury, N.C., and won a national reputation. Richardson never fully recovered from the exposure and hardships he suffered in captivity. Meanwhile his wife had died, leaving him three small children. Richardson remained with the *Tribune* as a special writer, mainly of books. He died about 5 a.m. Thursday, 2 Dec. 1869, eight days after being shot by a friend who thought Richardson was having an illicit affair with the man's ex-wife.

Jesse Quinn Thornton

Jesse Quinn Thornton was born 24 Aug. 1810 near Point Pleasant, W. Va. His ancestors apparently came to eastern Virginia in 1633 from England and family members became widely scattered over the southern and western states. While still a child, Thornton moved with his parents to Champaign County, Ohio. He grew up a studious boy and was an avid reader. Thornton's mother wanted him to become a minister, but instead he went to London and studied law for almost three years — "living in retirement and learning little of the great world about him." After an apprenticeship with a Staunton, Va., law firm, Thornton was admitted to the bar in May 1833. He later attended the University of Virginia. In 1835, Thornton opened a law office in Palmyra, Mo., and edited a political paper for Martin Van Buren, the eventual winner, during the 1836 presidential campaign. Thornton married Nancy M. Logue, of Hannibal, Mo., on 8 Feb. 1838. Three years later the couple moved to Quincy, Ill., and to Oregon in 1846. On 9 Feb. 1847, about six weeks after his arrival, Thornton was appointed supreme judge of the provisional government which American settlers established in 1843 to conduct their affairs until Oregon could become U.S. territory. In November 1847 he resigned, to lobby in Washington, D.C., on Oregon's behalf. After his return in the summer of 1848, Thornton served as the U.S. sub-agent for Indian affairs north of the Columbia River, but soon resigned. The following year he published *Oregon and California in 1848*, which was based in part on the writings of earlier pioneers. He lived in Oregon City for several years, and then moved to Albany to practice law. It was here that Mrs. Victor was introduced to him in 1865. "Judge Thornton and wife . . . entertained me at their place . . . for two days, during which time the judge told me the early history of Oregon from the Hudson Bay company's [British] point of view," Frances recalled. "Afterwards he wrote me several letters in the same vein; but when I published my 'River of the West,' he came out savagely against the very statements he had given me." Thornton spent

1870-1871 in Portland, and lived in Salem until his death on 5 Feb. 1888, at the age of 77, just a few days before his 50th wedding anniversary.

Orville C. Pratt

A native of Ontario County, N. Y., where he was born on 24 Apr. 1819, Orville C. Pratt entered the United States Military Academy in 1837, by appointment of President Martin Van Buren, but resigned as a cadet after about two years. Pratt returned to New York to study law and on 3 June 1840 was admitted to practice before the Oswego County courts. Three years later he moved to Galena, Ill. In 1847, the War Department sent Pratt on a secret political mission to Mexico, California and Oregon. On the way north, he stopped at Los Angeles, Monterey, San Jose and San Francisco. Pratt arrived in Oregon in January 1849 and became a judge. His only colleague soon resigned to go back east, and from October 1849-April 1851 Pratt was the territory's only judge. The salary was only $2,000 a year, so Pratt had to engage in business on the side. He was a shrewd trader and before long he became wealthy. A partisan Democrat, Pratt made few friends and was defeated when he stood for nomination in 1855 as Oregon's territorial delegate to Congress. The following June, he and his family left for San Francisco, where Pratt profited in law and land speculation. In 1875, Pratt's wife came into possession of amorous letters that her husband wrote to another woman, and Pratt had to give her $750,000 in property in exchange for her promise not to emphasize the adultery part of her divorce suit. Still a multi-millionaire, Pratt soon married the other woman and lived in San Francisco until his death, after a short illness, on 24 Oct. 1891, at the age of 72. Looking back, a historian wrote: "Pratt was a person of unusual characteristics. A man of large stature, dignified and impressive in appearance, he had a mien of austerity and pompousness. Undoubtedly he had a mind of some depth, and possessed considerable legal ability and acumen. His prejudices however often swayed his judgments. He was an opportunist and frequently permitted his personal predelictions [sic], his prejudices and his interests to influence his conclusions. But withal he was a forcible person, and a pioneer character of note."

Joseph Lane

Born 14 Dec. 1801 in Buncombe County, N.C., Joseph Lane moved with his parents to Henderson, Ky., and attended the public schools. The young man went to Vanderburgh County, Ind., when he was 20. Lane was elected to the Indiana house of representatives in 1822, 1823, 1831-1833, 1838 and 1839, and to the state senate 1844-1846. During the Mexican War he was commissioned a colonel commanding the Second Indiana Volunteer Regiment on 25 June 1846, and a week later was promoted to brigadier-general. On 9 Oct. 1847 Lane was given the temporary rank of major-general "for gallant and meritorious conduct in the Battle of Huamantla,

Mexico," and honorably discharged 20 July 1848. Congress formally placed the Oregon Territory under federal jurisdiction on 14 Aug. 1848, and President James Polk appointed Lane as its first governor. Lane served from 3 Mar. 1849-18 June 1850, when he resigned. Lane acted as delegate to Congress from 4 Mar. 1851-14 Feb. 1859, when Oregon became a state, and then was elected U.S. senator for the short term, until 3 Mar. 1861. Lane did not seek re-election in 1860, having been nominated for Vice President on the Democratic ticket with John Breckinridge of Kentucky. Lane died in Roseburg, Oreg., on 19 Apr. 1881.

Helen Hunt Jackson

Helen Fiske Hunt Jackson, an American poet and novelist, was born in Amherst, Mass., 15 Oct. 1830, and baptized 8 May 1831. Her father was a professor at Amherst College. In October 1852, she married Lieutenant Edward Bissell Hunt (1822-1863), of the U.S. Army's Corps of Engineers. Her writing appeared under her married name of Helen Hunt ("H.H."). In 1870, she published a small volume of meditative *Verses*, which won praise four years later from the noted poet Ralph Waldo Emerson in the preface of his *Parnassus*. In 1875, she wed William S. Jackson, a banker, of Colorado Springs, Colo. Mrs. Jackson became a prolific writer of prose and poetry, including stories for children, books of travel, household hints and novels. *Ramona* (1884), a defense of Indian character, is considered her best work. Previously, she had written *A Century of Dishonor* (1881), an indictment of the United States' treatment of Indians. In 1883, as a special commissioner, she helped investigate the condition and needs of the Mission Indians in California. Helen Hunt Jackson died 12 Aug. 1885, of cancer, in San Francisco. She was buried near Colorado Springs in the "Garden of the Gods," so named, one early traveler said, for the "red and white sedimentary strata which have been upheaved to a perfect perpendicular on a narrow plain at the base of the foot-hills, with summits worn by the action of wind and weather into their present statuesque appearance. . . . These masses, upon their east and west faces, are nearly tabular. Some of them reach a height of four hundred feet, with the proportions of a flat grave-stone. Two of the loftier ones make a fine portal to the gateway of the garden."

John McLoughlin

John McLoughlin, widely known today as the "Father of Oregon," was born of Irish parents in the city of Quebec, Canada, in 1784. He studied medicine in Paris before joining the North West Company, a British fur trader based in Montreal, and worked at several of its posts. In 1821, the Hudson's Bay Company absorbed the North West Company. Three years later McLoughlin arrived at Fort George, at the mouth of the Columbia River. In 1825, he moved about 120 miles upriver to establish Fort Vancouver. Here, for twenty years, McLoughlin held sway as absolute monarch over the district of the Columbia, which included all of the Hudson's Bay Company's trapping-grounds west of the Rocky Mountains and extending as far south as trapping parties could penetrate. His was a "commanding presence" — 6'6", stout, with "flowing white hair, . . . a benevolent expression, . . . courtly manners, and great affability in conversation." As more and more Americans came to Oregon, McLoughlin decided to accept the situation gracefully and offer a helping hand. He extended credit to many immigrants so they could obtain food and provisions. During the winter of 1842-1843 there was talk of establishing an independent government for Oregon, and McLoughlin reportedly favored the scheme. But the Methodist missionaries suspected him of undercutting their influence by inviting Catholics to settle in the territory. This suspicion was heightened when McLoughlin joined the Catholic Church in 1842, and two years later a legislative committee voted down bills and petitions presented in his interest. It was clear that Oregon soon would become U.S. territory. McLoughlin decided to cast his fate with the Americans, and he resigned in the autumn of 1845 as head of the Hudson's Bay Company in Oregon. The following spring, he took up residence at Oregon City, planning to become an American citizen when the Northwest boundary question was settled. (See Chapter 13.) "The missionary party . . . made war on him after he came to Oregon City," Mrs. Victor wrote. "In addition, he lost heavily through the debts of the settlers, which the company put upon him, if not wholly, at least to a great amount, and was severely attacked by English writers." By making his declaration as an American citizen, McLoughlin not only forfeited his British holdings but lost his right, as a British subject, to compensation under the boundary treaty. This was important, for Samuel R. Thurston, the territory's delegate to Congress, managed to insert in the Oregon land bill a provision depriving McLoughlin of his Oregon City property, which he took possession of in 1828 before there was a town. But Thurston's course, Frances noted, "had been marked out for him by those who stood high in society, and who were leaders of the largest religious body in Oregon. He had been elected by a majority of the people. The people had been pleased and more than pleased with what he had done. . . . Almost the only persons to protest against the robbery of McLoughlin were those who were made to suffer with him." After Oregon became a state in 1859, the legislature restored his property rights to his heirs, but McLoughlin would be fated to spend his last years struggling to vindicate himself. He died 3 Sept. 1857, at the age of 73, and was buried in the enclosure of the Catholic Church in Oregon City. On his tombstone is engraved this epitaph: "The Pioneer and Friend of Oregon; also The Founder of this City."

Elliott Coues

Coues was born in Portsmouth, N.H., on 9 Sept. 1842. He was educated in Washington, D.C., at Gonzaga College and Columbia University, graduating from the latter in 1861. Coues resided in the capital, though he wrote and traveled extensively. His interests included ornithology, mammalogy, herpetology, comparative anatomy, natural philosophy and psychic research. He was affiliated with the Smithsonian Institution and for several years edited various scientific publications. He also served, as an officer and assistant surgeon, in the U.S. Army. Coues' correspondence with Mrs. Victor began in January 1898 when he asked her to send a copy of *The River of the West* and to clear up some historical ambiguities for him. "He understood that an author is pretty sure to find 'erroneous passages' in books that an honest writer must be willing to correct," Frances recalled, "besides, he wished to avoid quoting others' errors." She told Frederic George Young that Coues should be made an honorary member of the Oregon Historical Society for his work pertaining to the state. Before the nomination could be acted upon, Coues spent several weeks examining ancient ruins in Arizona and New Mexico, and in "roughing it" too long, contracted a serious illness that detained him for a month on the way home. Coues seemed to have recovered from his summer ordeal, and was back at his desk, but he died 25 Dec. 1899 at Johns Hopkins Hospital.

Joseph Gaston

A native of Belmont County, Ohio, Joseph Gaston worked on a farm until the age of 16, when he started out on his own with but a public school education. The young man took odd jobs while he studied law. In 1862 Gaston came to southern Oregon, but railroad projects drew him northward. A San Francisco-Portland line was envisioned. On 25 July 1866, to facilitate construction to meet the Central Pacific at the Oregon boundary, Congress offered to give builders the land for twenty miles on either side of the right-of-way. Gaston was among the men who on 21 Nov. 1866 incorporated the Oregon Central Railroad Company to fulfill terms of the land grant. They proposed a route south from Portland on the west side of the Willamette River. The Oregon legislature designated this company to receive the land. Enter Ben Holladay, a Kentucky native who made his fortune in the 1860s by combining stagecoach companies into a transcontinental link with steamships at San Francisco. Holladay, eyeing the same prize as the Oregon men, had organized a rival company of the same name, which planned a railroad on the east side of the Willamette River. He insisted that Gaston's railroad had never been legally organized. On 20 Oct. 1868, after a lavish and intense lobbying campaign, Holladay got legislators to invalidate their original decision and award *his* company the land grant. Two years later Holladay bought all of his competitor's capital stock and formed the Oregon & California Railroad, which later went bankrupt. The Southern Pacific Railroad acquired its assets and finally completed the San Francisco-Portland line on 17 Dec. 1887. Gaston actively promoted railroads until 1880 when he settled on a farm in Washington County, west of Portland. Before he sold out and moved into the city 16 years later, Gaston had drained a lake and added 1,000 acres of fertile farmland to his holdings. He edited a couple of newspapers, and in 1894 was an unsuccessful Populist (People's Party) candidate for the Oregon Supreme Court. In 1911, Gaston published *Portland, Oregon; Its History and Builders*, a historical volume of 700 pages with two volumes of bibliographies; and *The Centennial History of Oregon*, a similar work published in 1912 with three volumes of bibliographies to commemorate the 100th anniversary of the founding of Astoria, at the mouth of the Columbia River. Gaston died 20 July 1913, at the age of 79, after a short illness, in Pasadena, Calif.

Notes

In California, gold and silver were the sole means of payment. U.S. currency did circulate, but only at the discount which the newspapers announced each day. No merchant or businessman would risk being paid in legal tender as long as the precious metals were favored. Contracts specified the kind of money in which debts were to be paid. The state legislature passed a specific contract law to regulate these transactions; Oregon and Nevada soon did likewise. The U.S. Supreme Court finally settled matters by ruling that a contract to pay in any kind of legal tender was valid, whether written or not.

. . . Is the effect of our system of civilization to impart to the savage only its vices? So it would seem, to the observer of Indian character and history in Oregon. . . .

. . .

When the first trading-ship entered the Columbia River, its shores were bordered with Indian villages, from the Capes to the Cascades, and from the Cascades to the Dalles; and so on, to its sources. They were well clad in skins and cloth made of cedar-bark. They had abundance of food, in the game which the land and water supplied, besides roots and berries in ample variety. In all respects, they were a prosperous and contented, though a savage, race.

The settlement of the fur companies in their midst dated the commencement of the destruction which has come upon them so overwhelmingly. Gradually, diseases, with whose character they were previously entirely unacquainted, and vices, of which . . . they had heretofore been innocent, were introduced among them. . . . In . . . 1829, five years subsequent to the settlement of Vancouver by the Hudson Bay Company, thirty thousand natives were estimated to have died from malarial fever in the Columbia River and Willamette valleys, west of the Cascade Mountains.

The Indians understood nothing of the cause, or the treatment, of the disease; and, although the gentlemen at the Fort did all they could to save life, yet with such numbers needing assistance, and with the native ignorance and superstition against them, very little, comparatively, could be effected. . . .

. . .

The advent among the Indians of missionaries, in 1835, did not improve their condition. Of the few who could be induced to alter their nomadic habits, nearly all died. The children and young persons taken into the mission-school, although they displayed an aptitude for learning, and even seemed to comprehend the vital truths of Christianity, perished like wild-wood flowers set in the sunny parterres of a garden. The causes are evident: change of diet, change of dress, and malarial poisons from the upturned sods of the mission-farm. The missionaries themselves suffered much from intermittent fever and chills; but the disease proved fatal to the Indians, while the White Men's constitutions were able to throw it off. By this time, too, [something] worse than malarial poison was working in the veins of the natives, resulting from their intercourse with a vicious class of men — the dregs of white races — floated to these shores, by chance, in trading-ships, or seeking here adventure more exciting than civilized countries afforded. From these causes — to which may be added the deprivation of their old means of abundant subsistence, and natural habits and recreations — the Oregon Indians have been reduced from many to few.

The valley of the Columbia, west of the Cascades, and the Willamette and other valleys of western Oregon, contained, fifty years ago, a native population numbering between two and three hundred thousand. The last census places the sum total of the Indian population of western Oregon at two thousand five hundred and fifty-one. Adding to these the few hundreds on the Washington Territory side of the river, we may have three thousand. A loss like this is really astounding. Averaging the numbers who have died in the last fifty years, we have nearly six thousand deaths annually. . . . .

. . .

The extinguishment of the native populations has not gone on with quite the same rapidity east of the Cascades as west: a fact which is undoubtedly owing to the Indian wars which drove the Whites from their country, and kept them out of it for a number of years, until the Government had made treaties with the different tribes owning it. Some other local circumstances were also in favor of their superior preservation: such as a more healthful climate, and inexhaustible pastures for their horses and cattle, which meant inexhaustible means of living, so long as they occupied these pastures.

Voters of Portland, The Book of Remembrance is this day opened, and you are called upon to choose "whom ye will serve." On one hand are found prostitutes, gamblers, rumsellers, whisky topers, beer guzzlers, wine bibbers, rum suckers, hoodlums, loafers, and ungodly men. On the other hand are found Christian wives, mothers, sisters, and daughters of the good people of Portland. You cannot serve two masters. You must be numbered with one or the other. Whom will ye choose?

Remember the Temperance Ticket. Vote for it early, and work for it earnestly all day. It is the safe side.

Remember that this is a struggle between virtue and vice. May you be found on the side of virtue.

Remember that the success of either of the other tickets is the success of whisky — supported by bad men and polluted women.

Remember that the whisky advocates employ prostitutes to insult Christian women while praying and reading the Holy Bible.

Remember that the police of Portland arrest, fine, and imprison the Christian women of Portland for reading the Bible and praying.

Remember that the police of Portland are devoted to the protection of prostitution, drunkenness, and debauchery, and the persecution and punishment of virtue.

Remember that persons are known by the company they keep. Birds of a feather flock together.

Remember that R. R. Thompson, one of the whisky candidates on one of the whisky tickets, served on the jury that fined and imprisoned Christian women in Portland for reading the Bible and praying.

Remember that the police and city police authority, wink at the flaunting of prostitutes and silently endorse their insulting language, applied to Christian women on the public streets of Portland.

Remember the honored name of our city and its inhabitants, and shield them from disgrace and the rule of prostitutes and rumsellers, by voting the Temperance ticket.

Vote for Temperance, and thereby cast your influence on the side of God and humanity, for the upbuilding of a better civilization. If you vote for the opponents of temperance, you vote for crime, hatred and violence; for misrule, oppression and wrong; for debauchery, pauperism and the long catalogue of vices that load the soul with heavy burdens of shame and disgrace.

Remember your duty, and do it so well that it will stay done forever.

Remember thy duty to the mother that bore thee; to the wife that confides in thee; to the sister that cherishes thee; to the children of thy love, that they may not be cursed into being by a father unworthy to bear that sacred name.

Remember thy duty; quit you like men and be strong. Vote for temperance, virtue, morality, and all the blessings they confer. Be loyal to the requirements of a better life, and thy name shall be honored among men, and thy life be made a blessing to all who know thee.

Vote for school-houses instead of rum-hells; industry instead of pauperism; factories instead of prisons, and churches instead of houses of infamy, and thy conscience shall be thy great reward, and thy children and thy children's children shall arise and call thee blessed.

Let your name be enrolled this day in the Book of Life. Be ye workers together with God for the putting down of the strongholds of sin, and great shall be thy reward. Thy journey shall be made peaceful and prosperous, and thy end-life everlasting.

Mrs. Victor was referring to the 1876 presidential election. Democratic candidate Samuel J. Tilden won a popular majority but was one undisputed vote short of a clear margin in the electoral college. Twenty-two electoral votes were at issue because Florida, Louisiana, Oregon and South Carolina each submitted two sets of election returns. Republican election boards in the three southern states threw out enough Democratic votes to certify the Republican candidate, Rutherford B. Hayes. But Oregon's governor disqualified a Republican elector, replacing him with a Democrat. Since the U.S. Senate was Republican and the House of Representatives was Democratic, it seemed useless to refer the disputed returns to the two houses for solution. Instead an Electoral Commission was established, with five senators, five representatives, and four U.S. Supreme Court justices who were to choose a fifth. He was a Republican who first favored Tilden, but switched under pressure from his party. The commission elected Hayes on a straight party-line vote of 8 to 7.

In 1855-1856, there was serious fighting between white settlers and various Indian tribes in Oregon and Washington. Civilian militias were organized and took the field, but General John E. Wool, commander of the Army's Department of the Pacific headquartered in San Francisco, did not allow U.S. soldiers to act in conjunction with these forces. This hampered the war effort. Worse, the general accused settlers of making attacks to provoke the Indians. Wool visited Fort Vancouver in mid-winter to look into the conduct of several of his officers in the Yakima Indian war in eastern Washington, "and to censure and insult, as they thought, both them and the governors of Oregon and Washington," a historian wrote. Washington Gov. Isaac Stevens, who had been designated a U.S. commissioner to negotiate with the Blackfoot tribe in council at Fort Benton (Mont.), was further angered by Wool's refusal to provide an escort that Stevens thought he would have while passing through hostile Indian country. This was the ultimate indignity and the general, who was considered "so much at variance with the civil authorities on the Pacific coast," was transferred in the summer of 1857.

Sources

CHAPTER 1

1. Hubert Howe Bancroft, *Literary Industries* (San Francisco: The History Company, publishers, 1890), pp. 259-261; William Alfred Morris, "Historian of the Northwest," *Oregon Historical Quarterly* (December 1902), p. 429; Albert Johannsen, *The House of Beadle and Adams and Its Dime and Nickel Novels, the Story of a Vanished Literature* (Norman: University of Oklahoma Press, 1950), Vol. 2, p. 29; Oregon Historical Society Scrapbook No. 120, p. 137; Frances E. Willard and Mary A. Livermore, *American Women*, Vol. 2 (1897). Reprint (Detroit: Gale Research Company, 1973), pp. 734-735.

2-5. Frances Fuller Victor [Florence Fane], *The* (San Francisco) *Golden Era*, Sunday, 9 October 1864, p. 5 c. 2.

6. "Talk with a Woman Who Writes Poems," Portland *Evening Telegram*, Tuesday, 11 September 1900, p. 8 c. 1.

7-15. Victor, *The Golden Era*, 9 October 1864, p. 5 c. 2.

16. "One of Our Poets," *The* (New York) *Home Journal*, Saturday, 27 May 1848, p. 4 c. 1; Victor, *The Golden Era*, 9 October 1864, p. 5 c. 2.

17. "Talk with a Woman Who Writes Poems," Portland *Evening Telegram*, 11 September 1900, p. 8 c. 1.

18-19. "Well, What Say?" *The* (New York) *Home Journal*, Saturday, 10 June 1848, p. 2 c. 5.

20. "Our Western Contributors," *The* (New York) *Home Journal*, Saturday, 14 October 1848, p. 2 c. 5.

21-23. "The Stars of the West," *The* (New York) *Home Journal*, Saturday, 30 September 1848, p. 2 c. 7.

24. Ibid., p. 2 c. 7, p. 3 c. 1.

25. "Our Western Contributors," *The* (New York) *Home Journal*, 14 October 1848, p. 2 c. 5.

26. Bancroft, *Literary Industries*, p. 261.

27. "Talk with a Woman Who Writes Poems," Portland *Evening Telegram*, 11 September 1900, p. 8 c. 2.

28. James A. Harrison, ed. *The Complete Works of Edgar Allan Poe* (New York: AMS Press Inc., 1965), pp. 159-160.

29. New York *Message Bird*, cited in Detroit *Monthly Hesperian and Odd-Fellows' Literary Magazine*, Vol. 2, No. 7 (1851), p. 33.

CHAPTER 2

1. Hubert Howe Bancroft, *Literary Industries* (San Francisco: The History Company, publishers, 1890), p. 260; *Monthly Hesperian and Odd-Fellows' Literary Magazine*, Detroit (May and July 1850); William Lee Jenks, *St. Clair County, Michigan: Its History and Its People* (Chicago: The Lewis Publishing Company, 1912), pp. 307-308.

2. Edmund Janes Cleveland and Horace Gillette Cleveland, *The Genealogy of the Cleveland and Cleaveland Families* (Hartford, Conn.: The Case, Lockwood & Brainard Company, 1899), Vol. 3, p. 2318; "Marriages," Detroit *Daily Advertiser*, Monday, 20 June 1853, p. 2 c. 5; Michigan Historical Commission, *Michigan Biographies* (Lansing: 1924), Vol. 1, p. 56.

3. William T. Coggeshall, *The Poets and Poetry of the West: with Biographical and Critical Notices* (Columbus, Ohio: Follett, Foster and Company, 1860), p. 511.

4. U.S. Veterans' Administration, military pension file Navy WC 7962 of Henry C. Victor and Frances Fuller Victor, widow, 1890-1902; Frances Fuller Victor, *Poems* (Author's Edition: 1900), pp. 87-89.

5. Coggeshall, *Poets and Poetry of the West*, p. 511.

6. Frances Fuller Victor, "Manifest Destiny in the West," *Overland Monthly*, San Francisco (August 1869), p. 158.

7. Albert Johannsen, *The House of Beadle and Adams and Its Dime and Nickel Novels, the Story of a Vanished Literature* (Norman: University of Oklahoma Press, 1950), Vol. 1, pp. 4-5.

8. Johannsen, *The House of Beadle and Adams*, Vol. 2, p. 30; "The Woman Historian," San Francisco *Call*, Sunday, 7 July 1895, p. 20 c. 4.

9. William Alfred Morris, "The Origin and Authorship of the Bancroft Pacific States Publications: A History of a History," *Oregon Historical Quarterly* (December 1903), p. 315; Frances E. Willard and Mary A. Livermore, *American Women*, Vol. 2 (1897). Reprint (Detroit: Gale Research Company, 1973), p. 734.

10. "Talk with a Woman Who Writes Poems," Portland *Evening Telegram*, Tuesday, 11 September 1900, p. 8 c. 1.

11. Mary Clemmer Hudson, *A Memorial of Alice and Phoebe Cary, with Some of Their Later Poems*, 31st ed. (Boston and Cambridge: Houghton, Mifflin and Company and The Riverside Press, 1898), p. 61.

12. Ibid., pp. 60-61.

13. U.S. Veterans' Administration, military pension file Navy WC 7962 of Henry C. Victor and Frances Fuller Victor, widow, 1890-1902.

14. *Annual Report of the Adjutant General of the State of Michigan for the Year 1864* (Lansing: John A. Kerr & Co., Printers to the State, 1865), p. 233.

15-16. U. S. Veterans' Administration, military pension file Navy WC 7962 of Henry C. Victor and Frances Fuller Victor, widow, 1890-1902.

17. U. S. Serial Set, Vol. 1183, 38th Cong., 1st sess., 1863, *Annual Report of the Secretary of the Navy*, House Executive Document 1, pp. 162-180.
18. *New York Times*, Monday, 9 February 1863, p. 1 c. 1-2.

CHAPTER 3

1. Frances Fuller Victor, "A Short Stay in Acapulco," *Overland Monthly*, San Francisco (March 1871), p. 214.
2. Charles H. Webb, "The Nicaragua Route," San Francisco *Evening Bulletin*, Thursday, 23 April 1863, p. 1 c. 1.
3. Victor, "A Short Stay in Acapulco," pp. 214-215.
4-5. Ibid., p. 215.
6-9. Webb, "The Nicaragua Route," p. 1 c. 2.
10. Victor, "A Short Stay in Acapulco," p. 215.
11. Frances Fuller Victor [Florence Fane] *The* (San Francisco) *Golden Era*, Sunday, 9 August 1863, p. 5 c. 5.
12. Victor, "A Short Stay in Acapulco," p. 215.
13. Victor, *The Golden Era*, p. 5 c. 5.
14. Victor, "A Short Stay in Acapulco," p. 215.
15-16. Ibid., p. 216.
17. Victor, *The Golden Era*, p. 5 c. 5.
18-19. Victor, "A Short Stay in Acapulco," p. 216.
20. Victor, *The Golden Era*, p. 5 c. 5.

CHAPTER 4

1. "Arrival of the Golden Age," San Francisco *Daily Alta California*, Tuesday, 7 April 1863, p. 1 c. 2; "Arrival of the 'Golden Age,'" San Francisco *Evening Bulletin*, Tuesday, 7 April 1863, p. 3 c. 5; Frances Fuller Victor, "A Short Stay in Acapulco," *Overland Monthly*, San Francisco (March 1871), p. 216.
2-3. Victor, "A Short Stay in Acapulco," p. 217.
4. Ibid., pp. 217-218.
5-9. Ibid., p. 218.
10. Ibid., p. 219.
11-12. Frances Fuller Victor [Florence Fane], *The* (San Francisco) *Golden Era*, Sunday, 16 August 1863, p. 5 c. 3.
13. Victor, "A Short Stay in Acapulco," pp. 219-220.
14. Ibid., p. 220.
15. Ibid., p. 221.
16. Ibid., p. 222.
17-20. Ibid., p. 220.
21. Ibid., p. 219.
22. "Our Letter from Mexico," *Daily Alta California*, Monday, 9 February 1863, p. 1 c. 8.
23-24. Victor, "A Short Stay in Acapulco," p. 221.
25. "Letter from Mexico," *Daily Alta California*, Tuesday, 27 January 1863, p. 1 c. 7.

26. Victor, "A Short Stay in Acapulco," p. 221.
27-28. Ibid., p. 222.
29. Ibid., pp. 220-221.

CHAPTER 5

1. "Arrival of the Sonora," San Francisco *Daily Alta California*, Sunday, 19 April 1863, p. 1 c. 2; "Commercial and Financial," San Francisco *Evening Bulletin*, Monday, 20 April 1863, p. 3 c. 1; Frances Fuller Victor, "A Short Stay in Acapulco," *Overland Monthly*, San Francisco (March 1871), p. 222.
2. Frances Fuller Victor [Florence Fane], *The* (San Francisco) *Golden Era*, Sunday, 1 November 1863, p. 5 c. 2.
3. Frances Fuller Victor autobiographical sketch, Salem *Daily Oregon Statesman*, Sunday, 16 June 1895, p. 2 c. 1.
4. Frances Fuller Victor [Florence Fane], *The* (San Francisco) *Golden Era*, Sunday, 16 August 1863, p. 5 c. 3.
5-10. Ibid., p. 5 c. 6.
11-14. Frances Fuller Victor [Florence Fane], *The* (San Francisco) *Golden Era*, Sunday, 9 August 1863, p. 5 c. 6.
15. Frances Fuller Victor [Florence Fane], *The* (San Francisco) *Golden Era*, Sunday, 30 August 1863, p. 5 c. 5.
16-18. Frances Fuller Victor [Florence Fane], *The* (San Francisco) *Golden Era*, Sunday, 23 August 1863, p. 5 c. 5.
19-20. Frances Fuller Victor [Florence Fane], *The* (San Francisco) *Golden Era*, Sunday, 25 October 1863, p. 4 c. 4.
21. Frances Fuller Victor [Florence Fane], *The* (San Francisco) *Golden Era*, Sunday, 6 September 1863, p. 5 c. 5.
22. Victor, *The Golden Era*, 25 October 1863, p. 4 c. 4.
23. Victor, *The Golden Era*, 6 September 1863. p. 5 c. 4.
24. Ibid., p. 5 c. 5.
25-27. Victor, *The Golden Era*, 23 August 1863, p. 5 c. 5.
28-33. Frances Fuller Victor [Florence Fane], *The* (San Francisco) *Golden Era*, Sunday, 27 September 1863, p. 1 c. 1.
34. Ibid., p. 1 c. 1-2.
35. Ibid., p. 1 c. 1.
36. Ibid., p. 1 c. 2.
37. Frances Fuller Victor [Florence Fane], *The* (San Francisco) *Golden Era*, Sunday, 13 September 1863, p. 5 c. 4.
38. Ibid., p. 5 c. 5.
39-42. Victor, *The Golden Era*, 23 August 1863, p. 5 c. 6.
43-48. Ibid., p. 5 c. 4.
49. Victor, *The Golden Era*, 16 August 1863, p. 5 c. 5.
50. Frances Fuller Victor [Florence Fane], *The* (San Francisco) *Golden Era*, Sunday, 15 November 1863, p. 4 c. 3.

CHAPTER 6

1. F. A. Golder, "The Russian Fleet and the Civil War," *American Historical Review* (July 1915), pp. 801-812; Edward Crankshaw, *The Shadow of*

the Winter Palace: Russia's Drift to Revolution, 1825-1917 (New York: The Viking Press, 1976), pp. 203-206; Drew Middleton, "Russian Attitude Toward Poland Has Changed Little Since Days of the Czars," *New York Times*, Sunday, 17 January 1982, p. 12.

2. Ernest Schell, "Our Good Friends, the Russians," *American History Illustrated* (January 1981), p. 20; Golder, "The Russian Fleet and the Civil War," pp. 805, 807, 808.

3. "Our Russian Naval Visitors," *New York Times*, Saturday, 26 September 1863, p. 4 c. 4-5; Schell, "Our Good Friends, the Russians," p. 20; Golder, "The Russian Fleet and the Civil War," p. 807.

4. Golder, "The Russian Fleet and the Civil War," pp. 804-805.

5-6. Golder, "The Russian Fleet and the Civil War," p. 809; Schell, "Our Good Friends, the Russians," p. 25.

7. "The Great Fire This Morning," San Francisco *Evening Bulletin*, Friday, 23 October 1863, p. 3 c. 3.

8. "The Ball to the Russians To-Night," San Francisco *Evening Bulletin*, Tuesday, 17 November 1863, p. 3 c. 3.

9-10. "The Russian Ball Last Night," San Francisco *Evening Bulletin*, Wednesday, 18 November 1863, p. 5 c. 3.

11. "Answers to Correspondents," *The* (San Francisco) *Golden Era*, Sunday, 29 November 1863, p. 4 c. 1. Original text reads: "Intellecktewly speakin', it wus a tremenjus sucksess. . . . The ladys luked Gay, and eye say it with a big gee. . . . The hull thing wus a *feet*, well 'wurthy uv our steel.'"

12. Ibid. Original text reads: "Pork-off konfidently towld me he wus *still on gude terms with the Sar*, and thort the *decky*-rashins uv the haul brillint in the ex *stream*."

13. Ibid. Original text reads: "Pork-off . . . wus hiley embellished with lee-gins uv meduls, gee enerisly bestowed onter him — fer grate merrytorius konduck in late Kry Mary-Ann konflicks — bi his troo friend the Sar."

14. San Francisco *Evening Bulletin*, 18 November 1863, p. 5 c. 3.

15-19. Frances Fuller Victor [Florence Fane], *The* (San Francisco) *Golden Era*, Sunday, 29 November 1863, p. 4 c. 3.

20. "Answers to Correspondents," *The Golden Era*, 29 November 1863, p. 4 c. 1. Original text reads: "The gran' supper wus well rendered, and reflecktid grate kredit on the geitters up thurov. The Wushshin kramberry sawse wus pertickalerly fine. . . . The Wushshin pickerls wus tew sour tew bee perfick. The spunge-kake was gude, howiver, and no doubt konsisted uv the best material. The Kastill uv Ise wus alser well dun, though a leetle tew keold — 'Yung pigings, kontainin' sham-paine sause, fried on a hot stove' fully realised awl eggspecktashins. *It exackly sooted the publick taste*."

21. "The Russian Ball Last Night," *Evening Bulletin*, 18 November 1863, p. 5 c. 3.

22. Victor, *The Golden Era*, 29 November 1863, p. 4 c. 4.

CHAPTER 7

1. Frances Fuller Victor [Florence Fane], *The* (San Francisco) *Golden Era*, Sunday, 6 December 1863, p. 4 c. 4.

2-5. Frances Fuller Victor [Florence Fane], *The* (San Francisco) *Golden Era*, Sunday, 3 January 1864, p. 4 c. 6.

6. Ibid., p. 4 c. 7.

7-8. Ibid., p. 4 c. 6.

9-10. Frances Fuller Victor [Florence Fane], *The* (San Francisco) *Golden Era*, Sunday, 14 February 1864, p. 4 c. 6.

11-12. Frances Fuller Victor [Florence Fane], *The* (San Francisco) *Golden Era*, Sunday, 28 August 1864, p. 4 c. 5.

13-15. Ibid., p. 4 c. 6.

16-18. Frances Fuller Victor [Florence Fane], *The* (San Francisco) *Golden Era*, Sunday, 4 September 1864, p. 4 c. 6.

19-21. Frances Fuller Victor [Florence Fane], *The* (San Francisco) *Golden Era*, Sunday, 11 September 1864, p. 1 c. 1.

22-23. Frances Fuller Victor [Florence Fane], *The* (San Francisco) *Golden Era*, Sunday, 16 October 1864, p. 5 c. 2.

24. "The Election," *The* (San Francisco) *Golden Era*, Sunday, 13 November 1864, p. 4 c. 1.

25-26. Victor, *The Golden Era*, 16 October 1864, p. 5 c. 2.

27. Frances Fuller Victor [Florence Fane], *The* (San Francisco) *Golden Era*, Sunday, 6 November 1864, p. 4 c. 6.

28. "The Election," *The Golden Era*, 13 November 1864, p. 4 c. 1.

29. Frances Fuller Victor [Florence Fane], *The* (San Francisco) *Golden Era*, Sunday, 13 November 1864, p. 4 c. 7.

30-32. Ibid., p. 4 c. 6.

33-42. Frances Fuller Victor [Florence Fane], *The* (San Francisco) *Golden Era*, Sunday, 27 November 1864, p. 4 c. 6.

43-45. Ibid., p. 4 c. 7.

46-47. Frances Fuller Victor [Florence Fane], *The* (San Francisco) *Golden Era*, Sunday, 20 November 1864, p. 4 c. 6.

48. Ibid., p. 4 c. 6-7.

49-52. Ibid., p. 4 c. 7.

53. Ibid., p. 4 c. 7, p. 5 c. 1.

CHAPTER 8

1-7. Frances Fuller Victor [Florence Fane], *The* (San Francisco) *Golden Era*, Sunday, 8 January 1865, p. 4 c. 5.

8. Frances Fuller Victor [Florence Fane], *The* (San Francisco) *Golden Era*, Sunday, 25 December 1864, p. 5 c. 1.

9. "Iron Works," *Albany* (Oreg.) *Journal*, Friday, 30 December 1864, p. 3 c. 1; U. S. Veterans' Administration, military pension file Navy WC 7962 of Henry C. Victor and Frances Fuller Victor, widow, 1890-1902; Frances Fuller Victor autobiographical sketch, Salem *Daily Oregon Statesman*, Sunday, 16 June 1895, p. 2 c. 1; "A Special Correspondent," Victoria (B.C.) *British Colonist*, Thursday, 8 September 1864, p. 3 c. 1.

10. Frances Fuller Victor [Florence Fane], *The* (San Francisco) *Golden Era*, Sunday, 20 November 1864, p. 4 c. 7.

11-20. Frances Fuller Victor, "A Winter Trip to Victoria and Portland," San Francisco *Evening Bulletin*, Friday, 20 January 1865, p. 2 c. 2.

21. Victor autobiographical sketch, p. 2 c. 1.

22-24. Victor, "A Winter Trip to Victoria and Portland," p. 2 c. 2.

25. Victor autobiographical sketch, p. 2 c. 2.

26. "Marine Intelligence," Portland *Morning Oregonian*, Wednesday, 28 December 1864, p. 3 c. 2; Victor, "A Winter Trip to Victoria and Portland," p. 2 c. 2.

27-28. Victor, "A Winter Trip to Victoria and Portland," p. 2 c. 2.

29. Victor autobiographical sketch, p. 2 c. 2.

30. Frances Fuller Victor, "The Webfoot History," Salem *Daily Oregon Statesman*, Sunday, 24 February 1895, p. 2 c. 3.

31-32. Victor autobiographical sketch, p. 2 c. 2.

33. [Matthew P. Deady], "Letter from Oregon," San Francisco *Evening Bulletin*, Thursday, 19 January 1865, p. 1 c. 4.

34-35. Victor autobiographical sketch, p. 2 c. 2.

36. William Alfred Morris, "Historian of the Northwest," *Oregon Historical Quarterly* (December 1902), p. 431.

37. Victor autobiographical sketch, p. 2 c. 1.

CHAPTER 9

1-4. Frances Fuller Victor, "Wayside Pictures from Oregon," San Francisco *Evening Bulletin*, Friday, 14 July 1865, p. 1 c. 1.

5. Ibid., p. 1 c. 2.

6-9. Ibid., p. 1 c. 1.

10-12. Ibid., p. 1 c. 2.

13. Jesse Applegate to Elwood Evans, 13 October 1867, in Elwood Evans collection, Mss 603, Oregon Historical Society Library, Portland.

14. Frances Fuller Victor autobiographical sketch, Salem *Daily Oregon Statesman*, Sunday, 16 June 1895, p. 2 c. 2-3.

15. Applegate to Evans, 13 October 1867.

16-23. Frances Fuller Victor, "A Voyage Up the Columbia River," San Francisco *Evening Bulletin*, Saturday, 2 September 1865, p. 1 c. 1.

24-27. Ibid., p. 1 c. 2.

28. Ibid., p. 1 c. 3.

29. Frances Fuller Victor, "Summer Wanderings," Portland *Morning Oregonian*, Tuesday, 21 June 1870, p. 1 c. 7.

30-33. Victor, "A Voyage Up the Columbia River," p. 1 c. 3.

CHAPTER 10

1. "Belching Again," Portland *Morning Oregonian*, Monday, 25 September 1865, p. 3 c. 1; San Francisco *Evening Bulletin*, Saturday, 7 October 1865, p. 1 c. 4; Frances Fuller Victor, "The Late Eruption of Mount Hood," San Francisco *Evening Bulletin*, Saturday, 28 October 1865, p. 1 c. 2.

2-6. Victor, "The Late Eruption of Mount Hood," p. 1 c. 2.

7. "Frightful Earthquake at San Francisco," Portland *Morning Oregonian*, Thursday, 12 October 1865, p. 1 c. 6.

8. Victor, "The Late Eruption of Mount Hood," p. 1 c. 2.

CHAPTER 11

1-3. Frances Fuller Victor to Elwood Evans, 15 November 1865. Microfilm copy at Oregon State Library, Salem, taken from originals in Evans' Correspondence and Papers, 1843-1894. In Western Americana Collection, Yale University Library, New Haven, Conn.

4. Frances Fuller Victor, "Railroads and Railroad Routes in Oregon," Portland *Morning Oregonian*, Wednesday, 11 October 1865, p. 1 c. 6-7.

5. [Matthew P. Deady], "Letter from Oregon," San Francisco *Evening Bulletin*, Tuesday, 17 October 1865, p. 1 c. 1.

6-7. Frances Fuller Victor to Matthew P. Deady, 17 March 1866, in Matthew P. Deady collection, Mss 48, Oregon Historical Society Library, Portland.

8. Frances Fuller Victor, *The River of the West* (Hartford, Conn., and San Francisco: R. W. Bliss & Co. and R. J. Turnbull & Co., 1870), p. 41.

9. Frances Fuller Victor autobiographical sketch, Salem *Daily Oregon Statesman*, Sunday, 16 June 1895, p. 2 c. 3.

10. U. S. Veterans' Administration, military pension file Navy WC 7962 of Henry C. Victor and Frances Fuller Victor, widow, 1890-1902.

11. Frances Fuller Victor et al. vs. Walter S. Davis, Supreme Court case files 1855-1904, RG S-5 61 A-20 No. 01524, p. 20; [Frances Fuller Victor], *History of Oregon, 1848-1888* (San Francisco: The History Company, publishers, 1888), pp. 735-736; Victor autobiographical sketch, p. 2 c. 1.

12. Victor to Deady, 30 July 1868.

13. Victor to Deady, 5 August 1868.

14-15. [Harvey W. Scott], "The River of the West," Portland *Morning Oregonian*, Tuesday, 8 March 1870, p. 2 c. 2.

16. Ibid., p. 2 c. 3.

17. Victor to Deady, 25 March 1870.

18. Victor to Deady, 5 April 1870.

CHAPTER 12

1. Frances Fuller Victor, "Summer Wanderings," Portland *Morning Oregonian*, Tuesday, 21 June 1870, p. 1 c. 6.

2-4. Ibid., p. 1 c. 7.

5-8. Frances Fuller Victor, "Summer Wanderings," Portland *Morning Oregonian*, Wednesday, 22 June 1870, p. 1 c. 6.

9. Frances Fuller Victor, *All Over Oregon and Washington* (San Francisco: John H. Carmany & Co., 1872), p. 96.

10. Victor, "Summer Wanderings," 22 June 1870, p. 1 c. 6.

11-12. Ibid., p. 1 c. 7.

13-14. Frances Fuller Victor, "Summer Wanderings," Portland *Morning Oregonian*, Saturday, 2 July 1870, p. 1 c. 5.

15-20. Frances Fuller Victor, "Summer Wanderings," Portland *Morning Oregonian*, Monday, 27 June 1870, p. 1 c. 6.

21. Ibid., p. 1 c. 6-7.

22-26. Victor, "Summer Wanderings," 2 July 1870, p. 1 c. 5.

27-34. Ibid., p. 1 c. 6.

35-42. Frances Fuller Victor, "Summer Wanderings," Portland *Morning Oregonian*, Thursday, 7 July 1870, p. 1 c. 4.

43-46. Ibid., p. 1 c. 5.

47. Jesse Quinn Thornton, "The River of the West," Portland (Oreg.) *Pacific Christian Advocate*, Saturday, 21 May 1870, p. 1 c. 1.

48. Frances Fuller Victor, "Mr. Thornton's Review of 'The River of the West,'" Portland (Oreg.) *Pacific Christian Advocate*, Saturday, 11 June 1870, p. 2 c. 5.

CHAPTER 13

1-6. Frances Fuller Victor, "Summer Wanderings," Portland *Morning Oregonian*, Wednesday, 27 July 1870, p. 1 c. 6.

7-12. Ibid., p. 1 c. 7.

13-26. Frances Fuller Victor, "Summer Wanderings," Portland *Morning Oregonian*, Monday, 1 August 1870, p. 2 c. 2.

27-31. Frances Fuller Victor, "Summer Wanderings," Portland *Morning Oregonian*, Tuesday, 2 August 1870, p. 2 c. 3.

32. *U. S. Serial Set*, Vol. 478, 29th Cong., 1st sess., 1845, Senate Document 489, p. 14.

33. Victor, "Summer Wanderings," 2 August 1870, p. 2 c. 3.

34. "The Treaty: Full Text of the Document As It Was Submitted to the Senate," *New York Times*, Friday, 12 May 1871, p. 5 c. 5.

35. *History of the Pacific Northwest: Oregon and Washington* (Portland: North Pacific History Company, 1889), Vol. 2, p. 44.

36. Victor, "Summer Wanderings," 2 August 1870, p. 2 c. 3.

37-40. Frances Fuller Victor, "Summer Wanderings," Portland *Morning Oregonian*, Wednesday, 10 August 1870, p. 1 c. 6.

41. Ibid., p. 1 c. 7.

CHAPTER 14

1-3. Frances Fuller Victor, "A Stage Ride in Oregon and California," *The American Publisher* (Hartford, Conn.: August 1871), p. 2 c. 1.

4. Ibid., p. 2 c. 1-2.

5-16. Ibid., p. 2 c. 2.

17-33. Frances Fuller Victor, "A Stage Ride in Oregon and California," *The American Publisher* (Hartford, Conn.: September 1871), p. 2 c. 2.

34-35. Ibid., p. 2 c. 3.

CHAPTER 15

1. Frances Fuller Victor to Elwood Evans, 15 December 1871. Microfilm copy at Oregon State Library, Salem, taken from originals in Evans' Cor-

respondence and Papers, 1843-1894, in Western Americana Collection, Yale University Library, New Haven, Conn.

2. Frances Fuller Victor to Matthew P. Deady, 3 May 1872, in Matthew P. Deady collection, Mss 48, Oregon Historical Society Library, Portland.

3-4. Victor to Deady, 27 October 1872.

5. Frances Fuller Victor to Oliver C. Applegate, 11 May 1873, in Special Collections, Knight Library, University of Oregon, Eugene.

6-8. "Letter from Mrs. Victor," *The* (Portland, Oreg.) *New Northwest*, Friday, 5 September 1873, p. 1 c. 4.

9. Ibid., p. 1 c. 5.

10-11. Frances Fuller Victor, *Atlantis Arisen; or, Talks of a Tourist About Oregon and Washington* (Philadelphia: J. B. Lippincott Company, 1891), p. 178.

12-17. "Letter from Mrs. Victor," 5 September 1873, p. 1 c. 5.

18-19. Ibid., p. 1 c. 6.

20. Victor to Applegate, 9 February 1875.

21. "Letter from Mrs. Victor," 5 September 1873, p. 1 c. 6.

22. Victor, *Atlantis Arisen*, p. 179.

23. Ibid., p. 180.

24. Ibid., pp. 180-181.

25-26. Victor to Applegate, 27 August 1873.

27-28. Oliver C. Applegate to Frances Fuller Victor, 9 September 1873, in Special Collections, Knight Library, University of Oregon, Eugene.

29-33. Victor to Applegate, 17 September 1873.

34-35. Victor to Applegate, 23 October 1873.

36-38. Victor to Applegate, 15 November 1873.

39-42. Victor to Applegate, 22 December 1873.

43-48. Victor to Applegate, 18 January 1874.

49. U. S. Congress, House, *Congressional Record*, 43rd Cong., 1st sess., 1874, Vol. 2, pt. 2, p. 1490.

50. Ibid., p. 1491.

51-55. Victor to Applegate, 19 February 1874.

56-59. Frances Fuller Victor to Oliver C. Applegate, 28 March 1874, in Special Collections, Knight Library, University of Oregon, Eugene.

CHAPTER 16

1. [Abigail Scott Duniway], "Praying Down Saloons," *The* (Portland, Oreg.) *New Northwest*, Friday, 6 March 1874, p. 2 c. 1.

2. Victor to Applegate, 28 March 1874.

3. Frances Fuller Victor, *The Women's War with Whisky; or, Crusading in Portland* (Portland: Geo. H. Himes, Steam Book and Job Printer, 1874), p. 12.

4-5. Ibid., p. 14.

6. Ibid., p. 11.

7. Ibid., p. 12.

8. "Crusaders Arrested," Portland *Morning Oregonian*, Wednesday, 8 April 1874, p. 3 c. 2.

9. Victor, *Women's War with Whisky*, p. 21; "Crusaders Arrested," p. 3 c. 2.

10. Victor, *Women's War with Whisky*, p. 21.

11. "Crusaders Arrested," p. 3 c. 2.

12. Victor, *Women's War with Whisky*, p. 21.

13-14. Ibid., p. 15.

15-16. "The War on Whisky," Portland *Morning Oregonian*, Friday, 17 April 1874, p. 3 c. 2.

17. Victor, *Women's War with Whisky*, p. 25.

18. "Trial of the Crusaders," Portland *Morning Oregonian*, Tuesday, 21 April 1874, p. 3 c. 2.

19. Victor, *Women's War with Whisky*, p. 33.

20-21. "Crusaders' Trial Concluded," Portland *Morning Oregonian*, Wednesday, 22 April 1874, p. 3 c. 2.

22-23. "Crusaders Sentenced," Portland *Morning Oregonian*, Thursday, 23 April 1874, p. 3 c. 3.

24. Victor, *Women's War with Whisky,* p. 35.

25. "Crusaders Sentenced," p. 3 c. 3.

26. Victor, *Women's War with Whisky*, p. 36.

27. "The End of It," *The* (Portland, Oreg.) *New Northwest*, Friday, 24 April 1874, p. 2 c. 4.

28-30. Victor to Applegate, 23 April 1874.

31-32. Victor, *Women's War with Whisky*, p. 38.

33. Ibid., p. 39.

34-36. Ibid., p. 40.

37. Ibid., p. 46.

38. Ibid., p. 45.

39-40. Ibid., p. 52.

41-42. Frances Fuller Victor, "A Word in Defense of the Crusaders," Portland *Morning Oregonian*, Friday, 19 June 1874, p. 1 c. 3.

43. Victor, *Women's War with Whisky*, p. 53.

44. Victor, "A Word in Defense of the Crusaders," p. 1 c. 3.

45-47. Victor, *Women's War with Whisky*, p. 55.

48. "Another Victory for the People," Portland *Morning Oregonian*, Tuesday, 16 June 1874, p. 2 c. 2-3.

49-50. Victor, "A Word in Defense of the Crusaders," p. 1 c. 3.

51-54. Victor, *Women's War with Whisky*, p. 49.

55-56. Ibid., p. 58.

57. Ibid., pp. 59-60.

58-61. [Abigail Scott Duniway], "'Women's War with Whisky,'" *The* (Portland, Oreg.) *New Northwest*, Friday, 11 September 1874, p. 2 c. 4.

62. *Journal of the House of Representatives of the Eighth Biennial Session of the Legislative Assembly of the State of Oregon, 1874* (Salem: Mart. V. Brown, State Printer, 1874), pp. 195, 196, 283.

63. Frances Fuller Victor autobiographical sketch, Salem *Daily Oregon Statesman*, Sunday, 16 June 1895, p. 2 c. 3.

64-70. Victor to Applegate, 8 October 1874.

CHAPTER 17

1. Frances Fuller Victor, "Some Thoughts About Ourselves," *The* (Portland, Oreg.) *New Northwest*, Friday, 27 February 1874, p. 4 c. 1.
2-3. Ibid., p. 1 c. 7, p. 4 c. 1.
4. Ibid., p. 4 c. 1-2.
5. Frances Fuller Victor, "Suffrage and Religion," *The* (Portland, Oreg.) *New Northwest*, Friday, 28 August 1874, p. 4 c. 1.
6-14. Ibid., p. 4 c. 2.

CHAPTER 18

1. Frances Fuller Victor autobiographical sketch, Salem *Daily Oregon Statesman*, Sunday, 16 June 1895, p. 2 c. 4.
2. Frances Fuller Victor to Oliver C. Applegate, 9 February 1875, in Special Collections, Knight Library, University of Oregon, Eugene.
3-13. Frances Fuller Victor [Dorothy D.], " 'Poor Ladies,' " San Francisco *Daily Morning Call*, Sunday, 25 April 1875, p. 1 c. 6.
14-18. Frances Fuller Victor [Dorothy D.], "The 'Girl of the Period,' " San Francisco *Daily Morning Call*, Sunday, 20 June 1875, p. 1 c. 7.
19. Ibid., p. 1 c. 7-8.
20-33. Frances Fuller Victor [Dorothy D.], " 'Cultivated Women,' " San Francisco *Daily Morning Call*, Sunday, 27 June 1875, p. 1 c. 7.
34-37. Ibid., p. 1 c. 8.

CHAPTER 19

1-14. Frances Fuller Victor [Dorothy D.], "Love Letters," San Francisco *Daily Morning Call*, Sunday, 18 July 1875, p. 1 c. 7.
15. Ibid., p. 1 c. 8.

CHAPTER 20

1-13. Frances Fuller Victor [Dorothy D.], "She Discourseth Upon Popular Literature," San Francisco *Daily Morning Call*, Sunday, 22 August 1875, p. 1 c. 6.
14-19. Ibid., p. 1 c. 7.

CHAPTER 21

1. *Scribner's*, July 1875, quoted by Frances Fuller Victor [Dorothy D.] in San Francisco *Daily Morning Call*, Sunday, 25 July 1875, p. 1 c. 7.
2-5. Frances Fuller Victor [Dorothy D.], " 'Common-Place Women,' " San Francisco *Daily Morning Call*, Sunday, 25 July 1875, p. 1 c. 7.
6. *Scribner's*, July 1875, quoted by Victor in San Francisco *Daily Morning Call*, 25 July 1875, p. 1 c. 7.
7-9. Victor, *Daily Morning Call*, 25 July 1875, p. 1 c. 7.
10. Ibid., p. 1 c. 7-8.

11. Ibid., p. 1 c. 8.
12-16. Frances Fuller Victor [Dorothy D.], "High-Steppers," San Francisco *Daily Morning Call*, Sunday, 13 June 1875, p. 8 c. 3.
17-31. Frances Fuller Victor [Dorothy D.], "Contrasts Masculine and Feminine Nature," San Francisco *Daily Morning Call*, Sunday, 1 August 1875, p. 5 c. 7.
32-36. Ibid., p. 5 c. 8.
37-47. Frances Fuller Victor [Dorothy D.], "The Etiquette and Manners of Street Cars and the Street," San Francisco *Daily Morning Call*, Sunday, 8 August 1875, p. 1 c. 6.
48. Ibid., p. 1 c. 6-7.
49-50. Ibid., p. 1 c. 7.

CHAPTER 22

1. *The* (Portland, Oreg.) *New Northwest*, Friday, 24 September 1875, p. 2 c. 7.
2-3. Frances Fuller Victor to Oliver C. Applegate, 22 April 1876, in Special Collections, Knight Library, University of Oregon, Eugene.
4. *The* (Portland, Oreg.) *New Northwest*, Friday, 15 September 1876, p. 3 c. 1.
5-8. "Correspondence of the O.S.W.S.A.," *The* (Portland, Oreg.) *New Northwest*, Friday, 30 March 1877, p. 2 c. 5.
9-11. Victor to Applegate, 18 March 1877.
12-16. Victor to Applegate, 29 June 1877.
17. *The* (Portland, Oreg.) *New Northwest*, Friday, 17 August 1877, p. 3 c. 1.

CHAPTER 23

1. William Alfred Morris, "The Origin and Authorship of the Bancroft Pacific States Publications: A History of a History," *Oregon Historical Quarterly* (December 1903), p. 337.
2. Ibid., p. 288.
3. Hubert Howe Bancroft, *Literary Industries* (San Francisco: The History Company, publishers, 1890), p. 472; Morris, "Origin and Authorship of the Bancroft Pacific States Publications," p. 312.
4-5. Bancroft, *Literary Industries*, p. 543.
6. Frances Fuller Victor autobiographical sketch, Salem *Daily Oregon Statesman*, Sunday, 16 June 1895, p. 2 c. 4.
7. Hubert Howe Bancroft to Frances Fuller Victor, 1 August 1878. Quoted in Morris, "Origin and Authorship of the Bancroft Pacific States Publications," pp. 295, 340.
8. Frances Fuller Victor to Matthew P. Deady, 8 December 1878, in Matthew P. Deady collection, Mss 48, Oregon Historical Society Library, Portland.
9. Hubert Howe Bancroft, quoted in Victor autobiographical sketch, p. 2 c. 4.

10. Victor autobiographical sketch, p. 2 c. 4.

11. Bancroft, quoted in Victor autobiographical sketch, p. 2 c. 4.

12. Victor autobiographical sketch, p. 2 c. 4.

13. Morris, "Origin and Authorship of the Bancroft Pacific States Publications," p. 341.

14. Frances Fuller Victor to Elwood Evans, 9 December 1879. Microfilm copy at Oregon State Library, Salem, taken from originals in Evans' Correspondence and Papers, 1843-1894, in Western Americana Collection, Yale University Library, New Haven, Conn.

15. Victor autobiographical sketch, p. 2 c. 4.

16. Victor to Evans, 7 January 1880.

17. Hubert Howe Bancroft, *Literary Industries*, pp. 237-238.

18-19. Victor to Evans, 7 January 1880.

20. Victor to Deady, 10 April 1880.

21. Frances Fuller Victor to Frederic George Young, 31 December 1900. The original Victor-Young correspondence is part of the manuscript collections of the Oregon Historical Society Library in Portland; while a microfilm copy reposes in the Special Collections of the Knight Library, University of Oregon, Eugene.

22. Victor to Deady, 17 June 1880.

23. Victor to Evans, 17 February 1881.

24-26. Frances Fuller Victor, "Bancroft's Methods," *The* (Salt Lake City) *Daily Tribune*, Friday, 14 April 1893.

27. Bancroft, *Literary Industries*, p. 202.

28. Ibid., p. 205.

29. Ibid., p. 203.

30. Ibid., pp. 562-563.

31. Victor to Deady, 1 November 1882.

32. Victor to Deady, 18 June 1883.

33. Victor to Deady, 25 April 1885.

34. Bancroft to Victor, 20 October 1885. Quoted in Morris, "Origin and Authorship of the Bancroft Pacific States Publications," p. 329.

35. Bancroft to Victor, 17 November 1885. Quoted in Morris, "Origin and Authorship of the Bancroft Pacific States Publications," pp. 329-330.

36. Ibid., p. 330.

37. Victor to Evans, 23 September 1886.

38. Bancroft, *Literary Industries*, p. 773.

39. Victor to Deady, 3 November 1886.

40. Victor to Deady, 12 July 1888.

41-43. Victor to Deady, 24 December 1888.

44. Hubert Howe Bancroft quoted in Victor to Deady, 24 December 1888.

45-47. Victor to Deady, 5 April 1889.

48. Bancroft to Victor, 16 October 1886. Quoted in Morris, "Origin and Authorship of the Bancroft Pacific States Publications," p. 342.

49. Victor autobiographical sketch, p. 2 c. 4.

50. Ibid., p. 2 c. 5.

51. Henry L. Oak, *"Literary Industries" in a New Light* (San Francisco: Bacon Printing Company, 1893), p. 38.

52-53. Victor to Evans, 23 September 1886.

54. Morris, "Origin and Authorship of the Bancroft Pacific States Publications," p. 362.

55. Frances Fuller Victor, "Bancroft's Histories," Portland *Sunday Oregonian*, 8 July 1900, p. 11 c. 6.

56. Oak, *"Literary Industries" in a New Light*, p. 38.

57. Victor autobiographical sketch, p. 2 c. 5.

58-59. Hubert Howe Bancroft, quoted in Victor, "Bancroft's Histories," p. 11 c. 5.

60. Victor, "Bancroft's Histories," p. 11 c. 6.

CHAPTER 24

1. Frances Fuller Victor et al. vs. Walter S. Davis. Supreme Court case files 1855-1904, RG S-5 61 A-20 No. 01524, p. 20.

2-4. Frances Fuller Victor to Matthew P. Deady, 7 December 1882, in Matthew P. Deady collection, Mss 48, Oregon Historical Society Library, Portland.

5. Victor vs. Davis, Supreme Court case files, p. 8.

6. Ibid., p. 9.

7. Ibid., p. 17.

8. F. F. Victor and M. E. V. Sampson, appellants, vs. W. S. Davis, respondent, *Appellant's Brief in the Supreme Court of the State of Oregon. Appeal from Columbia County*, October term, 1884, E.D. Shattuck, and Robt. L. McKee, attorneys for appellants (Portland: A. G. Walling, printer, 1884), p. 6. In Oregon Supreme Court case file No. 01524.

9. Oregon Supreme Court judgment roll, filed 26 February 1885. In Oregon Supreme Court case file No. 01524.

10. Victor to Deady, 25 April 1885.

CHAPTER 25

1. Frances Fuller Victor to Matthew P. Deady, 9 July 1889, in Matthew P. Deady collection, Mss 48, Oregon Historical Society Library, Portland.

2. Frances Fuller Victor, *Atlantis Arisen; or, Talks of a Tourist About Oregon and Washington* (Philadelphia: J. B. Lippincott Company, 1891), p. 3.

3. "Mrs. Frances Fuller Victor," Portland *Morning Oregonian*, Friday, 13 June 1890, p. 4 c. 2. Copied from Spokane (Wash.) *Spokesman*.

4-6. Victor to Deady, 19 August 1890.

7. Frances Fuller Victor statement dated 7 August 1891 in U. S. Veterans' Administration, military pension file Navy WC 7962 of Henry C. Victor and Frances Fuller Victor, widow, 1890-1902. Microfilm copy in Oregon State Library, Salem.

8. "An Oregon Book," Portland *Morning Oregonian*, Wednesday, 3 September 1890, p. 6 c. 2.

9. Victor to Deady, 9 November 1891.

10. "'Atlantis Arisen,'" Portland *Morning Oregonian*, Saturday, 7 November 1891, p. 10 c. 3-4.

11. Victor to Deady, 9 November 1891.

CHAPTER 26

1. *Journal of the House of the Legislative Assembly of the State of Oregon for the Sixteenth Regular Session, 1891* (Salem: Frank C. Baker, State Printer, 1891), pp. 559, 880.

2. Frances Fuller Victor, *The Early Indian Wars of Oregon* (Salem: Frank C. Baker, State Printer, 1894), p. v.

3. Quoted by Frances Fuller Victor in "The Webfoot History," Salem *Daily Oregon Statesman*, Sunday, 24 February 1895, p. 2 c. 3.

4. Frances Fuller Victor, "The Webfoot History," Salem *Daily Oregon Statesman*, Sunday, 24 February 1895, p. 2 c. 3.

5. Frances Fuller Victor, "Review of a Criticism," Portland *Morning Oregonian*, Thursday, 25 March 1897, p. 6 c. 5.

CHAPTER 27

1. "The Oregon Essayists," Salem *Daily Oregon Statesman*, Sunday, 13 May 1894, p. 5 c. 2.

2-3. "Writer of Oregon History," Portland *Sunday Oregonian*, 3 June 1900, p. 9 c. 3.

4-6. Frances Fuller Victor to Ellen M. White, 18 August 1894, incomplete. In Ellen M. White's *Diaries, Salem, Oregon, 1891-1900, 1902-1909, 1912, 1914-1917*. Microfilm copy in Oregon State Library, Salem. Mmes. Victor and White were sisters-in-law of Sebastian C. Adams, of Salem.

7-9. Frances Fuller Victor to Oliver C. Applegate, 10 September 1895, in Special Collections, Knight Library, University of Oregon, Eugene.

10. Frances Fuller Victor, "The Webfoot History," Salem *Daily Oregon Statesman*, Sunday, 24 February 1895, p. 2 c. 3.

11. Victor to Applegate, 10 September 1895.

12-14. "The Woman Historian," San Francisco *Call*, Sunday, 7 July 1895, p. 20 c. 4.

15. Ibid., p. 20 c. 5.

16. Victor to Applegate, 16 September 1896.

17. Hiram Martin Chittenden quoted in Victor to Applegate, 16 September 1896.

18-20. Victor to Applegate, 16 September 1896.

21. Frances Fuller Victor to Frederic George Young, 20 September 1897. The original Victor-Young correspondence is part of the manuscript collections of the Oregon Historical Society Library in Portland; while a microfilm copy reposes in the Special Collections of the Knight Library, University of Oregon, Eugene.

22. Victor to Young, 5 December 1898.

23-24. Frances Fuller Victor to William Gladstone Steel, 9 February 1899, in Frances Fuller Victor collection, Mss 1199, Oregon Historical Society Library, Portland.

25-28. Victor to Young, 24 August 1899.
29. Victor to Applegate, 21 November 1899.

CHAPTER 28

1. Frances Fuller Victor, "Dr. Marcus Whitman . . . An Exhaustive Examination . . . of all the Points in the So-called Whitman Controversy," Portland *Morning Oregonian*, Thursday, 6 November 1884, p. 3 c. 3.
2. Marcus Whitman quoted by Frances Fuller Victor in *Morning Oregonian*, 6 November 1884, p. 3 c. 3.
3. Ibid. Italics added by Mrs. Victor to denote the personal interest Dr. Whitman had in going east.
4. Victor, "Dr. Marcus Whitman," p. 3 c. 4.
5. Ibid., p. 3 c. 3.
6. Ibid., p. 3 c. 4.
7. Ibid., p. 3 c. 6.
8-9. Frances Fuller Victor, "The Whitman Controversy," Portland *Sunday Oregonian*, 29 March 1891.
10. Frances Fuller Victor to Oliver C. Applegate, 10 September 1895, in Special Collections, Knight Library, University of Oregon, Eugene.
11. Frances Fuller Victor to Frederic George Young, 5 December 1898. The original Victor-Young correspondence is part of the manuscript collections of the Oregon Historical Society Library in Portland; while a microfilm copy reposes in the Special Collections of the Knight Library, University of Oregon, Eugene.
12. Victor to Young, 23 January 1900.
13. J. Franklin Jameson quoted in Victor to Young, 10 December 1900.
14. Edward Gaylord Bourne, *Essays in Historical Criticism* (New Haven: Yale University Press, 1913), p. 36.
15. Ibid., p. 41.
16-17. Victor to Young, 10 December 1900.
18. Victor to Young, 25 January 1901.
19. Victor to Young, 9 November 1901.
20. Victor to Young, 30 March 1902.

CHAPTER 29

1. Frances Fuller Victor to Frederic George Young, 23 January 1900. The original Victor-Young correspondence is part of the manuscript collections of the Oregon Historical Society Library in Portland; while a microfilm copy reposes in the Special Collections of the Knight Library, University of Oregon, Eugene.
2. Frances Fuller Victor autobiographical sketch in Salem *Daily Oregon Statesman*, Sunday, 16 June 1895, p. 2 c. 4; Victor to Young, 23 January 1900.
3-7. Victor to Young, 23 January 1900.
8. "Writer of Oregon History," Portland *Sunday Oregonian*, 3 June 1900, p. 9 c. 3.

9-11. Victor to Young, 13 September 1900.

12. Victor to Young, 16 December 1900.

13. Victor to Young, 22 November 1901.

14-15. Victor to Young, 9 November 1901.

16-17. Victor to Young, 11 January 1902.

18-20. Victor to Young, 28 February 1902.

21. Victor to Young, 25 January 1901.

22. Victor to Young, 22 March 1902.

23. Victor to Young, 26 April 1902.

24-25. Victor to Young, 30 March 1902.

26. Victor to Young, 26 April 1902.

27-28. Victor to Young, 10 November 1902.

29. "Frances Fuller Victor," Portland *Sunday Oregonian*, 16 November 1902, p. 4 c. 4.

Bibliography

Annual Report of the Adjutant General of the State of Michigan for the Year 1864. Lansing: John A. Kerr & Co., Printers to the State, 1865.

Applegate, Jesse to Elwood Evans. 13 October 1867. In Elwood Evans collection, Mss 603, Oregon Historical Society Library, Portland.

Applegate, Oliver C. to Frances Fuller Victor. 9 September 1873. In Special Collections, Knight Library, University of Oregon, Eugene.

Bancroft, Hubert Howe to Frances Fuller Victor. 1 August 1878. Quoted in *Oregon Historical Quarterly*, December 1903.

_____. 20 October 1885. Quoted in ibid.

_____. 17 November 1885. Quoted in ibid.

_____. 16 October 1886. Quoted in ibid.

_____ to Matthew P. Deady. 15 May 1883. In Matthew P. Deady collection, Mss 48, Oregon Historical Society Library, Portland.

_____. *California Inter Pocula.* San Francisco: The History Company, publishers, 1888.

_____. *History of California, 1848-1859.* San Francisco: The History Company, publishers, 1888.

_____. *History of California, 1860-1890.* San Francisco: The History Company, publishers, 1890.

_____. *Literary Industries.* San Francisco: The History Company, publishers, 1890.

Biennial Report of the Secretary of State of the State of Oregon to the Legislative Assembly, Seventeenth Regular Session, 1893. Vol. I. Salem: Frank C. Baker, State Printer, 1893.

Biennial Report of the Secretary of State of the State of Oregon to the Legislative Assembly, Eighteenth Regular Session, 1895. Vol. I. Salem: Frank C. Baker, State Printer, 1894.

Biennial Report of the State Treasurer of the State of Oregon to the Legislative Assembly, Eighteenth Regular Session, 1895. Salem: Frank C. Baker, State Printer, 1894.

Biographical Directory of the American Congress, 1774-1971. Washington: Government Printing Office, 1971.

Bourne, Edward Gaylord. *Essays in Historical Criticism.* New Haven: Yale University Press, 1913.

Clarke, Samuel A. "The Oregon Central Railroad." *Oregon Historical Quarterly,* June 1906.

Cleveland, Edmund Janes, and Cleveland, Horace Gillette. *The Genealogy of the Cleveland and Cleaveland Families.* Vol. 3. Hartford, Conn.: The Case, Lockwood & Brainard Company, 1899.

Coggeshall, William T. *The Poets and Poetry of the West: with Biographical and Critical Notices.* Columbus, Ohio: Follett, Foster and Company, 1860.

Congressional Directory, 1774-1911 (Washington: Government Printing Office, 1913).

Douglas, Benjamin. *History of Wayne County, Ohio.* Indianapolis, Ind.: R. Douglass, 1878.

Drury, Clifford Merrill, Ph.D. *Marcus Whitman, M.D., Pioneer and Martyr.* Caldwell, Idaho: The Caxton Printers, Ltd., 1937.

Encyclopaedia Britannica. 11th ed. Vols. 3 and 7. Cambridge, England: at the University Press, New York, 1910.

————————————. 11th ed. Vols. 15 and 25. Cambridge, England: at the University Press, New York, 1911.

Fuller, Frances Auretta. *Anizetta, the Guajira; or, the Creole of Cuba.* Boston: "Star Spangled Banner" Office, 1848. Microfilm copy in Special Collections, Knight Library, University of Oregon, Eugene.

———, and Fuller, Metta Victoria. *Poems of Sentiment and Imagination, with Dramatic and Descriptive Pieces.* New York: A. S. Barnes & Co., publishers, 1851.

Gaston, Joseph. "The Genesis of the Oregon Railway System." *Oregon Historical Quarterly,* June 1906.

Griswold, Rufus Wilmot. *The Female Poets of America.* Philadelphia: Carey and Hart, 1849.

Harrison, James A., ed. *The Complete Works of Edgar Allan Poe.* Vol. 11. New York: AMS Press Inc., 1965.

Hines, Rev. Harvey K., D.D. *An Illustrated History of the State of Oregon.* Chicago: The Lewis Publishing Company, 1893.

History of the Pacific Northwest: Oregon and Washington. 2 vols. Portland: North Pacific History Company, 1889.

Hudson, Mary Clemmer. *A Memorial of Alice and Phoebe Cary, with Some of Their Later Poems.* 31st ed. Boston and Cambridge: Houghton, Mifflin and Company and The Riverside Press, 1898.

Irving, Washington. *Astoria.* 2 vols. 1836. Reprint (2 vols. in 1). Portland, Oreg.: Binfords & Mort, publishers, [1950].

Jenks, William Lee. *St. Clair County, Michigan: Its History and Its People.* Vol. 1. Chicago: The Lewis Publishing Company, 1912.

Johannsen, Albert. *The House of Beadle and Adams and Its Dime and Nickel Novels, the Story of a Vanished Literature.* 2 vols. Norman: University of Oklahoma Press, 1950.

Journal of the House of Representatives of the Eighth Biennial Session of the Legislative Assembly of the State of Oregon, 1874. Salem: Mart. V. Brown, State Printer, 1874.

Journal of the House of the Legislative Assembly of the State of Oregon for the Sixteenth Regular Session, 1891. Salem: Frank C. Baker, State Printer, 1891.

Ledger Appropriations 1891-1892 State of Oregon. In Oregon State Archives. Archives Division, Office of the Secretary of State, Salem.

Ludlow, Fitz Hugh. *The Heart of the Continent.* New York and Cambridge: Hurd and Houghton and Riverside Press, 1870.

McCormick, Stephen J. *Portland Directory for the Year Commencing January, 1865.* Portland: Oregon Farmer Book and Job Printing Office, 1865.

Michigan Historical Commission. *Michigan Biographies.* Vol. 1. Lansing: 1924.

Miller, David Hunter. *San Juan Archipelago.* Bellows Falls, Vt.: Wyndham Press, 1943.

Monthly Hesperian and Odd-Fellows' Literary Magazine (Detroit). John N. Ingersoll and Henry Barns, publishers.

Morris, William Alfred. "Historian of the Northwest." *Oregon Historical Quarterly,* December 1902.

_____. "The Origin and Authorship of the Bancroft Pacific States Publications: A History of a History." *Oregon Historical Quarterly,* December 1903.

Nordhoff, Charles. *Northern California, Oregon, and the Sandwich Islands.* New York: Harper & Brothers, publishers, 1877.

Oak, Henry L. *"Literary Industries" in a New Light.* San Francisco: Bacon Printing Company, 1893. Copy in Oregon Historical Society Library, Portland.

Odell, Ruth. *Helen Hunt Jackson.* New York and London: D. Appleton-Century Company, Incorporated, 1939.

Oregon Blue Book, 1973-1974. Salem: Clay Myers, Secretary of State, compiler and publisher, 1973.

Oregon Historical Society Scrapbook No. 120.

Schell, Ernest. "Our Good Friends, the Russians." *American History Illustrated,* January 1981.

Steel, William G. *The Mountains of Oregon.* Portland: David Steel, 1890.

Teiser, Sidney. "First Associate Justice of Oregon Territory: O. C. Pratt." *Oregon Historical Quarterly,* September 1948.

The Laws of Oregon, and the Resolutions and Memorials of the Sixteenth Regular Session of the Legislative Assembly Thereof. Salem: Frank C. Baker, State Printer, 1891.

Thwaites, Reuben Gold, ed. *Original Journals of the Lewis and Clark Expedition, 1804-1806.* 8 vols. New York: Arno Press, 1969.

U.S. Congress, House. *Congressional Record.* 43rd Cong., 1st sess., 1874. Vol. 2, pt. 2.

U.S. Serial Set. Vol. 478. 29th Cong., 1st sess., 1845. Senate Document 489. _____. Vol. 1183. 38th Cong., 1st sess., 1863. *Annual Report of the Secretary of the Navy.* House Executive Document 1.

U.S. Veterans' Administration. Military pension file Navy WC 7962 of Henry C. Victor and Frances Fuller Victor, widow, 1890-1902. Microfilm copy in Oregon State Library, Salem.

Victor, Frances Fuller to Elwood Evans. 15 November 1865. Microfilm
copy at Oregon State Library, Salem, taken from originals in Evans' Correspondence and Papers, 1843-1894, in Western Americana Collection,
Yale University Library, New Haven, Conn.
_____. 5 February 1866.
_____. 15 December 1871.
_____. 9 December 1879.
_____. 7 January 1880.
_____. 17 February 1881.
_____. 23 September 1886.
_____ to Matthew P. Deady. 17 March 1866. In Matthew P. Deady collection, Mss 48, Oregon Historical Society Library, Portland.
_____. 30 July 1868.
_____. 5 August 1868.
_____. 25 March 1870.
_____. 5 April 1870.
_____. 3 May 1872.
_____. 27 October 1872.
_____. 8 December 1878.
_____. 10 April 1880.
_____. 17 June 1880.
_____. 1 November 1882.
_____. 7 December 1882.
_____. 18 June 1883.
_____. 25 April 1885.
_____. 3 November 1886.
_____. 12 July 1888.
_____. 24 December 1888.
_____. 5 April 1889.
_____. 9 July 1889.
_____. 19 August 1890.
_____. 5 September 1890.
_____. 2 October 1891.
_____. 9 November 1891.
_____ et al. vs. Walter S. Davis. Supreme Court case files 1855-1904, RG
S-5 61 A-20 No. 01524. In Oregon State Archives. Archives Division,
Office of the Secretary of State, Salem.
_____. "Manifest Destiny in the West." *Overland Monthly* (San Francisco),
August 1869.
_____. *The River of the West*. Hartford, Conn., and San Francisco: R. W.
Bliss & Co. and R. J. Turnbull & Co., 1870.
_____. "A Short Stay in Acapulco." *Overland Monthly* (San Francisco),
March 1871.
_____. "A Stage Ride in Oregon and California." *The American Publisher*
(Hartford, Conn.), August and September 1871.
_____. "The Oregon Indians." *Overland Monthly* (San Francisco), October
1871.
_____. *All Over Oregon and Washington*. San Francisco: John H. Car-
many & Co., 1872.

_____ to Oliver C. Applegate. 11 May 1873. In Special Collections, Knight Library, University of Oregon, Eugene.

_____. 27 August 1873.

_____. 17 September 1873.

_____. 23 October 1873.

_____. 15 November 1873.

_____. 17 December 1873.

_____. 22 December 1873.

_____. 18 January 1874.

_____. 19 February 1874.

_____. 28 March 1874.

_____. 23 April 1874.

_____. 8 October 1874.

_____. 9 February 1875.

_____. 22 April 1876.

_____. 18 March 1877.

_____. 29 June 1877.

_____. 10 September 1895.

_____. 5 September 1896.

_____. 16 September 1896.

_____. 27 September 1896.

_____. 21 November 1899.

_____. *The Women's War with Whisky; or, Crusading in Portland*. Portland: Geo. H. Himes, Steam Book and Job Printer, 1874.

_____. *The New Penelope*. San Francisco: A. L. Bancroft & Company, printers, 1877.

_____. "Did Dr. Whitman Save Oregon?" *The Californian* (San Francisco), September 1880.

_____. *Eleven Years in the Rocky Mountains*. Hartford, Conn.: R. W. Bliss and Company, 1881.

_____. "The Bancroft Historical Library." *The Californian and Overland Monthly* (San Francisco), December 1882.

[_____]. *History of Oregon, 1832-1847*. San Francisco: The History Company, publishers, 1886.

[_____]. *History of Oregon, 1848-1888*. San Francisco: The History Company, publishers, 1888.

[_____]. *History of Washington, Idaho and Montana, 1845-1889*. San Francisco: The History Company, publishers, 1890.

[_____]. *History of Nevada, Colorado and Wyoming, 1540-1888*. San Francisco: The History Company, publishers, 1890.

_____. *Atlantis Arisen; or, Talks of a Tourist About Oregon and Washington*. Philadelphia: J. B. Lippincott Company, 1891.

_____ to Ellen M. White. 18 August 1894, incomplete. Mmes. Victor and White were sisters-in-law of Sebastian C. Adams, of Salem. See White's *Diaries, Salem, Oregon, 1891-1900, 1902-1909, 1912, 1914-1917*. Microfilm copy in Oregon State Library, Salem.

_____. *The Early Indian Wars of Oregon*. Salem: Frank C. Baker, State Printer, 1894.

_____ to Frederic George Young. 20 September 1897. The original Victor-Young correspondence is part of the manuscript collections of the Oregon Historical Society Library in Portland; while a microfilm copy reposes in the Special Collections of the Knight Library, University of Oregon, Eugene.

_____. 5 December 1898.

_____. 24 August 1899.

_____. 23 September 1899.

_____. 23 January 1900.

_____. 8 June 1900.

_____. 13 September 1900.

_____. 10 December 1900.

_____. 31 December 1900.

_____. 25 January 1901.

_____. 9 November 1901.

_____. 22 November 1901.

_____. 2 January 1902.

_____. 11 January 1902.

_____. 28 February 1902.

_____. 22 March 1902.

_____. 30 March 1902.

_____. 26 April 1902.

_____. 10 November 1902.

_____ to William Gladstone Steel, 9 February 1899. In Frances Fuller Victor collection, Mss 1199, Oregon Historical Society Library, Portland.

_____. 20 February 1899.

_____. "Dr. Elliott Coues." *Oregon Historical Quarterly*, June 1900.

_____. *Poems*. Author's Edition: 1900.

_____. "The American Fur Trade in the Far West." *Oregon Historical Quarterly*, September 1902.

Victor, Henry Clay. Oregon Central Military Road Company. Records, 1864-1877. Mss 993, Oregon Historical Society Library, Portland.

Willard, Frances E., and Livermore, Mary A. *American Women*. Vol. 2. 1897. Reprint. Detroit: Gale Research Company, 1973.

Wright, Edgar W., ed. *Lewis & Dryden's Marine History of the Pacific Northwest*. Portland, Oreg.: Lewis & Dryden Printing Company, 1895.

ABOUT THE AUTHOR

Jim Martin was born in Eugene, Oregon, and has lived in the Willamette and Rogue valleys. He graduated in 1971 from the University of Santa Clara, Santa Clara, California, with a Bachelor of Arts degree in History, and then worked as a reporter and editor for weekly newspapers. He later was a correspondent for *The* (Portland, Oreg.) *Oregonian*, and for several years regularly contributed articles on state history to *The* (Salem, Oreg.) *Statesman-Journal*. His work also has appeared in *The* (Eugene, Oreg.) *Register-Guard*; *Old West* magazine; *Oregon Business* magazine in Portland; and *The Wall Street Journal*. He has been employed part time since 1976, by the Legislative Counsel Committee of the Oregon Legislature, as a copy editor for bill drafts and other legal documents. He does historical research and freelance writing in his spare time, and has been at work on this book for the past fifteen years.

E 175.5 .V53 M37 1992
Martin, Jim, 1949-
A bit of a blue